THE WHOLE ISLAND

The publisher gratefully acknowledges
the generous support provided by
the Humanities Endowment Fund of the
University of California Press Foundation
and by Edmund and Jeannie Kaufman
as members of the Literati Circle of the
University of California Press Foundation.

THE WHOLE ISLAND

Six Decades of Cuban Poetry

A Bilingual Anthology

EDITED BY MARK WEISS

University of California Press   Berkeley Los Angeles London

University of California Press, one of the most distinguished
university presses in the United States, enriches lives around the
world by advancing scholarship in the humanities, social sciences,
and natural sciences. Its activities are supported by the UC Press
Foundation and by philanthropic contributions from individuals
and institutions. For more information, visit www.ucpress.edu.

University of California Press
Berkeley and Los Angeles, California

University of California Press, Ltd.
London, England

Library of Congress Cataloging-in-Publication Data

The whole island : six decades of Cuban poetry, a bilingual
anthology / edited by Mark Weiss.
    p.   cm.
Includes bibliographical references.
ISBN 978-0-520-25034-5 (cloth : alk. paper)
ISBN 978-0-520-25894-5 (pbk. : alk. paper)
1. Cuban poetry—Translations into English.   2. Cuban
poetry.   I. Weiss, Mark.
PQ7384.5.E5W56   2009
861'.608097291—dc22   2009030687

Manufactured in the United States of America

18   17   16   15   14   13   12   11   10   09
10   9   8   7   6   5   4   3   2   1

This book is printed on Natures Book, which contains 30% post-
consumer waste and meets the minimum requirements of ANSI/
NISO Z39.48–1992 (R 1997) (*Permanence of Paper*).

Contents

xi

xv

Cuban Tightrope

Public and Private Lives of the Poets

Relations with Cuba have preoccupied the North American imagination far more than one might expect, given the island's small size and minimal power.[1] North American understanding of Cuba has, at the same time, been obscured by longings for the exotic, as well as mythologies of both right and left, in which Cubans have also been known to indulge. It's been imagined as a place simpler than our own, whose people are less inhibited and more passionate, friendly to strangers and prone to dancing in the street, a land strangely set apart in a childhood fantasy, as evidenced by the opulent hulks that cruise its streets. For those of the left, there's the equally simplified Cuba of heroes, where the new man, freed from the shackles of exploitive cultures, has managed to create a society based on cooperation and compassion rather than greed, despite the opposition of the giant to the north. And for those of the right there's a gray, joyless, island-wide gulag, where all spirits are crushed under the weight of oppression.

The reality has always been more complex. Except for a period of relative cultural isolation and attendant provincialism between the collapse of the Spanish empire on the mainland in the 1820s and Cuba's own achievement of independence in 1902, Havana has been a cosmopolitan city. It was one of the major entrepôts of Spanish America, and all the currents of European thought and culture passed through its port. Cuba has had an active literary culture for four hundred years, which since the late nineteenth century has had a disproportionate influence on the literatures of all of the Spanish-speaking Americas. Even before the Revolution, when literacy rates hovered around 70 percent, the education of those who received one was often extraordinary. Among the first actions of the revolutionary government was a massive literacy campaign and a large investment in education at every level, as a result of which Cuba has one of the highest literacy rates and one of the best-educated populations anywhere. Presses and journals, though plagued by censorship and worse, and under government control, like almost everything else in Cuba, have proliferated, publishing an endless outpouring of books, a portion of each press run made available to the general population at giveaway prices in subsidized bookstores. Those who have chosen or been forced into exile have often been of the educated classes, and they, too, have spawned a publishing industry and a major efflorescence of literature and thought, which, because of the successive waves of emigration, has remained closely allied to the development of poetry on the island.

Very little of the poetry of Cuba and its diaspora has made its way into the awareness of non-Spanish speakers. The long postrevolutionary U.S. embargo is partly to blame, limiting the flow of information, but also limiting imports of paper to the island, so that books have been produced in small editions and rarely reprinted.

Perhaps more important than the effects of the embargo is the unsystematic way in which writing makes its way from one language to another. Faced with the overwhelming presence of the source culture, translators tend to translate work that flatters their preconceptions and the preconceptions of publishers and readers. Which is to say that politics often figures in the choice. This is especially true for poetry, a hard sell at the best of times. So, for instance, Heberto Padilla, a fine poet, was being published in translation by major New York publishers almost as soon as he left the island, for reasons that will become apparent, while the poetry of essential figures like José Lezama Lima and Eliseo Diego has had to wait for decades.

Between the late 1960s and early 1990s another factor came into play. Cuban poets needed government permission to have their work published, whether on or off the island, and until recently only the favored were allowed to travel abroad, as promoters of Cuba and their own work. A small cadre of what have come to be called the *oficialistas*, poets who, like Pablo Armando Fernández, Roberto Fernández Retamar, Miguel Barnet, and Nancy Morejón, often hold important government posts, became the public face of Cuban poetry in the outside world and have tended to be disproportionately published in translation. That most of them have also been victims of repression is often forgotten.

The reception of poets of the diaspora has also been influenced by politics. José Kozer, perhaps Cuba's most influential living poet and a resident of the United States since 1960, speaks of being shunned by the left in his adoptive country as a *gusano*, a worm, the term of abuse for anti-Castro exiles of the far right, while right-wing exiles themselves have sometimes rejected him as a communist because of his liberal politics; he, and those like him, have had a difficult time breaking into print in English.

Little of the work included here will be familiar to English-language readers, regardless of its source: most of the few translations that exist have been published in fugitive journals and books that have vanished from the bookshelves, and despite the lively interest in all things Cuban, there have been only a handful of narrowly focused bilingual anthologies.[2] *The Whole Island*, surprisingly, is the first attempt at a comprehensive picture of Cuban poetry in the modern period. I have tried to present a range of poetries that represent the best of what's been published in book form by native-born or naturalized Cubans writing in Spanish on or off the island, beginning with the founding of the seminal journal *Orígenes* in 1944 by Lezama Lima and the critic José Rodríguez Feo, and to present as well the full range of Cuban practice in this period.

It's worth bearing in mind that the discussion that follows inevitably suffers from a kind of tunnel vision. Cuban poetry in this account may seem separate from other arts and thought, even those produced by the poets themselves, many of whom are also novelists, essayists, and playwrights. It may also seem more Cuba-centered than the poetry itself, although a strong strain of exceptionalism in Cuba long predates the official messianism of the current regime.

It's also helpful to remember that Cuba's culture is in some ways very different from ours. North American readers may notice, for instance, the relative paucity of women in this anthology—only twelve of the fifty-five poets included. This proportion appears consistent with the relative numbers of women published on the island, although there may be a change in the works in the generation too young to be represented here, and it's not true of Cuban-born poets in the United States, where the gender division approximates that of North American poetry in general. My numbers are, at any rate, consistent with the proportions in the standard anthologies in Spanish.[3]

The relative scarcity of Cuban women poets has not been a hot-button issue on the island, although poets like Nancy Morejón and Reina María Rodríguez tend not to be shy about their displeasures. There don't appear to be any cultural or official barriers that women have to overcome to write or publish, and there have been important women writers in Cuba since the late nineteenth century. Some women have also wielded considerable power in literary bureaucracies, among them Morejón, who heads the Caribbean section of Casa de las Américas, the preeminent arts organization on the island, and Haydée Santamaría, who founded it in 1959 and was its director for twenty years until her death.

None of those I have asked about this subject have offered an explanation for the imbalance. Cubans of both genders have in fact been surprised by the question—it had simply never been raised.

Race plays a very different role in Cuba than in the United States, and although there is certainly plenty of racism, and economic inequality tends to cling to color lines as it does in the United States, it's considerably less poisonous than here.[4] One difference is the lack of a sense that ownership of African culture is restricted to those of African descent. It raises no eyebrows, for instance, that Miguel Barnet, a White ethnographer of Afro-Cuban culture, writes "ethnographic novels" from the point of view of Afro-Cubans, any more than Pablo Armando Fernández' right to compose his *santería*-derived poems would be questioned because of his color.[5]

The *negrista* poems (as Latin Americans refer to writing in Afro-Spanish dialect) familiar to non-Cubans from the early work of Nicolás Guillén had passed from fashion by 1944, and the major poets have rarely written in black dialect since. Like most of their white compatriots, Afro-Cuban poets tend to come from educated, urban backgrounds, and with the enormous extension of quality education in the generations since the Revolution I doubt that many of them would be able to speak or write dialect unselfconsciously.

Skin tone also functions differently in Cuban culture; those of mixed heritage are seen, and tend to see themselves, as a separate group. Guillén, for instance, would react indignantly if called black, insisting that he was *mulato*. For this reason the translators have retained the Spanish *mulato/mulata*, rather than using the English language mulatto, which carries very different cultural baggage.

At least nine of the included poets are *mulato* or black, and several others may be as well. It's not customary to include author portraits or mentions of race on book jackets in Cuba.

My goal, in any case, has been to present a collection of the most significant poems and poets within an evolving context that Cuban poets and readers might recognize, not as North Americans might wish it.

Among Cuban poets and readers there is general agreement about who the most important poets are, and I have included these, except for Dulce María Loynaz, whose estate's demands were exorbitant.[6] I have included as well a selection of other fine poets, many of them younger, from among the large number who had to be excluded because of limitations of space. Inevitably, this has led to injustices, but I hope that my choices are at least plausible.

Anthologies are about choices. My hope has been to display something of the complex matrix of ways of thinking about poetry and their environments that Cuban poets have woven, to create something of a group portrait through time of an extraordinary poetic culture very different from our own. Political considerations have played no part, though I am well aware that one polemic or another will inevitably be read into my inclusions and exclusions, and even into the line and page counts allocated to each poet.

Within Cuban poetry there's a mini-genre centered around the metaphor of the tightrope walker, deriving from Eliseo Diego's "The Rope Dancer's Risks" (p. 147). It's been put to different uses, but for me it has become something of an overarching metaphor for the Cuban poet's suspension between the external—the political—and the demands of craft and psyche.

The connection between politics and poetry has in fact been expressed by a tradition of poetic exile and martyrdom. Among Cuba's most important nineteenth-century poets, José María Heredia (1803–1839) was forced into exile; Gabriel de la Concepción Valdés, known by his pen-name Plácido (1809–1844), was executed for his supposed participation in a slave rebellion; and Juan Clemente Zenea (1832–1871) was executed as a rebel during Cuba's interminable and brutal wars of independence.

The most significant figure by far was José Martí (1853–1895), universally known as the Apostle of Independence, who was killed in the first engagement of Cuba's final struggle for freedom from Spain. His contemporary, Julián del Casal (1863–1893), has been assigned the role of an apolitical counterweight of sorts, not least by Lezama. Both are usually considered early members of or participants in the loosely organized hemisphere-wide movement known as *modernismo*, the idiosyncratic Latin American adaptation of French Romantic and Symbolist poetry of the second half of the nineteenth century. Their impact was felt during their lifetimes, but most of their work only became available in the 1920s, when the poets of the *Orígenes* group were first learning their craft.

Martí was the chief propagandist and theorist of Cuba's final War of Independence. He is ubiquitous, in public statuary and on the walls of every schoolroom and government office in Cuba, and in the opening lines of his "Versos sencillos" ("Simple Verses"), appropriated for the lyrics of "Guantanamera," Cuba's unofficial national anthem. Thanks to the Cuban exile community, he joins the other liberators of Latin America at the northern end of New York's Avenue of the Americas, where it gives way to Central Park, frozen in monumental bronze on his rearing horse at the moment before he was to be struck down in battle.

Martí was also one of Latin America's most influential poets. He was largely responsible for the introduction of Whitman to Spanish-language poetry, as well as for the introduction of free verse, though much of his own verse was rhymed. While poetry in rhyme, especially sonnets, is still written, free verse, and the long Whitmanic line, have become the dominant forms of Latin American verse.

In Martí's work can be found germs of the three tendencies that have governed most of Cuban poetry since: his often difficult syntax, extreme imagery, and nervous line are reminiscent of the *neobarroco;* there are poems that have the proselike cadences of what's come to be called *conversacionalismo;* and there are the poems that justify his position as a *modernista.*

A large part of Martí's impact has been as a role model, the quintessential revolutionary and patriot, the politically committed poet. "Every Cuban," according to José Kozer, "in his heart of hearts wants to be José Martí. But we lack two things that would be necessary to make this possible: the breadth of language as total knowledge and expression, and an ethical sense of life whose daily character is absolute, demanding of us a maximum of compassionate and spiritual behavior. . . . It's impossible to live with the language and ethical purity of the Apostle."[7] He has become the demanding conscience of Cuban poetry.

The poetry and life of Julián del Casal more closely approximate the standard image of *modernismo.* A dandy and *flâneur,* he dressed the part of the poet, as he had learned it from Baudelaire, whose crucial influence he introduced to Latin America, along with Baudelaire's invention, the prose poem (translating and imitating several of the master's), although most of Casal's poetry is in conventional rhymed forms. He cultivated an aesthete's eye in his personal collecting, in his poetry (introducing the *japonisme* that remains a part of Cuban culture), and in the remarkable *crónicas* that he wrote for the Havana newspapers to earn his keep. These journalistic pieces range from keenly noted society reportage to portraits of Havana's slums, all recounted with an ironic detachment. He has become the model for the poet as poet first and last, and for the creation of a politically inviolable aesthetic and personal realm.

It's tempting to elevate Martí and Casal into champions of the two arms of a dichotomy that can serve as the key to understanding the dialogue of Cuban poetry since 1944, but the choices taken have seldom been that stark. One needn't, however, exaggerate the explanatory power of the conflict between the ideal or necessity of a politically engaged poetry and the hope for a more private verse to appreciate its centrality. For a Cuban poet to be apolitical is so counter to expectations that it's inevitably interpreted as a political statement in itself.

By the late 1930s, when Lezama began publishing, *modernismo's* moment had passed (though it continued, notably, in the work of Dulce María Loynaz and remained an influence on a great deal that was to follow, including the lyrics of the *origenista* Eliseo Diego and the persistence of the figure of poet as *flâneur*). It was replaced as the dominant mode by what Latin Americans call *vanguardismo* (which is no more related to what we call in English the avant-garde than *modernismo* is related to what we call modernism). In Cuba, by the 1940s, the aspect of *vanguardismo* called *coloquialismo* or *conversacionalismo* had become dominant.[8]

Conversacionalismo eschewed the ornate imagery and vocabulary of *modernismo*, as well as its symbolism and indirection, in favor of a syntactically straightforward verse written in the language of everyday speech, a "poetry that does not inevitably have to be subjected to abstraction and the systematic chain of metaphors which have tyrannized poetics in the Spanish language over the centuries," as Heberto Padilla put it.[9] Eugenio Florit's epistolary "Poets Alone in Manhattan," and the work of Guillén, Virgilio Piñera, Fayad Jamís, and of course Padilla, are examples of *conversacionalismo*'s range, and it has remained the majority strain in Cuban poetry. Not incidentally, it has proven particularly useful for writers of political verse.

Padilla, to a degree that his contemporaries (who allied themselves with French surrealist and existentialist poetry) probably would have found disturbing, saw Cuban poetry as in need of an infusion of influence from the poetry of his English-language contemporaries, especially Robert Lowell. Lowell, in Padilla's estimation, "had brought back to American poetry a vigor of language that had dissipated—he was different from Eliot, Auden, Stevens, and William Carlos Williams," all published in *Orígenes*, and "he distanced himself also from the Beat poets. . . ."[10] The goal was a poetry in which the shaping hand of the poet was invisible.

Like most forms of thought, poetry usually requires that the overwhelming amount of language and other phenomena that are always present be radically filtered. For *conversacionalistas*, as for their English-language counterparts, that filtering is in the service of the presentation of a logically coherent argument that should be understandable by any competent reader. As such, its focus is on the end to be reached—an end known to the poet beforehand—rather than on what's encountered in the process of getting there. Since 1937, when his first book was published, but reaching its fulfillment in his poetry of the 1940s and thereafter, Lezama elaborated a very different practice. Taking his cue not from the poetry of another culture but from Spain's Baroque, out of which had grown its New World colonies, and particularly from the work of Luis de Góngora, he brought attention back to the world of undifferentiated phenomena that we all inhabit. So, in his major poems, the reader confronts an unfiltered glut of information, presented without syntactic or ideational hierarchy. The "Ode to Julián del Casal," for instance, presents details of Casal's Havana and the Havana of Lezama's day; obscure, sometimes private, references; allusions to the *crónicas*; objects from Casal's, as well as Lezama's, collection of art and oddities; inner thought and outer experience presented without boundaries or inhibitions—all, apparently, thrown at us helter-skelter, by means of an enormous vocabulary borrowing from the idioms of different trades, times, dialects, and places.

Padilla was to tell us in his memoir that reading Lezama "I found myself violently dispatched to a realm of pure language, his one and only kingdom."[11] From the beginning Lezama had confronted the accusation that his work was obscurantist, hermetic, a mere construct of language, disengaged from ordinary life, disinterested in social reality. He would answer, famously, that "sólo lo difícil es estimulante,"[12] only the difficult stimulates growth (which I find myself recasting as a statement at once Darwinian and from the realm of religious and therapeutic practice, "only hardship begets change"), but also that "understanding" was beside the point—the poem was to be experienced as a thing in itself, not as a subject for paraphrase. An analogy that comes to mind is a first encounter with a forest or any complex ecosystem. One can deconstruct the forest, catalog its species and their interactions, but it can't be paraphrased, one has to experience it as simply there. The Lezamian moment is of that order of reality—all the confusion of the unfiltered moment present at once. As such, he claimed, it was a more profound engagement with everyday life than the clarified narrative of *conversacionalismo*.[13]

There is no way to cope with this flood of phenomena except to submit oneself to the moment and be carried along in a fugal current, where words, references, and motifs recur and recombine in changing, progressive guises, creating an inexorable propulsive force.

Haroldo de Campos and Sévero Sarduy were to name this kind of art *neobarroco*,[14] a term that Lezama and his companions never used, but it's apt enough that it's become the term of choice, not only, I think, because Lezama had invoked the Baroque masters, but also because behind his practice is the central metaphor of the Baroque, the neoplatonic *concordia discors*, harmony out of discord.

To paraphrase a large body of theology, from the apparent chaos of the disjunct phenomena of a moment, a life, the natural world, and all of human history arises a harmony only perceivable to the mind of their maker, who alone is capable of simultaneous awareness of all things. To approach that state (and it is the function of the immense polyphonic structures of Baroque music, art and architecture to help us do so) is to approach the state of profound, endless ecstasy of the saved, who in the afterlife are joined to the mind of God, recapturing the harmony of the paradise garden from which humans were expelled for their discordant sin.[15]

Lezama thought of himself as a Catholic, but his version of Catholicism scandalized the more orthodox members of his circle. Hell, he thought, didn't exist, or if it did, it was and had always been empty.[16] He seems also not to have had a strong personal sense of a sinful nature to be overcome. And he apparently wasn't willing to consign paradise to the next life, pointedly naming his autobiographical novel *Paradiso*, in Italian, rather than the Spanish *paraíso*, so that his reference to the final book of Dante's allegorical *Divine Comedy* would be unmistakable. For Lezama, the ecstatic moment was in the full experience of the garden of this world, not the next.[17]

Orígenes, the first important organ for the dissemination of the *neobarroco*, began life in 1944 with an edition of three hundred hand-delivered copies. By the late 1940s the *neobarroco* had become a force with which hostile critics had to reckon, inspiring an essay in the large-circulation weekly *Bohemia* (which at the time was something like a combination of *Newsweek*, *People,* and the *New Yorker*).[18] In the three decades since Lezama's death it has become perhaps the dominant strain in Latin American poetry, among poets Catholic or otherwise.

What Kozer said of the demands posed by Martí could be applied equally to Lezama, and very few Cuban poets, other than the entirely secular Kozer, have risen to the challenge. Only Cintio Vitier (a Catholic), Samuel Feijóo (a Communist), Lorenzo García Vega (secular), and Raúl Hernández Novás (secular) have fully embraced it, though it has powerfully influenced the work of others, particularly Ángel Escobar and Soleida Ríos.

Orígenes emerged in a rare interval of relative calm in Cuba's tortured history, when Fulgencio Batista, who had been the de facto power on the island since he seized control of the military in 1933, was content to allow a civil government to rule. It was a uniquely permissive government in matters of censorship, and writers were basically ignored, which meant that a nonpolitical poetry became conceivable.

Most of the poets who have become known as the *Orígenes* group or generation, among them Piñera, Gastón Baquero, Diego, Vitier, Fina García Marruz, and, somewhat later, García Vega, had originally come together around three earlier short-lived journals that Lezama had edited, and they were united as much by Lezama's commanding presence and example (even his enemies saw him as something of a poetic saint for his total devotion to his art) as by his practice. It's helpful to remember how young they were in

1944. Lezama, at 34, was the oldest. Piñera was 32, Baquero 28, Diego 24, Vitier 23, García Marruz 21, and García Vega 17. It was a close-knit group. Lezama and Piñera's tortured, passionate friendship was already a decade old. Vitier and García Marruz were to marry, and Diego would marry García Marruz' sister. The poet and priest Ángel Gaztelu, Lezama's confessor and himself a member of the group, officiated at their weddings. Except for Piñera and García Vega, they all espoused a meditative Catholicism, and Lezama was something of a pontifical figure for his younger compatriots.

Orígenes was to publish forty issues, surviving until 1956, well into Batista's final thuggish presidency. It included work by Cuban poets who never identified themselves with the *Orígenes* group, including Eugenio Florit, Samuel Feijóo, Fayad Jamís, Pablo Armando Fernández, and Roberto Fernández Retamar, as well as a Who's Who of French, North American and English, and Spanish-language poets. But the seeds of its fracture were evident from the first, in Lezama's high-handedness, its perceived failure to engage politically, and also, as Piñera was to admit, its Catholicism.[19] Rodríguez Feo was to withdraw his co-editorship, and, crucially, his financial support, after issue 34, producing two parallel issues under his sole editorship before ceding the title to Lezama's version, which published its final issues with Baquero's financing. Immediately thereafter, Rodríguez Feo founded *Ciclón*, which continued publication until its voluntary dissolution shortly after the Revolution. Piñera was its guiding voice, and he published none of his erstwhile colleagues.

The entry of the revolutionary army into Havana early in January of 1959 irrevocably changed the lives of all Cubans. In the discussion that follows I will not attempt a balance sheet of the Revolution's impact for good or ill. My interest here is in the lives and work of Cuba's poets, who, like intellectuals in general, have probably been subject to greater scrutiny and repression than the population at large, although most of them were early and enthusiastic supporters of the Revolution. Almost all have suffered losses, though some have also gained.

It's also not my intention to judge the reactions and accommodations of men and women who have lived through a period of sometimes extreme psychological, political, and material stress, with which they have coped with varying degrees of grace. Sustained heroism and purity of motive are given to very few.

With the coming of the Revolution the place of the poet in relation to power structures became critical. Some, like Florit, denounced the new regime, from the safety of a comfortable life abroad, for its secularism and its impact on the old elite. A very few fled immediately, among them Baquero, who had been a member of the Batista government. Uniquely, he settled in Franco's hyper-Catholic, hyperauthoritarian Spain. Some who were too young to decide for themselves left with their families and much of the middle class between 1960 and 1965. Two, Iraida Iturralde and Lourdes Gil, were sent ahead by their families into exile, in the notorious Pedro Pan airlift, the product of rumors, spread by the CIA and elements of the U.S. Catholic church, that Cuban children were to be imprisoned in slave labor camps in the Soviet Union.

A far larger group of poets returned from abroad to take part in the new regime. There had been growing colonies of Cubans in the United States and elsewhere since the 1850s, and Paris had long been a place of refuge for Cuban writers.[20] Whether to leave or stay has always entailed a calculation of levels of comfort and discomfort. Those who were less attached to life on the island left voluntarily. I have mentioned Florit. José Kozer, who had been preparing to leave since adolescence, was another, although the expropriation of his father's business and the family's subsequent emigration made return unlikely.

Some of the poets who were to leave in subsequent waves of emigration, from 1980s Marielitos to those who have left legally in the past decade, have been victims of repression and worse, and others have left for reasons of ideology, but it's probably fair to say that the desire for a life with fewer material constraints has usually been a factor, perhaps increasingly so as leaving has become less dangerous.

Guillén, Pablo Armando Fernández, Jamís, Padilla, and José Álvarez Baragaño were among the large number of artists and intellectuals who returned, for reasons as varied as their reasons for leaving had been. Some, like Guillén, had been in political exile; others, like Pablo Armando Fernández, had left as part of the economic diaspora; and others had left because of discomfort with the political or cultural limitations of life on the island. There is no doubt that an enthusiasm for the creation of a new kind of society was a powerful motivation for return—it's difficult to deny the sincerity of the post-1959 poems of Jamís and Álvarez Baragaño, for instance—but they must also have been drawn by the probability of employment in a rapidly expanding cultural sector. These same motivations probably influenced the decisions of many intellectuals already on the island to stay.

It became the norm for writers to be employed in government ministries or government-funded arts and publishing.

Almost immediately after the Revolution, the clandestine newspaper of Castro's July 26th Movement, *Revolución,* surfaced and became Cuba's leading newspaper. Its weekly cultural supplement, *Lunes de Revolución,* under the direction of Guillermo Cabrera Infante and Pablo Armando Fernández, and with the active editorial participation of Piñera, Padilla, and Álvarez Baragaño, quickly grew from twelve to forty-eight pages with a weekly circulation of 250,000. Almost all of the older generation of poets (with the notable exception of Baquero, who had been written out of history) and most of those who, coming of age in the 1950s, have come to be known as the Generation of the Fifties, contributed. Reading *Lunes'* weekly supplement's table of contents, one is struck by the vast optimism of the time: its enormous array of Cuban and foreign authors and subject matter is witness to unlimited curiosity and the freedom to satisfy it.[21]

It also contains, in the issue of December 7, 1959, a strange diatribe by Padilla against Lezama and the entire *Orígenes* group that recasts earlier complaints about their mystical bent and distance from ordinary speech and reality into the much more dangerous language of the Revolution. For Padilla, Lezama and company are "the evidence of our literary colonialism and our subservience to enslaving literary forms. It's not an accident that the words, the vocabulary of those poets retains everywhere a repeated allusion to monarchy: kingdom, crown, prince, princess, heralds. . . ." In the new Cuba, by contrast, "the poet who expresses his anguish or joy will have this primary responsibility: he will have to oppose to gratuitous song a voice of service. . . ." The *Orígenes* group will survive, he writes, as a reminder of "the stupidities that we put an end to in 1959."[22]

Two weeks later Pablo Armando Fernández, who a few months earlier had written similarly about Lezama and *Orígenes* in *Ciclón,*[23] included Lezama's work in *Lunes* for the first time, with the tacit agreement of Piñera and over the opposition of Padilla and Álvarez Baragaño.[24]

The dream of a new Cuba in which the writers gathered around *Lunes* hoped to participate began to disintegrate almost immediately. From the very beginning there were signs—criticisms, attempts at coercion. By early 1961, in the wake of the crisis begun by the imposition of the U.S. embargo in November 1960 and the 1961 Bay of Pigs invasion, the slow train wreck that was to be the next decade had started.

The first blow was an attack on *Lunes,* not, ostensibly, because of its inclusion of opinions at odds with the increasingly hardening stance of the regime, but over Sabá Cabrera and Orlando Jiménez' sixteen-minute film *PM, a cinéma vérité* stroll through Havana's working-class black night life, for which *Lunes* had financed postproduction. The film was almost immediately withdrawn from exhibition by the government, criticized for showing an aspect of Cuban life that was unflattering to the nation, but the real issue seems to have been centralization of power and control. Castro was moving quickly toward the Communist Party, perhaps in order to flatter the Soviet regime, potentially a source of desperately needed hard currency and a guarantor of security against U.S. aggression, and the newly formed Instituto Cubano del Arte e Industria Cinematográficos (ICAIC) was run by Communist bureaucrats intent on consolidating the party's power.[25]

The resolution was that all film production would be placed under the control of ICAIC and *Lunes* would be shut down, and a meeting of artists, intellectuals, and the government, including Castro—billed as a town meeting where all viewpoints could be expressed freely—was called for Friday, June 16, 1961, and the following two Fridays in the auditorium of the National Library. In the event, the floor was largely left to the government and those who agreed with it. Only a few of the more skeptical artists and writers ventured to speak, among them Piñera, who let it be known that there was a suspicion in the artistic community of repression to come. He was assured that those who agreed with the Revolution had nothing to fear.[26]

In *Palabras a los intelectuales*, which Castro delivered at the final session, he addressed at length what he saw as "the fundamental question raised here . . . the question of artistic freedom." His answer is a long, chilling justification of censorship and a series of slightly veiled threats. Only those even among the honorable who were not sufficiently sure of their revolutionary convictions, he says, would raise the issue of artistic freedom, "because the revolutionary places the Revolution above all such questions, above his own creative spirit; he places the Revolution above everything else, and the most revolutionary artist would be willing to sacrifice even his artistic vocation for the Revolution."[27]

"We are . . . revolutionaries," he continued. "Those who are artists first and revolutionaries second don't think as we do. . . . We must think of the people first and ourselves after, and that is the only attitude that can be called truly revolutionary. And it's for those who don't have that attitude, but are nonetheless honorable, that the problem exists, and just as the Revolution is a problem for them, they constitute a problem that the Revolution must deal with." The solution is that the Revolution must give artists "who are not truly revolutionaries . . . a space within the Revolution where they can work and create and where their creative spirit, even if they are not revolutionary writers or artists, will have the opportunity and liberty to be expressed, within the Revolution. Which means: within the Revolution, everything; against the Revolution, nothing. . . . I think this is sufficiently clear. What rights do writers and artists have, whether or not they are revolutionaries? Within the Revolution, everything; against the Revolution, no rights at all."[28] It was sufficiently clear for many. Cabrera Infante, for one, secured a diplomatic post abroad.

In the remainder of his speech Castro outlined plans for the greatly expanded system of artistic education that remains one of the Revolution's great achievements, as well as for a centralized organization of artists and writers. Two months later the First National Congress of Cuban Writers and Artists created the Union of Writers and Artists of Cuba (UNEAC). Nicolás Guillén was its first president; Lezama Lima was one of its vice presidents, and largely responsible for its aesthetic direction. Its publishing arm, Ediciones Unión, which also produces the journal *Unión,* very quickly became, and remains, one of Cuba's most important publishers of poetry.

Membership in UNEAC conveyed privileges, as it still does: a monthly stipend, and access to employment in publishing and government arts bureaucracies. It was also an instrument of control. Of the artists and writers active in 1961 perhaps a third were allowed to join. Then as now nonmembers have had to find other ways to make a living. For its first two decades it was not uncommon for writers to be expelled. This still happens on occasion, as we shall see.

The night of October 11, 1961, which has become known as *La Noche de las Tres Pes*—the Night of the Three Ps—saw the first of a series of roundups of suspected prostitutes, pimps, and pederasts. Many were arrested while cruising, but some, including Piñera, simply because they were known or assumed to be gay. Unusually for Cuba, Piñera had always been open about his orientation. He was quickly released, out of fear that his celebrity would bring embarrassing attention to the regime.

Homosexuality had been illegal in Cuba since 1938, but the law had rarely been enforced. Gays and lesbians in general led closeted lives, socializing with each other at home or in private clubs. With the Revolution, a more open, flamboyant gay nightlife blossomed. The change in the regime's attitude two years later was probably a further flattery of Soviet ideas of normalcy, and an expression of the idea that deviant behavior was a product of corrupt capitalist societies. In any event, the change in policy fell particularly heavily on artists and writers, and accusations of homosexuality (as in the United States in the same period) were a weapon always at hand.

Even now, despite the legalization of homosexuality—a process begun in 1979 and completed in 1988—many gay and lesbian Cuban poets are circumspect about making their orientation public. To give a sense of the impact of persecution and innuendo, in an environment where innuendo always contains a threat, of the fifty-five poets included in this anthology I am aware of only twelve who are gay or lesbian. Probably several others are as well. However, writing explicitly from a gay perspective remains rare. Havana is one of the world capitals of gossip, and *habaneros* seem to have always known who is gay and who straight, which has meant that for much of the past forty-five years gays and lesbians have lived in fear, even those who held and still hold high offices in the arts establishment or the government itself.

Accusations of homosexuality were one of the pretexts for shutting down Ediciones El Puente, one of the last of the independent presses, in 1965, though the real motive was probably further consolidation of state control of the publishing industry. Some of El Puente's authors were homosexual, but sexual orientation hardly defined it. Among the poets it published were Miguel Barnet, Belkis Cuza Malé, and Nancy Morejón. Its editor, José Mario Rodríguez, was drafted into the Military Units to Help Production (UMAP), forced labor battalions made up of "social undesirables," among them Jehovah's Witnesses and gays. UMAPs were certainly used as an assertion of government power, but also as a response to the need to generate hard currency from the labor-intensive sugar industry. Conditions were always spartan and sometimes brutal. The UMAPs were shut down officially in 1967, and the camps were in fact empty by 1969, largely because of protests from the leadership of the government-run dance and theater establishments. By then Rodríguez had left Cuba and reestablished El Puente in Madrid, where he published Delfín Prats, among others.[29]

In the arts, as well as in the rest of Cuban life, a change was taking place, whose implications were more apparent to some than to others. Cabrera Infante tells us that Lezama warned him in 1966 that it would be a mistake to return to Cuba.[30] Heberto Padilla, on the other hand, came back from his government duties abroad and gave his name to what has become known as the Padilla Affair. It was to inaugurate a very dark time.

From the outside what unfolded seems odd to say the least, like a conflict between the right and left hands of the same body. There had been from 1959 onwards criticisms on the island of the directions the Revolution was taking in terms of individual rights, as in the successful protests against the UMAPs, and Padilla took part in these. His work nonetheless continued to be published in highly visible state-supported journals. In 1968 his book *Fuera del juego (Out of the Game, or On the Sidelines),* from which all of the selections in this anthology are taken, was awarded the Premio Julián del Casal by UNEAC. The jury included Padilla's *bête noire,* Lezama Lima. The prize for drama was awarded to Antón Arrufat's *Los siete contra Tebas (The Seven Against Thebes).* The prizes were to include publication by Ediciones Unión.

Immediately after the prizes were announced, both, but especially *Fuera del juego*, were denounced as counterrevolutionary by Cuba's Interior Ministry and by a range of periodicals, including some, like *El Caimán Barbudo (The Bearded Crocodile)*, under the editorship of Luis Rogelio Nogueras and then of Lina de Feria, that had recently published Padilla's poems, and significantly in *Verde Olivo (Olive Drab)*, the journal of the Cuban armed forces. This put UNEAC (which, like virtually all arts organizations in Cuba, regardless of claims to the contrary, has always been a de facto arm of the government) in a difficult position. Bowing to pressure while maintaining the fiction of independence, it published both books, but prefaced with a "Declaration of UNEAC concerning the prizes awarded to Heberto Padilla in Poetry and Antón Arrufat in Theater." The declaration, signed by the governing committee of UNEAC in "the year of the heroic guerrilla," states that "after several hours of full debate, in which every attendee expressed himself entirely freely," the committee and the deciding jurors agreed that the books would be published, but with the inclusion in each book of a note expressing the governing committee's disagreement with the choice as ideologically at variance with "our Revolution," and listing the names of the jurors. In brief, the declaration asserts that UNEAC had published, in accordance with "the respect that the Revolution has for freedom of expression," several books that had pushed the limits (presumably a veiled reference to Lezama's *Paradiso,* published two years earlier), and that this tolerance of difference had been seen as a weakness to be taken advantage of. *Los siete contra Tebas* was indicted as a counterrevolutionary allegory, and *Fuera del juego,* at much greater length, as a liberal capitalist assertion of individualism at the expense of the overriding need to subsume individualism to the collective action of the Revolution.[31]

The jurors noted, in a separate document, that many of the poems under attack had been published, without controversy, in unimpeachably pro-Revolution journals, like that of the Casa de las Américas. "The book's power and what gives it its revolutionary feeling," they concluded, "is precisely that it isn't justificatory, but critical, polemical, and in its essence wedded to the Revolution as the only possible solution for the problems with which the author is obsessed."[32]

Padilla's and Arrufat's books were removed from the shelves of bookstores and libraries shortly after publication. Three years later (during which time the regime had hardened considerably), on March 20, 1971, Padilla and his wife, Belkis Cuza Malé, were arrested. Cuza Malé was released after a few days, but Padilla was held until April 27, accused of "having plotted against the powers of the state." His interrogation during those five weeks didn't quite meet the definition of torture espoused by the Bush administration, but it was harsh enough.[33] The night of his release he delivered a coerced public confession before a gathering at UNEAC.

His confession took the familiar form of similar acts of contrition under Stalin's and Mao's regimes, but bears as well an uncanny resemblance to the public confessions of born-again sinners in charismatic sects, complete with an admission of something like original sin: "I was more concerned with my own intellectual and literary importance than with the importance of the Revolution." He also admitted being guilty of the sins of unhappiness and skepticism, despite Roberto Fernández Retamar's attempts to enlighten him.

Padilla was aware of what he was doing. By adopting a conventional rhetoric of grandiose repetitions pushed to the limits of bathos he sought to signal that he was acting under duress, but also that he was outsmarting his interrogators. It's doubtful that they missed his intent, and they probably didn't care. They had achieved their goal: there was to be little public dissent by writers for the next two decades.

Padilla had been asked to denounce others, and he complied. He asked his wife, Pablo Armando Fernández, César López, and Lezama (as well as several poets and novelists not included in this anthology) to confess their sins and repent. It is worth quoting in full the passage concerning Lezama:

> I know that this experience of mine, comrades, will be an example, will serve as an example to all the others. I know, for example . . . I don't know if he's here, but I venture to mention his name here with all the respect that his work deserves, with all the respect that his conduct deserves on so many levels, with all the respect that his person deserves; I know that I can mention Lezama. I can mention him for one simple reason: the Cuban Revolution has been very fair to Lezama, this very year the Revolution has published two of his books in the most beautiful editions.
>
> But Lezama's judgments have not always been fair to the Cuban Revolution. And all of these judgments, comrades, all of these attitudes and activities . . . are well known, and are well known, moreover, everywhere, are well known, moreover, by State Security; I'm not telling anything new here to anybody, much less to State Security; State Security knows about these attitudes, these opinions exchanged between Cubans and foreigners, opinions that are much more than merely opinions, opinions that constitute an entire point of view that orchestrates an analysis of books that afterward defame the Revolution by leaning upon the opinions of famous writers.
>
> And I have said it: Lezama is not fair and has not been fair, in my conversations with him, in conversations he has had with foreign writers in my presence, he has not been fair to the Revolution. I'm now convinced that Lezama would be capable of coming here to acknowledge it, to recognize it; I am convinced,

because Lezama is an extraordinarily honest man, with a limitless capacity for correction. And Lezama would be capable of coming here to acknowledge it, and to say: yes, *chico*, you're right; and the only possible way to make things right is the correction of our conduct.

Because what else can explain that a Revolution whose principles are Marxist-Leninist, what else but the breadth of its judgment, the extraordinary understanding that the Revolution possesses, [what else can explain] that it publishes even a work like Lezama's, which depends on other political and philosophical concepts, on other interests?[34]

Through Padilla, the state claims to be all-seeing and all-knowing, and it also takes down what must have been its major target. Lezama was vulnerable for several reasons, not least of which was his exuberant depiction of gay sex in his 1966 novel *Paradiso*. But he was also the arbiter of Cuban letters, despite his strange form of Catholicism, the difficulty of his work, and its almost total lack of political and politicizable content. And he had chosen Padilla's book for publication and defended his choice publicly after its condemnation.

The First National Congress of Education and Culture, which began while Padilla was in jail, ended three days after his release. The closing session featured an address by Castro that was filled with contempt for writers and intellectuals, in the midst of which he set forth the policy that had been evolving since 1961, which was to govern publishing for the next decade and beyond:

> We, a revolutionary people in a revolutionary process, value cultural and artistic creations according to their usefulness for the people, according to what they contribute to man, according to what they contribute to mankind's demand, to the liberation of mankind, to mankind's happiness.
>
> Our evaluation is political. There can be no aesthetic value that is against man. There can be no aesthetic value that is against justice, against the well-being, against the liberation, against the happiness of mankind. It can't exist!
>
> For a bourgeois anything can be an aesthetic value if it amuses, or diverts, or helps to entertain the leisure and boredom of the idle, the unproductive parasites. But this can't be a worker's, or a revolutionary's, or a communist's valuation.[35]

This meant in practice that for the next ten years both the apolitical, nonlinear Lezamian mysticism that Padilla had come very close to labeling counterrevolutionary in 1960 and the plainspoken, ironic, politically engaged *conversacionalismo* that Piñera and Padilla had championed, among other things, as a vehicle for debate within the Revolution, were sidelined in favor of an exhortatory, relentlessly optimistic version of the conversational style, a poetry whose engagement with the Revolution was marked by a critical stance only toward its opponents, a total lack of reflectiveness, the virtual elimination of the pronoun "I" in favor of "we," and a plethora of odes to the Revolution's martyrs and heroes. The term "socialist realism" applies. Almost none of it remains in print, even on the island.

Luis Rogelio Nogueras provides some of the very few bright moments in this grim time. Even his poems that most closely match the opinions of the regime manage a lightness of touch and a personal tone, and he created for some of the poems an ironic distance by signing them with the names of fictitious poets, whose biographies he provided.

The political establishment continued to promote the revolutionary need for an ongoing critique within an ongoing revolutionary process, but it was amply clear that it intended to monopolize that privilege.

Lezama was forced into involuntary retirement; he was not to be published again in Cuba until 1977, the year after his death, although his reputation outside the country continued to grow. Pablo Armando Fernández, who would deliver the eulogy at Lezama's grave, would not publish in Cuba or abroad, except for a brief chapbook that he printed at his own expense, until 1983. César López would not publish again until 1983, and Antón Arrufat would not be published nor have his plays performed until 1986. Belkis Cuza Malé's book *Juego de damas (Checkers;* literally, *The Game of Ladies),*[36] which had just been published at the time of her arrest, was withdrawn from circulation. Her next Cuban publication was in the anthology *Las palabras son islas (Words Are Islands)* in 1999.[37] She left Cuba in 1979. Padilla's next Cuban publication was also in *Las palabras son islas.* He left the island in 1980. All of their books were removed from the shelves of bookstores and libraries.

The early 1970s was a period of increased hardship on the island, and that, combined with their suffering at the hands of the regime, would certainly have caused a great many other poets to leave, but exit visas had become almost impossible to obtain, except for trusted allies of the regime, who traveled incessantly as its cultural emissaries.

Of those not immediately involved in the Padilla-Arrufat controversy, Piñera was never published (nor his plays produced) again in his lifetime, Vitier and García Marruz collaborated on two works of scholarship, their only publications until the 1980s; and García Vega, who had left the island in 1968, remained unpublished there until *Las palabras son islas.* Francisco de Oraá didn't publish again until 1978. Perhaps because of their association with El Puente, Miguel Barnet was not to publish again in Cuba until 1980, Nancy Morejón, except for two scholarly works, until 1979, and Delfín Prats (whose first book, *Lenguaje de mudos,* had won UNEAC's Premio David but was never published in Cuba) until 1987.[38] All of their books became unavailable.

Of the *origenistas* who remained in Cuba only Eliseo Diego managed to remain in print. Of their contemporaries, Samuel Feijóo, who had sided with the regime's anti-gay policies in the 1960s, also continued to publish. As for the Generation of the Fifties, only three of the poets represented in this anthology were allowed to publish: Roberto Branly; Fayad Jamís (vulnerable because he had accepted *Paradiso* for publication and drawn its cover art), who spent most of the 1970s and 1980s as a diplomat in Mexico; and Roberto Fernández Retamar, who took on the job of answering the worldwide outburst of criticism from writers previously friendly to the regime.[39]

It's difficult not to read Francisco de Oraá's "De tres fotos de Mella" ("On Three Photos of Mella"), written in 1980 but not published until 1986, as a reflection on the failures of the preceding decade. Mella, the martyred founder of Cuba's Communist Party, becomes a disapproving superego:

> in his reproachful father's brow I seemed to hear Mella's questions:
> "What are you doing in the world? What are you doing with your life?"
> I answered as my strange self allowed
> —strange always to others and alien to my desire,
> so that I wasn't what I wanted to be
> and I didn't live the way I wished.
> I only know that, deep down, I would have wanted to be let loose in the
>   garden,
> and that the garden would grow and become the whole world.[40]

By the late 1970s Cuba had entered into its period of greatest prosperity and security since the Revolution, thanks in large part to direct subsidies and favorable trade agreements with the Soviet Union and its allies, and with the change came a gradual relaxation of the demands placed on writers. Even after the catastrophic economic collapse following the end of the Soviet Union (in a single year the Cuban economy lost 60 percent of its value), this process continued. A new generation of writers emerged, most of whom had little access to much of the most important work of the *origenistas* and the Generation of the Fifties until they were in their twenties, when the work of the older poets began to emerge in the form of new publications and new editions of their earlier books, and some of them, including Cintio Vitier, Pablo Armando Fernández, Miguel Barnet, and Nancy Morejón, became members of the ruling elite. Francisco de Oraá, César López, Cintio Vitier, Fina García Marruz, and Antón Arrufat have become elder statesmen of Cuban letters, Piñera has assumed the status of martyr and hero for younger Cuban poets, and Lezama's modest apartment in one of Havana's most dilapidated quarters is now a museum and cultural center.

Even exiles, some of whom, like Baquero, had been written out of history, their names removed from the captions of group photographs, were once again published on the island. Many of them first appeared in *Las palabras son islas*, the first anthology published on the island since the Revolution to include writers in exile. *La patria sonora de los frutos (The Sonorous Homeland of Fruit)*, a large selection of Baquero's poetry, and Kozer's *No buscan reflejarse (They Don't Seek to Be Reflected)*, the first two books by poets of the diaspora to be published in Cuba since the early 1970s, appeared in 2001.[41]

In 2000, when I was just beginning to think about the contents of this anthology, I spoke with Roberto Fernández Retamar. "Let me assure you," he told me, "that I have always been and still am a true revolutionary. Nonetheless, you must include Baquero in your anthology." Fernández Retamar always speaks for the regime, and he was signaling a change that would bring the publication on the island of almost every writer of any importance in the diaspora. Many of them had been known to some extent: baggage is rarely inspected for books at Cuban airports, which has meant, for instance, that a few copies of Kozer's books have been in circulation since the early 1980s. By the mid-1990s there was greater access to the Internet, which has meant that Cuban writers are in constant, if guarded, contact, and there are now dozens of ezines and websites, both on- and off-island, allowing access to the work of writers of all camps.[42]

A major difference in the lives of poets after the 1980s has been the greater ease with which poets who have left the island visit and those who live on the island leave. In the 1990s the Clinton administration greatly liberalized visiting rights for Cubans living in the United States, allowing them to visit the island legally once a year. Temporary U.S. visas for Cuban writers also became relatively easy to obtain. The Bush administration enforced the much stricter limit of one visit in three years for Cubans living in the United States (if they have parents, siblings, or children in Cuba), and it virtually eliminated temporary U.S. visas for Cubans resident in Cuba (even for openly dissident writers). Any Cuban who manages to set foot on U.S. soil illegally receives residency for the asking. As of this writing, the Obama administration has lifted restrictions on travel to Cuba for Cuban-Americans with immediate family on the island, but the Bush restrictions on travel in the other direction remain in force.

From the Cuban side, exit visas, once restricted to writers strongly connected to the regime, have become pro forma, and writers who obtain exit visas and then become foreign residents are free to return with no fear of being held, which for many has greatly eased the decision to leave.

The regime's apparent liberalization has had a motive. In the financial crisis that followed the collapse of the Soviet Union, and with the U.S. embargo still in place, one of Cuba's few potential sources of the hard currency it has needed to keep the economy running has been tourism, and overt oppression is very bad advertising. And the hard currency that Cubans from abroad have brought with them or sent to their families under somewhat liberalized U.S. rules, as well as the money that Cubans have earned in their travels, enters the government's reserves, because all markets and financial institutions are government-controlled.

This has created a bizarre situation. Cuba now has two currencies—pesos (known as *moneda nacional*, or MN) and convertible pesos—and two economies. Those in the tourist trade, which is run entirely in hard currency (currently euros and Canadian dollars), or who receive remittances or earn money abroad, can convert their hard currency into convertible pesos for otherwise scarce items, or exchange them for MN at twenty-five to one. Salaries continue to be paid in MN. Only with great effort can one find the minimal provisions provided by one's ration book; everything beyond that has been enormously inflated. Those who have a product or service to sell often do so on the black market, for hard currency.

Most Cuban writers are entirely dependent on their peso salaries, which means that their standards of living have fallen catastrophically. And while they suffer less repression than in the past and tend to express their disagreements with the regime more openly, particularly on the Internet, there is still censorship. None of Antonio José Ponte's fiction or his 2004 book of essays *El libro perdido de los origenistas (The Lost Book of the Origenistas)* have been published in Cuba, for instance, although they are available elsewhere in several languages. And open dissent has consequences. Ponte has been expelled from UNEAC, which means he can't earn the meager living of a writer in Cuba. In his case the financial loss is inconsequential: his books earn foreign royalties and he has had no trouble attracting invitations from abroad; in fact, he has been a resident of Spain for several years. For most other writers the threat of any loss of income often remains a crucial deterrent. And there's the further threat, evidenced by occasional repressive acts, that an unrestrained government that hasn't been shy about disrupting lives in the past could do so again.

The result has been that poets leave. Of the twenty-one living members of the generations of the 1980s and 1990s included in this anthology, eleven are currently resident abroad and three others have deliberately left their status ambiguous. All managed to leave Cuba legally, with legitimate invitations from foreign cultural institutions in hand, except for one, who claims to have forged his invitation. His success may indicate how casual the regime's oversight has become. Most have settled in Europe or Latin America. A few, after some years in other countries, have become legal residents of the United States. One crossed the border from Mexico with a *coyote,* becoming a legal immigrant the moment his foot touched U.S. soil.

Poetry of the 1980s and after, both on and off the island, has tended to continue the conversational tradition, though with a far more intimate, personal focus, and frequently a retreat into fantasy or childhood or an imagery of dreams or the surreal reminiscent of Eliseo Diego, upon which are sometimes built layers of subtle irony. Overwhelmingly, there has been a turning inwards toward an often hermetic conversation with the self and away from the public sphere.

But the poets of the 80s, 90s and beyond are an extremely varied group. While many poets on the island have claimed the long-sought territory of the private sphere, by dint of conscious or unconscious self-censorship, as an outsider one could easily miss the presence of a political critique hiding in plain sight. I asked Fernández Larrea about the expletive at the end of "El país de los elfos" ("The Land of Elves"), which appears until that final word to be the narrative of a childhood fantasy: ". . . in the land of elves / damn." "The land of elves," he explained, "is something like 'the promised future, idyllic communism.'"

Similarly, "the cynical head of the crocodile" in Rolando Sánchez Mejías' "Cálculo de lindes" ("A Calculus of Boundaries") would be instantly recognizable to Cubans as a swipe at Castro: the crocodile has long been a synonym for Cuba, because of its shape on the map.

It would be harder to miss the message within Soleida Ríos' baroque structures. "The important thing was—is— " she tells us in "Texto sucio" ("Dirty Text"), "that leading such regimented lives we haven't learned how to live. We haven't learned . . . We don't know how to solve the problems of our own lives. Without Divine Intervention. Without A Decision From Above." A decision from "He Who Is in Charge" in "Gathering Lemons," the insistence on a nonsensical path in "The Road to the Cemetery." It would be equally difficult to miss the import of the last two lines of Damaris Calderón's provocatively titled "This Will Be the Only Lie We'll Always Believe": "This is a sad business / this playing at being perfect."

The *neobarroco* has become again a major influence, certainly on Soleida Ríos' work, but also on the dense, involuted poetry of Ángel Escobar, and the hallucinatory, driven structures of Raúl Hernández Novás, where Lezama and John Lennon mix as equally the impetus for obsessive exploration.

For one group of poets, including Pedro Marqués de Armas, Rolando Sánchez Mejías, Rogelio Saunders, Ismael González Castañer, and Carlos A.

Aguilera, the *neobarroco* has been decisive. Like the *origenistas,* they have given themselves a name and created a journal, *Diáspora(s),* edited by Sánchez Mejías and Aguilera, seven issues of which appeared between 1996 and 2002. Produced in photocopied editions of never more than a hundred, and without the legally required government sanction, it was never shy about publishing materials that in a previous decade would have led to arrest. Here, for instance, the first paragraph of Saunders' "El Fascismo. Apuntes" ("Fascism. Notes"), which appeared in the second issue: "A State that never wants to appear to be the cause of any evil, that wants to appear to be instead the Great Benefactor, when in reality it is in every instance the *only* cause of the evil that erupts in a million places at once like a huge incurable pustule." [43] It would be easy to multiply examples, and the political is rarely absent from the poetry of the *diasporistas.* They reject, in fact, the distinction between the personal and the political as a false dichotomy—theirs is a politically involved reinvention of the *neobarroco.*

Along with Antón Arrufat, Soleida Ríos, Juan Carlos Flores, Omar Pérez López, Antonio José Ponte, Alessandra Molina, and Javier Marimón, the *Diáspora(s)* poets were frequent guests of Reina María Rodríguez' salon, known by its location, her rooftop apartment, or *azotea.* In a country where until recently private parties were illegal, its very existence was subversive. It was subversive fun, but also a venue for sharing one's latest writing and ideas, in an environment where the state held no sway.

Despite the addition of a new generation of writers, today the *azotea* is considerably depleted. Rodríguez, Arrufat, Ríos, and Flores remain; the rest have left the island. Ríos expresses the poignancy of being left behind in her "Dirty Text."

A recent controversy about the appearance of three of the key figures in the implementation of the persecutions and censorship of the 1960s and 1970s, in a Cuban television documentary, dramatizes the changing position of writers and intellectuals within the current avatar of the Cuban regime. A very public storm of protest erupted on the Internet and in newspapers and journals around the Spanish-speaking world. Among the most vocal were Arrufat (who had been a victim of those persecutions), Rodríguez, and Ponte. The fear was that the re-emergence of the three ex-officials into public view might be a harbinger of a new round of repression.

The response from the regime was astonishing. In an interview in the Mexican newspaper *La Jornada* Abel Prieto, Cuba's minister of culture, said that the appearance of the three in the documentary had been a mistake, not a change in cultural policy. He continued, by way of an ingenious reading of Castro's *Palabras a los intelectuales,* "The government of this country now views very critically that period, when we moved away from the cultural politics that the Revolution initiated in 1961, in which artists and writers of every tendency, of every generation; Catholics, Communists, even honorable nonrevolutionaries, were invited to join the cultural enterprise."[44] It has apparently become dogma that the years of the worst repression were an aberration.

Signs of change have become commonplace. On October 20, 2007, Antón Arrufat's *Las siete contra Tebas* was performed in Cuba for the first time. A few weeks later, on November 16, Prieto declared on an Internet forum that "there is no censorship of artists and intellectuals" in Cuba.[45]

While his assertion was greeted by titters in some quarters, the regime has undoubtedly allowed larger areas of freedom to writers in recent years, and Prieto's words may come to be true in the near future, but no one, I think, ever forgets that it's the regime that decides what to allow. And while it may appear that this softening of repression is a sign of the regime's impending dissolution, few are assuming that to be the case. On the contrary, it may be that the regime now feels so secure that it no longer needs to control what's written, spoken or published as tightly as it used to. Maybe Cuban writers will become as irrelevant to those in power as their counterparts in the United States.

But no one is making a lot of predictions. One would like to imagine a democratic, prosperous Cuba free of foreign domination or embargo and not dependent economically on either remissions from abroad or the fickle and often degrading demands of a tourist economy, a Cuba in which poets will have the choice of embracing or ignoring the political without compunction. When or if this will happen or if it's even possible—certainly no other country in the Caribbean or Central America has managed it—remains an open question.

What is beyond dispute is that despite enormous pressures Cuban poets have produced a poetic culture of extraordinary wealth and originality that has been largely unavailable to North Americans for far too long.

July 15, 2009

Notes

1. With apologies to Canadian readers, I have used "North American" to indicate a citizen of the United States. Most Latin Americans find it annoyingly presumptuous that we call ourselves Americans to the exclusion of the hemisphere's other inhabitants. Thus far the English language offers no equivalent to the Spanish *estadounidense,* "unitedstatesian."

The primary audience for this introduction (as for the anthology itself) is, of course, North American; I have accordingly focused on issues with which North Americans will find themselves dealing in reading Cuban poetry. I have also focused on Cuba's relationship, cultural and political, with the United States, which has been primary, as Louis A. Pérez has documented for the period 1898 to 1959 in his *On Becoming Cuban: Identity, Nationality, and Culture* (Chapel Hill: University of North Carolina Press, 1999), and which I would contend has been equally dominant since, despite, and, paradoxically, because of the post-1960 U.S. embargo. As evidence, one need look no further than the frequent references within the poems to the English-speaking giant to the north, and the almost total lack of reference to the rest of Latin America.

Cuba has always been awash with the poetry of the rest of Latin America, and in the past its influence has been significant. Since 1944 Cuban poetry has been decidedly an export commodity. No Brazilian, Chilean, or Mexican poet has facilitated paradigm shifts on the island, while Guillén, Lezama, and Kozer have been the instruments of major change on the mainland. And of course Cuba's revolution, widely read as a revolution against U.S. hegemony, has been seen, even by its Latin American detractors, as a second declaration of Latin American independence.

All of this would be subject for another book.

2. Of the anthologies, *Cuban Poetry, 1959–1966,* edited by Claudia Beck, Sylvia Carranza, Heberto Padilla, and Luis Suardíaz (Havana: Book Institute, 1967; there was also a Spanish-French bilingual edition), is overwhelmingly political in intent. Nathaniel Tarn's *Con Cuba: An Anthology of Cuban Poetry of the Last Sixty Years* (London: Cape Goliard & Grossman, 1969) was produced hurriedly as a reaction to the growing awareness of dangers faced by Cuban poets. As its title indicates, Margaret Randall's *Breaking the Silences: An Anthology of Twentieth-Century Poetry by Cuban Women* (Vancouver, B.C.: Pulp Press, 1982) leaves out male poets. Lori Marie Carson and Oscar Hijuelos' *Burnt Sugar Cana Quemada: Contemporary Cuban Poetry in English and Spanish* (New York: Simon & Schuster, 2006) consists largely of poems written in English by the U.S.-born children or grandchildren of émigrés. Francisco Morán's *Island of My Hunger: Cuban Poetry Today* (San Francisco: City Lights, 2008) limits itself to poets born since 1950.

3. A brief glance at sixteen anthologies of modern Cuban poetry in Spanish yielded an average of 17 percent women.

4. For a history of race relations in Cuba, see Alejandro de la Fuente, *A Nation for All: Race, Inequality, and Politics in Twentieth-Century Cuba* (Chapel Hill: University of North Carolina Press, 2001). In his otherwise excellent study, de la Fuente fails to mention Gastón Baquero's seminal essays written in the 1960s, 1970s and 1980s, collected in *Indios, blancos y negros en el caldero de América* (Madrid: Ediciones de Cultura Hispánica, 1991), especially "Hay razos o no hay razos?" (1963) and "El negro en Cuba" (1972).

5. Jorge Luis Morales' anthology *Poesía afroantillana y negrista* (Río Piedras: Universidad de Puerto Rico, 1976, 1981, and 2000), one of the standard works on the subject, includes numerous white writers. An indication of cultural differences about race is that this would be inconceivable in an English-language anthology.

6. I refer the reader to the two bilingual collections of Loynaz's poetry: *A Woman in Her Garden: Selected Poems of Dulce María Loynaz,* translated by Judith Kerman (Buffalo, N.Y.: White Pine Press, 2002), and *Against Heaven,* translated by James O'Connor (Manchester, U.K.: Carcanet, 2007). Those knowledgeable about Cuban poetry may wonder at the absence of two important poets, Emilio Ballagas (1908–1954) and José Zacarias Tallet (1893–1989), both of whom continued to publish poetry into the period covered by *The Whole Island.* All of Ballagas' best work was in fact published by 1941; to include his later

poetry would have been a disservice to his memory. Tallet, an important influence on Cuban *conversacionalismo* (see below) along with Guillén and Florit, wrote poetry only sporadically; most of his work, including all of his best and most influential poems, was produced in the 1930s, when it was widely circulated in newspapers and journals, although Tallet didn't gather it into a book until 1951.

7. José Kozer, "Martí, una ansiedad," *Encuentro de la Cultura Cubana* 3 (Winter 1996–1997): 64. See also José Antonio Ponte's discussions of the influence of Martí and Casal in *El libro perdido de los origenistas* (Mexico City: Aldus, 2002).

8. My account of the different schools of Cuban poetry is necessarily brief and perhaps oversimplified. *Vanguardismo*, in particular, involved a lot more than the *conversacionalismo* of its final phase. But that's a story for another time. It's worth remembering that discussions of literary taxonomy often shed more heat than light, and that a great many, perhaps most, poets avoid identifying themselves with any school.

9. Heberto Padilla, *Self-Portrait of the Other*, translated by Alexander Coleman (New York: Farrar, Straus, Giroux, 1990), p. 29.

10. Ibid.

11. Ibid., p. 169.

12. José Lezama Lima, "Mitos y cansancio clásico," in *La expresión americana* (Santiago, Chile: Editorial Universitaria, 1969), p. 1. The first edition, published in Havana in 1957, is extremely scarce.

13. For an early statement of what became the standard objections to Lezama and the *neobarroco*, and Lezama's customary answers, see Jorge Mañach, "El arcano de cierta poesía nueva. Carta abierta al poeta José Lezama Lima," *Bohemia*, Sept. 25, 1949; and José Lezama Lima, "Respuesta y nuevas interrogantes. Carta abierta a Jorge Mañach," *Bohemia*, Oct. 2, 1949.

14. Haroldo de Campos, "A obra de arte aberta," *Diário de São Paulo*, July 3, 1955. Sarduy wrote exhaustively about the Baroque and the *neobarroco* for several decades. Of special importance is his "Barroco y neobarroco," in César Fernández Moreno, *América Latina en su literatura* (Mexico City: UNESCO/Siglo XX, 1972), pp. 24–27.

15. Useful discussions of the *concordia discors* can be found in C. S. Lewis, *The Discarded Image: An Introduction to Medieval and Renaissance Literature* (Cambridge, U.K.: Cambridge University Press, 1964); and Robert E. Stillman, *Sydney's Poetic Justice* (Lewisburg, Penn.: Bucknell University Press, 1986). For the concept's neoplatonic origins, see Andrew Scholtz, *Concordia Discors: Eros and Dialogue* (Washington, D.C.: Center for Hellenic Studies, 2007).

16. Recounted by David Huerta, in "Trece motivos para Lezama," the introduction to his selected Lezama, *Muerto de Narciso. Antología poética* (Mexico City: Era, 1988), p. 9.

17. For an important reading of the Baroque and the *neobarroco*, though for the most part focused on prose, see Roberto González Echevarría, *Celestina's Brood: Continuities of the Baroque in Spanish and Latin American Literature* (Durham, N.C.: Duke University Press, 1993), particularly the last chapter.

Lezama elaborated a complex metaphysical system of the image, the poem, and history, not dealt with here. For an introduction in Lezama's words, see "Interview with José Lezama Lima" by Armando Álvarez Bravo (translated by James Irby), in *José Lezama Lima: Selections,* edited by Ernesto Livon-Grosman (Berkeley: University of California Press, 2005), pp. 122–137. For a concise summary of Lezama's system, see Emilio Bejel, *Gay Cuban Nation* (Chicago: University of Chicago Press, 2001), pp. 117–120.

18. Lezama Lima, "Mitos y cansancio clásico."

19. Piñera recounts and documents the reasons for his disagreements with Lezama (and their history, dating back to the 1930s) in "Cada cosa en su lugar," *Lunes de Revolución* 39 (Dec. 14, 1959): 11–12. For an anecdotal account of the difficult friendship of Lezama and Piñera, the founding and dissolution of *Orígenes* and *Ciclón*, and the hostility toward Lezama of the group surrounding *Lunes de Revolución*, see the memoirs gathered in Roberto Pérez León, *Tiempo de Ciclón* (Havana: Unión, 1991).

20. See Jason Weiss' encyclopedic *The Lights of Home: A Century of Latin American Writers in Paris* (New York: Routledge, 2002).

21. For an account of *Lunes*, the memories of its publisher, Carlos Franquí, and its editor and assistant editor, Guillermo Cabrera Infante and Pablo Armando Fernández, and a complete table of contents of its 129 issues, see William Luis, ed., *Lunes de Revolución: Literatura y cultura en los primeros años de la Revolución Cubana* (Madrid: Verbum, 2003).

22. "La poesía en su lugar," *Lunes de Revolución* 38 (Dec. 7, 1959): 5–6. This translation, like all translations not otherwise credited, is mine.

23. Pablo Armando Fernández, "Refutación a Vitier," *Ciclón* 4, no. 1 (Jan.–Mar. 1959); translated by Stephen D. Gingerich in *New Centennial Review* 2, no. 2 (Summer 2002): 134–150 (an issue devoted entirely to *Orígenes* and *Cíclon*).

24. Guillermo Cabrera Infante, "Un mes lleno de *Lunes*," in Luis, ed., *Lunes de Revolución*, p. 142.

25. I refer to the Partido Socialista Popular (People's Socialist Party), one of the several Communist parties that had been active in Cuba since the 1920s. In 1962 it was to join with Castro's 26th of July Movement and the Revolutionary Directory March 13th student party to form Cuba's current Communist Party.

ICAIC appears to many as being anomalously liberal, producing films like *Fresa y chocolate* (*Strawberries and Chocolate*, 1994), an international hit that seemed to signal a new openness by the regime to criticism. It should be noted, however, that the film, set ten years in the past, deals with a subject that had become less controversial; its distribution on the island was extremely limited and short-lived; and it was not shown on Cuban television until 2008. Like many of ICAIC's more open films, it was intended primarily for export.

26. "Encuentro de los intelectuales cubanos con Fidel Castro (Fragmentos de la primera sesión), Biblioteca Nacional, La Habana, 16 de junio, 1961," *Encuentro de la Cultura Cubana* 43 (Winter 2006/2007): 157–175. Among the participants were Baragaño and Padilla. The exchange between Piñera and Castro is on pages 163–164, Castro's reaction continuing until p. 168.

27. Fidel Castro Ruz, *Palabras a los intelectuales* (Havana: Departamento de Ediciones de la Biblioteca Nacional "José Martí," 1991), p. 6, 9–10.

28. Ibid., p. 11, 12–13.

29. My account of the varying status of homosexuals in Cuba is largely drawn from Ian Lumsden, *Machos, Maricones, and Gays: Cuba and Homosexuality* (Philadelphia: Temple University Press, 1996).

30. Cabrera Infante, "Un mes lleno de *Lunes*," p. 146.

31. The most important documents of the Padilla Affair are included in *Fuera del juego: Edición conmemorativa, 1968–1998* (Miami: Ediciones Universal, 1998). "Declaración de la UNEAC" is on pp. 115–121.

32. "Dictamen del jurado del concurso de la UNEAC 1968," in *Fuera del juego. Edición conmemorativa*, pp. 87–88.

33. Padilla's account of his imprisonment is in his memoir, *La mala memoria* (1989), translated by Alexander Coleman as *Self-Portrait of the Other* (New York: Farrar, Straus, Giroux, 1990), pp. 143–166.

34. *Fuera del juego. Edición conmemorativa*, p. 148. After he delivered his confession, Padilla and Lezama dined together. By all accounts they had become friends before the confession and were to remain so until Lezama's death. Parts of Padilla's memoir read like an apology to Lezama the man, if not Lezama the poet. Piñera and Lezama had reconciled after the publication of *Paradiso* and remained very close, as did Lezama and Pablo Armando Fernández. Words that may seem to us unforgivable are often considerably less so within the context of the unrestrained verbal ferocity of Latin American literary controversies.

35. Ibid., p. 157.

36. Belkis Cuza Malé, *Juego de damas*, 2d ed. (Cincinnati: Termino Editorial, 2002).

37. Jorge Luis Arcos, ed., *Las palabras son islas: Panorama de la poesía Cubana, siglo XX (1900–1998)* (Havana: Letras Cubanas, 1999)—the essential Cuban anthology.

38. Delfín Prats, *Lenguaje de mudos* (Madrid: El Puente, 1970).

39. Roberto Fernández Retamar, "Calibán. Apuntes sobre la cultura en nuestra América" (1971) and its 1986 appendix, "Calibán revisitado," both included in Edward Baker's translation, *"Caliban" and Other Essays* (Minneapolis: University of Minnesota Press, 1989).

40. Translated by Christopher Winks. See page 223.

41. Gastón Baquero, *La patria sonora de los frutos. Antología poética*, edited by Efrain Rodriguez Santana (Havana: Letras Cubanas, 2001); José Kozer, *No buscan reflejarse. Antología poética*, edited by Jorge Luis Arcos (Havana: Letras Cubanas, 2001).

42. Among the more important of those produced on the island, and very much supportive of the regime, are *Cubaliteraria* (www.cubaliteraria.com) and *La Jiribilla* (www .lajiribilla.cu). On the other side are two of the most important of those produced off-island, *Encuentro de la Cultura Cubana* (www.cubaencuentro.com/revista; also available in print) and *La Habana Elegante* (www.lahabanaelegante.com), which includes "La azotea de Reina," edited by Reina María Rodríguez. Writers on- and off-island increasingly participate in all of them, and *La Jiribilla* includes on its site a link to *Encuentro*.

43. In *Tsé-tsé* 13, "ni orden ni desorden," Oct. 2003, p. 31. Pages 3–77 of *Tsé-tsé* 13 are dedicated to *Diáspora(s)*.

44. "Encuentro en la Red," on the *Encuentro de la Cultura Cubana* website, Mar. 25, 2007. A dossier of the email exchanges is to be found in the print edition of *Encuentro* 43 (Winter 2006/2007): 253–269.

45. For an account of the long-delayed premiere of *Las siete contra Tebas*, see *Encuentro en la Red*, Nov. 21, 2007. For a report of Prieto's declaration, see Cuba-L, http://cuba-l .unm.edu/?nid=41543&q=prieto&h=.

A Note on the Text

The poets are arranged by birth order, the poems by date of publication. Dates at the ends of poems are as originally published with the poems.

Spanish texts are as published or as supplied by the poets. In Cuba, as in the rest of Latin America, proofreading is often lax, and errors tend to be reproduced from edition to edition. Where there is no ambiguity, I have corrected errors in the Spanish silently; otherwise, I have erred on the side of caution. Where they are clearly intentional, I have retained idiosyncrasies of spelling and punctuation.

All poems are complete. There are no excerpts from longer poems, although in a few cases a poem, meant by the poet to be able to stand alone, has been selected from a sequence.

Nicolás Guillén

de El gran zoo

EL CARIBE

En el acuario del Gran Zoo,
nada el Caribe.

    Este animal
marítimo y enigmático
tiene una cresta de cristal,
el lomo azul, la cola verde,
vientre de compacto coral,
grises aletas de ciclón.
En el acuario, esta inscripción:
                "Cuidado: muerde".

GUITARRA

Fueron a cazar guitarras,
bajo la luna llena.
Y trajeron ésta,
pálida, fina, esbelta,
ojos de inagotable mulata,
cintura de abierta madera.
Es joven, apenas vuela.
Pero ya canta
cuando oye en otras jaulas
aletear sones y coplas.
Los sonesombres y las coplasolas.
Hay en su jaula esta inscripción:
                "Cuidado: sueña".

Nicolás Guillén

from The Great Zoo

THE CARIB

In the aquarium of the Great Zoo
swims the Carib.

  This animal,
seagoing and enigmatic,
has a crystal crest,
a blue back, a green tail,
a belly of dense coral,
a hurricane's gray fins.
In the aquarium, this inscription:

  "Caution; it bites."

GUITAR

Beneath the full moon,
they went hunting guitars.
And brought back this one,
pale, delicate, shapely,
eyes of inexhaustible *mulata*,
waist of wood with an opening.
She's young, barely flies.
But already she sings
when she hears
songs and couplets
flutter their wings in other cages.
Sombersongs and lonelycouplets.
There's this inscription on her cage:

  "Beware: she dreams."

LA PAJARITA DE PAPEL

Sola, en su jaula mínima,
dormitando,
la Pajarita de Papel.

LA OSA MAYOR

Esta es la Osa Mayor.
Cazada en junio 4, 64,
por un sputnik cazador.
(No tocar las estrellas
de la piel).
                              Se solicita
un domador.

EL ACONCAGUA

El Aconcagua. Bestia
solemne y frígida. Cabeza
blanca y ojos de piedra fija.
Anda en lentos rebaños
con otros animales semejantes
por entre rocallosos desamparos.

En la noche,
roza con belfo blando
las manos frías de la luna.

LOS RÍOS

He aquí la jaula de las culebras.
Enroscados en sí mismos,
duermen los ríos, los sagrados ríos.
El Mississippi con sus negros,
el Amazonas con sus indios.
Son como los zunchos poderosos
de unos camiones gigantescos.

LITTLE PAPER BIRD

Alone, in its minute cage,
sleeping,
the Little Paper Bird.

URSA MAJOR

This is Ursa Major.
Caught on June 4, '64,
by a hunter sputnik.
(Don't touch the stars
on its skin.)
               Wanted:
a trainer.

ACONCAGUA

Aconcagua. Solemn and frigid
beast. White
head and eyes of immobile stone.
Travels in slow herds
with others like itself
through gravel desolations.

At night,
its bland lip nibbles
the cold hands of the moon.

THE RIVERS

Here is the cage of the snakes.
Coiled within them
sleep rivers, the sacred rivers.
The Mississippi with its blacks,
The Amazon with its Indians.
They are like powerful springs
on gigantic trucks.

Riendo, los niños les arrojan
verdes islotes vivos,
selvas pintadas de papagayos,
canoas tripuladas
y otros ríos.

Los grandes ríos despiertan,
se desenroscan lentamente,
engullen todo, se hinchan, a poco más revientan,
y vuelven a quedar dormidos.

SEÑORA

Esta señora inmensa
fue arponeada en la calle.

Sus pescadores arrojados
se prometían el aceite,
los bigotes delgados y flexibles,
la grasa . . . (Descuartizarla sabiamente).

Aquí está.

Convalece.

LA SED

Esponja de agua dulce,
la Sed.
Espera un río, lo devora.
Absorbe un aguacero.
Estrangula
con una cinta colorada.
¡Atención! ¡Las gargantas!

EL HAMBRE

Este es el hambre. Un animal
todo colmillo y ojo.
Nadie le engaña ni distrae.
No se harta en una mesa.

Laughing, children throw at them
small green living islands,
forests painted with parrots,
manned canoes,
and other rivers.

The great rivers wake up,
slowly uncoil,
swallow it all, swell, almost to bursting,
and go back to sleep.

LADY

This enormous lady
was harpooned in the street.

The foolhardy fishermen
anticipated her oil,
her delicate and flexible whiskers,
her fat . . . (To dismember her skillfully).

Here she is.

Convalescing.

THIRST

A freshwater sponge,
Thirst.
Awaits a river, devours it.
Absorbs a downpour.
Strangles
with a red ribbon.
Throats! Watch out!

HUNGER

This is hunger. An animal
all fang and eye.
No one can fool or distract it.
It's not satisfied with one meal.

No se contenta
con un almuerzo o una cena.
Anuncia siempre sangre.
Ruge como león, aprieta como boa,
piensa como persona.

El ejemplar que aquí se ofrece
fue cazado en la India (suburbios de Bombay),
pero existe en estado más o menos salvaje
en otras muchas partes.

No acercarse.

LAS NUBES

El Nubario.
Capacidad: 84 nubes.
Una experiencia nueva, porque hay
nubes de todo el día,
y de muchos países diferentes.
(La Dirección anuncia más).

Larguilenguas de pájaro,
rojizas,
las matutinas
hechas al poco sueño labrador
y a las albas vacías.
Detenidas,
de algodón seco y firme,
las matronales fijas del mediodía.
Como serpientes encendidas
las que anuncian a Véspero.
Curiosidad: Las hay de Uganda,
movidas por los vientos del gran lago Victoria.
Las del Turquino, bajas.
Las de los Alpes Marítimos.
Las del Pico Bolívar.
Negras, de gordas tetas,
las de tormenta.
También nubes románticas,
como por ejemplo las que empeñan

It's not content
with one lunch or dinner.
It always prophesies blood.
Roars like a lion, constricts like a boa,
thinks like a person.

The specimen exhibited here
was caught in India (Bombay's suburbs),
but exists in a more or less savage state
in many other places.

Stand back.

CLOUDS

The nublary.
Capacity: 84 clouds.
A new experience, because there are
clouds all day
and from many different countries.
(The Director anticipates even more).

Long-tongued like a bird,
ruddy,
the morning clouds
made of the short sleep of the hired hand
and empty dawns.
The restrained immovable
matrons of noon,
made of firm dry cotton.
Those that like flaming serpents
announce the evening star.
A curiosity: those from Uganda,
moved by the winds of Lake Victoria.
Those low clouds of Turquino.
Those of the Maritime Alps.
Those of Pico Bolívar.
Black, full-breasted,
thunderclouds.
Romantic clouds, as well,
for example, those that sully

el cielo del amor. Las coloreadas
de hace sesenta años
en los augurios de Noel.
Nubes con ángeles.
Nubes con formas de titán,
de mapas conocidos (Inglaterra),
de kanguro, león.
En fin, un cargamento respetable.

Sin embargo,
las de raza Polar, rarísimas,
no hubo manera de traerlas vivas.
Llegaron en salmuera, expresamente
de Groenlandia, Noruega, Terranova.
(La Dirección ha prometido
exhibirlas al público en vitrinas).

LOS VIENTOS

Usted no puede imaginar
cómo andaban estos vientos anoche.
Se les vio,
los ojos centelleantes,
largo y rígido el rabo.

Nada pudo desviarlos
(ni oraciones ni votos)
de una choza, de un barco solitario,
de una granja,
de todas esas cosas necesarias
que ellos destruyen sin saberlo.

Hasta que esta mañana los trajeron atados,
cogidos por sorpresa,
lentos enamorados,
cuando vagaban pensativos
junto a un campo de dalias.

(Esos de allí, a la izquierda,
dormidos en sus cajas).

the sky with love. The red-colored
clouds of sixty-year-old
Christmas cards.
Clouds with angels.
Clouds in the shape of titans,
of familiar maps (England),
of kangaroo, lion.
In short, a respectable cargo.

Still,
there was no way to bring back alive
the rarest, those of the Polar species.
They arrived in brine, express
from Greenland, Norway, Newfoundland.
(The Board of Directors has promised
to exhibit them behind glass for the public.)

THE WINDS

You cannot imagine
how these winds carried on last night.
They were seen,
eyes flashing,
tails long and rigid.

Nothing could turn them away
(neither vows nor prayers)
from a hovel, from a solitary boat,
from a farm,
from all those necessary things
they unknowingly destroy.

Not until this morning were they brought back, bound,
lingering lovers,
caught by surprise
when they wandered pensively
near a field of dahlias.

(Over there, on the left,
asleep in their boxes.)

EL TIGRE

Anda preso en su propia jaula
de duras rayas negras.
El metal con que ruge
quema, está al rojo blanco.

(Un gangster.
El instinto sexual.
Un boxeador.
Un furioso de celos.
Un general.
El puñal del amor).

Tranquilizarse.
Un tigre
real.

CICLÓN

Ciclón de raza,
recién llegado a Cuba de las islas Bahamas.
Se crió en Bermudas,
pero tiene parientes en Barbados.
Estuvo en Puerto Rico.
Arrancó de raíz el palo mayor de Jamaica.
Iba a violar a Guadalupe.
Logró violar a Martinica.

Edad: dos días.

AVE-FÉNIX

Esta es la jaula destinada
a la resurrección del Ave-Fénix.
(En diciembre llegarán sus cenizas).

THE TIGER

Imprisoned, he paces his cage
of hard black stripes.
The metal which he roars
burns, is white hot.

(A gangster.
The sexual instinct.
A boxer.
An insane fury of jealousy.
A general.
The dagger of love.)

Calm yourself.
It's a real
tiger.

HURRICANE

An exemplary hurricane
recently arrived in Cuba from the Bahamas.
It was raised in Bermuda,
but has family in Barbados.
Has been to Puerto Rico.
It tore out the mainmast of Jamaica by its roots.
It was going to ravish Guadeloupe.
It succeeded in ravishing Martinique.

Age: two days.

PHOENIX

This is the cage destined
for the resurrection of the Phoenix.
(In December its ashes will arrive.)

LYNCH

Lynch de Alabama.
Rabo en forma de látigo
y pezuñas terciarias.
Suele manifestarse
con una gran cruz en llamas.
Se alimenta de negros, sogas,
fuego, sangre, clavos,
alquitrán.

                      Capturado
junto a una horca. Macho.
Castrado.

K K K

Este cuadrúpedo procede
de Joplin, Misuri.
Carnicero.
Aúlla largamente en la noche
sin su dieta habitual de negro asado.

Acabará por sucumbir.
Un problema (insoluble) alimentarlo.

LAS ÁGUILAS

En esta parte están las águilas.
La caudal.
La imperial.
El águila en su nopal.
La bicéfala (fenómeno)
en una jaula personal.
Las condecoratrices
arrancadas del pecho de los condenados
en los fusilamientos.
La pecuniaria, doble, de oro $20 (veinte dólares).
Las heráldicas.
La prusiana, de negro siempre como una viuda fiel.

LYNCHING

Alabama lynching.
Tail in the form of a whip
and tertiary cloven hooves.
Usually manifests itself
with a large burning cross.
Feeds on blacks, ropes,
fire, blood, nails,
tar.

                    Captured
near a gallows. Male.
Castrated.

KKK

This quadruped originates
in Joplin, Missouri.
Carnivorous.
Without its habitual diet of roast black man
it howls the whole night long.

It will certainly die.
Feeding it is an (insoluble) problem.

THE EAGLES

In this section are the eagles.
The golden.
The imperial.
The eagle on its prickly pear.
The two-headed (a freak)
in its personal cage.
The decorative ones
torn out of the breasts of those condemned
to the firing squad.
The coin, the double, gold (twenty dollars).
The heraldic.
The Prussian, always in black like a faithful widow.

La que voló sesenta años sobre el Maine, en La Habana.
La yanqui, traída de Viet Nam.
Las napoleónicas y las romanas.
La celestial,
en cuyo pecho resplandece Altaír.
En fin,
el águila
de la leche condensada marca "El Aguila".
(Un ejemplar
realmente original).

LUNA

Mamífero metálico. Nocturno.

Se le ve
el rostro comido por un acné.

Sputniks y sonetos.

TENOR

Está el tenor en éxtasis
contemplando al tenor
del espejo, que es el mismo tenor
en éxtasis
que contempla al tenor.

Sale a veces a pasear por el mundo
llevado de un bramante de seda,
aplaudido en dólares,
tinta de imprenta
y otras sustancias gananciales.
(Aquí en el zoo le molesta
cantar por la comida
y no es muy generoso con sus arias).

Milán Scala.
New York Metropolitan.
Opera de París.

The one that flew for sixty years over the Maine, in Havana.
The Yankee, brought from Viet Nam.
The Napoleonic and the Roman.
The celestial one,
Altair glittering on its chest.
And finally,
the eagle
of "Eagle Brand" condensed milk.
(A truly original
specimen.)

MOON

Metallic mammal. Nocturnal.

Its face can be seen
eaten by acne.

Sputniks and sonnets.

TENOR

The tenor is in ecstasy
contemplating the tenor
in the mirror, who is the same tenor
in ecstasy
who contemplates the tenor.

He leaves sometimes for a stroll around the world
led by a silk string,
applauded in dollars,
printer's ink,
and other lucrative substances.
(Here in the zoo he's annoyed
at having to sing for his supper
and is not very generous with his arias.)

La Scala, Milan.
The New York Metropolitan.
The Paris Opera.

RELOJ

Quiroptero
de una paciencia extraordinaria
no exenta de crueldad,
sobre todo
con los ajedrecistas y los novios.

Sin embargo,
es cordial a las 3 menos ¼
tanto como a las 9 h 15, los únicos momentos
en que estaría dispuesto a darnos un abrazo.

AVISO

GRAN ZOO DE LA HABANA

Museo de prehistoria abierto al público—todos los días menos los domingos.
—Idiomas: español, inglés y ruso.

Se avisa la llegada
de nuevos ejemplares, a saber:
La gran paloma fósil del jurásico
en la que son visibles todavía
sus dos dispositivos lanzabombas.
Hay una colección de hachas atómicas,
máscaras rituales de forma antiaerolítica
y macanas de sílex radioactivo.
Finalmente, un avión
(el tan buscado caza del plioceno)
que es una pieza de excepción.

¡Patria o Muerte!

EL DIRECTOR

CLOCK

A bat
of extraordinary patience
but not without cruelty
especially
for chess players and lovers.

Nevertheless
it's cordial at a quarter to three,
also at 9:15, the only times
when it would be inclined to embrace us.

ANNOUNCEMENT:

GREAT ZOO OF HAVANA

Prehistoric museum open to the public—daily except Sunday.
—Languages: Spanish, English, and Russian.

The arrival of new specimens
is announced, namely:
The great fossil dove of the Jurassic
whose two bomb-launching devices
are still visible.
There's a collection of atomic axes,
ritual masks of the antiballistic kind,
and clubs of radioactive flint.
Finally, an airplane
(the much-sought predator of the Pliocene),
which is an exceptional piece.

Our Country or Death!

THE DIRECTOR

Translated by Rebecca Seiferle

Eugenio Florit

Los poetas solos de Manhattan

El poeta cubano Alcides Iznaga vino a Nueva York, de paseo, en agosto de 1959. A su regreso a Cienfuegos me envió un poema, "Estamos solos en Manhattan," al que contesté con estos versos:

Mi muy querido Alcides Iznaga:
es cierto que ni Langston Hughes ni yo estábamos en casa.
Porque Langston, que vive con sus negros,
también baja hasta el centro.
Y yo, cuando llamaste por teléfono,
o mejor dicho, pasaste por mi casa,
estaba lejos, en el campo,
yo que vivo con mis blancos.
Pero es que aquí, por aquí arriba,
lo mismo da que vivas
en la calle 127
o en el número 7
de la Avenida del Parque.
Aquí todos andamos solos y perdidos,
todos desconocidos
entre el ruido
de trenes subterráneos, y de bombas de incendio,
y de sirenas de ambulancias
que tratan de salvar a los suicidas
que se tiran al río desde un puente,
o a la calle desde su ventana,
o que abren las llaves del gas,
o se toman cien pastillas para dormir
—porque, como no se han encontrado todavía,
lo que desean es dormir y olvidarse de todo—,
olvidarse de que nadie se acuerda de ellos,
de que están solos, terriblemente solos entre la multitud.

Ya ves, a Langston Hughes me lo encontré a fines de agosto
en un cóctel del *Pen Club*,
muy cortés y muy ceremonioso
y muy vestido de azul.
Y luego pasan los años, y lo más, si acaso,
nos cambiamos un libro: "Inscribed for my dear friend . . . "

Eugenio Florit

Poets Alone in Manhattan

The Cuban poet Alcides Iznaga came to visit New York in August 1959. On his return to Cienfuegos he sent me a poem, "We're alone in Manhattan," to which I answered with these lines:

My dear Alcides Iznaga:
it's true that neither Langston Hughes nor I was at home.
Because Langston, who lives in the black quarter,
also goes downtown.
And I, when you phoned,
or rather, passed by my house,
was far away in the country,
I who live among whites.
But up here
it makes no difference whether you live
on 127th Street
or at 7 Park Avenue.
Here we all go about lost and alone,
unknown
amid the noise
of subway trains and fire trucks,
and sirens of ambulances
trying to rescue suicides
who throw themselves from a bridge into a river,
or from their window to the street,
or who open the gas valves,
or swallow a hundred sleeping pills
—because, since they haven't been found yet,
what they want is to sleep and forget everything—
to forget that no one remembers them,
that they're alone, terribly alone among the multitude.

For instance, I ran into Langston Hughes around the end of August
at a party at the Pen Club,
very courteous and formal
dressed in blue.
And then the years pass, and at most we might
exchange books: "For my dear friend . . . "

"Recuerdo muy afectuoso . . . ," etc.
Y así nos vamos haciendo viejos
el poeta negro
y el poeta blanco,
y el mulato y el chino y todo bicho viviente.
Como se irán haciendo viejos
ustedes, los amigos de Cienfuegos;
los que aquel día inolvidable de febrero
(1955) me llevaron al Castillo de Jagua
donde me hizo temblar de emoción una vicaria
que me salió al encuentro entre las piedras.
Lo que pasa,
mi muy querido Alcides Iznaga,
es que aquí no hay vicarias,
ni Castillo de Jagua,
ni están conmigo mis poetas
ni mis palmas ("Las palmas, ay . . .")
ni las aguas azules de la bahía de Cienfuegos
ni las de la bahía de La Habana.
Aquí sólo las aguas perezosas y tristes
de los dos ríos que ciñen a Manhattan . . .

    Tú, mi querido Alcides,
viniste
en busca de nosotros a Nueva York, a esta ciudad en donde
nadie a nadie conoce . . .
Donde
todos nosotros, cada uno,
no somos otra cosa que una gota de agua,
una mota de polvo, de esas
que salen tristes por las chimeneas.
Tristes, es un decir. Que yo, a Dios gracias,
aún conservo serenas las palabras
con las que doy los buenos días al sol
que sale—cuando sale—enfrente de mi ventana.
Y si no sale, da lo mismo, al viento, al aire, a niebla y nube;
saludar a este mundo en que vivimos
con estas las palabras que escribimos.
Y dar gracias a Dios por el día y la noche
y por tener una palabra nuestra, aquí, en donde nadie nos conoce.

    23 DE OCTUBRE DE 1959.

"Recuerdo muy afectuoso . . . ," etc.
And so we grow old
the black poet
and the white poet,
and the *mulato* and the Chinese and every living creature.
As you, my friends in Cienfuegos,
will grow old,
you who on that unforgettable day in February (1955)
took me to the Castillo de Jagua
where I trembled with emotion upon seeing
a vicaria among the stones.
The thing is,
my dear Alcides Iznaga,
that here there are no vicarias,
nor Castillo de Jagua,
nor are my poets with me
nor my palm trees ("Las palmas, ay . . .")
nor the blue waters of Cienfuegos Bay
nor those of Havana.
Here the sad lazy waters
of the two rivers circling Manhattan . . .

    You, my dear Alcides,
came
searching for us in New York, this city where
no one knows anyone . . .
Where
all of us, each,
are nothing but a drop of water,
a mote of dust, one of those
rising sadly from the chimneys.
Sadly, as one says. Thank God,
I still have the serene words
with which to greet the morning sun
that rises—when it rises—before my window.
And if it doesn't rise, then to greet the wind, the air, the mist and clouds;
to greet this world in which we live
with these words we write.
And to give thanks to God for the day and the night
and for having a word of our own, here, where no one knows us.

OCTOBER 23, 1959

Juego

Nada más que la voz en la montaña
o tal vez la montaña sobre el mar
o acaso el mar encima del abismo.
Puede ser que lo mismo
resulte el mar sobre el abismo
que la montaña sobre el mar
o que la voz en la montaña.
Extraña
surge en la tarde la canción serena
y el quieto verde sobre el verde trémulo,
y la inquietud posada en el trasfondo
hondo
donde ha de parar el movimiento
del abismo a la estrella.
Y en mitad del camino
como una columna de viento
detenida en el aire fino,
ella:
la voz de la montaña en la canción.

Brujas

(Lago de Amor)

Cuando la luz de arriba, la gris de hoy, se apaga,
antes de que se muera sale otra luz del suelo
que va haciendo de verde los árboles de noche,
de amarillo los cisnes y los puentes, de rojo.
Es la respuesta de la tierra, y aun del agua,
a la ausencia del sol, apenas en las lluvias entrevisto.
Es el sí irregular de los colores
al no del cielo y al tal vez del viento.
Caen al lago las torres desdobladas,
más fijas en el agua que en el aire;
cae todo al lago, luces y reflejos,
y hasta el agua se queda contenida en sí misma.
Ya no sabemos si al andar la orilla
somos sólo el reflejo de nosotros,
y que nuestra verdad está debajo de las aguas.

Game

Nothing more than the voice on the mountain
or maybe the mountain over the sea
or perhaps the sea above the abyss.
It could just as well be
the sea over the abyss
as the mountain over the sea
or the voice on the mountain.
Strange
the serene song rises in the evening
and the green quiet trembling over the green,
and the disquiet set in the deep
background
where the movement from abyss to star
must end.
And in the middle of the road
like a column of wind
halted in the thin air,
there it is:
the voice of the mountain in the song.

Bruges

(Lake of Love)

When the light from above, the gray of today, goes out,
before it dies another light comes up from the ground
that makes the trees green at night,
the swans yellow and the bridges red.
It's the response of earth, and even of water,
to the absence of sun, barely glimpsed through the rains.
It's the irregular yes of colors
to the no of sky and the maybe of wind.
The split towers fall to the lake,
steadier in the water than in the air;
everything falls to the lake, lights and reflections,
and even the water remains contained in itself.
We no longer know if walking the edge
we're merely our own reflection,
and that our truth is underneath the waters.

El eterno

No sabías que el mar con sus colores
—verde, amarillo, azul, gris, negro, de la luna—
iba a llegar a poseerte para siempre.
Su orilla pedregosa
tan de ayer y tan lejos,
te vio entrar en su amor cuando era manso
encerrado en su cerco de montañas severas,
y te vio sobre él hacia Occidente.
Iba contigo como sangre. Voces íntimas
de caracolas te sonaban
en los oídos que luego iban a enmudecerse.
Fue llegando después el mar de las arenas
bajo la luz terrible del Trópico. Terrible
luz, y tan suave por las tardes. Medrosa por las noches
cuando a lo negro se lo mira fantasmal.
Para siempre. Hasta ahora que en su ausencia
es un recuerdo al que una vez se llega
de paso, albatros volandero
de viene y va por aires y distancias.
Recuerdo solo y, más, presencia exacta
de su estar, ser, vivir, latir en donde siempre.
Desmarado, tenías que volverte hacia él;
ausente, regresar en recuerdo;
muerto, cuando lo estés, en viaje eterno,
ser, sí, ser sobre todo como la luz que se desliza
y en ondas de color prende su beso.

23 ABRIL 1969.

La niebla

Y allá a lo lejos, nada.
Una fila de casas que apenas se adivina
a través del blanco de la nieve y el sol.
Es mejor lo nublado.
Es mejor no ver nada claramente.
Es mejor que se cubra la ciudad con su niebla
para no ver lo sucio ni lo triste de dentro.
No ver, no ver. No mirar que la gente se resbala

The Eternal

You didn't know that the sea with its colors
—green, yellow, blue, gray, black, lunar—
would come to possess you forever.
Its rocky shore
so much yesterday, so far away,
saw you enter into its love when it was tame
enclosed in its circle of harsh mountains,
and saw you upon it headed west.
Like blood it was going with you. Intimate voices
of conch shells sounded
in your ears and then fell silent.
The sea of sands was arriving later
under the terrible light of the Tropics. Terrible
light, and so gentle in the evening. Fearsome at night
when the dark seems ghostly.
Forever. Until now where once it passed
it remains in absence
as a memory, a flying albatross
coming and going on breezes and distances.
A single memory and, more, the exact presence
of its being, existing, living, beating where it always had.
Unmoored, you had to return to it;
absent, to go back in memory;
dead, when you may be, on an eternal voyage,
to be, yes, to be above all like the light that slips away
and in waves of color catches its kiss.

APRIL 23, 1969

The Fog

And there in the distance, nothing.
A line of houses one can hardly make out
through the white of snow and sun.
Cloudy is better.
It's better not to see anything clearly.
It's better when the city is covered in fog
so as not to see the dirty or sad within it.
Not to see, not to see. Not to notice the people slip

y cae, y se levanta dando gracias ¿a quién?,
al buen chico que aunque sucio y despeinado
tiene una tentación de caridad y la realiza.
Ah, realizar la tentación de ser amable
entre el cochino suelo y los periódicos sin dueño.
Ser amable: decir gracias, perdón, esas palabras
que sin querer alivian la tristeza.
Mas, sobre todo, no ver, no mirar, estarse ciego.
Y poder ser feliz entre la niebla.

4 DE FEBRERO DE 1970.

José Lezama Lima

Pensamientos en La Habana

Porque habito un susurro como un velamen,
una tierra donde el hielo es una reminiscencia,
el fuego no puede izar un pájaro
y quemarlo en una conversación de estilo calmo.
Aunque ese estilo no me dicte un sollozo
y un brinco tenue me deje vivir malhumorado,
no he de reconocer la inútil marcha
de una máscara flotando donde yo no pueda,
donde yo no pueda transportar el picapedrero o el picaporte
a los museos donde se empapelan los asesinatos
mientras los visitadores señalan la ardilla
que con el rabo se ajusta las medias.
Si un estilo anterior sacude el árbol,
decide el sollozo de dos cabellos y exclama:
my soul is not in an ashtray.

Cualquier recuerdo que sea transportado,
recibido como una galantina de los obesos embajadores de antaño,
no nos hará vivir como la silla rota
de la existencia solitaria que anota la marea
y estornuda en otoño.
Y el tamaño de una carcajada,

and fall, and get up giving thanks, to whom?
to the good boy, dirty and unkempt, who
is tempted to be charitable and acts on it.
Ah, to act on the temptation to be kind
amid the filthy ground and abandoned newspapers.
To be kind: to say thanks, excuse me, those words
that unintentionally alleviate the sorrow.
But, above all, not to see, not to notice, to stay blind.
To be able to be happy amid the fog.

FEBRUARY 4, 1970

Translated by Jason Weiss

José Lezama Lima

Thoughts in Havana

Because I dwell in a whisper like a set of sails,
a land where ice is a reminiscence,
fire cannot hoist a bird
and burn it in a conversation calm in style.
Though that style doesn't dictate to me a sob
and a tenuous hop lets me live in bad humor,
I will not recognize the useless movement
of a mask floating where I cannot,
where I cannot transport the stonecutter or the door latch
to the museums where murders are papered
while the judges point out the squirrel
that straightens its stockings with its tail.
If a previous style shakes the tree,
it decides the sob of two hairs and exclaims:
mi alma no está en un cenicero.

Any memory that is transported,
received like a galantine from the obese ambassadors of old,
will not make us live like the broken chair
of the lonesome existence that notes the tide
and sneezes in autumn.
And the size of a loud laugh,

rota por decir que sus recuerdos están recordados,
y sus estilos los fragmentos de una serpiente
que queremos soldar
sin preocuparnos de la intensidad de sus ojos.
Si alguien nos recuerda que nuestros estilos
están ya recordados;
que por nuestras narices no escogita un aire sutil,
sino que el Eolo de las fuentes elaboradas
por los que decidieron que el ser
habitase en el hombre,
sin que ninguno de nosotros
dejase caer la saliva de una decisión bailable,
aunque presumimos como los demás hombres
que nuestras narices lanzan un aire sutil.
Como sueñan humillarnos,
repitiendo día y noche con el ritmo de la tortuga
que oculta el tiempo en su espaldar:
ustedes no decidieron que el ser habitase en el hombre;
vuestro Dios es la luna
contemplando como una balaustrada
al ser entrando en el hombre.
Como quieren humillarnos le decimos
the chief of the tribe descended the staircase.

Ellos tienen unas vitrinas y usan unos zapatos.
En esas vitrinas alternan el maniquí con el quebrantahuesos disecado,
y todo lo que ha pasado por la frente del hastío del búfalo solitario.
Si no miramos la vitrina, charlan
de nuestra insuficiente desnudez que no vale una estatuilla de Nápoles.
Si la atravesamos y no rompemos los cristales,
no subrayan con gracia que nuestro hastío puede quebrar el fuego
y nos hablan del modelo viviente y de la parábola del quebrantahuesos.
Ellos que cargan con sus maniquíes a todos los puertos
y que hunden en sus baúles un chirriar
de vultúridos disecados.
Ellos no quieren saber que trepamos por las raíces húmedas del helecho
—donde hay dos hombres frente a una mesa; a la derecha, la jarra
y el pan acariciado—,
y que aunque mastiquemos su estilo,
we don't choose our shoes in a show-window.

broken by saying that its memories are remembered,
and its styles the fragments of a serpent
that we want to solder together
without worrying about the intensity of its eyes.
If someone reminds us that our styles
are already remembered;
that through our nostrils no subtle air thinks forth
but rather that the Aeolus of the sources elaborated
by those who decided that being
should dwell in man,
without any of us
dropping the saliva of a danceable decision,
though we presume like other men
that our nostrils expel a subtle air.
Since they dream of humiliating us,
repeating day and night with the rhythm of the tortoise
that conceals time on its back:
you didn't decide that being should dwell in man;
your God is the moon
watching like a banister
the entrance of being into man.
Since they want to humiliate us we say to them:
el jefe de la tribu descendió la escalinata.

They have some show windows and wear some shoes.
In those show windows they alternate the mannequin with the stuffed
   ossifrage,
and everything that has passed through the forehead
of the lonesome buffalo's boredom.
If we don't look at the show window, they chat
about our insufficient nakedness that isn't worth a figurine from Naples.
If we go through it and don't break the glass,
they don't stress amusingly that our boredom can break the fire
and they talk to us about the living model and the parable of the ossifrage.
They who carry their mannequins to all the ports
and who push down into their trunks a screeching
of stuffed vultures.
They don't want to know that we climb up along the damp roots of the fern
—where there are two men in front of a table; to the right, the jug
and the bread that has been caressed—
and that though we may chew their style,
no escogemos nuestros zapatos en una vitrina.

El caballo relincha cuando hay un bulto
que se interpone como un buey de peluche,
que impide que el río le pegue en el costado
y se bese con las espuelas regaladas
por una sonrosada adúltera neoyorquina.
El caballo no relincha de noche;
los cristales que exhala por su nariz,
una escarcha tibia, de papel;
la digestión de las espuelas
después de recorrer sus músculos encristalados
por un sudor de sartén.
El buey de peluche y el caballo
oyen el violín, pero el fruto no cae
reventado en su lomo frotado
con un almíbar que no es nunca el alquitrán.
El caballo resbala por el musgo
donde hay una mesa que exhibe las espuelas,
pero la oreja erizada de la bestia no descifra.

La calma con música traspiés
y ebrios caballos de circo enrevesados,
donde la aguja muerde porque no hay un leopardo
y la crecida del acordeón
elabora una malla de tafetán gastado.
Aunque el hombre no salte, suenan
bultos divididos en cada estación indivisible,
porque el violín salta como un ojo.
Las inmóviles jarras remueven un eco cartilaginoso;
el vientre azul del pastor
se muestra en una bandeja de ostiones.
En ese eco del hueso y de la carne, brotan unos bufidos
cubiertos por un disfraz de telaraña,
para el deleite al que se le abre una boca,
como la flauta de bambú elaborada
por los garzones pedigüeños.
Piden una cóncava oscuridad
donde dormir, rajando insensibles
el estilo del vientre de su madre.
Pero mientras afilan un suspiro de telaraña
dentro de una jarra de mano en mano,
el rasguño en la tiorba no descifra.

The horse neighs when there's a shape
that comes in between like a toy ox,
that keeps the river from hitting it on the side
and kissing the spurs that were a present
from a rosy-cheeked adulteress from New York.
The horse doesn't neigh at night;
the crystals it exhales through its nose,
a warm frost, of paper;
the digestion of the spurs
after going through its muscles now glassy
with the sweat of a frying pan.
The toy ox and the horse
hear the violin, but the fruit doesn't fall
squashed on their backs that are rubbed
with a syrup that is never tar.
The horse slides over the moss
where there is a table exhibiting the spurs,
but the perked-up ear of the beast doesn't decipher.

The calm with stumble music
and drunken circus horses in a tangle,
where the needle bites because there's no leopard
and the surge of the accordion
elaborates some tights of worn taffeta.
Though the man doesn't leap, there's a sound
of divided shapes in each indivisible season,
because the violin leaps like an eye.
The motionless jugs stir up a cartilaginous echo:
the shepherd's blue belly
is displayed on a tray of oysters.
In that echo of the bone and the flesh, some snorts
come out covered with a spiderweb disguise,
for the delight to which a mouth is opened,
like the bamboo flute elaborated
by the boys always asking for something.
They ask for a hollow darkness
to sleep in, splitting open, with no sensitivity,
the style of their mothers' bellies.
But while they sharpen a spiderweb sigh,
inside a jug passing from hand to hand,
the scratch on the lute doesn't decipher.

Indicaba unas molduras
que mi carne prefiere a las almendras.
Unas molduras ricas y agujereadas
por la mano que las envuelve
y le riega los insectos que la han de acompañar.
Y esa espera, esperada en la madera
por su absorción que no detiene al jinete,
mientras no unas máscaras, los hachazos
que no llegan a las molduras,
que no esperan como un hacha o una máscara,
sino como el hombre que espera en una casa de hojas.
Pero al trazar las grietas de la moldura
y al perejil y al canario haciendo gloria,
l'étranger nous demande le garçon maudit.

El mismo almizclero conocía la entrada,
el hilo de tres secretos
se continuaba hasta llegar a la terraza
sin ver el incendio del palacio grotesco.
¿Una puerta se derrumba porque el ebrio
sin las botas puestas le abandona su sueño?
Un sudor fangoso caía de los fustes
y las columnas se deshacían en un suspiro
que rodaba sus piedras hasta el arroyo.
Las azoteas y las barcazas
resguardan el líquido calmo y el aire escogido;
las azoteas amigas de los trompos
y las barcazas que anclan en un monte truncado,
ruedan confundidas por una galantería disecada que sorprende
a la hilandería y al reverso del ojo enmascarados tiritando juntos.

Pensar que unos ballesteros
disparan a una urna cineraria
y que de la urna saltan
unos pálidos cantando,
porque nuestros recuerdos están ya recordados
y rumiamos con una dignidad muy atolondrada
unas molduras salidas de la siesta picoteada del cazador.
Para saber si la canción es nuestra o de la noche,
quieren darnos un hacha elaborada en las fuentes de Eolo.
Quieren que saltemos de esa urna
y quieren también vernos desnudos.

He indicated some moldings
that my flesh preferred to almonds.
Some delicious moldings riddled with holes
by the hand that wraps them
and sprinkles them with the insects that will accompany it.
And that waiting, waited for in the wood
by its absorption that doesn't stop the horseman,
while not some masks, the ax cuts
that do not reach the moldings,
which do not wait like an ax or a mask,
but like the man who waits in a house of leaves.
But in tracing the cracks in the molding
and making a glory of the parsley and the canary,
l'étranger nous demande le garçon maudit.

The musk ox itself knew the entrance,
the thread of three secrets
continued till it reached the terrace
without seeing the burning of the grotesque palace.
Does a door collapse because the drunken man
with no boots on yields to it his dream?
A muddy sweat fell from the shafts
and the columns collapsed in a sigh
that sent their stones tumbling down to the brook.
The flat roofs and the barges
safeguard the calm liquid and the chosen air;
the flat roofs so friendly to tops
and the barges anchored on a truncated hill,
are tumbled in confusion by a stuffed gallantry that catches unawares
the weaving and the obverse of the eye shivering together in masks.

To think that some crossbowmen
shoot at a funeral urn
and that from that urn leap
some pale people singing,
because our memories are already remembered
and we ruminate with a very bewildered dignity
some moldings that came out of the hunter's pecked siesta.
To know whether the song is ours or the night's,
they want to give us an ax elaborated in the sources of Aeolus.
They want us to leap from that urn
and they also want to see us naked.

Quieren que esa muerte que nos han regalado
sea la fuente de nuestro nacimiento,
y que nuestro oscuro tejer y deshacerse
esté recordado por el hilo de la pretendida.
Sabemos que el canario y el perejil hacen gloria
y que la primera flauta se hizo de una rama robada.

Nos recorremos
y ya detenidos señalamos la urna y a las palomas
grabadas en el aire escogido.
Nos recorremos
y la nueva sorpresa nos da los amigos
y el nacimiento de una dialéctica:
mientras dos diedros giran mordisqueándose,
el agua paseando por los canales de los huesos
lleva nuestro cuerpo hacia el flujo calmoso
de la tierra que no está navegada,
donde un alga despierta digiere incansablemente a un pájaro dormido.
Nos da los amigos que una luz redescubre
y la plaza donde conversan sin ser despertados.
De aquella urna maliciosamente donada,
saltaban parejas, contrastes y la fiebre
injertada en los cuernos de imán
del paje loco sutilizando el suplicio lamido.
Mi vergüenza, los cuernos de imán untados de luna fría,
pero el desprecio paría una cifra
y ya sin conciencia columpiaba una rama.
Pero después de ofrecer sus respetos,
cuando bicéfalos, mañosos correctos
golpean con martillos algosos el androide tenorino,
el jefe de la tribu descendió la escalinata.

Los abalorios que nos han regalado
han fortalecido nuestra propia miseria,
pero como nos sabemos desnudos
el ser se posará en nuestros pasos cruzados.
Y mientras nos pintarrajeaban
para que saltásemos de la urna cineraria,
sabíamos que como siempre el viento rizaba las aguas
y unos pasos seguían con fruición nuestra propia miseria.
Los pasos huían con las primeras preguntas del sueño.
Pero el perro mordido por luz y por sombra,

They want that death they have given us as a gift
to be the source of our birth,
and our obscure weaving and undoing
to be remembered by the thread of the woman beset by suitors.
We know that the canary and the parsley make a glory
and that the first flute was made from a stolen branch.

We go through ourselves
and having stopped point out the urn and the doves
engraved in the chosen air.
We go through ourselves
and the new surprise gives us our friends
and the birth of a dialectic:
while two dihedrals spin and nibble each other,
the water strolling through the canals of our bones
carries our body toward the calm flow
of the unnavigated land,
where a waking alga tirelessly digests a sleeping bird.
It gives us friends that a light rediscovers
and the square where they converse without being awakened.
From that urn maliciously donated,
there came leaping couples, contrasts and the fever
grafted into the magnet horns
of the crazy page boy making a slick torture even more subtle.
My shame, the magnet horns smeared with a cold moon,
but the scorn gave birth to a cipher
and now unconsciously swung on a branch.
But after offering his respects,
when two-headed people, crafty, correct,
strike with algal hammers the tenor-voiced android,
the chief of the tribe descended the staircase.

The beads they have given us as gifts
have fortified our own poverty,
but since we know we are naked
being will come to rest upon our crossed steps.
And while they were daubing us in wild colors
so we could leap out of the funeral urn,
we knew that as always the wind was rippling the waters
and some steps were following with delight our own poverty.
The steps fled with the first questions of sleep.
But the dog bitten by light and by shadow,

por rabo y cabeza;
de luz tenebrosa que no logra grabarlo
y de sombra apestosa; la luz no lo afina
ni lo nutre la sombra; y así muerde
la luz y el fruto, la madera y la sombra,
la mansión y el hijo, rompiendo el zumbido
cuando los pasos se alejan y él toca en el pórtico.
Pobre río bobo que no encuentra salida,
ni las puertas y hojas hinchando su música.
Escogió, doble contra sencillo, los terrones malditos,
pero yo no escojo mis zapatos en una vitrina.

Al perderse el contorno en la hoja
el gusano revisaba oliscón su vieja morada;
al morder las aguas llegadas al río definido,
el colibrí tocaba las viejas molduras.
El violín de hielo amortajado en la reminiscencia.
El pájaro mosca destrenza una música y ata una música.
Nuestros bosques no obligan el hombre a perderse,
el bosque es para nosotros una serafina en la reminiscencia.
Cada hombre desnudo que viene por el río,
en la corriente o el huevo hialino,
nada en el aire si suspende el aliento
y extiende indefinidamente las piernas.
La boca de la carne de nuestras maderas
quema las gotas rizadas.
El aire escogido es como un hacha
para la carne de nuestras maderas,
y el colibrí las traspasa.

Mi espalda se irrita surcada por las orugas
que mastican un mimbre trocado en pez centurión,
pero yo continúo trabajando la madera,
como una uña despierta,
como una serafina que ata y destrenza en la reminiscencia.
El bosque soplado
desprende el colibrí del instante
y las viejas molduras.
Nuestra madera es un buey de peluche;
el estado ciudad es hoy el estado y un bosque pequeño.
El huésped sopla el caballo y las lluvias también.
El caballo pasa su belfo y su cola por la serafina del bosque;

by tail and head;
the dog of dark light that cannot engrave it
and of stinking shadow; the light doesn't refine it
nor does the shadow nurture it; and so it bites
the light and the fruit, the wood and the shadow,
the mansion and the son, breaking the buzz
when the steps go away and he knocks at the portico.
Poor silly river that finds no way out
nor the doors and leaves swelling their music.
It chose, double against single, the cursed clods,
but I don't choose my shoes in a show-window.

As it lost its shape on the leaf
the worm sniffed and inspected its old home;
as it bit the waters that had come to the defined river,
the hummingbird touched the old moldings.
The violin of ice shrouded in reminiscence.
The colibri unbraids a music and ties a music.
Our forests don't force man to become lost,
the forest is for us a harmonium in reminiscence.
Every naked man that comes along the river,
in the current or in the glassy egg,
swims in the air if he suspends his breath
and stretches out indefinitely his legs.
The mouth of the flesh of our wood
burns the rippled drops.
The chosen air is like an ax
for the flesh of our wood,
and the hummingbird pierces it.

My back is irritated and furrowed by the caterpillars
that chew some wicker changed into centurion fish,
but I go on working the wood,
like a sleepless fingernail,
like a harmonium that ties and unbraids in reminiscence.
The forest, breathed upon,
releases the hummingbird of the instant
and the old moldings.
Our wood is a toy ox;
the city state is today the state and a small forest.
The guest breathes upon the horse and the rains, too.
The horse rubs its muzzle and its tail over the harmonium of the forest;

el hombre desnudo entona su propia miseria,
el pájaro mosca lo mancha y traspasa.
Mi alma no está en un cenicero.

Oda a Julián del Casal

Déjenlo, verdeante, que se vuelva;
permitidle que salga de la fiesta
a la terraza donde están dormidos.
A los dormidos los cuidará quejoso,
fijándose cómo se agrupa la mañana helada.
La errante chispa de su verde errante,
trazará círculos frente a los dormidos
de la terraza, la seda de su solapa
escurre el agua repasada del tritón
y otro tritón sobre su espalda en polvo.
Dejadlo que se vuelva, mitad ciruelo
y mitad piña laqueada por la frente.

Déjenlo que acompañe sin hablar,
permitidle, blandamente, que se vuelva
hacia el frutero donde están los osos
con el plato de nieve, o el reno
de la escribanía, con su manilla de ámbar
por la espalda. Su tos alegre
espolvorea la máscara de combatientes japoneses.
Dentro de un dragón de hilos de oro,
camina ligero con los pedidos de la lluvia,
hasta la Concha de oro del Teatro Tacón,
donde rígida la corista colocará
sus flores en el pico del cisne,
como la mulata de los tres gritos en el vodevil
y los neoclásicos senos martillados por la pedantería
de Clesinger. Todo pasó
cuando ya fue pasado, pero también pasó
la aurora con su punto de nieve.

Si lo tocan, chirrían sus arenas;
si lo mueven, el arco iris rompe sus cenizas.
Inmóvil en la brisa, sujetado
por el brillo de las arañas verdes.
Es un vaho que se dobla en las ventanas.

the naked man intones his own poverty,
the colibri stains and pierces him.
My soul is not in an ashtray.

Ode to Julián del Casal

Allow him, greening, to return;
permit him to leave the party
and come out to the terrace where they sleep.
The sleepers he will watch over and complain,
noticing how the chill morning gathers.
The errant spark of his errant green
will trace circles in front of the sleepers
on the terrace, the silk of his lapel
sheds the water gone over by the triton
and another triton on his back in dust.
Let him return, half plum tree
and half pineapple lacquered in front.

Allow him to accompany without speaking,
permit him, softly, to turn
toward the fruit bowl where the bears are
with the plate of snow, or the reindeer
on the writing stand, with the amber backscratcher
in back. His happy cough
sprinkles the Japanese warrior mask.
Inside a dragon of golden threads,
he walks quickly with the rain's requests
all the way to the Golden Shell at the Teatro Tacón,
where rigidly the chorus girl will place
his flowers on the swan's beak,
like the *mulata* of the three shouts in the vaudeville
and the neo-classical breasts hammered out by Clésinger's
pedantry. It all passed
when it had already passed, but the dawn also passed
at its exact snow point.

If they touch him, his sands squeak;
if they move him, the rainbow breaks his ashes.
Motionless in the breeze, held fast
by the gleam of the green chandeliers.
He's a mist that thickens on the windows.

Trae la carta funeral del ópalo.
Trae el pañuelo del opopónax
y agua quejumbrosa a la visita
sin sentarse apenas, con muchos
quédese, quédese,
que se acercan para llorar en su sonido
como los sillones de mimbre de las ruinas del ingenio,
en cuyas ruinas se quedó para siempre el ancla
de su infantil chaqueta marinera.

Pregunta y no espera la respuesta,
lo tiran de la manga con trifolias de ceniza.
Están frías las ornadas florecillas.
Frías están sus manos que no acaban,
aprieta las manos con sus manos frías.
Sus manos no están frías, frío es el sudor
que lo detiene en su visita a la corista.
Le entrega las flores y el maniquí
se rompe en las baldosas rotas del acantilado.
Sus manos frías avivan las arañas ebrias,
que van a deglutir el maniquí playero.
Cuidado, sus manos pueden avivar
la araña fría y el maniquí de las coristas.
Cuidado, él sigue oyendo cómo evapora
la propia tierra maternal,
compás para el espacio coralino.
Su tos alegre sigue ordenando el ritmo
de nuestra crecida vegetal,
al extenderse dormido.

Las formas en que utilizaste tus disfraces,
hubieran logrado influenciar a Baudelaire.
El espejo que unió a la condesa de Fernandina
con Napoleón Tercero, no te arrancó
las mismas flores que le llevaste a la corista,
pues allí viste el aleph negro en lo alto del surtidor.
Cronista de la boda de Luna de Copas
con la Sota de Bastos, tuviste que brindar
con *champagne gelé* por los sudores fríos
de tu medianoche de agonizante.
Los dormidos en la terraza,
que tú tan sólo los tocabas quejumbrosamente,
escupían sobre el tazón que tú le llevabas a los cisnes.

He brings the funeral card with the opal.
He brings the handkerchief with the opoponax
and complaining water to the visit
without hardly sitting down, with many
please stay, please stay,
that come closer to weep in his sound
like the wicker armchairs from the ruins of the plantation,
in whose ruins remained forever the anchor
from the sailor jacket of his childhood.

He asks and doesn't wait for a reply,
they pull his sleeve with trefoils of ashes.
Cold are the ornate little flowers.
Cold are his hands that never end,
he squeezes hands with his cold hands.
His hands are not cold, cold is the sweat
that halts him in his visit to the chorus girl.
He gives her the flowers and the mannikin
breaks on the broken tiles of the cliff.
His cold hands enliven the drunken chandeliers
that are going to swallow the beach mannikin.
Be careful, his hands can enliven
the cold chandelier and the chorus girls' mannikin.
Be careful, he goes on hearing how
his own maternal earth evaporates,
keeping time with the coral space.
His happy cough goes on structuring the rhythm
of our vegetal growth,
as it extends in sleep.

The forms in which you used your disguises
could have managed to influence Baudelaire.
The mirror that connected the Countess of Fernandina
with Napoleon III didn't extract from you
the same flowers you took to the chorus girl,
because there you saw the black aleph at the top of the fountain.
Chronicler of the wedding of the Moon of Cups
to the Page of Wands, you had to offer a toast
with *champagne gelé* because of the cold sweats
of your midnights as a dying man.
The sleepers on the terrace,
whom you only touched as you complained,
spat on the breakfast bowl you were taking to the swans.

No respetaban que tú le habías encristalado la terraza
y llevado el menguante de la liebre al espejo.
Tus disfraces, como el almirante samurai,
que tapó la escuadra enemiga con un abanico,
o el monje que no sabe qué espera en El Escorial,
hubieran producido otro escalofrío en Baudelaire.
Sus sombríos rasguños, exagramas chinos en tu sangre,
se igualaban con la influencia que tu vida
hubiera dejado en Baudelaire,
como lograste alucinar al Sileno
con ojos de sapo y diamante frontal.
Los fantasmas resinosos, los gatos
que dormían en el bolsillo de tu chaleco estrellado,
se embriagaban con tus ojos verdes.
Desde entonces, el mayor gato, el peligroso genuflexo,
no ha vuelto a ser acariciado.
Cuando el gato termine la madeja,
le gustará jugar con tu cerquillo,
como las estrías de la tortuga
nos dan la hoja precisa de nuestro fin.
Tu calidad cariciosa,
que colocaba un sofá de mimbre en una estampa japonesa,
el sofá volante, como los paños de fondo
de los relatos hagiográficos,
que vino para ayudarte a morir.
El *mail coach* con trompetas,
acudido para despertar a los dormidos de la terraza,
rompía tu escaso sueño en la madrugada,
pues entre la medianoche y el despertar
hacías tus injertos de azalea con araña fría,
que engendraban los sollozos de la Venus Anadyomena
y el brazalete robado por el pico del alción.

Sea maldito el que se equivoque y te quiera
ofender, riéndose de tus disfraces
o de lo que escribiste en *La Caricatura*,
con tan buena suerte que nadie ha podido
encontrar lo que escribiste para burlarte
y poder comprar la máscara japonesa.
Cómo se deben haber reído los ángeles,
cuando saludabas estupefacto
a la marquesa Polavieja, que avanzaba

They didn't respect the fact that you had glassed in the terrace
and taken the waning of the hare to the mirror.
Your disguises, like the samurai admiral
who blotted out the enemy squadron with a fan,
or the monk who doesn't know what he expects in the Escorial,
could have produced another chill in Baudelaire.
Those somber scratches, Chinese hexagrams in your blood,
equaled the influence your life
could have left on Baudelaire,
just as you managed to astonish Silenus
with his toad-like eyes and frontal diamond.
The resinous ghosts, the cats
who slept in the pocket of your star-studded vest,
were intoxicated with your green eyes.
Since then, the biggest cat of all, the dangerous kneeling one,
hasn't been caressed anymore.
When it finishes the skein,
the cat will like to play with your bangs,
just as the creases on the tortoise
give us the exact page of our end.
Your caressable quality,
that put a wicker sofa in a Japanese print,
the movable sofa, like the backdrops
of the hagiographic tales
that came to help you die.
The mail coach with trumpets,
arriving to wake the sleepers on the terrace,
interrupted your scant early-morning hours of sleep,
for between midnight and waking
your graftings of azaleas onto cold chandeliers
engendered the sobs of the Venus Anadyomene
and the bracelet stolen by the kingfisher's beak.

May anyone be damned who blunders and tries
to offend you, laughing at your disguises
or at what you wrote in *La Caricatura*,
so successfully that no one has been able
to find what you wrote for fun
so you could buy the Japanese mask.
How the angels must have laughed
when in astonishment you greeted
the Marquise of Polavieja, who came forward

hacia ti para palmearte frente al espejo.
Qué horror, debes haber soltado un lagarto
sobre la trifolia de una taza de té.
Haces después de muerto
las mismas iniciales, ahora
en el mojado escudo de cobre de la noche,
que comprobaban al tacto
la trigueñita de los doce años
y el padre enloquecido colgado de un árbol.
Sigues trazando círculos
en torno a los que se pasean por la terraza,
la chispa errante de tu errante verde.
Todos sabemos ya que no era tuyo
el falso terciopelo de la magia verde,
los pasos contados sobre alfombras,
la daga que divide las barajas,
para unirlas de nuevo con tizne de cisnes.
No era tampoco tuya la separación,
que la tribu de malvados te atribuye,
entre el espejo y el lago.
Eres el huevo de cristal,
donde el amarillo está reemplazado
por el verde errante de tus ojos verdes.
Invencionaste un color solemne,
guardamos ese verde entre dos hojas.
El verde de la muerte.

Ninguna estrofa de Baudelaire,
puede igualar el sonido de tu tos alegre.
Podemos retocar,
pero en definitiva lo que queda,
es la forma en que hemos sido retocados.
¿Por quién?
Respondan la chispa errante de tus ojos verdes
y el sonido de tu tos alegre.
Los frascos de perfume que entreabriste,
ahora te hacen salir de ellos como un homúnculo,
ente de imagen creado por la evaporación,
corteza del árbol donde Adonai
huyó del jabalí para alcanzar
la resurrección de las estaciones.
El frío de tus manos,

to pat you on the back in front of the mirror.
How awful, you must have let loose
a lizard on the trefoil of a teacup.
You make after your death
the same initials, now
on the wet copper shield of the night,
that had been evidenced by touch
by that dark-haired twelve-year-old girl
and her crazed father hanging from a tree.
You go on tracing circles
around the people strolling on the terrace,
the errant spark of your errant green.
We all know now that none of these were yours:
the fake velvet of green magic,
the steps counted out over carpets,
the dagger dividing the decks of cards,
so as to join them again with swan soot.
Nor was yours the separation
that the evil tribe attributes to you,
between the mirror and the lake.
You are the glass egg
where the yellow is replaced
by the errant green of your green eyes.
You invented a solemn color,
we keep that green between two leaves.
The green of death.

No stanza of Baudelaire's
can equal the sound of your happy cough.
We can retouch,
but in the last analysis what remains
is the form in which we've been retouched.
By whom?
Let the answer come from the errant green of your green eyes
and the sound of your happy cough.
The vials of perfume you began to open
now make you rise up from them like a homunculus,
an image-entity created by evaporation,
bark of the tree where Adonai
fled from the boar to attain
the resurrection of the seasons.
The cold of your hands

es nuestra franja de la muerte,
tiene la misma hilacha de la manga
verde oro del disfraz para morir,
es el frío de todas nuestras manos.
A pesar del frío de nuestra inicial timidez
y del sorprendido en nuestro miedo final,
llevaste nuestra luciérnaga verde al valle de Proserpina.

La misión que te fue encomendada,
descender a las profundidades con nuestra chispa verde,
la quisiste cumplir de inmediato y por eso escribiste:
ansias de aniquilarme sólo siento.
Pues todo poeta se apresura sin saberlo
para cumplir las órdenes indescifrables de Adonai.
Ahora ya sabemos el esplendor de esa sentencia tuya,
quisiste llevar el verde de tus ojos verdes
a la terraza de los dormidos invisibles.
Por eso aquí y allí, con los excavadores de la identidad,
entre los reseñadores y los sombrosos,
abres el quitasol de un inmenso Eros.
Nuestro escandaloso cariño te persigue
y por eso sonríes entre los muertos.

La muerte de Baudelaire, balbuceando
incesantemente: Sagrado nombre, Sagrado nombre,
tiene la misma calidad de tu muerte,
pues habiendo vivido como un delfín muerto de sueños,
alcanzaste a morir muerto de risa.
Tu muerte podía haber influenciado a Baudelaire.
Aquel que entre nosotros dijo:
ansias de aniquilarme sólo siento,
fue tapado por la risa como una lava.
En esas ruinas, cubierto por la muerte,
ahora reaparece el cigarrillo que entre tus dedos se quemaba,
la chispa con la que descendiste
al lento oscuro de la terraza helada.
Permitid que se vuelva, ya nos mira,
qué compañía la chispa errante de su errante verde,
mitad ciruelo y mitad piña laqueada por la frente.

is our fringe of death,
it has the same frayed edge
as the green-gold sleeve of the death disguise,
it is the cold of all our hands.
Despite the cold of our initial timidity
and the cold suddenly found in our final fear,
you took our green firefly down to the valley of Proserpina.

The mission entrusted to you,
to go down to the depths with our green spark,
you chose to carry out right away and that's why you wrote:
longings for annihilation are all I feel.
For all poets hasten unknowingly
to carry out the indecipherable orders of Adonai.
Now we know the splendor of that statement of yours,
you wanted to take the green of your green eyes
to the terrace of the invisible sleepers.
That's why, here and there, with the excavators of identity,
among the reviewers and the murky ones,
you open the parasol of an immense Eros.
Our scandalous love pursues you
and that's why you smile among the dead.

Baudelaire's death, muttering
over and over: Sacré nom, Sacré nom,
has the same quality as your death,
since, having lived like a dauphin dead tired,
you managed in the end to die laughing.
Your death could have influenced Baudelaire.
The one who among us said:
longings for annihilation are all I feel,
was covered by laughter like a layer of lava.
In those ruins, concealed by death,
now reappears the cigarette that was burning between your fingers,
the spark with which you went down
to the slow darkness of the chill terrace.
Allow him to return, he sees us now,
what great company the errant spark of his errant green,
half plum tree and half pineapple lacquered in front.

Translated by James Irby

Atraviesan la noche

En la medianoche un pisicorre,
lleno de músicos,
traquetea las viejas piedras,
con astillas de plata,
como las que vi en Taxco,
entrando en la ciudad.
La cómica gorda
y el galán enlombrizado
tropiezan con el cerrojo
de la ventanilla—melindres
y se arrancan cabellos—.
Gritos y campanillas,
los tintes de una mejilla
resbalan al vozarrón del orine
de los caballos nadantes,
con sombrillas
sobre las ancas infladas.
Pardo terrenal
y ráfagas violetas,
alardean los tumbos
que el farol descifraba.
Una casa sin nadie,
con vaciedad teatral,
apuntala los músicos
que pasan.
Ahí se detiene el apóstrofe
del brazo demandado
fuera de la ventanilla,
con escarcha de diferentes plumajes.
Entra entonces al grupo
un reloj de péndulo
que tropieza con las carcajadas
de los músicos hundidos
en su almohadón con cascabeles.
Las borlas del tiempo,
creadoras como las pistolas
de Montecristo y los bolsones
espermáticos desinflados en el río.
¿El gallo?
Abrió las piernas

They Pass Through the Night

At midnight a station wagon
filled with musicians
rattles old stones
shot through with silver
like the ones I saw
when I entered Taxco.
The fat actress
and the scrawny romeo
fall by accident
against the window crank—pretentiousness,
and they tear out their hair—.
Screams and bells,
the flush of a cheek,
slide to the roar of the piss
of swimming horses, parasols
above their inflated haunches.
Terrestrial brown
and violet flashes
boast of the bouncing
that the street light once deciphered.
A vacant house,
theatrically empty,
invigorates the passing musicians.
And there beyond the car's window
a covetous arm's apostrophe lingers
frosted with various feathers.
The great hall clock chimes in,
bumping into the raucous laughter
of those musicians sunk
in their ball-fringed pillows.
Time's tassels,
creative as Montecristo's pistols
or the river's deflated sperm sacs.
And the cock?
It spread its legs

y señaló con el índice.
Y el cacareo
en el ascua del cigarro.

7 DE OCTUBRE DE 1971

Las siete alegorías

La primera alegoría
es el puerco con los dientes de estrellas,
los dientes vuelan a su cielo de nubes bajas,
el puerco se extasía riendo de su desdoblamiento.
Al lacón, lacónicas preguntas.

Á tan capitosa sentencia eructos de aceituna.
La segunda alegoría
es la Diosa Blanca fornicando con un canguro.
El le da la hincada absoluta,
con gloria y dolor que es la hincada lasciva.
Lo lascivo son los labios
por un cristal en el rocío de la Navidad.
Sin embargo, el inca no era muy voluptuoso.

Después la otra alegoría, la que se apoya.
La Rueda de Rocío.
El ojo se hace tan transparente
que parece que nos quedamos ciegos,
pero la Rueda sigue agrandando el ojo
y el rocío dilata las hojas como orejas de elefantes.

Otro descansillo lo ocupa la tertalegoría.
Brilla cuanto más se reduce,
cuando ya es un punto es la semilla metálica.
Une el resplandor y la lisura de la superficie.
Se reproduce en gotas de resplandor.
Parir una de esas semillas
justifica la pareja.
Pero ese punto que no se ve y brilla
es el fruto del uno indual.
La lluvia cae sobre un casco romano.
La gota resplandor en el cuenco de la lanza de Palas.
Muestra la desnudez de su brazo
y con él penetra en las circunvoluciones de Júpiter.

pointed its finger
and crowed
in the glow of a cigarette.

OCTOBER 7, 1971

The Seven Allegories

The first allegory
is the pig whose teeth are the teeth of stars
that fly to their sky of low clouds,
the pig laughing in celebration of its double nature,
both bacon and laconic questions.

After so capricious a sentence the belch of olives.
The second allegory
is the White Goddess coupling with a kangaroo.
He gives her the thrust
which, glorious and painful, defines the thrust of lust.
It's the lips that are lustful,
the crystal in the dew of Christmas makes it so.
The Inca, on the other hand, wasn't particularly voluptuous.

Next, the other, the supporting allegory.
The Wheel of Dew.
One's eye become so transparent
it's as if we were blind,
but the Wheel keeps expanding it
the dew dilating the foliage like an elephant's ears.

The tetrallegory fills another landing.
The smaller it gets the brighter it shines,
until it's become, as now, a dot, a metallic seed.
Uniting the splendor and smoothness of surface
it reproduces itself in drops of splendor
the coupling justified
by the birth of even a single seed.
But this unseen and shining dot
is the fruit of the undivided singular.
Rain falls on a Roman helmet.
The resplendent drop in the groove of Pallas' spear.
She demonstrates her arm's nakedness
and with it penetrates the rotations of Jupiter.

Saltan las aguas sopladas por la gran boca.
De esa boca sale el espíritu que ordena
la sucesión de las olas.
Es la quinta alegoría,
como otra cuerda de la guitarra.
La alegoría del Agua Ígnea.
Un agua salta,
quema las conchas y las raíces.
Tiene de la hoguera y del pez,
pero se detiene y nombra el aire,
llevándolo de choza en choza,
quemando el bosque después de las danzas
que se esconden detrás de cada árbol.
Cada árbol será después una hoguera que habla.
Donde el fuego se retira
salta la primera astilla del mármol.
El Agua Ígnea demuestra que la imagen
existió primero que el hombre,
y que el hombre adquirirá ¿dónde?
el disfraz final del Agua Ígnea.

Teseo trae la luz
el sextante alegórico.
La luz es el primer animal visible de lo invisible.
Es la luz que se manifiesta,
la evidencia como un brazo
que penetra en el pez de la noche.
Oh luz manifestada
que iguala al ojo con el sol.
Un grupo de encinas
derribadas oculta las prolongaciones
de la luz sobre la repisa fría
con objetos inmutables.
Es lo primero que se manifiesta
y será lo último manifestado.
Teseo frente al monstruo cuadrado
trae la luz evidente
y la manifestada.
Las repisas brillan
y se hunden a los hachazos.

Volvemos a la tetralegoría,
a la Simiente Metálica.

Blown from that great mouth the waters pour forth.
From that mouth pours forth the spirit
that orders the succession of waves.
It is the fifth allegory,
like one more guitar string.
The allegory of Burning Water.
Water pours forth
burning shells and roots,
containing something of fish and fire,
but it pauses to name the breeze
carrying it from hut to hut
burning the forest at the end of those dances
hidden behind each tree.
Each tree afterwards will be a speaking fire.
There where the flame retreats
the first sliver of marble pours forth.
The Burning Water demonstrates that image
was there before man
and that man (but where?) will acquire
the Burning Water's last disguise.

Theseus brings the light
the allegorical sextant.
Light is the first visible of invisible animals.
The light manifests itself,
evidence, like an arm
penetrating the fish of night.
Oh manifest light
to the eye the sun's rival!
A felled copse of oaks hides
light's prolongations on the cold mantel
with its immutable objects.
First and last
of manifest things. Theseus
facing the inflexible monster
carries the evident
and manifest light.
The shining mantels
fall beneath ax blows.

Let us return to the tetrallegory,
the Metallic Seed.

La luz buscando la raíz
de las encinas.
Buscando la resina como un óleo,
tocado por la respiración manifestada
con la luz manifiesta.

La Simiente Metálica buscada por Licario.
Con la luz resinosa,
regalada por la raíz golpeada por el hacha,
comienza el frenesí de las danzas corales.
La ciudad bailando
en el desfile de las antorchas fálicas.

FEBRERO Y 1973

Virgilio Piñera

Los muertos de la Patria

Vamos a ver los muertos de la Patria.
En la pradera del silencio los árboles,
las aves, los saludos
son también muertos que a muertos corresponden.
Fusiles, metralletas y las manos empuñadoras
son sueños arrugados que soñara
un muerto nacido al mundo de los muertos.

Vamos a ver los muertos de la Patria.

En el montón ilustre nadie espera
recompensas, títulos, ni siquiera tierra;
podrían recabar monumentos, mármoles, honores,
pero eligieron ser muertos de la Patria.

Vamos a ver los muertos de la Patria.

Verlos con nuestros ojos dilatados por la vida.
Hay que tocarlos con nuestras manos.
Están como aves posadas en el árbol terrible,
donde el viento no suena,

Light searching for the roots
of the oaks.
Searching for oily resin,
touched, because of manifest breath,
by manifest light.

The Metallic Seed that Licario searched for.
In resinous light,
gift of the root struck by the ax,
the frenzied choral dance begins,
the city dancing
in a parade of phallic torches.

FEBRUARY 1973

Translated by Mark Weiss

Virgilio Piñera

The Fatherland's Dead

Let's go to see the Fatherland's dead.
In the field of silence trees,
birds, salutes
are dead as well and belong to the dead.
Rifles, machine guns and the hands that hold them
are wrinkled dreams that could have been dreamt
by a dead man born to the world of the dead.

Let's go to see the Fatherland's dead.

In the illustrious heap nobody seeks
rewards, or titles, or lands;
they could have earned monuments, marble, honors,
but chose to be the Fatherland's dead.

Let's go to see the Fatherland's dead.

To see them through eyes wide with life.
We are compelled to touch them with our hands.
They are like birds perched in terrible trees
where the wind makes no sound,

y en donde la noche misma
se aleja vencida por la Nada.

Vamos a ver los muertos de la Patria.

¡Ay!—diría yo ese muerto
en quien quedó un asomo
de sonrisa indestructible—:
¿Cómo se muere en el momento
en que la bala se funde con la risa?
Y tú
—muerto tirado en esa zanja,
con un zapato como casco guerrero en tu cabeza—,
¿qué mago consultaste para estar ahora
de cara al Tiempo y con la Patria adentro?

Vamos a ver los muertos de la Patria.

1962

Nunca los dejaré

Cuando puso los ojos en el mundo,
dijo mi padre:
"vamos a dar una vuelta por el pueblo".
El pueblo eran las casas,
los árboles, la ropa tendida,
hombres y mujeres cantando
y a ratos peleándose entre sí.
Cuántas veces miré las estrellas.
Cuántas veces, temiendo su atracción inhumana,
esperé flotar solitario en los espacios
mientras abajo Cuba perpetuaba su azul,
donde la muerte se detiene.
Entonces olía las rosas,
o en la retreta, la voz desafinada
del cantante me sumía en delicias celestiales.
Nunca los dejaré—decía en voz baja;
aunque me claven en la cruz,
nunca los dejaré.
Aunque me escupan,
me quedaré entre el pueblo.
Y gritaré con ese amor que puede

and even night withdraws,
overcome by Nothingness.

Let's go to see the Fatherland's dead.

"What's it like," I'd say to one of the dead
who wears on his face
a hint of an indestructible smile:
"What's it like to die at the very moment the bullet
melds with laughter?
And you"
—corpse tossed into that ditch
with a shoe on your head in place of a helmet—
"what wizard did you consult to be left
with your face to Time and the Fatherland within?"

Let's go to see the Fatherland's dead.

    1962

I Will Never Leave Them

When he opened his eyes to the world
my father said:
"Let's take a stroll around town."
The town was houses, trees,
clothes on the clotheslines,
men and women singing and
sometimes quarreling.
How many times I saw the stars.
How many times, fearing their inhuman attraction,
I hoped to float alone in space
while beneath me Cuba kept its blueness,
where death lingers.
Then I smelled the roses,
or in the military band, the out of tune voice
of the singer drowned me in heavenly delights.
I will never leave them—I whispered;
even if they nail me to the cross
I will never leave them.
Even if they spit at me,
I will remain among the people.
And I will shout with that love that can shout

gritar su nombre hacia los cuatro vientos,
lo que el pueblo dice cada instante:
"me están matando pero estoy gozando".

1962

En la puerta de mi vecino . . .

En la puerta de mi vecino
un papelito me dejó helado.
"No me molesten. Estoy llorando.
Y consolarme ya nadie puede".

Ahora yo sueño con mi vecino.
Y mientras sueño, abro la puerta.
Adentro veo mi propia cara,
mi propia cara bañada en lágrimas.

1962

Testamento

Como he sido iconoclasta
me niego a que me hagan estatua;
si en la vida he sido carne,
en la muerte no quiero ser mármol.

Como yo soy de un lugar
de demonios y de ángeles,
en ángel y demonio muerto
seguiré por esas calles . . .

En tal eternidad veré
nuevos demonios y ángeles,
con ellos conversaré
en un lenguaje cifrado.

Y todos entenderán
el yo no lloro, mi hermano . . .
Así fui, así viví,
así soñé y pasé el trance.

1967

its name to the four winds,
the phrase that the people constantly repeat:
"they're killing me but I'm having fun."

1962

On my neighbor's door . . .

On my neighbor's door
a chilling note.
"Go away. I'm weeping.
No one can comfort me."

Now I dream of my neighbor.
And in my dream I open the door.
Within I see my own face,
my own face, bathed in tears.

1962

Testament

As I was an iconoclast
I won't have them build me a statue;
in life I was flesh,
and I don't wish to be marble in death.

As I come from a place
of devils and angels,
as a dead angel or devil
I will walk those streets . . .

In that hereafter I'll see
new devils and angels,
and speak to them
in a secret language.

And they'll all understand
my "I don't weep, brother . . . "
That's how I was, that's how I lived,
how I dreamt and how I survived the bitter time.

1967

En el Gato Tuerto

En el Gato Tuerto no hay gatos.
En el Gato Tuerto hay gente,
con ojos como prismáticos,
con bocas como ventosas,
con manos como tentáculos,
con pies como detectores.

En el Gato Tuerto
hay una noche dentro de la noche,
con una luna que sale para algunos,
un sol que brilla para otros
y un gallo que canta para todos.

En el Gato Tuerto
hay el asiento de la felicidad,
hay el asiento de la desdicha,
y hay también el horrendo asiento de la espera.

En el Gato Tuerto,
¿me atreveré a decirlo?,
hay un pañuelo para enjugar las lágrimas,
y hay igualmente,
—casi no me atrevo—
un espejo para mirarse cara a cara.

En el Gato Tuerto
una noche se dieron el sí dos amantes,
y en el Gato Tuerto
otra noche mataron lo que amaban.

En el Gato Tuerto
hay un momento de expectación
cuando el amante imaginario
hace su aparición.

Mira amorosamente y dice:
"¡Soy de quien me espera!",
y entonces el *feeling* llega al corazón,
en el Gato Tuerto con Revolución.

1967

At the One-Eyed Cat

At the One-Eyed Cat there are no cats.
At the One-Eyed Cat there are people,
with eyes like binoculars,
mouths like vents,
hands like tentacles,
feet like detectors.

At the One-Eyed Cat
there's a night within night,
with a moon that emerges for some,
a sun that shines for others
and a cock that crows for all.

At the One-Eyed Cat
there's the seat of happiness,
the seat of misfortune
and also the terrible seat of hope.

At the One-Eyed Cat,
will I dare to say it?
there's a cloth to wipe away tears,
and there's also
—I scarcely dare it—
a mirror to look at yourself face to face.

At the One-Eyed Cat
on a certain night two lovers said yes to each other,
and at the One-Eyed Cat
another night they killed the one they'd loved.

At the One-Eyed Cat
there's an expectant moment
when the imagined lover
makes his appearance.

He casts an amorous glance and says:
"I belong to the one who waits for me!"
And then the *feeling* reaches the heart,
at the One-Eyed Cat plus Revolution.

1967

Pin, pan, pun

El niño me mató con su fusil de palo. Muerto empecé a verlo
en su lento crecimiento hacia la crueldad.
En estos días me gusta escuchar los disparos. Se tiñe
de sangre el horizonte. Todos afirmamos que la felicidad
es una bala.

1969

Quien soy

Poco importa mi nombre, y mucho menos mi edad.
No he de enumerar la caída del pelo ni decir "encanezco".
Tan sólo una sencilla confesión: no tengo ni un perro acompañante,
y tengo cantidades de soledad que regalar.

1969

Una noche

Una noche en la calle Zanja,
saltando entre chinos impávidos,
escuché una voz que me decía:
¡Qué bobo tú eres, Virgilio!
pensando todas esas marañas,
esos mares, esas montañas:
tomas el bosque por los árboles
y esperas un amor al paso.
Qué bobo eres. Si supieras,
o lograras adivinarlo,
no abrieras tanto los ojos,
y me tendieras la mano.
Una noche en la calle Zanja.
Pero yo pasé de largo.

1969

Bang Bang

The child killed me with his wooden gun. Dead now I begin to see him
in his slow growth towards cruelty.
These days I like to hear the shots. The horizon
is stained with blood. We all agree that happiness
is a bullet.

1969

Who I Am

My name is of little importance, even less my age.
I don't need to count my hair loss nor announce that I'm turning gray.
A simple confession, nothing more: I don't have even a dog for company,
and I have solitude to spare.

1969

A Night

One night on Zanja Street,
leaping between impassive Chinese,
I heard a voice that said:
"What a fool you are, Virgilio!
inventing all those swamps,
seas, mountains:
you mistake the forest for the trees
and hope for a love met by chance.
What a fool you are. If you had any foresight,
you wouldn't look around so much,
and you'd let me take your hand."
One night on Zanja Street.
But I kept walking.

1969

Bueno, digamos

• *A Lezama*

Bueno, digamos que hemos vivido,
no ciertamente—aunque sería elegante—
como los griegos de la polis radiante,
sino parecidos a estatuas kriselefantinas,
y con un asomo de esteatopigia.
Hemos vivido en una isla,
quizá no como quisimos,
pero como pudimos.
Aun así derribamos algunos templos,
y levantamos otros
que tal vez perduren
o sean a su tiempo derribados.
Hemos escrito infatigablemente,
soñado lo suficiente
para penetrar la realidad.
Alzamos diques
contra la idolatría y lo crepuscular.
Hemos rendido culto al sol
y, algo aún más esplendoroso,
luchamos para ser esplendentes.
Ahora, callados por un rato,
oímos ciudades deshechas en polvo,
arder en pavesas insignes manuscritos,
y el lento, cotidiano gotear del odio.
Mas, es sólo una pausa en nuestro devenir.
Pronto nos pondremos a conversar.
No encima de las ruinas, sino del recuerdo,
porque fíjate: son ingrávidos
y nosotros ahora empezamos.

1972

OK, Let's Say

• *to Lezama*

OK, let's say that we've lived,
not, surely—though it would be elegant—
like the Greeks of the shining city,
but like chryselephantine statues,
with a hint of steatopygia.
We have lived on an island,
not, maybe, as we'd wished,
but as we could.
Even so we tore down some temples,
and built others
which may last
or be leveled in turn.
We have written tirelessly,
dreamt enough
to penetrate reality.
We built dikes
against idolatry and twilight.
We have paid homage to the sun
and, more splendidly,
struggled to be more splendid still.
Now, quieted for a while,
we hear cities pounded to dust,
famous manuscripts reduced to embers,
and the slow, daily drip of hatred.
But it's only a pause in our future.
Soon we will speak to each other.
From the heights of memory, not ruins,
because listen: they are weightless,
and we are just beginning.

1972

Y cuando me contó . . .

Y cuando me contó que el asesino,
sus manos en la funda de mi almohada,
de la almohada en que mi cabeza se encabrita
víctima de los vaivenes del sueño,
me dijo: "¿nunca pensaste, Virgilio,
en el poco tiempo de vida que te queda?"
Me cagué en los pantalones,
puse un disco de alegría en conserva,
y me tomé un diazepán.
Me habían despertado los gatos
en su templeta homérica.
Todo normal:
temperatura entre veinticinco y treinta grados,
algunos chubascos, marejadas por la noche.
El día monótonamente programado
en su inevitable desarrollo hacia la noche,
que pese a su tan alabado misterio
no es otra cosa que una duración del tiempo.
Me había lavado los dientes
con esa holgazanería con que enfrentamos
al nuevo día en su terror creciente,
como si la muerte llegara de golpe
en mitad de una claridad deslumbrante.
Pasé entonces a la cocina,
hice café, lo tomé a sorbos,
prendí un cigarro, cogí una hoja de papel,
la puse en la máquina y escribí:
Y cuando me contó que el asesino . . .

II

Qué extraño
levantarse, tomar café,
ponerse a la máquina, escribir.
Pero el día tiene que marchar
y yo con él, y con el asesino,
hasta que llegue la noche

And when he told me . . .

I

And when he told me that the murderer,
his hands on my pillowcase,
on the pillow from which my head rebounds
victim of the drift of dreams,
he asked me: "Have you never thought, Virgilio,
how little time you have left?"
I shat in my pants,
played a disk of preserved happiness,
and swallowed a diazepam.
The homeric fucking of cats had awakened me.
Nothing unusual:
temperature in the eighties,
a few showers, storm surges through the night.
The day monotonously programmed
to unfold inevitably towards the night
that despite its famous mystery
is merely a stretch of time.
I had brushed my teeth
with that laziness with which we confront
the new day's rising terror,
as if death were about to burst upon us
in the midst of a dazzling light.
I went then into the kitchen,
made coffee, sipped it,
lit a cigarette, picked up a sheet of paper,
put it in the machine and wrote
"And when he told me that the murderer . . . "

II

How strange
to wake up, drink coffee,
sit at the machine and write.
But the day has to go on
and me and the murderer with it,
until night falls

y ponga la cabeza en la almohada,
mi cabeza, víctima de los espasmos del sueño,
del sueño donde el asesino me dice
el poco tiempo de vida que me queda.

1974

Reversibilidad

Rodeado de un bobo, un mudo y un ciego
—adornos monstruosos del negocio—,
esperas tu turno en la barbería.
Ellos te llevan la ventaja
de estar fuera del tiempo.
Sagrados y consagrados
por una muerte en vida,
nada podría herirlos.
Pero tú existes, existes a medias,
en una extraña manera de existir.
De los muchos paraísos de este mundo,
ninguno te tocó en suerte.
Tu papel es testificar
el tremendo gozar de los otros,
y mediante la palabra, convertir
ese gozo en algo más sublime.

Y mientras embellezco al prójimo,
me voy afeando hasta adquirir la máscara grotesca
de quien existe a medias, sufre en el cepo de sus días
imaginarios, y su máscara corroe su cara verdadera.

De niño ya simulabas ser otro.
Tú no podías ser tú.
Si veías un árbol no era un árbol,
era algo indescifrable.
Algo que, indescriptible, venía a ser tu otro yo.
Entretanto los frutos del paraíso terrenal
se alejaban de ti en una barca negra
construida con palabras herméticas,
tan indescifrables como tú mismo.

and I lay my head on the pillow,
my head, victim of the spasms of dream,
the dream in which the murderer tells me
how little time I have left.

1974

Reversibility

Surrounded by an idiot, a mute and a blindman
—the shop's monstrous décor—
you wait your turn at the barber's.
They have the advantage
of being outside of time.
Sacred and consecrated
by a death in life,
nothing could hurt them.
But you exist, you half-exist,
in a peculiar kind of existence.
You had no luck with any
of the paradises of this earth.
Your job is to testify
to the tremendous joy of others,
and to convert that joy
by means of words
into something more sublime.

And while I beautify my neighbor,
I grow uglier and uglier, until I've become the grotesque mask
of the half-alive, languishing in the snare of his imaginary
days, his mask eroding his true face.

Even as a child you pretended to be another.
You couldn't be you.
If you saw a tree it wasn't a tree,
it was an indecipherable thing.
Something that, indescribable, came to be your other self.
Meanwhile the fruit of the terrestrial paradise
drifted away from you in a black ship
of hermetic words,
as indecipherable as you yourself.

Ahora el barbero esgrime la navaja,
y se dispone a afeitar al cliente ciego,
quien experimenta casi el orgasmo
cuando la navaja le roza la nuez.
Pero es un cliente, y la navaja es inofensiva.
No se abatirá en la yugular ni segará su vida.
Pero yo veo ríos de sangre,
al barbero convertido en Jack el destripador,
al ciego, como una mujer fatal, recibiendo su merecido.
La escena es tan perfecta, tan propicia.
Acá el espejo multiplica las pasiones,
un asiento es la cama de la concupiscencia,
y esta toalla un raudal de lágrimas.
El amante traicionado esgrime la navaja.
Hay que ver cómo se superpone un barbero
a un hombre loco de pasión,
y un cliente ciego, a una cortesana degollada.
Lo irreal es realidad, lo minúsculo, grandioso.
Y aunque nadie se percate, acabo de transformar el mundo.
Mío tan sólo, intemporal. Ellos siguen intactos.

—Gracias—dice el ciego—. ¿Cuánto le debo?
Y el bobo repite: ¿Cuánto le debo?
Y se ríe sin saber de qué se ríe.
No lo ven. No pueden verlo.
Pero todos, ya fuera del tiempo, son figuras yacentes.
Las animo a medida que desarrollo la trama.
—Señor—me dice el barbero—. Es su turno.
—Señora—me dice el amante traicionado—, encomienda tu alma.
—Señor—me dice el barbero—, ¿lo afeito?
—Señora—me dice el amante traicionado—, voy a degollarla.
Brota la sangre de mi carótida, tiemblo como un poseso.
—¿Se siente mal, señor?, me pregunta el barbero inocente.

Perfectamente afeitado abandono la barbería,
y perfectamente degollado me llevan a la morgue.
Un mundo gelatinoso en el que resbalo a cada paso
me envuelve en sus oleadas de realidad luminosas.
El tiempo deja de transcurrir, aunque el sol
se ha ocultado, y la noche no existe.
El barbero lee en su casa el periódico,

Now the barber brandishes the razor,
preparing to shave the blind customer,
who experiences something like an orgasm
when the razor scrapes his adam's apple.
But he's a customer, and the razor is harmless.
It won't plunge into his jugular nor sever his life.
But me, I see rivers of blood,
the barber as Jack the Ripper,
the blind man a femme fatale meeting her maker.
The scene is so perfect, so propitious.
Here the mirror multiplies passions
and a barber chair is the bed of concupiscence,
this towel a torrent of tears.
The betrayed lover brandishes the razor.
One's forced to notice the barber superimposed
on a man crazy with passion,
and a blind customer on a courtesan with a slit throat.
The unreal is reality, the minuscule's the enormous.
No one notices as I finish transforming the world.
It's mine alone, outside of time. They remain intact.

"Thanks," says the blindman. "How much do I owe you?"
And the idiot repeats: "How much do I owe you?"
And he laughs without knowing why.
They don't see. They can't see it.
But all of them, outside of time now, are lying down.
I pull their strings as the plot unfolds.
"Sir," the barber tells me, "it's your turn."
"Madam," the betrayed lover tells me, "better start praying."
"Sir," the barber asks me, "a shave?"
"Madam," the betrayed lover tells me, "I'm going to slit your throat."
The blood sprouts from my carotid, I tremble like one possessed.
"Are you ok?" the unsuspecting barber asks.

Perfectly shaved I leave the barber,
and I'm taken to the morgue, my throat slit perfectly.
A gelatinous world where I slip at each step
envelops me in its waves of luminous reality.
Time stops passing, despite
the hidden sun and nonexistent night.
The barber reads the newspaper at home,

el mudo traga su bocado, el ciego se sumerge en el sueño,
con sus alaridos puebla el idiota la plaza desierta.
Pero todos ellos, sin saberlo siquiera,
siguen por una avenida mi cortejo fúnebre:
soy una puta famosa que acaba de ser degollada.

1978

Isla

Aunque estoy a punto de renacer,
no lo proclamaré a los cuatro vientos
ni me sentiré un elegido:
sólo me tocó en suerte,
y lo acepto porque no está en mi mano
negarme, y sería por otra parte una descortesía
que un hombre distinguido jamás haría.
Se me ha anunciado que mañana,
a las siete y seis minutos de la tarde,
me convertiré en una isla,
isla como suelen ser las islas.
Mis piernas se irán haciendo tierra y mar,
y poco a poco, igual que un andante chopiniano,
empezarán a salirme árboles en los brazos,
rosas en los ojos y arena en el pecho.
En la boca las palabras morirán
para que el viento a su deseo pueda ulular.
Después, tendido como suelen hacer las islas,
miraré fijamente al horizonte,
veré salir el sol, la luna,
y lejos ya de la inquietud,
diré muy bajito:
¿así que era verdad?

1979

the mute swallows his morsel, the blindman submerges himself in dream,
the idiot fills the empty plaza with his shrieks.
But all of them, unknowing,
follow my cortege down the avenue:
I'm a famous whore who's had her throat slit.

1978

Island

Although I'm about to be reborn,
I won't proclaim it to the four winds
nor feel myself among the elect:
it came to me by chance,
and I accept it because it's not for me
to refuse, and besides, it would be bad manners
if a man of distinction were to do so.
It was announced to me that tomorrow
at six after seven in the evening
I would become an island,
an island like any other.
My legs will be turning to earth and sea,
and little by little, like a Chopin andante,
trees will begin to sprout from my arms,
from my eyes roses, and sand from my breast.
Words will die in my mouth
so that the wind may howl at will.
Afterwards, as islands do,
I will stare at the horizon,
see the sun and moon emerge,
and far now from anxiety
whisper softly:
"did that really happen?"

1979

Translated by Mark Weiss

Samuel Feijóo

En la muerte por fuego de Gladys, la joven de los canarios

¿Dónde está el precioso diálogo
que anunciaban los canarios junto al rostro
de la doncella quemada?
                                    ¿Hubo algo
más hermoso de oir dentro de la fresca casa,
que el pico rubio trinador
cerca de la boca que nadie protegió?

Las impuras llamas rayaron devorando
a las flautas en su pausa de la delicadeza,
a los cabellos, y al rostro.
Ceñía el fuego
a las sensatas conclusiones deseadas, a las amadas
bocas rosas con canciones de penas
entre los ásperos lauros del anochecer y los cabos
de las soledades . . .
                                    Por los rocajes del mar del tiempo
ya dialogan los canarios,
                                    simulan silbar.
En la boca entreabierta de la virgen incendiada.
                                                        Cantan
en medio de las llamas de la joven carne,
tersa y rosa, crujiendo, chispeando. Maldicen
al azar y su retórica, al escriba, al lector, al estanque
con sus espaldas de verde eterno, y al neblinar nocturno
que va deslizando su baba idílica en las fuentes
mientras el fuego come los muslos dulces
con el oro del carbón maloliente.

Tumba con palmas

Pasaba la bicicleta a veinte varas
de la fosa y me detuvo el ángel de la piedra,
en gris. Por un instante
quedé absorto. Hasta que dije: "Aquí

Samuel Feijóo

On the Death by Fire of Gladys, the Young Girl Who Kept Canaries

Where are the lovely words
the canaries proclaimed to the face
of the burnt maiden?
                                        Was there any sound
more beautiful within that fragrant house
than the blond beak warbling
beside that unprotected mouth?

The impure flames streaked forth
devouring in their delicate rest the flutes,
the hair, the face.
Fire constrained
the hoped-for rational endings, stopped the beloved
pink mouths with songs of grief
amid the harsh laurels of nightfall and the tethers
of solitude . . .
                                By the sea-boulders of time
the canaries have already begun to speak,
                                        pretending to whistle
through the half-open mouth of the burnt virgin.
                                                            They sing
amid flames of young flesh,
firm and pink, crackling with sparks. They curse
chance and its rhetoric, the scribe, the reader, the pond
with its eternally green surface, and the night-mist
that slides its idyllic drool into the fountains
while fire consumes the sweet thighs
with the gold of malodorous coal.

Tomb with Palm-Trees

My bicycle was passing twenty yards
from the grave when the gray stone angel
stopped me. For a moment I was lost in thought. And then I said: "Here

aquel que me acompañara en la montaña,
en aventuras incontables, roe
su robusto esqueleto." Silbaban
las memorias. Sumido en la zona
estaba, campesina, con aire de aguinaldos
oloroso de sonido de rama en paz.

Apoyé los tarros de la bicicleta
contra la palma primera. Entré
al diminuto pueblo de mármoles.
Por la limpia vegetación
la soledad del campo
se sentaba bajo las alas de piedra.

Trémulo surgió mi pensamiento:
"Aquí yace Tomás Feijóo, el
andarín de Siguanea. Envenenada espada
de mosquito le mató. ¡Loor
a él, vendedor de billetes de lotería
y el holgazán rural
marchando entre montañas! ¡Loor
al navegante de las palmeras,
al ausente de una lluvia,
que jamás enjoyó sus visiones de guajiro!"
Tomás, ayer errante por las lomas,
me apena tomarte de pretexto
para hacer unos renglones
con mi recuerdo tuyo por las tinajas
y las hamacas. Ante tu polvo
que me habla, me acoge
una ignorante tristeza impávida.

Suave, sacudido de tu conocimiento,
uno el limo mortal con otras voces:
quiero ser vasto y
nadar mis aguas densas,
e introducir mi rostro en la penumbra
afortunada. Para llegar a esa
soltura feliz
afinaré las entrañas en distintas
soledades, cruzaré sobre los puentes
de la conversación de los sentidos,
de las luces en ellos descubiertas.

corrodes the robust skeleton
of he who accompanied me
into the mountains on countless adventures."
Memories whistled through me. I was immersed
in the region, rural, a breath of convolvulus
fragrant with the sounds of a peaceful bough.

I leaned the handlebars
against the first palm-tree. I entered
the tiny village of marble slabs.
Through clean vegetation
the rural solitude
rested beneath wings of stone.

Trembling, my thought came forth:
"Here lies Tomás Feijóo, of Siguanea,
who loved to walk. A mosquito's
venomous sword killed him. All praise
to him, seller of lottery tickets
and country loafer
strolling among the mountains! All praise
to the navigator of palm-trees,
he whom the rain finds absent,
who never embellished his peasant's visions."
Tomás, once wanderer of hills,
it saddens me that you become
an excuse to make some lines
filled with my memory of you among jugs
and hammocks. Before your speaking dust
a fearless
ignorant sadness welcomes me.

Gently, shaken by your knowledge,
I join the mortal slime with other voices:
I want to be vast and
swim in my own dense waters,
to introduce my face into the fortunate
shadow. To reach that
happy freedom
I will refine my heart with different
solitudes, I will cross bridges
of the conversation of feelings,
and the lights found in them.

Y seré vasto, callado tono
por inmensos dominios solitarios
y no alejado por el salto insomne
de mi enemigo alerta, sin figura
de estas voces cernidas del alma
que caen con la gracia natural
del cotidiano fruto de la frente.

Así, ya la simpleza
de mi desoída voz de poeta
hallará el puro acento: como
el golpe que oigo del ramo de la palma
contra su tronco, como el sonido
de la yagua, universal
y uno. No mi filosofía
agrestemente reunida entinte
la flor asomada a mis labios
ni la concha del pétalo
pierda en un humo de lejanas chozas.

Pero con gemas puras
puedo yo sustentarme
del acertado acento. Pueda
en el trágico instante
hallar la palma criolla al lado
tocando la nube con su lanza,
cuidando con su sombra
los yerbajos de mi polvareda.

¿Podré, ya, ser tan simple
como el arroyo del aire echando su ruido a mi hombro,
como el zumbido gris
de la tojosa? (En la tradición
de los campos de mi tierra
llenos de jades transparentes
y golpes de blanquísima luz niña.)
Sigo los sonidos vegetales,
sus cuerdas del ocaso tan pálido
que se posa en el cañaveral goteante.

(Ay, aún guardo
entre mis umbríos tesoros la visión
de una cabellera rubia

And I will be a vast, silent note
sounding through immense solitary domains
not pushed away by the sleepless leap
of my vigilant, shapeless enemy,
of these hovering voices of the soul,
that fall with the natural grace
of the daily fruit of the mind.

So, now the simplicity
of my unheard poet's voice
will find the pure tone: like
the beat I hear of the frond
against the palm-tree's trunk, like the sound
of its husk, universal
and one. Let not my philosophy,
that rural assemblage, tinge
the flower visible on my lips
nor let the shell of the petal
be lost in a smoke of distant huts.

But now with pure gems
of the proper tone
I can sustain myself. Oh let me
in the tragic moment
find the creole palm-tree nearby
touching the cloud with its lance,
sheltering with its shade
the grasses of my dust.

Will I come, then, to be as simple
as the stream of air pouring its noise at my shoulder,
like the dove's gray hum?
(In the tradition
of the fields of my country,
full of transparent jades
and the pounding of the whitest young light.)
I follow the vegetal sounds
their strings of so pale a sunset
perching on the dripping cane-fields.

(Ah! I still keep
among my shadowy treasures the vision
of blond tresses

en las manos del sepulturero
de un cementerio desechado.) Este trébol
de memorias tocadas de espanto
esparce suave delirio
entre las letras con acaso grávido.
Sí, visiones he escrito
cambiándome la faz. Y su música
cuidadosamente he cubierto de mi sabiduría
para ofrendarla en trabajado emblema.

Natural en mi
artificio, miro esta luz
bajando entre los ángeles funerarios
que me rodean con sílabas verdes
y muy grises y negramente pétreas,
arrebujada la luz en sus alas densas, impenetrables.

Quedo lanzado contra la pared blanca
interminable de todos los cementerios
de las cosas que se van
tocando mis labios que también huyen
(no las llamo: me llevan
a sus escondites, enredijos y misterios
y mi tallo o aguja de oro
esconden en los libros del suspiro
o de la roca recia en que reposo).

Adiós, tío mío,
junto a tu tumba breves pensamientos
te debo. Así, ayer,
te agradecí aquel nudo en la hamaca de Pueblo Viejo,
fresco caserío sobre una
cresta de monte con arroyo.
Muera, como tú en lo tuyo,
yo en lo mío.

Yo: sobre el libro ligero de la memoria,
entre palmas y tormentosas nubes;
tú: en tu camino morado en la loma
donde el mosquito te mató
(sin que de nada te valiera el sello postal
que te pegó en la frente tu salvaje hermano).

in the hands of the gravedigger
of an abandoned cemetery.) This clover
of memories touched with fright
spreads a soft delirium
among letters freighted with fate.
Yes, I have written visions
changing my face. And their music
I have carefully covered with the patina
of my wisdom
to offer it as a wrought emblem.

Natural in my
artifice, I look at this light
descending among funereal angels
that surround me with green
and very gray and dark stony syllables,
the light wrapped in their dense, impenetrable wings.

I stay, thrown against the white
endless wall of all the cemeteries
of things that leave
touching my lips that also flee
(I don't call them: they take me
to their hideouts, their entanglements and mysteries,
and hide my stem or golden needle
in books of sighs
or of the hard rock on which I rest).

Goodbye, my uncle,
I owe you these brief thoughts
beside your tomb. As once
I thanked you for that knot in the hammock from Pueblo Viejo,
a cool village with a stream
at the crest of a mountain.
May I die—like you—
in my proper place.

I: bent over the slender book of memory,
among palms and storm clouds;
you: on your purple road on the hillside
where the mosquito killed you
(of no avail the postage stamp your wild brother
stuck to your forehead).

Muera yo como tú
con la majestad de un árbol hachado.
Yo, como tú, hombre de largas jornadas y
jugador (con otras barajas), ligado
al hechizo del bosque en cuya ventana me sentaste.

. . . Al correr de los años
alguien vendrá también a este pueblo de tiznados ángeles de mármol
suspendidos sobre el dulce paisaje, y ante
mi nombre de borrosas letras
del panteón familiar, dirá sencillo:
"Aquí Samuel
dio su nocturno claro y aquí yace
más solo ya, bajo esta
losa donde apoyó una vez la página para escribir otro poema
desordenado y puro. Es increíble . . . "

Tres blues

I

BLUE DEL VULGAR

Cuando lejos esté,
lejos, lejos,
en aquel valle
tan lejano.

¡Cuando en aquel
valle
tan
lejano
vea el agua
vea el agua
dorada
y
tranquila!

II

BLUE DEL SUEÑO

La libélula,
amor mío,
vuela de mí

Let me die like you
with the majesty of a felled tree.
I, like you, a man of long workdays and
a gambler (with other cards), bound
to the spell of the woods in whose window you sat me.

. . . As the years fly by
someone else will come to this village of blackened marble angels
hanging above the sweet landscape and, before
the faded letters of my name
on the family vault, will say:
"Here Samuel
performed his limpid nocturne and here he lies
more alone now, under this
gravestone where he once rested the page to write another pure
chaotic poem. Who could believe it . . . "

Three Blues

I

VERNACULAR BLUES

When I'm far,
far away, far away,
in that valley
so far away.

When in that
valley
so
far away
I see the water
I see the water
golden
and
peaceful!

II

DREAM BLUES

The dragonfly,
my love,
flies from me

a ti, de ti
a mí.
Gris y azul.
¡Azul y gris,
mi amor!

Abrázame,
sol de otoños,
esqueleto
helado.

Vuela de mí
a ti y es bella
la música.
La música, el día
azul y gris,
y gris y gris,
gris en el azul
más gris del gris.

III

BLUE DEL HIJO

Pájaro, pájaro,
yo soy un hijo
deforme:
tengo los pies rotos,
la cabeza grande,
no puedo mover
mis manos.
Mis ojos miran
a mi madre.
Pájaro, pájaro,
mi madre se fue,
abrió la puerta y se fue,
mi mamá se fue.

CIENFUEGOS, 31 DE MARZO DE 1968

to you, from you
to me.
Gray and blue.
Blue and gray,
my love!

Embrace me,
autumn sun,
frozen
skeleton.

It flies from me
to you, and the music
is beautiful.
The music, the day
blue and gray,
gray within gray's
grayest blue.

III

THE SON'S BLUES

Bird, bird,
I am a deformed
son:
my feet are broken,
my head is huge,
I can't move
my hands.
My eyes watch
my mother.
Bird, bird,
my mother left,
she opened the door and left,
my mama left.

CIENFUEGOS, MARCH 31, 1968

Son del loco

Los árboles se han cerrado.
El agua se ha cerrado.
El rocío se ha cerrado.
El cielo
inmensamente cerrado.

En las yerbas cerradas
       cerrado.
La tiniebla de la nieve.
La sombra sellada.
Palabras cerradas, sellos cerrados.
Signos, olas, luces, cerrados.
Caminan las espaldas.
Sangrantes lomas.
Con esta luz espantosa
dándoles vasos de agua.

    PARÍS, OCTUBRE 25 DE 1971

Caonao adentro

Cruzaba.
De un rancho solitario
en el monte,
        escuché una guitarra.

Entré.
Una mujer enferma
rasgaba sus cuerdas
en el humilde lecho.

Le di las buenas tardes suavamente.
"Si tiene sed beba de esa tinaja."

Ay hermana
bebo del aire que sale de sus dedos . . .

"Tocaba para mí, si estoy enferma" . . .

Tocabas para mí
al tocar para ti,

The Madman's *Son*

The trees have closed
The water has closed.
The dew has closed.
The sky
immensely closed.

Closed within the closed
            grass.
The darkness of the snow.
The sealed shade.
Closed words, closed seals.
Signs, waves, lights—closed.
Buttocks travel.
Bleeding hills.
Offering glasses of water
with this hideous light.

PARIS, OCTOBER 25, 1971

Deep Within the Caonao

I was passing by.
From a solitary hut
in the woods,
            I heard a guitar.

I entered.
A sick woman
was plucking its strings
on her humble bed.

Gently I bade her good evening.
"If you are thirsty, drink of this cup."

Oh sister,
I drink of the air coming out of your fingers . . .

"I was playing for myself, because I'm sick . . . "

Playing for yourself
that happy and gentle tune

ese aire alegre y suave
en tu guitarra llena de yerbas.

Sonreía rasgando las cuerdas
mientras mis labios bebían
del agua en la tinaja.

SEPT. 29/77

Gastón Baquero

Breve viaje nocturno

Según la leyenda africana, el alma del durmiente va a la luna.

Mi madre no sabe que por la noche,
cuando ella mira mi cuerpo dormido
y sonríe feliz sintiéndome a su lado,
mi alma sale de mí, se va de viaje
guiada por elefantes blanquirrojos,
y toda la tierra queda abandonada,
y ya no pertenezco a la prisión del mundo,
pues llego hasta la luna, desciendo
en sus verdes ríos y en sus bosques de oro,
y pastoreo rebaños de tiernos elefantes,
y cabalgo los dóciles leopardos de la luna,
y me divierto en el teatro de los astros
contemplando a Júpiter danzar, reír a Hyleo.

Y mi madre no sabe que al otro día,
cuando toca en mi hombro y dulcemente llama,
yo no vengo del sueño: yo he regresado
pocos instantes antes, después de haber sido
el más feliz de los niños, y el viajero
que despaciosamente entra y sale del cielo,
cuando la madre llama y obedece el alma.

1962

on your guitar full of herbs
you played for me.

She smiled, plucking at the strings
while my lips drank
of the water from that clay cup.

SEPTEMBER 29, 1977

Translated by Michael Smith

Gastón Baquero

A Brief Nocturnal Voyage

According to African legend, the soul of the sleeper travels to the moon.

My mother doesn't know that at night,
when she sees my sleeping body
and smiles with contentment to feel me at her side,
my soul, guided by pale pink
elephants, goes off on a journey
and leaves the earth bereft,
and I no longer belong to the prison of the world,
but reach the moon, descend
into its green rivers and forests of gold,
and pasture flocks of affectionate elephants,
and ride on the backs of the moon's tame leopards,
and amuse myself in the theater of the stars
watching Jupiter dance and laughing at Hylus.

And my mother doesn't know that when the new day dawns,
when she touches my shoulder and softly calls,
I don't emerge from the dream: I've returned
moments before, after being
the happiest of boys, the traveler
who slowly enters and leaves the sky
when his mother calls and his soul obeys.

1962

Pavana para el Emperador

Napoleón tenía un manto lleno de abejitas de oro.
Cuando el dolor de lumbago acometía al Emperador,
Las viejas hechiceras de Córcega le aconsejaban:
—Polioni, vuelve el manto al revés, ponte las abejas en la piel.
Y las fieras abejitas picoteaban a lo largo del espinazo imperial;
Sin la menor reverencia clavaban sus aguijoncitos arriba y abajo,
Hasta que transfundían sus benévolos ácidos en la sangre del Corso,
Y el lumbago salía dando gritos, vencido por el vencedor de Austerlitz.

La risa reaparecía en el rostro imperial, y la corte se vestía de encarnado;
Napoleón, libre de penas, volvía al derecho el manto, el de las abejitas de
    oro,
Y tomando con la punta de los dedos los extremos del armiño,
Echábase a bailar una pavana por todos los salones de las Tullerías:
Tra-la-lá, tra-la-lá, bailaba y cantaba, y decía olé, y viva la vida, y olé.
Y en tanto bailaba de nuevo feliz el Señor del Mundo,
Las doradas abejitas de su manto, felices también, reían y cantaban,
Como rayos de sol en la cabeza de un niño.

1963

El viento en Trieste decía

El viento en Trieste decía tan extrañas canciones al amanecer,
que a nada temíamos tanto como al anuncio de que el alba llegaba.
Allí fuimos por una vez hijos felices de las tinieblas,
allí aprendimos a amar como si fuera la más hermosa luz
el rostro entero de la noche.

El viento en Trieste decía tales sufrimientos y horrores en lo alto,
que aprendíamos a desconfiar de las candorosas nubes,
y tomábamos por verdaderos centinelas de oscuras ceremonias
la antes cristalina bandada de aves blancas.

                          El viento,
el viento en Trieste abatía premeditadamente cuanto fuera hermoso,
y metidos en el último rincón de nuestros refugios sentíamos que el viento,
el viento bramador, el de la enajenada y espectral sinfonía,
hería, y estrujaba, y arrastraba gozosamente entre la inmundicia,

Pavane for the Emperor

Napoleon had a cloak covered with gold bees.
When lumbago attacked the Emperor
The old witches of Corsica advised him:
"Nappy, reverse your cloak, bees to skin."
And the cruel bees stung the length of the imperial spine;
Without the least reverence they plunged their little stingers up and down,
Until their benevolent acids entered the blood of the Corsican,
And the lumbago ran off screaming, victim of the victor of Austerlitz.

Laughter reappeared on the imperial face, and the court dressed in red;
Napoleon, free of pain, turned his bee-covered cloak right-side out
Seized its ermine border with his fingertips
And began to dance a pavane through all the salons of the Tuileries:
Tra-la-la, Tra-la-la, he danced and sang, shouting Olé! and Long live life!
    and Olé.
The Lord of the Earth danced with renewed happiness,
And the bees on his cloak, also happy, laughed and sang
Like rays of the sun in a child's head.

  1963

The Wind in Trieste Told

The wind in Trieste told such strange songs at dawn
that more than anything we dreaded the announcement of the sun's arrival.
There for once we were happy children of darkness,
there we learned to love as if the face of night itself
were the loveliest light.

The wind in Trieste told such sufferings and horrors on high,
that we learned to distrust the innocent clouds,
and we took for true sentinels of dark ceremonies
the once-crystalline flock of white birds.

                              The wind,
the wind in Trieste at its whim flattened all that was beautiful,
and, squeezed into the deepest corner of our refuge, we sensed that the wind,
the wind that brayed like a crazed and spectral symphony,
wounded, crushed, and joyfully dragged through the filth

las vestiduras blanquísimas de los ángeles, los velos de la futura deposada,
los últimos depósitos de la sangre conservada como reliquia en el secreto
   del sagrario.

El viento en Trieste decía la pena de las estrellas,
la guerra incesante que hay allá, en las regiones donde nosotros
queríamos ver astros límpidos, armonía pautada en persona por Santa
   Cecilia,
paz del cielo.

                              El viento,
el viento en Trieste nos hacía desear como refugio la vida de la tierra,
la propia vida que nos habíamos empeñado en repudiar. El viento en
   Trieste decía
cuántos infiernos moran allá entre las estrellas, y nos hacía buena la tierra,
y del pecho se escapaban bendiciones cuando el viento rugía contra el sueño,
y nos daba sin tregua y sin consuelo
la inesperada enemistad del alba.

Los lunes me llamaba Nicanor

Yo los lunes me llamaba Nicanor.
Vindicaba el horrible tedio de los domingos
Y desconcertaba por unas horas a las doncellas
Y a los horóscopos.

El martes es un día hermoso para llamarse Adrián.
Con ello se vence el maleficio de la jornada
Y puede entrarse con buen pie en la roja pradera
Del miércoles,
Cuando es tan grato informar a los amigos
De que por todo ese día nuestro nombre es Cristóbal.

Yo en otro tiempo escamoteaba la guillotina del tiempo
Mudando de nombre cada día para no ser localizado
Por la señora Aquella,
La que transforma todo nombre en un pretérito
Decorado por las lágrimas.

Pero al fin he aprendido que el jueves Melitón,
Recaredo viernes, sábado Alejandro,
No impedirán jamás llegar al pálido domingo innominado.

the pearly vestments of angels, the veils of the promised wife,
the final store of blood preserved as a relic in the coffers of the tabernacle.

The wind in Trieste told the sorrow of the stars,
the incessant war waged there, in those regions where we
wished to see limpid stars, a harmony conducted by Saint Cecilia herself,
a heavenly peace.

                                      The wind,
the wind in Trieste made us desire life on earth as a refuge,
the very life that we had determined to renounce. The wind in Trieste told
how many hells dwell among the stars, and made us value earth,
and from our hearts went forth blessings when the wind roared against the
    dream
and gave us relentlessly and without consolation
the unhoped-for enmity of sunrise.

On Mondays My Name Was Nicanor

On Mondays my name was Nicanor.
It avenged the terrible boredom of Sundays
And upset for a few hours those young ladies
And their horoscopes.

Tuesday is a fine day to call oneself Adrian.
With it the curse of the day is conquered
And one can enter confidently the red meadow
Of Wednesday,
When it's pleasant to inform one's friends
That all day long our name is Christopher.

Once I tricked the guillotine of time,
Changing name each day to evade
My Lady She
Who transforms each name into a preterit
Adorned with tears.

But I have learned at last that Thursday Meliton,
Friday Recaredo, Saturday Alexander
Can't keep nameless, pallid Sunday from beginning

Cuando ella bautiza y clava certera su venablo
Tras el antifaz de cualquier nombre.

Yo los lunes me llamaba Nicanor.
Y ahora mismo no recuerdo en qué día estamos
Ni cómo me tocaría hoy llamarme en vano.

1965

El héroe

El héroe pasó su vida a caballo.
Su esposa misma creía que él era un Centauro.
Sus hijos creyeron siempre que su padre era un Centauro.
Sus compañeros de armas le llamaban el Centauro.
Pues nadie, nunca, le había visto sino a caballo.
Montado día y noche, año tras año, cabalgando en su caballo,
Como un Centauro.

El héroe llegó a viejo y nunca descendió de su caballo.
"Es el Centauro", decían los nuevos soldados con envidia
"Es el Centauro", decían las novias llenas de pena por sus años.
Pero el viejo héroe se mantenía erguido en su caballo,
Y nadie pudo nunca, ni por dormir ni por nada,
Verle descendido de su hermoso caballo de pelea,
Como un Centauro.

Y el héroe un día aceptó, él también, morir, pero a caballo.
Fue llevado a su tumba encima de su caballo, como viviera,
Pues ni aún después de muerto quiso dimitir de su existencia.
Y ahora seguimos viéndole, en medio de la plaza, heroico,
En ese monumento que niños y palomas toman por viviente.
Erguido está en su caballo, el héroe de siempre, aquel Centauro,
Cuyos hijos no le vieron sino a caballo, cuya esposa misma
No llegó a enterarse nunca de si aquel a quien amaba
Era un hombre a caballo, o era un Centauro.

1965

Fábula

Mi nombre es Filemón, mi apellido es Ustariz.
Tengo una vaca, un perro, un fusil y un sombrero;

When she baptizes and sticks her dart unerringly
Through the mask of any name at all.

On Monday my name was Nicanor.
And now I have forgotten what day it is
And what I would have named myself in vain.

1965

The Hero

The hero spent his life on horseback.
His very wife thought him a Centaur.
His children always thought their father a Centaur.
His companions in arms called him the Centaur.
No one, ever, had seen him except on horseback.
Day and night, year after year, mounted, riding his horse,
Like a Centaur.

The hero grew old and never dismounted his horse.
"He's the Centaur," the new soldiers said, enviously
"He's the Centaur," said their brides, pitying his years.
But the old hero stayed erect on his horse,
And no one could ever, asleep or otherwise,
See him dismount from his beautiful steed,
Like a Centaur.

And one day the hero, even he, accepted death, but on horseback.
He was led to his tomb atop his horse, as if alive,
Because not even after death did he wish to resign his existence.
And we still see him, in the center of the plaza, heroic,
In that monument that children and pigeons take for alive.
Erect on his horse, the eternal hero, that Centaur,
Whose sons never saw him except on horseback, whose very wife
Never learned if he she'd loved
Was a man on horseback or a Centaur.

1965

Fable

My name is Filemon, my family name Ustariz.
I have a cow, a dog, a rifle and a hat;

vagabundos, errantes, sin más tierra que el cielo,
vivimos cobijados por el techo más alto;
ni lluvias ni tormentas, ni océanos ni ríos,
impiden que vaguemos de pradera en pradera.
Filemón es mi nombre, Ustariz mi apellido.
No dormimos dos veces bajo la misma estrella;
cada día un paisaje, cada noche otra luz,
un viajero hoy nos halla junto al río Amazonas,
y mañana es posible que en el río Amarillo
aparezcamos justo al irrumpir el sol.
Somos como las nubes, pero reales, concretos:
un hombre, un perro, una vaca, un sombrero,
apestamos, queremos, odiamos y nos odian,
vagabundos, errantes, sin más tierra que el cielo
—Filemón es mi nombre, Ustariz mi apellido—;
los míos me acompañan, lucientes o sombríos,
pero con nombres propios, con sombras bien corpóreas,
seres corrientes, sueños, efluvios de una magia
que hace de lo increíble lo solo que creemos.
Filemón es mi nombre, Ustariz mi apellido;
somos materia cierta, cifras, humareda,
llevados por el viento, hambrientos de infinito,
un perro, una vaca, un palpable sombrero;
simples y sin misterio seguiremos el viaje:
por eso yo declaro al tomar el camino,
que es Filemón mi nombre y Ustariz mi apellido,
que la vaca se llama Rosamunda de Hungría,
y que al perro le puse el nombre de una estrella:
le digo Aldebarán, y brinca, y ríe, y canta,
como un tenor que quiere romperse la garganta.

Charada para Lydia Cabrera

Uno caballo, dos mariposa, tres marinero,
mira el caballo, mira el marino,
mira la mariposa.
Va de blanco vestido el marino,
blanca es la pelliza del caballo,
ríe la mariposa blanca.
Tres marinero, dos mariposa, uno caballo,
sobre el blanco caballo vuela el marino,

vagabonds, wanderers, with no land but the sky,
we live beneath the loftiest roof;
neither rain nor storm nor ocean nor river
keeps us from wandering from meadow to meadow.
My name is Filemon, my family name Ustariz.
We never sleep twice beneath the same star;
Each day a landscape, each night another light,
A traveler today may find us near the Amazon,
and tomorrow perhaps by the Yellow
at the moment the sun breaks above the horizon.
We are like clouds, but real, solid:
a man, a dog, a cow, a hat,
we sicken, we love, we hate and are hated,
vagabonds, wanderers, with no land but the sky
—my name is Filemon, my family name Ustariz;
my own come with me, bright or in shadow,
but with their own names, their own physical shadows,
real creatures, dreams, vapors of a magic
that out of the unbelievable builds all we believe.
My name is Filemon, my family name Ustariz;
matter, ciphers, smoke,
carried by the wind, hungry for the infinite,
a dog, a cow, an actual hat;
simple, without mystery, we continue our voyage:
that's why when we take to the road, I say
that my name is Filemon and my family name Ustariz,
that the cow's name is Rosamund of Hungary,
and that I took the dog's name from a star:
I call it Aldebaran, and it leaps, and it laughs, and it sings
like a tenor bursting his throat with song.

Charada for Lydia Cabrera

One horse, two butterfly, three sailor,
look at the horse, look at the sailor,
look at the butterfly.
The sailor is dressed in white
the horse's hide is white,
the white butterfly laughs.
Three sailor, two butterfly, one horse,
the sailor flies over the white horse,

sobre el marino va la mariposa,
dos mariposa, uno caballo, tres marinero,
mira el caballo a la mariposa,
mira el marino la blanca risa de su caballo,
la mariposa mira al marino, mira al caballo,
vuela el caballo, canta el marino
canción de cuna a la mariposa,
duerme el caballo y sueña con el marino,
duerme la mariposa y sueña que es el caballo,
duerme el marino y sueña ser mariposa,
uno caballo, dos mariposa, tres marinero,
tres mariposa, dos marinero, uno caballo,
uno marinero, uno caballo, uno mariposa.

1968

Marcel Proust pasea en barca por la bahía de Corinto

A la sombra de la juventud florecida
sentábase todos los días el viejo Anaximandro.
Tan viejo estaba el famoso mandrita,
que no despegaba los labios, ni sonreía, ni parecía comprender
la fiesta de aquellas cabelleras doradas, de aquellas
risas y picardías de las muchachas más bellas de Corinto.

Fue hacia el final de su vida,
cuando ya decíase la gente a sí misma al verle pasar:
a Anaximandro le quedan, cuando más, tres o cuatro girasoles por
    deshojar;
fue en aquel pedacito de tiempo que antecede al morirse,
cuando Anaximandro descubrió la solución del enigma del tiempo.

Fue allí en Corinto, junto a la bahía, rodeado de muchachas florecidas.
Le había dado por la inofensiva manía
de protegerse con un quitasol mitad verde mitad azul a la hora del
    mediodía;
no saludaba a las gentes de su edad, no frecuentaba los sitios de los
    ancianos,
ni parecía tener en común con los del ágora
otra cosa que senectud y nieve alrededor de las mandíbulas: Anaximandro
se había mudado al tiempo de la juventud florecida,
como quien cambia de país para curarse una dolencia vieja.

the butterfly over the sailor,
two butterfly, one horse, three sailor,
the horse looks at the butterfly,
the sailor looks at his horse's white laughter,
the butterfly looks at the sailor, looks at the horse,
the horse flies, the sailor sings
the butterfly a lullaby,
the horse sleeps and dreams of the sailor,
the butterfly sleeps and dreams it's the horse,
the sailor sleeps and dreams of becoming a butterfly,
one horse, two butterfly, three sailor,
three butterfly, two sailor, one horse,
one sailor, one horse, one butterfly.

    1968

Marcel Proust Cruises the Bay of Corinth

Each day old Anaximander
sat beneath the shade of youth in flower.
The famous sage had grown so old
that his lips no longer parted, nor did he smile nor seem even to understand
the play of golden hair the laughter, the sly, flirtatious games
of the loveliest girls in Corinth.

It was towards the end of his life
when as he passed folk would comment
that there was left to him at most
the wilting of three or four sunflowers.
It was in that small morsel of time preceding death
that Anaximander discovered
the solution to the enigma of time.

There, in Corinth, by the bay, encircled by the flowering girls.
That he would shelter at noon beneath a green and blue parasol
was his harmless eccentricity.
He had ceased greeting his age-mates, no longer frequenting the places
    where the old would gather,
nor did he seem to share with those in the agora
anything other than years and the snow encircling their jaws: Anaximander
had moved to the time of flowering youth,
like one who goes abroad to cure an old illness.

Llegaba con el mediodía a la sombra sonora de aquellas muchachas de
   Corinto;
arrastrando los pies, impasible, con su quitasol abierto, y sentábase calladito,
sentábase en medio de ellas a oír sus gorjeos, a observar la delicada
   geometría de aquellas rodillas de color de trigo, a atisbar alguna fugitiva
   paloma de rosado plumaje,
volando bajo el puente de los hombros.
                              Nada decía el viejo Anaximandro
ni nada parecía conmoverle bajo su quitasol, sintiendo el tiempo pasar entre
   las dulces muchachas de Corinto, el tiempo hecho una finísima lluvia
de alfileres de oro, de resplandor de cerezas mojadas,
el tiempo fluyendo en torno a los tobillos de las florecidas palomas de
   Corinto,
el tiempo que en otros sitios acerca a los labios del hombre una copa de
   irrechazable veneno,
ofrecía allí el néctar de tan especial ambrosía,
como si él, el tiempo, también quisiese vivir, y hacerse persona, y deleitarse
en el raso de una piel o en el rayo de una pupila entre verde y azul.
                              Silencioso Anaximandro
como un cisne navegaba cada día entre las nubes de la belleza, y permanecía;
estaba allí, dentro y fuera del tiempo, paladeando lentos sorbitos de
   eternidad, con el ronroneo del gato junto a la estufa. Al atardecer volvía
   a su casa,
y pasaba la noche dedicado a escribir pequeños poemas para
las rumorosas palomas de Corinto.

Los otros sabios de la ciudad murmuraban sin descanso.
Anaximandro había llegado a ser, más que el rito de las cosechas y que el
   vaivén de los navíos,
el tema predilecto de los aburridos conciliábulos:
                              —"Siempre os dije,
oh ancianos de Corinto, afirmaba su viejo enemigo Pródico, que éste no era
   un sabio verdadero ni siquiera un hombre medianamente formal. ¿Su obra?
Todo copiado. Todo repetido. Pero vacío por dentro. Vacío como un tonel
   de vino cuando los hijos de Tebas vienen a saborear la luz de los viñedos
   de Corinto".
Anaximandro cruzaba impasible las calles de la ciudad, rumbo a la bahía.
Llevaba abierta su sombrilla azul, y cazaba al vuelo los rumores de cuanto
   ocurría:
un día tras otro se iba hacia los sótanos del tiempo algún profundo anciano.

It began at noon in the sonorous shade of the girls of Corinth;
impassive, his parasol open, he dragged his feet to where he would sit in
    silence,
to where he would seat himself among them, listening to their cooing,
    observing the delicate geometry of knees the color of wheat, glancing
    furtively at those fugitive pink doves
that flew beneath the bridge of shoulders.
                                        He said nothing,
and nothing seemed to stir him beneath his parasol, sensing, among the
    sweet girls of Corinth, time's passage, time become a shower
of golden pins, resplendent as ripe cherries,
time flowing around the ankles of the flowering doves of Corinth,
time, which in other places brings to the lips of men a draught of poison
    none may refuse,
here offered the nectar of an ambrosia so singular
one would have thought that time itself wished also to live, to become
    incarnate, to delight
in smooth skin or in the reflection of a blue-green eye.
                            Silently Anaximander
floated like a swan each day between clouds of beauty, and endured;
there, within time and beyond it, he sipped the slow fragrance of eternity,
    while his cat purred beside the fire. At evening he would return home
and pass the night writing tiny poems
for the noisy doves of Corinth.

The city's other sages muttered ceaselessly.
More even than the harvest festival or the comings and goings of ships,
    Anaximander had become
the preferred topic of tiresome conversations:
                        "Always have I told you,
wise men of Corinth," his old enemy Prodicos proclaimed, "that he was no
    true sage nor even of average importance. His work?
Plagiarized. Repetitious. And hollow at the core. Hollow as a barrel of
    wine after the Thebans have come to taste the sunlight of Corinthian
    vineyards."
Impassive, Anaximander walked through the streets of Corinth to the bay,
his blue parasol open above him, catching the latest news in passing:
day after day some wise old man would pass below. Day after day the sages

Los sabios eran talados, día a día, por las mensajeras de Proserpina, y sólo sus cenizas
pasaban, rumbo al mar, entre las aguas cubiertas de violetas que es el mar de Corinto.

Todos se iban, y Anaximandro seguía allí, rodeado de muchachas, sentado bajo el sol.
Un pliegue de la túnica de Atalanta, la garganta de Aglaé,
cuando Aglaé lanzaba hacia el cielo su himno para imitar las melodías del ruiseñor,
una sonrisa de Anadiomena, eran todo el alimento que Anaximandro requería: y estaba allí, seguía allí, cuando todo a su alrededor se había evaporado.

  Un día, allá, desde lo lejos,
se vio dibujarse una pequeña barca
  en el trashorizonte de la bahía de Corinto.
Venía en ella, remando con fatigada tenacidad de asmático, un hombrecito:
cubría su cabeza un sombrero de paja, un blanco sombrero de paja encintado de rojo. Desde su confín
el hombrecito miraba hacia el corazón de la bahía, y descubría a lo muy lejos una sombrilla azul, un redondelito aureolado como el sol. Hacia allí bogaba.
Terco, tenaz, tarareando una cancioncilla, el hombrecito de manos enguantadas
remaba sin cesar. Anaximandro comenzó a sonreír. La barca, inmóvil en medio de la bahía,
vencía también el tiempo. Despaciosamente el blanco sombrero de paja anunció que el hombre regresaba.

  Esa noche, poco antes de irse a dormir,
Marcel Proust gritaba exaltado desde su habitación:
"Madre, traígame más papel, traiga todo el papel que pueda.
Voy a comenzar un nuevo capítulo de mi obra.
Voy a titularlo: 'A la sombra de las muchachas en flor'".

1973

El gato personal del conde Cagliostro

Tuve un gato llamado Tamerlán.
Se alimentaba solamente con poemas de Emily Dickinson,
y melodías de Schubert.

would be summoned by Proserpina, their ashes only
flowing towards the sea, the violet-covered waters of the sea at Corinth.

All passed, and Anaximander remained, encircled by the girls, seated
     beneath the sun.
A fold of Atalanta's blouse, Aglae's voice
when she sang to the heavens her hymn in imitation of the nightingale,
Anadiomena's smile, were all the sustenance Anaximander needed, and he
     was there, still there, when everything around him had vanished.

     One day he saw in the distance
a small boat on the horizon of the Bay of Corinth.
Within, a little man rowed with an asthmatic's exhausted tenacity.
His head was covered with a straw hat, a white straw hat with a red band.
     From its confines
the little man looked out upon the entire bay and saw, on its furthest
     shore,
a blue parasol, a small circle as golden as the sun. He rowed
towards it. Stubborn, tenacious, whistling a tune, the little man with
     gloved hands
rowed ceaselessly. Anaximander began to smile. The boat, immobile on the
     bay,
had also conquered time. Slowly the white straw hat announced that the
     little man was receding into the distance homeward.

     That night, shortly before retiring,
Marcel Proust, exhilarated, called from his room:
"Mother, bring me more paper, bring me all the paper you can.
I'm going to begin a new chapter. I'm going to call it
'In the Shade of the Flowering Girls.'"

     1973

Count Cagliostro's Cat

I had a cat named Tamerlaine.
And all he ate were poems by Emily Dickinson
and Schubert melodies.

Viajaba conmigo: en París
le servían inútilmente, en mantelitos de encaje Richelieu,
chocolatinas elaboradas para él por Madame Sévigné en persona,
pero él todo lo rechazaba,
con el gesto de un emperador romano
tras una noche de orgía.

Porque él sólo quería masticar,
hoja por hoja, verso por verso,
viejas ediciones de los poemas de Emily Dickinson,
y escuchar incesantemente,
melodías de Schubert.

(Conocimos en Munich, en una pensión alemana,
a Katherine Mansfield, y ella,
que era todo lo delicado del mundo,
tocaba suavemente en su violoncelo, para Tamerlán,
melodías de Schubert).

Tamerlán se alejó del modo más apropiado:
paseábamos por Amsterdam, por el barrio judío de Amsterdam
     concretamente,
y al pasar ante la más arcaica sinagoga de la ciudad,
Tamerlán se detuvo, me miró con visible resplandor de ternura en sus ojos,
y saltó al interior de aquel oscuro templo.

Desde entonces, todos los años,
envío como presente a la vieja sinagoga de Amsterdam,
un manojo de poemas.
         De poemas que fueron llorados, en Amherst, un día,
por la melancólica señorita llamada Emily,
Emily, Tamerlán, Dickinson.

El viajero

J'ai bâti de si beaux châteaux que les ruines m'en suffiraient.
                                                    JULES RENARD

La Barcarola de "Los Cuentos de Hoffmann":
solo esta melodía quedó en la memoria del viajero
cuando echó a andar sin más finalidad que sacudirse
el tedio de estar vivo.

He traveled with me: in Paris
they served him on lace doilies
chocolate confections made for him and him alone
by Madame de Sévigné herself.
To no avail: he waved them off
like a Roman emperor
after a night of orgies.

Page by page, verse by verse,
he wished only to chew on
old editions of Emily Dickinson's poems
and he listened incessantly
to Schubert melodies.

(In Munich, in a German *pension*, we met
Katherine Mansfield, and she,
who held within her all the world's
delicacy, for Tamerlaine played sweetly on her cello
Schubert melodies.)

Tamerlaine passed away in the most appropriate manner:
we were on our way through Amsterdam, through the ghetto, to be exact,
and as we passed the front of the oldest synagogue
Tamerlaine stopped, looked at me with all love's splendor in his eyes
and leaped into the interior of that dark temple.

Since then, each year,
I send a bunch of poems as a present to the old
synagogue of Amsterdam.
        Poems that were wept one day in Amherst
by Emily, that melancholy lady,
Emily Tamerlaine Dickinson.

The Traveler

J'ai bâti de si beaux châteaux que les ruines m'en suffiraient.
JULES RENARD

The Barcarolle from the *Tales of Hoffmann*:
that tune alone remained in the traveler's memory
when he set out to walk with no other end than to relieve
the boredom of being alive.

Luego de recorrido paso a paso
el gran bosque de ciervos que va de Alaska a Punta del Este,
con su bastón de fibra
y con el gran sombrero tejido a ciegas por indios
de dedos iluminados por rayos puros de luna bajo el río,
decidió concentrar su viaje sobre castillos y bellas estatuas,
y emprendió, así, la última etapa de su peregrinar,
que consistía, y consiste todavía,—porque el viajero
ni ha terminado de andar, ni conoce el cansancio o el sueño—
en ir y volver a pie, incesantemente,
desde Lisboa hasta Varsovia, y desde Varsovia hasta Lisboa,
silbando la Barcarola de "Los Cuentos de Hoffmann".

Si alguien le pregunta, él, sin dejar de andar, explica:
"Silbar en la oscuridad para vencer el miedo es lo que nos queda.
No creais que me haya dejado, jamás, distraer por la apariencia
de la luz: desde pequeño supe que la luz no existe, que es
tan solo uno de los disfraces de las tinieblas,
porque sólo hay tinieblas para el hombre. Silbo en la oscuridad
a ver si de alguna parte acude un perro a socorrerme:
el perro que la Virgen dejaba como guardián de su hijo
cuando ella se iba a su menester de cantante en el coro
de la sinagoga, para alabar a Abraham, a David, a Salomón,
y a todos sus hieráticos parientes de barbas taheñas
y crótalos de marfil, y balidos de corderos sacrificados
cuando la luna se ofrece como arco para enviarle
saetas al corazón del Creador: inútil todo, inútil".

Y el viajero seguía murmurando para sí:
"Lleno de miedo pero abroquelado en el castillo
de escucharme silbar, compruebo todos los días
que es sólo noche cerrada e irrompible lo que nos rodea;
percibo el desdén de la Creación por nosotros, la orfandad del planeta
en la siniestra llanura del universo, la soledad
absoluta de este puntito de polvo que tan importante creemos,
pero que es apenas el sucio corpúsculo de mugre
que revuela en la habitación cuando el señorito
se mira al espejo, ciñe su corbata, y displicentemente
sacude con la punta de sus dedos
ese poquito de polvo que no sabe cómo ha llegado hasta allí,
ni qué hace en medio de su impecable traje".

After touring step by step
the great forest of deer that extends from Alaska to Punta del Este,
with his fiberglass walking stick
and the big hat that Indians weave blindly
with fingers lit by the pure rays of the moon beneath the river,
he decided to focus his travels on castles and beautiful sculpture,
and began the final stage of his peregrination,
which consisted, and still consists—because the traveler
has neither stopped walking, nor known weariness nor sleep—
of coming and going on foot, incessantly,
from Lisbon to Warsaw, from Warsaw to Lisbon,
whistling the Barcarolle from the *Tales of Hoffmann.*

If someone asks, he explains, as he walks:
"Whistling in the dark to overcome fear is what's left us.
Don't think that I've ever allowed myself to be distracted
by the appearance of light: from my earliest years I've known that light
    doesn't really exist,
that it's merely one of the faces of darkness,
because darkness is all man has. I whistle in the dark
to see if from somewhere a dog will come to help me:
the dog that the Virgin left to guard her son
when she went to her job as a singer in the choir
of the synagogue, praising Abraham, David, Solomon,
and all their priestly relatives with their red beards
and marble castanets, and the bleating of lambs sacrificed
when the moon takes the form of a bow to shoot arrows
at the heart of the Creator: useless, completely useless."

And the traveler went on mumbling:
"Full of fear but protected within the castle
from the sound of my whistling, I prove again each day
that it's the locked unbreakable night alone that surrounds us;
I sense Creation's disdain for us, the orphanhood of the planet
on the sinister plains of the universe, the absolute
aloneness of this speck of dust that we think so important,
but which is scarcely the dirty corpuscle of muck
that stirs in the room when the fop
looks at himself in the mirror, tightens his tie, and carelessly
flicks with the tip of his fingers
that bit of dust whose presence he can't account for,
nor why it rests on his impeccable suit."

"Voy desde Lisboa hasta Varsovia,
me apiado otra vez
de la pavorosa soledad de
la tierra en el Cosmos,
acaricio su rostro para aliviarle, quizá, su eterna pena,
y vuelvo desde Varsovia hasta Lisboa, silbando
muy suavemente la Barcarola,
la Barcarola de "Los Cuentos de Hoffmann" del Tuerto de Offenbach,
una melodía, tan tonta e inútil
como el nacimiento de un niño, o como
el descender de un cadáver al castillo iluminado finalmente".

Eliseo Diego

Bajo los astros

Es así que la casa deshabitada, por la tarde, suena de pronto como el cordaje de un barco.

Vibran a solas los cristales vacíos, la penumbra quisiera conmovernos,

y el animal pequeño, el de lustrosa piel en los rincones, trémulo huye, como siempre, a los altos distantes.

Es aquí donde decíamos: qué tiempo maldito hace debajo de los álamos, suerte que vino usted a tiempo, buenas tardes, oh padre, qué mala noche, qué buen día siempre.

Aquí, en el umbral que los nortes menudos de las puertas asuelan de gris y leve polvo,

alguno de nosotros, los de casa, debe vestir los pesarosos, los oscuros

ropajes del sacrificio para decir: aquí esperaba, y aquí cosía mamá sus misteriosas telas blancas

y aquí entró aquel día el tímido lagarto, y aquí la mosca extraña que zumbaba, y aquí la sombra y los cubiertos, y aquí el fuego, y aquí el agua.

"I go from Lisbon to Warsaw,
I pity once more
the terrible loneliness of
the earth in the Cosmos,
caress its face to soothe, perhaps, its eternal sorrow,
and return from Warsaw to Lisbon, whistling
very softly the Barcarolle
the Barcarolle from the *Tales of Hoffmann* by one-eyed Offenbach,
a tune as foolish and useless
as the birth of a child, or the descent
of a corpse at last to the shining castle."

Translated by Mark Weiss

Eliseo Diego

Beneath the Stars

And so at night without warning the empty house resounds like a ship's
rigging.

The empty panes vibrate alone, the semidarkness would wish to move us,

and the small beast, the one in the corner with the lustrous skin, trembling,
flees, as always, to the furthest heights.

It's here we would say: what lousy weather we're having beneath the poplars,
thank god you arrived in time, good evening, oh father, what a nasty
night, what a lovely day always.

Here, on the threshold that the small north winds from the door attack with
a fine gray dust,

one of us, of this house, must wear the dreary, dark

vestments of sacrifice to pronounce: here he would wait, and here mother
would sew her mysterious white cloths

and it was here one day the timid lizard entered, and over here the strange
fly would buzz, and here the shadow and the silverware, and here the fire,
and here the water.

Porque llega una hora en que todas las casas se despueblan de sus ruidos mortales

y las vidrieras son frías como esos invernaderos desolados, lisos ojos de muerto, que nadie supo nunca dónde quedan,

es preciso que alguien, alguno de nosotros, venga y diga: los cubiertos de casa, qué se hicieron, alguien sin duda los ha robado.

Grave silencio, sobre mi hombro descansas como el peso conmovedor de una muchacha sollozante.

Es así que ahora todo nos falta. Si alguien nos ofreciera un poco de café nos salvábamos

porque la casa deshabitada es adusta como la justicia del fin

y el viento que pasea por los altos no es sino el viento, las estancias no son más que las estancias de la casa vacía

y es como si no hubiese venido nadie, como si nadie mirase los recintos del hombre, bajo los astros.

El oscuro esplendor

Juega el niño con unas pocas piedras inocentes
en el cantero gastado y roto
como paño de vieja.

        Yo pregunto:
qué irremediable catástrofe separa
sus manos de mi frente de arena,
su boca de mis ojos impasibles.

        Y suplico
al menudo señor que sabe conmover
la tranquila tristeza de las flores, la sagrada
costumbre de los árboles dormidos.

        Sin quererlo
el niño distraídamente solitario empuja
la domada furia de las cosas, olvidando
el oscuro esplendor que me ciega y él desdeña.

Because an hour comes when all houses lose their mortal sounds

and window panes are as cold as abandoned greenhouses, smooth eyes of
death, which no one ever knew how to find,

someone, one of us, must come to say: the silverware that once was here has
surely been stolen.

A somber silence, you rest on my shoulder like the moving weight of a sob-
bing girl.

And so it is that everything is lost to us now. If someone were to offer us a
sip of coffee we would be saved

because the empty house is as stern as final justice

and the wind that blows above us is merely wind, the rooms are merely
rooms of an empty house

and it's as if no one had ever come, no one had ever seen the place of man,
beneath the stars.

The Dark Splendor

The boy plays with a few simple stones
in a quarry spent and broken
as a worn-out rag.

> I ask:
what irremediable catastrophe separates
his hands from my forehead of sand,
his mouth from my impassive eyes.

> And I pray
to the little lord who knows how to move
the peaceful sadness of flowers, the sacred
habit of sleeping trees.

> Without meaning to
the solitary boy absentmindedly incites
the tame rage of things, forgetting
the dark splendor that blinds me and that he ignores.

En memoria

Fue capitán de navío y el carbón
de las altas chimeneas y la sal
y la profunda libertad del mar
conocieron su rostro.

          Yo lo he visto
pasando sus días entre cosas de costumbre
sacra y espesa.

        Lo recuerdo
inclinado hacia el clamor de la boca
incesante del puerto, sosteniendo
con sus manos de ámbar esa colcha de colores
que hacen las viejas con la tarde
y el esplendor hiriente de su tedio.

Cartagena de Indias

Ah! he was the flower of the flock, was Flint.
       TREASURE ISLAND

Ávidamente solo escondiste las monedas cansadas
y las joyas crueles e inocentes como los ojos de un lagarto
entre la suave tierra madura.

Los mapas que ornamentan los delfines de oro,
los surtidores escarlatas, la verdinegra malla,
sostuvieron tus manos de humo.

Y luego lavó el mar la miseria de tu barco podrido
y en las noches elogiaron tu silencio
las blandas horcas de Cartagena de Indias.

Muy rápidamente atraviesa el cuerpo de un hombre
la insaciable frescura de las inmensas aguas.
Te acompañó el escándalo de las gaviotas ávidas.
Sólo tu hambre conoce las joyas escondidas.

In Memoriam

He was captain of a ship and the soot
of tall smokestacks and the salt
and the deep freedom of the sea
knew his face.

I have seen him
passing his time in the daily round
of the sacred and profane.

I remember him
bent towards the incessant noise of the mouth
of the port, holding up
with his amber hands the colored quilt
that the old women make of evening
and the painful splendor of its boredom.

Cartagena of the Indies

Ah! he was the flower of the flock, was Flint.
TREASURE ISLAND

Alone, greedily, you hid the tired coins
and the cruel and innocent gems like a lizard's eyes
in the soft ripe earth.

Your misty hands held maps
ornamented with golden dolphins,
scarlet waterspouts, the dark green coat of mail.

And later the sea washed the misery of your rotted boat
and at night the gentle gallows of Cartagena
praised your silence.

A man's body quickly pierces
the insatiable cold of immense waters.
The din of greedy gulls was your companion.
Only your hunger knows the hidden gems.

Versiones

La muerte es esa pequeña jarra, con flores pintadas a mano, que hay en todas las casas y que uno jamás se detiene a ver.

La muerte es ese pequeño animal que ha cruzado en el patio, y del que nos consuela la ilusión, sentida como un soplo, de que es sólo el gato de la casa, el gato de costumbre, el gato que ha cruzado y al que ya no volveremos a ver.

La muerte es ese amigo que aparece en las fotografías de la familia, discretamente a un lado, y al que nadie acertó nunca a reconocer.

La muerte, en fin, es esa mancha en el muro que una tarde hemos mirado, sin saberlo, con un poco de terror.

La casa del pan

"Entra en la nave blanca: mira la mesa donde está la harina—la harina blanca.

"Fuera del pueblo, apenas tuerce el camino a la intemperie, allí está la casa del pan—la nave blanca.

"Donde un negro de sonrisa vaga saca del horno las palas con el pan crujiente. Saca del horno inmenso, quieto, las palas con el pan crujiente.

"¿Desde cuándo estás tú aquí—se le pregunta—, desde cuándo estás entre la harina?

"Responde con veloces zumbas: desde las ceremonias y las máscaras, desde el velamen y las fugas, desde las candelillas y las máquinas, desde los circos y las flautas.

"Desde que se encendió el fuego en el horno."

Riesgos del equilibrista

Allá va el equilibrista, imaginando
las venturas y prodigios del aire.
No es como nosotros, el equilibrista,
sino que más bien su naturalidad comienza
donde termina la naturalidad del aire:
allí es donde su imaginación inaugura los festejos

Versions

Death is this little jug, with hand-painted flowers, found in every house, that no one stops to look at.

Death is that little animal that crossed the yard, its illusion, felt like a puff of air, consoling us, but it's only the household cat, the usual cat, the cat that's passed that we'll never see again.

Death is the friend who appears in family photos, discreetly to one side, that no one has ever been sure he recognized.

Death, finally, is that stain on the wall that we noticed, unconsciously, one evening, with a whiff of fear.

The House of Bread

"Enter the white shop: see the table covered with flour—white flour.

"Outside the town, the path barely twists towards the open air, and there it is, the house of bread—the white shop.

"Where a black with a distant smile removes from the oven palettes of crusty bread. He removes the palettes of crusty bread from the enormous, quiet oven.

"How long have you been here?" you ask him, "how long have you spent with flour?"

"He answers with ready jokes: since ceremonies and masks, since sails and escapes, since tobacco bugs and machines, since circuses and flutes.

"Since they lit the fire in the oven."

The Rope Dancer's Risks

There goes the rope dancer, imagining
the luck and the wonders of air.
He's not like us,
his nature begins where the air's nature ends
it's there that his imagination opens

del otro espacio en que se vive de milagro
y cada movimiento está lleno de sentido y belleza.

Si bien lo miramos qué hace el equilibrista
sino caminar lo mismo que nosotros
por un trillo que es el suyo propio:
qué importa que ese sendero esté volado
sobre un imperioso abismo si ese abismo
arde con los diminutos amarillos y violetas,
azules y rojos y sepias y morados
de los sombrerillos y las gorras y los venturosos
pañuelos de encaje.

      Lo que verdaderamente importa
es que cada paso del ensimismado equilibrista
puede muy bien ser el último de modo
que son la medida y el ritmo los que guían
esos pasos.

      La voluntad también de aventurarse
por lo que no es ya sino un hilo de vida
sin más esperanza de permanencia
que el ir y venir de ayer a luego,
es sin duda otra distinción apreciable.

Sin contar que todo lo hace por una gloria tan efímera
que la misma indiferencia del aire
es por contraste más estable, y que no gana
para vivir de los sustos y quebrantos. El equilibrio
ha de ser a no dudarlo recompensa
tal que no la imaginamos.

      ¡ADELANTE!,
decimos al equilibrista, retirándonos
al respaldo suficiente de la silla
y la misericordiosa tierra: nosotros
pagamos a tiempo las entradas y de aquí no nos vamos.

La niña en el bosque

Caperuza del alma, está en lo oscuro
el lobo, donde nunca
sospecharías,

the festivities of another space in which he lives
miraculously and every motion is filled with feeling and beauty.

Although we see what the rope dancer's doing
walking as we do
on a path that's his alone:
what does it matter that that path be strung
above an imperious abyss if the abyss
burn with the tiny yellows and violets
blues and reds and sepias and purples
of caps and bonnets and fortunate squares
of lace.

    That each step of this intent rope dancer
could easily be his last
is what really matters,
which is why it's measure and rhythm
that guide his steps.

    The will also to venture
onto what's now nothing but a thread of life
with no hope of permanence
except for the back and forth, the before and after,
is another important distinction.

And let's remember that he does it all for a glory so ephemeral
even the indifference of the air
is more stable, and that it's not from near-misses and broken bones
that he earns his keep. Doubtless
balance is a recompense
that we can't imagine.

    GET GOING!
we tell the rope dancer, retiring
to the sufficient support of our seats
and the merciful earth: we paid
for our tickets promptly and we're not about to leave.

The Girl in the Forest

My soul's Red Riding Hood, the wolf
lurks in the shadows where no one expects him

y te mira
desde su roca de miseria,
su soledad, su enorme hambre.

Tú le preguntas: ¿por qué tienes
esos ojos redondos?
                    Y él responde,
ciego, para mirarte
mejor, llorando.
                    Y en seguida

tú vuelves: las orejas,
¿por qué tan grandes?
                    Y él,
para escucharte, oh música
del mundo, sólo
para escucharte.
                    Y luego

lo demás es la sombra—indescifrable.

La casa abandonada

Hacia el final de la escalera
te has dado vuelta: en el vacío de abajo
el viento solitario hace
las veces del trajín, y la penumbra
está sucia de olvido. Pero arriba,
en el piso de arriba, el cúmulo
de inútil sueño aguarda. ¿Vas
a entrar en él, a sumergirte? Con la mano
puesta en el balaústre, acariciándolo
te quedas. Poco a poco,
no vas así a bajar la vista: escucha el torvo
zumbido de la mosca que se afana
contra el ciego cristal: hay alguien
en el primer peldaño. Espera.
                    Mira:
tú estás en el primer peldaño. Lívido
te estás mirando a ti con toda el alma
como si fuese para siempre.
                    Y ya

and he watches you
from his miserable rock,
his solitude, his enormous hunger.
You ask him: why
are your eyes so big and round? Blind, he answers,
"for to see you better," weeping.
You ask again: why
are your ears so big, and he, "oh music
of the world, to hear you, only
to hear you." And then
the rest is darkness,
impossible to understand.

The Deserted House

Towards the top of the stairs
you've turned: in the empty space below
the solitary wind
goes back and forth, and the half-light
is filthy with forgetting. But above,
upstairs, the heap
of useless dreams awaits. Will you
enter, to drown yourself in it? You stop, resting your hand
on the baluster, stroking it.
Descending like this,
a bit at a time, you don't have to look down: listen to the grim
buzz of the fly struggling
against the blind glass: there's someone
on the first step. Wait.
                    Look:
it's you on the first step. Pallid,
you watch yourself
as if forever.
                    And now

no estás arriba, ni
tampoco abajo.
                    Zumba
sola por fin la torva prisionera.

Oda a la joven luz

En mi país la luz
es mucho más que el tiempo, se demora
con extraña delicia en los contornos
militares de todo, en las reliquias
escuetas del diluvio.

                    La luz
en mi país resiste a la memoria
como el oro al sudor de la codicia,
perdura entre sí misma, nos ignora
desde su ajeno ser, su transparencia.

Quien corteje a la luz con cintas y tambores
inclinándose aquí y allá según astucia
de una sensualidad arcaica, incalculable,
pierde su tiempo, arguye con las olas
mientras la luz, ensimismada, duerme.

Pues no mira la luz en mi país
las modestas victorias del sentido
ni los finos desastres de la suerte,
sino que se entretiene con hojas, pajarillos,
caracoles, relumbres, hondos verdes.

Y es que ciega la luz en mi país deslumbra
su propio corazón inviolable
sin saber de ganancias ni de pérdidas.
Pura como la sal, intacta, erguida,
la casta, demente luz deshoja el tiempo.

Testamento

Habiendo llegado al tiempo en que
la penumbra ya no me consuela más
y me apocan los presagios pequeños;

you're neither above
nor below.
            In the end it's just
the buzzing of the grim prisoner.

Ode to the Young Light

Light in my country
is much more than time, it lingers
with a strange delight in the military
contours of all things, in the simple
relics of the flood.

                Light
in my country resists memory
as gold resists the sweat of avarice,
endures within itself, indifferent to us
in its alien being, its transparency.

Who courts the light with ribbons and drums
bowing here and there with the cunning
of an archaic, incalculable sensuality,
wastes his time, argues with waves
while the rapt light sleeps.

Light, then, in my country doesn't notice
the sense's modest victories
nor the delicate disasters of luck,
but dallies among leaves, small birds,
shells, lusters, deepest greens.

Blind, the light in my country dazzles
its own inviolable heart
knowing nothing of profit or loss.
Pure as salt, untouched, upright,
the chaste, demented light strips time of its leaves.

Testament

Having come to the time when dusk
no longer consoles me
and small omens frighten me;

habiendo llegado a este tiempo;

y como las heces del café
abren de pronto ahora para mí
sus redondas bocas amargas;

habiendo llegado a este tiempo;

y perdida ya toda esperanza de
algún merecido ascenso, de
ver el manar sereno de la sombra;

y no poseyendo más que este tiempo;

no poseyendo más, en fin,
que mi memoria de las noches y
su vibrante delicadeza enorme;

no poseyendo más
entre cielo y tierra que
mi memoria, que este tiempo;

decido hacer mi testamento.
Es
éste: les dejo

el tiempo, todo el tiempo.

Mi madre la oca

La vieja inmensa, inmóvil junto al fuego.
Largo rostro rugoso,
manos rudas.
Las llamas charlan en la chimenea
con el obeso calderón de cobre.
Las ristras cuelgan lacias,
las magistrales ristras
de cebollas.

En la penumbra el fuego escoge
bien un surco reseco
junto a una boca mustia, bien
el voraz amarillo de unos ojos.
Hay gente allí muy quieta en la penumbra.
Tan callada, la gente,

having come to that time;

and as the dregs of coffee
suddenly open their round
and bitter mouths for me;

having come to that time;

all hope lost of any
well-earned gain, of seeing
the serene flow of darkness;

and owning nothing but this time;

owning, finally, nothing
except my memory of nights and
their enormous vibrant softness;

owning nothing
between earth and sky except
my memory, except this time;

I have decided to make my will.
It's this:
I leave you

time, all of time.

Mother Goose

The enormous old woman, motionless by the fire.
Broad wrinkled face
callused hands.
Flames and the copper cauldron chatter on the hearth.
Onions, magisterial braids
of onions
hang from the ceiling.

In the semidarkness the firelight finds
a dry crease, a withered mouth
the rapacious yellow of a pair of eyes.
There are people, very still, in the semidarkness, as silent

como las ristras blancas,
esas tan blancas ristras de cebollas.

Mira, tú estás allí también, un poco aparte,
aunque nunca, lo sabes, podrán verte.
Como un ratón en la pared,
al otro lado, quedo, inmóvil.
Qué bajas son las vigas, y qué oscuras.
Por fin bulle el caldero entre las llamas.
La enorme vieja ahora suspira.
Dónde se fue tu aliento, dónde el aire.

Tan pura es la quietud
que oyes la leve
huella de la ceniza. Entonces,
entre el oro del fuego, la caverna
de la gran boca. Un huracán susurra
"había una vez..."
                    Y nace todo.

Comienza un lunes

La eternidad por fin comienza un lunes
y el día siguiente apenas tiene nombre
y el otro es el oscuro, el abolido.
Y en él se apagan todos los murmullos
y aquel rostro que amábamos se esfuma
y en vano es ya la espera, nadie viene.
La eternidad ignora las costumbres,
le da lo mismo rojo que azul tierno,
se inclina al gris, al humo, a la ceniza.
Nombre y fecha tú grabas en un mármol,
los roza displicente con el hombro,
ni un montoncillo de amargura deja.
Y sin embargo, ves, me aferro al lunes
y al día siguiente doy el nombre tuyo
y con la punta del cigarro escribo
en plena oscuridad: aquí he vivido.

as the white braids, the pale
white braids of onions.

Look, you too are there, a little distant,
though none, you are sure, can see you.
Like the mouse, immobile on the far wall.
How low, how dark, the beams are.
At last the pot begins to boil.
The enormous old woman sighs.
Where's your breath now, where the air—

the silence so profound
you can hear
the footstep of a flake of ash. Then
amid the golden flames
that cavernous mouth.
A hurricane whispers:
"Once upon a time . . . "
                              And everything is born.

On a Monday

On a Monday eternity finally begins
and the day that follows is scarcely named,
and the other is the dark, the done.
On that day are extinguished all whispers
and the face we loved dissolves in mist—
hope becomes hopeless: no one is coming.
Eternity knows nothing of our habits,
indifferent to red and the softest blue, it prefers
gray, smoke, ashes. You scratch
a name and a date on a piece of marble
and it rubs them out
with a careless shoulder, not even
a pinch of bitterness left behind. Yet see,
I cling to Mondays
and I give the next your name;
in total darkness I write
with the tip of my cigarette:
here have I lived.

A una muchacha

Como si el Caballero de la Mano al Pecho
a través del abismo nocturno de los años
extendiera su mano y te rozara
con la fría punta de sus dedos idos
la cálida mejilla transparente.

Como si el Caballero de la Mano al Pecho.

Así apenas me atrevo yo a tocar
la trémula fragancia que tú eres.

En mi mano está el frío de los años.

Cintio Vitier

El bosque de Birnam

> *Thou com'st to use thy tongue; thy story quickly.*
> MACBETH AL MENSAJERO,
> ACTO V, ESCENA V

Tantas cosas que he visto y sin embargo
caben en un papel, pues la memoria,
idéntica a la línea del horizonte
que es el alimento único de mis ojos,
puede vaciarse entera en el olvido.
Todo en Matanzas era igual a París,
quiero decir equivalente a escala de crepúsculo.
Sentado allí en el parque, oyendo los danzones
giratorios bajo las estrellas, se asistía con respeto
a la novelización vehemente de un futuro
que yace desbaratado en el domingo
de la calle de Moscú. El respeto pierde grados
como un alcohol que nadie quiere, vuela antiguo
con la hopalanda suelta de las nubes, y el futuro
de la memoria que ya lo era en el fulgor del cornetín
pasa arrastrando el ala por la cubierta del naufragio.

To a Girl

As if the Knight with His Hand on His Breast
were to extend his hand across the nocturnal
abyss of time and touch your warm
transparent cheek with the frigid tips
of what were once his fingers.

As if the Knight with His Hand on His Breast.

Like him I scarcely dare to touch
the tremulous fragrance that you are.

In my hand is the cold of time.

Translated by Mark Weiss

Cintio Vitier

Birnam Wood

> *Thou com'st to use thy tongue; thy story quickly.*
> MACBETH TO THE MESSENGER,
> ACT V, SCENE V

So many things have I seen and yet
they fit on page, since memory,
like the line of the horizon
which is the only food for my eyes,
can empty itself entirely in forgetfulness.
Everything in Matanzas was the same as Paris,
I mean equal on the scale of twilight.
Sitting there in the park, before the whirling
dances beneath the stars, was to witness respectfully
the vehement romanticizing of a future
that lies spoiled on a Sunday
on Moscow Street. Respect loses degrees
like an unwanted drink, ancient it flies
with the loose robes of the clouds, and the future
of memory that was already present in the glow of the cornet
passes dragging its wing through the cover of shipwreck.

Palabras demasiado grandes. Habría que decir
cositas, alfileres que buscaba por las losas, gestecillos
de las gentes que esperan en los parques cuando están
a punto de convertirse en espectros del morado.
En todo caso el puntillismo es el amor del tiempo.
Un cuadro de Seurat puede absorber tanta materia
inflamable como la que desprendía de aquel Eros
que frotaba las piedras en procura de un cocuyo.
Así aparece algo que no estaba preparado
por la nada, ni mucho menos por las leyes de la física,
sin ser tampocó metafísico, algo hechizante y sabio
colándose en el fresco memorioso de los naranjales.

Cierto, señor, que vine a usar mi lengua,
y lo que tengo que decirte es:
por ella viene a hablar el bosque andante,
armadura nupcial de tu enemigo.
Desde el origen fuimos destinados.
La humedad de la vida apetece un lenguaje
que el industrioso tiempo ha construido
con la materia misma de lo mudo.
Lo mudo ruge, silba, estalla en la floresta
con el trueno general los gorjeos.
Lo mudo articulando su imposible
dialoga con las páginas en blanco . . .

En un recodo
de los jardines del Palazzo Pitti
pueden verse meriendas antológicas,
y si fuera necesario dar otros ejemplos de dulzura,
sin recurrir al melocotón pensante de Giorgione,
podría volver a amanecer en Nueva Orleáns,
goteando los sicomoros sobre un lúcido portal
que se alquilaba indiscriminadamente a los voraces.
No se trata de analogías ni de resonancias,
allí empieza la miseria donde termina el músico
que alargaba su violín hasta la sílaba del fuego.
He aquí de qué se trata, el fuego quiere hablar
aunque sea utilizando un lápiz romo y un papel
que presume turbiamente de toda transparencia:
no por ser el fuego, pues también el tocoloro
atraviesa las hojas con velada fama, también nunca,

Overblown words. One should say
little things, pins sought along the flagstones, small gestures
of people waiting in parks when they're
about to turn into spectras of purple.
In any case, pointillism is the love of time.
A painting by Seurat can absorb as much inflammable
material as flew off that Eros
who struck the stones in search of a firefly.
Thus something appears unbidden
out of nothingness, unimagined even by the laws of physics,
without being metaphysical either, something bewitching and wise
slipping into the retentive coolness of the orange groves.

Certainly, lord, I came to use my tongue,
and what I have to tell you is:
through it speaks the errant wood,
nuptial armature of your enemy.
Since the beginning we were destined.
The moisture of life yearns for a language
that industrious time has built
of the very substance of the silent.
The silent roars, whistles, explodes in the thicket
with the general thunder of warbling.
The silent articulating its impossible
dialogue with the blank pages . . .

In a corner
of the Pitti Palace gardens
you can see all sorts of snacks,
and were other examples of sweetness needed,
without resorting to Giorgione's thinking peach,
you could wake up again in New Orleans,
the sycamores dripping on a lucid porch
rented out indiscriminately to the voracious.
It's not a matter of analogies or resonances,
there the misery starts where the musician finishes
who stretched his violin to the syllable of fire.
This is what it's about, the fire wants to speak
even using a dull pencil and a sheet of paper
that vaguely pretends to be transparent:
not because of being fire, since the trogon likewise
flutters through the leaves with veiled fame, never likewise,

ojo, sangre, piedra, hijo, quieren decidirse
a atravesar el límite de sus instalaciones
que humean arrasadas por la infantería.
Naturaleza dice: verme, recorrerme, ay, ser vista,
no valdría la pena sino por el acto de parirme
proyectada en un móvil que me lleva a la otra parte.
La zambullida dura mundos y tú estás de posta
en el fuerte Belvedere o en la luna del agua del San Juan.
Escoge si quedarte en esa orilla que no habla
o castamente fecundar la sola esposa.
Entonces la merienda y sus palabras son un rostro,
los viajes son un viaje, el fuego alumbra a un hombre, comenzamos.

Lo mudo rompe a hablar, usando lengua
que venía de la bruma de las aguas,
como un sol que se parte en el arco iris.
Por necesidad y caridad la lengua
lo dice todo ayudada por la mano,
sostenida fieramente por el ojo
donde lo cóncavo se ajusta a lo convexo.
Todo lo dicho adquiere otra sustancia.
El bosque ha echado a andar hacia el castillo
de la mudez diabólica y la sangre maldita.
La vida no es el cuento narrado por un idiota
sino la marcha del bosque y el giro de los astros
en la voz del mensajero que no acaba.
Esa es mi historia, la historia de mi lengua.
La vida es eso, la lengua de la historia.
Sucumbe tú, poder endemoniado, usurpador y mudo,
ahogado por el bosque. Yo seguiré anunciando.

Lo que comienza ya había comenzado,
la garza se insinúa como flor de la justicia.
La historia es el milagro de la naturaleza
cuando el bosque de Birnam comienza a caminar
en el asedio del castillo alquilado por el demonio.
Pero el bosque siempre había estado avanzando hacia el castillo.
Un destino pequeñísimo, enviciado
por el disfrute de persianas clandestinas,
equivale de súbito a la Batalla de San Romano
pintada por Uccello como si devolviera
la historia endemoniada a las ecuaciones de la tierra.

eye, blood, stone, son, want to
cross the limit of their installations
that are smoking ruins leveled by the infantry.
Nature says: to see me, go through me, oh, to be seen,
would only be worth the trouble in the act of giving birth to myself
projected in a moving body that carries me to the other place.
The plunge lasts for worlds and you are at your post
in Fort Belvedere or on the moon in the water of the San Juan.
Choose whether to remain on that unspeaking shore
or to chastely fecundate the only wife.
Then the snack and its words are a face,
the journeys are one journey, the fire gives light to a man, let us begin.

The silent bursts into speech, using language
that rose from the mist on the water,
like a sun splitting into a rainbow.
Out of charity and need the tongue
says it all helped by the hand,
fiercely supported by the eye
where the concave adjusts to the convex.
All that's said acquires another substance.
The wood has started walking toward the castle
of diabolical silence and cursed blood.
Life is not the tale told by an idiot
but the march of the wood and the wheeling of the stars
in the voice of the messenger who isn't done.
That is my story, the story of my tongue.
That's what life is, the tongue of the story.
Succumb, infernal power, usurping and silent,
drowned by the wood. I will keep proclaiming.

What begins had already begun,
the heron insinuates itself like a flower of justice.
History is the miracle of nature
when Birnam Wood begins to walk
in the siege of the castle the devil rented.
But the wood had always been advancing toward the castle.
A tiny destination, corrupted
by the enjoyment of secret venetian blinds
suddenly equals the Battle of San Romano
painted by Uccello as if he were returning
infernal history to the earth's equations.

La tierra matemática, la tierra tocadora de flauta.
"Agua, amoníaco, ácido carbónico, flotan ya,
bañados por los rayos solares: desdeñar esa bruma
sería privar al astro juvenil de su más esencial ornato",
dice Teilhard enamoradamente.
De esa nostálgica bruma sale Atila galopando hacia el azul
de Teresita de Lisieux. En esa bruma
estamos los viejos músicos y yo, niño, tocando
el *Stabat Mater* de Rossini, mientras el bote
con mi hermano avanza hacia la desembocadura
cubierta por la neblina rubia del amanecer.
No existieron el Turner, el Ruskin del San Juan,
pero tampoco el Milanés del Támesis. Las complementarias
inexistencias clavan la aurora con un clavo de oro.
No falta nada que no sea un impulso para el bote.
Avanzamos en la bruma que flota sobre todo,
madre de los adentros del peciolo y del ojo de tigre,
disfrazados con las ramas del bosque inmemorial que avanza
en el asedio del castillo, y no sabemos ya
si somos el ejército armado hasta los dientes
o la novia campesina en la mañana de sus bodas.

Enero de 1971

Plegaria

Sensación general de algo abierto.

La ventana da al cielo,
el cielo al cielo.

El mar abierto.

La vena abierta.

La llaga abierta.

El cielo al cielo al cielo al
cielo. Los cielos a los cielos.

Rotura, salidero.

El balancín zafado del sillón de hierro:
ya lo soldaron.

The mathematical earth, the flute-playing earth.
"Water, ammonia, carbonic acid, float now,
bathed in solar rays: to scorn that mist
would be to deprive the young star of its most essential ornament,"
says Teilhard smitten.
From that nostalgic mist emerges Attila galloping toward the blue
of little Thérèse of Lisieux. In that mist
the old musicians and I, a child, are playing
the *Stabat Mater* of Rossini, while the boat
with my brother advances toward the outlet
covered by the blond haze of dawn.
There was no Turner nor Ruskin for the San Juan,
but there was also no Milanés for the Thames. The complementary
nonexistences nail daybreak with a golden nail.
All that's needed is a push for the boat.
We advance in the mist that floats over everything,
mother of the petiole's heart and the tiger's eye,
disguised with the branches of the immemorial wood that advances
in the siege of the castle, and we don't know
if now we're troops armed to the teeth
or the country bride on the morning of her wedding.

JANUARY 1971

Prayer

The sense of something open.

The window open to the sky,
the sky to the sky.

The open sea.

The open vein.

The open wound.

The sky onto the sky onto the sky onto
the sky. The skies to the skies.

Breakage, escape.

The loose runner of the iron rocker:
they've soldered it now.

Vino entero, sano, estaba suelto
y las dos patas que lo agarraban, sueltas,
cojo,
atascado el sillón en la terraza.

La terraza abierta
con el sillón roto, ahora sano.

Pero estuvo roto, abierto,
al cerrarse su forma ha denunciado
la desarticulación de lo cerrado.

En lo cerrado lo abierto
como su parte principal,
la que lo abre
a lo cerrado,
la que lo sella como cerrado,
cerrado-abierto.

Desaguadero, desangramiento
¿dónde?

Siempre hacia arriba, o difuso
por las entrañas, hacia los cielos
que se abren unos a otros
con la velocidad de lo inmóvil.

Estoy inmóvil volando
a la velocidad del pensamiento,
del deseo, de la nada,
de la crueldad, de la plegaria.

El mundo está saliéndose de sí,
vuela conmigo lento como un águila
que es el espacio que a sí mismo se perfora.

Estoy inmóvil en mi silla
mirando el sillón entero pero vacío
en la terraza hueca
subiendo como un rayo velocísimo, columna
que transparentemente lleva árboles,
la paz del azul cerrado
hacia otra herida que se cierra, se abre, se cierra.

It arrived in one piece, whole, it came loose
and the two legs that held it in place, loose,
the rocker wobbly, stock-still on the veranda.

The open veranda
with the broken rocker, whole again.

But it was broken, open,
when it closed its shape denounced
the disarticulation of the closed.

In the closed the open
as its principal part,
that which opens it
to the closed,
that which seals it as closed,
open-closed.

Drainage, bleeding
where?

Always upward, or diffused
through the heart of it to the skies
that open onto each other
with the speed of the motionless.

I am motionless flying
at the speed of thought,
of desire, nothingness,
cruelty, prayer.

The world is escaping itself,
it flies with me slow as an eagle
which is space piercing itself.

I am motionless in my seat
looking at the rocker whole but empty
on the empty veranda
rising like a lightning bolt, a pillar
that transparently carries trees.
The peace of blue closed
toward another wound that closes, opens, closes.

Lo final es lo abierto
pero dónde
si el dónde es un cerrojo.

Isla abierta, mar abierto, cielo abierto,
hombre abierto, Dios abierto
por el lanzazo en el costado.

Dios de cabeza
desde su espacio, manando hacia arriba
la sangre de su costado, el agua.

El agua siempre abierta,
sin orillas, encima de los cielos, primer cielo,
las aguas del principio
donde se empolla la vida.

La vida, la hembra hendida,
hendible, fecundable, paridora,
la mujer abierta por amor hasta los cielos.

El falo derramándose en lo abierto,
en lo cerrado, hasta los cielos.

Los labios de la herida, la sutura.

El inmenso torrente de la ausencia
desplomándose hacia arriba,
hacia afuera, succionando
cada partícula visible.

Lo visible como cerrado:
parte de lo abierto, lo invisible,
que bondadosamente, a cada instante,
lo ayuda a estar cerrado, a parecerlo.

Pacto de lo visible y lo invisible,
de lo ya visto con lo que todavía no se ve,
con lo que se verá pero ¿cuándo?
¿dónde?

Pacto de lo cerrado con lo abierto.

El grito, el alarido, la sangre derramada,
el mar furioso

The last is the open
but where
if the where is the bolt of a door.

Open island, open sea, open sky,
open man, God opened
by the thrust of the lance into his side.

Upside down God
from his space, the blood flowing upward
from his side, the water.

The water always open,
without shores, above the skies, first sky,
the waters of the beginning
where life wells up.

Life, cloven female,
cleavable, fertile, birthgiving,
the woman opened by love to the skies.

The phallus spilling itself into the open,
into the closed, to the skies.

The lips of the wound, the suture.

The immense torrent of absence
tumbling upward,
outward, sucking in
each visible particle.

The visible as closed:
part of the open, the invisible,
that kindly, at each instant,
helps it to be closed, to seem so.

Pact of the visible and the invisible,
of the already seen with what is not yet seen,
with what will be seen but when?
where?

Pact of the closed with the open.

The shout, the shriek, the spilled blood,
the sea raging

contra sus límites, los ríos que se salen
de madre.

Pero no ahora.

Sin dudas estallaremos.

Pero no ahora.

Ahora estamos en la serenidad del estallido,
volando hacia lo abierto con velocidad de una plegaria.

Mi plegaria es mirar
el sillón de hierro que estaba roto,
ahora sano,
inmóvil en la terraza abierta.

24 DE JUNIO DE 1988
DÍA DE SAN JUAN

Fina García Marruz

Visitaciones

I

Cuando el tiempo ya es ido, uno retorna
como a la casa de la infancia, a algunos
días, rostros, sucesos que supieron
recorrer el camino de nuestro corazón.
Vuelven de nuevo los cansados pasos
cada vez más sencillos y más lentos,
al mismo día, el mismo amigo, el mismo
viejo sol. Y queremos contar la maravilla
ciega para los otros, a nuestros ojos clara,
en donde la memoria ha detenido
como un pintor, un gesto de la mano,
una sonrisa, un modo breve de saludar.
Pues poco a poco el mundo se vuelve impenetrable,
los ojos no comprenden, la mano ya no toca
el alimento innombrable, lo real.

against its limits, the rivers overflowing
their beds.

But not now.

No doubt we will explode.

But not now.

Now we are in the calm of the explosion,
flying toward the open with the speed of a prayer.

My prayer is to look
at the iron rocker that was broken,
now whole,
motionless on the open veranda.

JUNE 24, 1988
FEAST OF SAINT JOHN

Translated by Jason Weiss

Fina García Marruz

Visitations

I

When the time has come, one returns
as if to one's childhood home, to certain
days, faces, events that knew how
to travel our heart's pathway.
Each time more simply
and slowly, those tired steps return to
the same day, the same friend, the same
old sun. And we want to recount the wonder
blind to others, but clear to our eyes,
where memory, like a painter,
has captured the gesture of a hand,
a smile, a quick hello. Because the world
bit by bit becomes impenetrable,
the eyes don't understand, the hand no longer touches
the real, the unnamable food.

2

Uno vuelve a subir las escaleras
de su casa perdida (ya no llevan
a ningún sitio), alguien nos llama
con una voz querida, familiar.
Pero ya no hace falta contestarle.
La voz sola nos llama, suficiente,
cual si nada pudiera hacerle daño,
en el pasillo inmenso. Una lluvia
que no puede mojarnos, no se cansa
de rodear un día preferido.
Uno toca la puerta de la casa
que le fue deparada a nuestras manos
mortales, como un tímido consuelo.

3

El que solía visitarnos, el que era
de todos más amado, suave vuelve
a la sala sencilla, cada día
más real y más leve, ya de humo.

¿Cuándo tocó la puerta? No podemos
recordarlo. Estaba allí, estaba!
Y no se irá jamás ni puede irse.
No nos trae la memoria las palabras
del adiós. Sólo podrá volverse
por la puerta de un ruido, de un llamado
de ese mundo que borra, ignora y vence.

4

¿Qué caprichosa y exquisita mano
trazó, eligió ese gesto perdurable,
lo sacó de su nada, como un dios,
para alumbrar por siempre otra alegría?
¿Participabas tú del dar eterno
que dejaste la mano humilde llena
del tesoro? En su feliz descuido
adolescente ¿derramaste el óleo?
¿Qué misterio fue el tuyo, instante puro,
silencioso elegido de los días?

2

Once again one climbs the stairs
of the lost house (that no longer
lead anywhere), someone calls us
with a familiar, beloved voice.
But there's no need to answer now.
The voice alone, entire, calls us,
as if nothing could harm it
in the enormous corridor. A rain
that can't wet us, that never tires
of encircling a favorite day.
One knocks at the door of the house
that's been prepared for our mortal
hands, like a shy comfort.

3

He who would usually come, he who of all
was the most beloved, softly returns
to the simple room, each day
more real and more ethereal, become vapor now.

When did he knock at the door? We can't
remember. He was there, he was there!
And he never left nor can.
Memory brings no words
of parting. A noise, a cry is all that can return
from the world that erases, ignores and conquers.

4

What whimsical delicate hand
sketched, selected this enduring gesture,
drew it forth from its nothing, like a god,
forever illuminating another happiness?
Did you partake of the eternal gift
that left the humble hand filled
with treasure? In your adolescent
carelessness did you spill the oil?
What was your mystery, pure, silent
moment, chosen from all the days?

Pues ellos van tornándose borrosos
y tú te quedas como estrella fija
con potencia mayor de eternidad.

5

Y cuando el tiempo torna impuro un rostro,
una vida que amamos en su hora
cierta de dar, por siempre más reales
que su verdad presente, lo veremos
cuando lo rodeaba aquella lumbre,
cuando el tiempo era apenas un fragmento
de un cuerpo más espléndido, invisible.
Todo hombre es el guardián de algo perdido.
Algo que sólo él sabe, sólo ha visto.
Y ese enterrado mundo, ese misterio
de nuestra juventud, lo defendemos
como una fantástica esperanza.

6

Y lo real es lo que aún no ha sido!
Toda apariencia es una misteriosa
aparición. En la rama de otoño
no acaba el fruto sino en la velada
promesa de ser siempre que su intacta
forma ofreció un momento a nuestra dicha.
Pues toda plenitud es la promesa
espléndida de la muerte, y la visitación
del ángel en el rostro del más joven
que todos sabíamos que se iría antes
pues escogía el Deseo su sonrisa nocturna.

7

A aquel vago delirio de la sala
traías el portal azul del pueblo
de tu niñez, en tu silencio abríase
una lejana cena misteriosa.
Cayó el espeso velo de los ojos
y al que aguardó toda la noche abrimos.
Partía el pan con una mano de nieve.
Con las espaldas del pastor huiste,

They become a blur, while you
survive as a fixed star
with the brightness of eternity.

5

And when time turns a face impure we will see,
forever more real than its present being,
a life that we love in its appointed hour of giving
when a kind of glow surrounded it,
when time was scarcely a fragment
of a more splendid, invisible body.
Every man is the keeper of something lost.
Something that only he knows, only he has seen.
And we defend that buried world,
that mystery of our youth,
like a fantastic hope.

6

And the real is what has not yet been!
All appearance is a mysterious
apparition. On the autumn branch
the fruit is not finished except in the veiled
promise of always being that its intact
form offered for a moment to our happiness.
All plenitude, then, is the splendid
promise of death, and the angel's
visitation in the face of the youngest
who we all knew would precede us,
its nocturnal smile chosen by The Wished-For.

7

To that vague delirium of the room
you brought the blue gate of the city
of your childhood, in your silence a distant
mysterious supper was begun.
The thick veil fell from our eyes
and we opened the gate to the one who'd waited
all night long. He was breaking the bread with a snowy hand.
You fled on the shepherd's shoulders,

cuando volviste el rostro era la noche,
todo había cambiado y sin embargo
en la granja dormían tranquilas las ovejas.

8

¿No sentías que ardía tu corazón
cuando nos hablaba de las Escrituras?
LOS PEREGRINOS DE EMMAÚS

Huésped me fue palabra misteriosa.
Huésped es el que viene de muy lejos,
de algún pueblo que nunca habremos visto.
Huésped es el que viene por la noche,
toca la aldaba de la puerta y todo
el umbral resplandece como nieve.
Huésped es quien se sienta a nuestra mesa
sólo por una noche, y no se acierta
sino ya a oír lo que su boca dijo.
Huésped es el que alegra con su rostro,
y alumbra con sus manos nuestro pan
y no logramos recordar su nombre.
Huésped es el que ha de partir, al alba.

9

There is a wind where the rose was.
WALTER DE LA MARE

Oh, vosotras, lámparas de otoño,
más fragante que todos los estíos!
¿Por qué ha de ser aquel que devenimos
con el tiempo, más real, menos efímero,
que aquel que fuimos a tus luces pálidas?
¿Por qué el polvo desierto, la agonía
junto a las armas bellas, quedan sólo
del resplandor de la victoria? Lejano
es todo vencimiento. En otro espacio
sucede, más allá del moribundo
rostro que hunde la gloria y deja ciego
junto al viento que lleva las banderas
espléndidas que huyen. Fiera es toda victoria.

when you looked back it was night,
everything had changed but nonetheless
the sheep slept peacefully in the fold.

8

Didn't you feel your heart burning
when he spoke to us of the Scriptures?
THE PILGRIMS OF EMMAUS

Guest was a mysterious word to me.
A guest is he who comes from afar,
from a town that we have never seen.
A guest is he who comes at night,
knocks at the door and the threshold
glitters like snow.
A guest is he who sits at our table
for just a night, and one is sure of nothing
but hearing the words of his mouth.
A guest is he whose face cheers us,
who illuminates our bread with his hands
and we don't remember his name.
A guest is he who must depart at dawn.

9

There is a wind where the rose was.
WALTER DE LA MARE

Oh you, lamps of autumn,
more fragrant than all summers!
Why must what time makes of us
be realer, less ephemeral,
than what we were in your pallid light?
Why do only the empty dust, the throes
of death amidst beautiful swords
remain of the splendor of victory? Every ending
is far away, elsewhere,
elsewhere, far from the dying face
that glory sinks and leaves blind
next to the wind that lifts the shining, retreating
flags. All victory is savage.

10

Amigo, el que yo más amaba,
venid a la luz del alba.

Cómo ha cambiado el tiempo aquella fija
mirada inteligente que una extraña
ternura, como un sol, desdibujaba!
La música de lo posible rodeaba tu rostro,
como un ladrón el tiempo llevó sólo el despojo,
en nuestra fiel ternura te cumplías
como en lo ardido el fuego, y no en la lívida
ceniza, acaba. Y donde ven los otros
la arruga del escarnio, te tocamos
el traje adolescente, casi nieve
infantil a la mano, pues que sólo
nuestro fue el privilegio de mirarte
con el rostro de tu resurrección.

11

Since I have walk'd with you through shady lanes . . .
KEATS

¿Quién no conoce ese sendero en sombras,
ese continuo hablar, interrumpiéndose
el uno al otro amigo, en el gozoso
diálogo hasta la puerta de la casa,
servida ya la cena? ¿Quién no escucha
las nocturnas pisadas en la acera
tornarse más opacas al cruzar por la yerba
que nos trae al amigo, al bien llegado?
¿A quién, ya tarde, no le cuesta mucho
despedirse y murmura generosos deseos,
inexplicables dichas, bajo los fríos astros?

12

. . . qui laetificat juventutem meam . . .

Sólo vosotras, bestias, claros árboles,
podéis seguir! Mas, eterno es el hombre.
Salvaje privilegio de la muerte,
heredad sólo nuestra, mientras derrama el astro

10

Friend who most I loved,
come at the light of dawn.

How time has changed that intent intelligent
gaze, softened by a strange
sunlike affection!
The music of the possible surrounded your face,
time, like a thief, stole your remains,
but in our faithful affection you were fulfilled
as warmth, not ashes,
fulfills the flame. Where others see
a mocking wrinkle we touch
the clothes of youth, like the snow of childhood
in our hands, because the privilege
was ours alone to see you
with the face of your resurrection.

11

Since I have walk'd with you through shady lanes . . .
                                                          KEATS

Who doesn't know that shady path,
that endless talking, each friend
interrupting the other in playful
dialogue to the door of the house,
where supper's already served? Who doesn't hear
the nightly clack of footsteps
that soften as they cross the grass,
bringing our friend, our welcome friend?
And when it's late is it ever easy
to say goodbye, murmuring fondest wishes,
inexplicable joys, beneath the cold stars?

12

. . . qui laetificat juventutem meam . . .

You only, beasts, bright trees,
may continue! But man is eternal.
The savage privilege of death,
our inheritance alone, while the star spills

su luz sobreviviente sobre ese rostro altivo
de ser fugaz, junto a los ciclos fijos,
y ese verdor, eterno! Se fue yendo
la gloria de los rostros más amados,
y tornamos, como la ola ciega, al tiempo
del cuerpo incorruptible que esperaste
y no pudimos retener, llorando
en la perdida lámpara, las voces,
lo que encuentro creímos y es partida.

Oh lo real, el mundo en el misterio
de nuestra juventud, que nos aguarda!
Nos ha sido prometida su alegría.
Nos ha sido prometido su retorno.
Eres lo que retorna, oh siempre lo supimos.
Pero no como ahora, amigo mío.

El momento que más amo

(Escena final de Luces de la ciudad*)*

El momento que más amo
es la escena final en que te quedas
sonriendo, sin rencor,
ante la dicha, inalcanzable.

El momento que más amo
es cuando dices a la joven ciega
"Ya puedes ver?" y ella descubre
en el tacto de tu mano al mendigo,
al caballero, a su benefactor desconocido.

De pronto, es como si te quisieras
ir, pero, al cabo, no te vas,
y ella te pide como perdón
con los ojos, y tú le devuelves

la mirada, aceptándote en tu real
miseria, los dos retirándose y quedándose

its enduring light on the upraised face
of a brief being, attached to fixed cycles,
and eternal verdure! The glory
of the most beloved faces was leaving,
and we return, like the blind wave, to the time
of the incorruptible body that you hoped for
and we could not keep, weeping
by the lost lamp, the voices, the departure
that we thought was a meeting.

Oh the real, the world in the mystery
of our youth, that awaits us!
We have been promised its joy.
We have been promised its return.
You are what returns, oh we have always known it.
But not as now, my friend.

My Favorite Moment

(Last scene of City Lights*)*

My favorite moment
is the last scene, when
without rancor
in the face of unattainable happiness
you smile.

My favorite moment
is when you ask the blind girl
"Do you see now?" and she discovers
in the touch of your hand the beggar,
the gentleman, her unknown benefactor.

Torn, it's as if you wanted
to leave, but you don't,
as if with her eyes
she asks your absolution
and you return her gaze

accepting, both of you, your true
misery, at once drawing apart

a la vez, cristalinamente mirándose
en una breve, interminable, doble piedad,

ese increíble dúo de amor,
esa pena de no amar que tú
—el infeliz—tan delicadamente
sonriendo, consuelas.

de Gramática inglesa

PEQUEÑA ELEGÍA

—Dónde estás, hijo mío?
—Oh, estoy aquí!

—Dónde está tu hermana?
—En la cocina.

—Tiene Emma dos gatos?
—Solamente dos.

—Tenemos una boca
y sólo dos orejas.

—Es rico tu hermano?
—Oh, sí lo es.

—Y tú, eres pobre?
—Oh, sí lo soy.

—La casa es vieja.
—El libro es gris.

¿Dónde estás, mariposa?

DÍGAME

—Dígame, puedo hacer algo
por usted?

—Yo tenía un pájaro.
¿Sabe usted su nombre?

and remaining, seeing yourselves
with crystal clarity
in a brief, endless, double compassion,

that love duet,
the sorrow of not loving that you—
unhappy one—console
with a tender smile.

from English Grammar

LITTLE ELEGY

"Where are you, my son?"
"Oh, I'm here!"

"Where is your sister?"
"In the kitchen."

"Does Emma have two cats?"
"Only two."

"We have one mouth
and just two ears."

"Is your brother rich?"
"Oh yes."

"And are you poor?"
"Oh yes."

"The house is old."
"The book is gray."

Where are you, butterfly?

TELL ME

"Tell me, can I do anything
for you?"

"I had a bird.
Do you know its name?"

USO DE PLURALES

(Cambiar del plural al singular y del singular al plural)

Son los cuartos grandes?
Son los sótanos húmedos?
—Mi madre tiene un jardín
con un caballo pequeño.

Los hermanos tienen plumas?
Las hermanas tienen naranjas?
—El día tiene noche, señor.
El mes tiene días y noches.

El cuarto, la cocina, el sótano.
El tulipán, el paraguas.
¿Y tú, tienes naranjas o plumas?
¿Tienes hermanos o hermanas?

HERALDO

El gallo
se engríe, ciertamente.

Pero tiene sus motivos.

ADÁN

—Adán,
dónde has estado tú
toda la mañana?

—Estuve en el jardín
de mi padre.
Fui muy feliz.

(¡Yo era tan joven
cuando tuve la desgracia
de perder mis parientes!)

USE OF THE PLURAL

(Changing plural to singular and singular to plural)

Are the rooms large?
Are the basements damp?
"My mother has a garden
with a small horse in it."

Do the brothers have feathers?
Do the sisters have oranges?
"Day has night, sir.
The month has days and nights."

The room, the kitchen, the basement.
The tulip, the umbrella.
And you, do you have oranges or feathers?
Do you have brothers or sisters?

HERALD

The rooster
is certainly conceited.

But he has his reasons.

ADAM

"Adam,
where have you been
all morning?"

"I have been
in my father's garden.
I have been very happy."

(I was so young
when I lost
my parents!)

PARTICIPIOS PASIVOS

Abandonado,
oculto,
ido.

(Caminamos lentamente.)

Llueve recio.

QUIÉN HA VISTO

Quién ha visto
el palacio del Rey?

El panadero, la roca
y la lluvia.

¿Quién quiere
hablar con mi padre?

El vaso de vino,
las pantuflas
y el cochero.

Cuidado con los caminos.

ESTE LIBRO DE GRAMÁTICA

Este libro de gramática
tiene algunos ejemplos cómicos,
otros son, sin embargo, melancólicos,
y acaso no debieran
dárselos a los niños.

Dice tan tranquilamente:
"El relojero ha vendido todos los relojes."
Y después (hay cierta lógica)
"María está triste."
"Aquel señor tenía muchos amigos
pero los ha perdido todos. Es muy viejo."
"Yo quiero ir al teatro."

PAST PARTICIPLES

Forsaken,
hidden,
gone.

(Let us walk slowly.)

It's raining hard.

WHO HAS SEEN

Who has seen
the King's palace?

The baker, the rock
and the rain.

Who wants to speak
to my father?

The glass of wine,
the slippers
and the coachman.

Be careful on the road.

THIS GRAMMAR BOOK

In this grammar book
there are funny examples, but others
are very sad, and perhaps
they should not be shown
to children.

Calmly it says:
"The watchmaker has sold all his watches."
And then (there's a certain logic to this)
"Mary is sad."
"That man had many friends,
but he's lost them all. He is very old."
"I want to go to the theater."

"Los pájaros hacen sus nidos."
"Quién es el que compra dos camisas
al pobre muchacho?"

"—Siempre usted me vende el periódico de ayer!"

Lorenzo García Vega

Variaciones

De la tarde a la noche no hubo tránsito. Estaba ahí. La lluvia la presiente, la
envuelve. Va como encapsulada en cada gota. Promesa de un otoño eterno.
Con acre sabor en los oídos.

El chubasco al lado de la noche persistía. Lamiendo en ondas el agua
emponzoñada. Ligeras corrían en breves presagios. Juego minúsculo: peque-
ñas amazonas que agitadas atravesaban la calle.

Breve mueca que hace la lluvia al tocar la acera. Desgestos y vieja mueca.
Mueca de parroquia al insinuar sus campanas.

El estremecimiento de lo viejo, de un algo impensado retenía. Tú. Tú.
Parecían venidas de muy lejos las puertas y ventanas. El sueño desenvolvién-
dose por las casas (confianza de extraños recovecos y dulce melodía).

¡Noches de lluvia que al pellejo se adhieren como gatos! Noches, resba-
lar. ¡Noches de inhumado eco, con sus pestañas tentando el vértigo de luz!
Caminan las calles, son descubiertas en relampagueante zigzag de casa con
relicario antiguo. Y encogidos gatos de esparcidos ojos. ¿Luminosos?

¿Tentación? ¿Cruce de calles? ¿Caminar? Oh, sí, tarde como un manto,
vívido paisaje. Reminiscencia de cansados niños en el portal tendidos.

Despaciosos pinos se mueven. Carretera de cristal por la luna empapada.
Cañaverales meciendo sus ensueños: Torpes. Quedo guiños de estrellas.

La locomotora cargada de tesoros sucios.

Me hieren los minutos. Siento el estremecimiento delirante. Desgárrenseme
las carnes: percibo el devenir plástico del día.

Mi mirada inmadura quiere besar las cosas. Tengo el miedo terrible de
perder el devenir, perseguido en la colina y en el río.

Las cosas se me presentan, ay, en majestuosidad imponente. Quiero ele-
varlas al sol y esconderlas en estuche.

"The birds build their nests."
"Who is buying two shirts
for the poor boy?"

"You always sell me yesterday's paper!"

Translated by Mark Weiss

Lorenzo García Vega

Variations

Between afternoon and nighttime, no transition. Night was there. Rain anticipates it, envelops it. It walks along as if contained in every drop. Promise of eternal autumn. With a bitter taste in its ears.

The downpour continued at the edge of night. Lapping in waves the envenomed water. Swiftly they flowed in brief premonitions. A tiny game; wee Amazons that crossed the street nervously.

Brief grimace of rain touching the pavement. Expressionless old grimace. The church's grimace when its bells insinuate.

The shudder of the aged retained something unthought-of. You. You. The doors and windows seemed to have come from far away. Sleep spreading through the houses (confidence of strange nooks and sweet melody).

Rainy nights that stick to the skin like cats! Nights, slipping. Nights of buried echoes, their eyelashes tempting light's vertigo! They walk the streets, they are revealed in the zigzag of lightning of a house with an ancient reliquary. And shrunken cats with scattered—luminous?—eyes.

Temptation? Crossroads? Walking? Oh yes, afternoon like a cloak, vivid landscape. A memory of weary children stretched out in the doorway.

Slow pines are moving. Crystal highway drenched by the moon. Cane fields rocking their reveries. Sluggish. Quietly, wink of stars.

The locomotive laden with dirty treasures.

The minutes wound me. I feel the frenzied shudder. Tear my flesh apart: I see day's expressive transformation.

My immature gaze wants to kiss things. I have the terrible fear of losing the transformation, pursued on hill and river.

Things present themselves, alas, in imposing majesty. I want to raise them to the sun and hide them in my drawer.

LORENZO GARCÍA VEGA   189

Quiero seguir en círculos creciendo.

Es la hora nocturna del buitre, ya sus alas azotan los balaústres.

Más, no he de mirarlo. Callo. Es un triste resabio de ancestral desilusión.

Se insinúa el buitre por las rejas. Con mirada de águila, y latir afiebrado, insinúa torrentes de palabras calladas y parece que esconde mil mares de antaño.

Solitario buitre. De mirada madura, témole a tu pico y a tu canto, desesperadamente. He de seguir tocando el fantasma dormido.

He de vivir por siempre. Me bañaré en los ríos y habrá lumbre encendida.

Sí, allá en la ciudad de la jerga dulce, el cantar afiebrado ilumina las murallas.

Después, me puedes destrozar buitre. Es mi precio a mi ansia de vida.

(El buitre se extraña inútilmente, con meneo de cola escucha a las estrellas.)

Meridiano. Y las porfías de niños se retuercen entre las flores. Y los organillos cercanos a la mar anuncian la llegada del velero.

Reloj. Exactitud y los blancos cristales de las copas. Y los altisonantes gritos del vendedor: últimos gritos y la parranda de las frondas. Y se abren las compuertas de la calle. Mientras las quejas se disipan en la nimiedad de la blancura.

Girar instantáneo. Vuelo de nubes. Las casas flotan en su diluvio estremecido. Nimiedad, luz clara. Mediodía.

En las lágrimas de las focas

Frío en las guardines terrosos
Parada la luna a estribor en la quinta hora de la tarde
Ahora todos nos iremos como un corcel
torcidamente muertos para llorar la injuria de las cortinas
y los llantos triples de las paredes dormidos truenos
Vaivén de desplegados cabezas hipnóticas calabazas calvas
Crines del estudiante musitan en las cuevas del Rey
lloran las pamelas
Coral absorto en pastillas de luna
Absalón húmedo remiendo lavanderas en las tropas
de la sal
        Panderetas para la huida
para los morteros doctores a cruce de jabalinas
así tramposos humeantes piedras jacarandá en la casa vacía

I want to keep growing in circles.

It is the vulture's nocturnal hour, already its wings are beating the balusters.

But I don't have to look at it. I keep quiet. It's a sad vestige of ancestral disillusion.

The vulture makes its way through the bars. With an eagle's gaze, and feverish wingbeats, it hints at torrents of silent words and seems to be hiding a thousand seas of yore.

Solitary vulture. With a ripe old gaze, I am in desperate dread of your beak and your song. I must keep touching the sleeping phantom.

I must live forever. I will bathe in the rivers and a fire will be lit.

Yes, over there in the city of sweet slang, feverish singing lights up the walls.

Afterwards, you can rip me apart, vulture. It's what I pay for my yearning for life.

(The vulture is pointlessly surprised, with a flick of his tail he listens to the stars.)

High noon. And the children's tiffs are entangled in flowers. And the hurdy-gurdies by the sea announce the sailboat's arrival.

Clock. Precision and the goblets' white glass. And the resonant cries of the vendor: last shouts and the binge of branches. And the street's floodgates open. As the complaints dissipate into the excessive whiteness.

Instantaneous whirl. Flight of clouds. The houses float in their shuddering flood. Excess, bright light. Midday.

In the Seals' Tears

Cold on the muddy tiller ropes
The moon halted at starboard around five in the afternoon
Now we'll all be off like a steed
twisted and dead to mourn the curtains' insult
and the triple laments of the walls sleeping thunderclaps
Swaying of hypnotic heads bald pumpkins on display
The student's horsehairs are mumbling in the King's caverns
the sombreros weep
Coral absorbed in lunar tablets
Damp Absalom patching up washerwomen in troops
of salt
        Tambourines for flight
for the mortar doctors crossing javelins
that kind of swindler smoking stones jacaranda in the empty house

frío el acordeón de la luna focas lloren sus precipicios
así en las fábricas los cadáveres elefantes
cuando los cuaternarios avancen cenicientos
lupa para Dios en los mosquiteros sonrosados
      encantos en los cuartos de baño
gritan las bombas para los inquilinos pacíficos
listones acuáticos en la tierra embadurnada tantanlin

Túnel

Túnel de mi espera. ¿Por qué tu noche labrada
de equívocas cenizas? ¿Por qué tu noche sostenida
por el tributo oscuro, extinguido? (Mi vida
perdiéndose por tus rotas imágenes) Oh morada,

¡oh silencio! ¿acaso anhelada? ¿acaso en el recodo, mía?
Si estabas, todo temblor, como un engaño,
a romper las esquinas de mi sueño. Si estabas por el regaño
de tus paredes rotas, espectrales. Sí, y retenía

tu fulgor la extraña tarde, como una bella
sensación de hastío (un soplo cansado colora
este último tributo de mi frente a tu enjuto

sueño ironizado). Oh leve, oh grande, oh aurora
de lo extraño, oh túnel: rompiendo en el instante, con la estrella
tenaz de tus insomnios, el hosco fulgor de mi tributo.

El santo del Padre Rector

    Llega ese día, el día de fiesta en el colegio: lo siente como un frío.
Sin embargo, él va también hasta allí, hasta el borde de ellos. Cerca de ellos,
pero no más que para pensar en sus cosas, en sus casi cosas, en su historia.
Por eso, no puede saber cómo son los gritos, las risas, los juegos. Y cuando
el jesuita—gordo, sofocado—tira caramelos por una ventana, él se levanta
con los demás, se agacha como los demás, llega a recoger bombones en un
rincón; pero luego se ve, entrando en la alegría de ellos como el que desenfa-
dadamente penetra en una casa ajena, y se avergüenza.

    Ahora unos montan a caballo; otros, cerca del campo de pelota, se
acercan al camión que tiene los refrescos: se sofocan, pelean, ríen: él nunca

cold the moon's accordion seals weep their cliffs
thus in the factories elephant corpses
when the ashen quaternaries advance
magnifier for God in the rosy mosquito nets
     enchantment in the bathrooms
bombs scream for the peaceful tenants
acoustic strips on the daubed earth teedadum

Tunnel

Tunnel of my waiting. Why is your night carved
from equivocal ashes? Why is your night sustained
by the dark, extinguished tribute? (My life
losing itself in your broken images) Oh dwelling,

oh silence perhaps longed-for? perhaps, in the recesses, my own?
You were there, trembling, like a trick,
breaking into the corners of my dream. You were there in the reproach
of your broken, spectral walls. Yes, and the strange

afternoon retained your splendor, like a beautiful
feeling of boredom (a tired breath colors
this final tribute of my brow to your skinny

ironical dream). Oh light, oh great, oh dawn
of strangeness, oh tunnel: that moment breaking, with the tenacious
star of your sleeplessness, my tribute's gloomy splendor.

The Rector's Saint's Day

That day arrives, a party in the school: it's like a blast of cold to
him. But he's going there too, right up to their edge. Close to them, but only
to think about what they're up to, what they're almost up to, their story.
That's why he can't know what their cries, laughter, games are like. And
when the Jesuit—fat and out-of-breath—throws caramels out a window,
he gets up with the others, bends over like them, even picks up candies in
a corner; but then he sees himself entering their joy like someone boldly
intruding into another's house, and feels ashamed.

Some play horsie; others, near the baseball field, approach the
soft-drink truck: breathless, they fight, they laugh: he'll never know their

conocerá su secreto. Pero aún insiste, va a quedarse para la *sesión de la tarde,* ensaya una que otra carrereta y, al final, siente sobre sus brazos el forro empapado en sudor de su saco. Ellos, los otros, sin embargo, giran con una luz, con un calor distinto.

Ya, nítidos, los ve. Los precisa, los dibuja. En las filas, en el comedor o en los juegos: palpitante, un solo organismo lleno de ruido y sudor, surge de sus cuerpos unidos. Y él intenta vivir un poco como ellos, doblar para sí, como si fuera un pañuelo, el tapiz de sus gritos. Y se acerca al banco de madera de la galería donde está sentado Ramón López: gordo, anodino, fofo, con barquillo de helado en una mano. Y se pone a imitar sus gestos de niño cándido—casi idiota—, como para remendar la soledad.

Pero, no hay salida, tiene que verlos de lejos. Tiene que ver su inmensa masa, globo de ruidos y colores fulgurantes, que suena con la nostalgia de los lugares adonde no ha estado, con las risas del circo donde estuvo solo. Porque esa inmensa presencia, porque ese ruido de ellos, es la presencia y el ruido, de una carpa grande, tan grande como el mundo, en que él no penetra.

Ahora ya es de noche. Ha terminado el día del santo del Padre Rector. Desde un pequeño paradero de tranvías—mortecina luz donde nacen chicharras, un solo banco de piedra para un viajero de humo—él, de la mano de sus padres, va entendiendo, lentamente, por la soledad, como el que escala, cautelosamente, una ladera nocturna. Y no es que deje de verlos, no: sabe que están allí, en el colegio; sabe que están dentro de una carpa grande, tan grande como el mundo. Y sabe, también, que ellos han de reírse, siempre, con ruido voluptuoso y alucinante, sobre la estéril pantomima de sus gestos.

El: soledad, títere: lanza su lamentable mímesis, cubierto con el forro empapado en sudor del uniforme de gala del colegio. Ellos: surgiendo, entrando, saliendo, por esa calle siempre prestigiosa, donde los cinematógrafos están cubiertos con la sombra de un gigante familiar.

Eso es así, lo sabe desde entonces, lo sabrá siempre. Y, cuando después de haber tomado el tranvía, apoya su frente en el cristal de la ventanilla, comprende que esas pequeñas luces que ruedan por lo oscuro de la noche, tienen la misteriosa dulzura del frío que se acepta, del frío en que se penetra por secreta vocación.

secret. But he still insists, he's going to stay for the *afternoon session*, he tries some cartwheels, and feels the sweat-soaked jacket lining under his arms. They, however, the others, whirl with a light, a different heat.

Now, in sharp outline, he sees them. He defines, draws them. Standing in line, at the dining hall, and at play; palpitating, a single organism full of noise and sweat emerges from their combined bodies. And he's trying to live like them a bit, to fold for himself like a handkerchief the tapestry of their shouts. And he approaches the wooden bench in the gallery where Ramón López—fat, insignificant, flabby, holding an ice cream cone—is sitting. And he starts imitating his innocent—almost idiotic—boy's gestures, as if to mend the solitude.

But there's no escape, he can only see them from a distance. He can only see their immense mass, a globe of noises and dazzling colors, which sings of nostalgia for places he's never been, with the laughter of the circus he went to alone. Because this immense presence, because this noise of theirs, is the presence and noise of a big tent, as big as the world, which he can't enter.

Now it's night. The Rector's saint's day is over. From a small trolley stop—fading light in which cicadas are born, a single stone bench for a traveler of smoke—he, at his parents' hand, will come to understand, slowly, through solitude, like someone cautiously climbing a nocturnal slope. And it's not that he stops seeing them, no: he knows they're there, in the school; he knows they're inside a big tent, as big as the world. And he also knows that they always have to laugh, with a voluptuous, beguiling noise, at the sterile pantomime of his gestures.

He: solitude, puppet: he hurls his lamentable mimesis, covered in the sweat-soaked lining of the school uniform. They: emerging, entering, leaving, through this always high-toned street, where the movie theaters are covered with the shadow of a familial giant.

That's how it is, he knows it now, he'll always know it. And, when, on the trolley, he leans his forehead on the windowpane, he understands that those tiny lights whirling through the darkness of the night have the mysterious sweetness of the cold one accepts, the cold one enters through a secret calling.

El viejo Maldoror

Como una boca desdentada: del otoño era la mañana una abertura gris. Labios había que al vacío trituraban.

El viejo y carcomido Maldoror se limpiaba los dientes mientras simulaba, frente al espejo del lavabo, el gesto estereotipado del tiburón textual.

Pues en gorgoritos lanzaba sus labios, pero sólo alcanzaba las descascaradas parcelas de un suntuoso y anacrónico grabado, grabado de folletinesco monstruo marino. O dicho de otra manera: con rotas, estériles, enclenques metamorfosis, intentaba saltar—como con velocípedo intenta un payaso saltar—por entre las distintas pieles que cubren a una legión de estatuas; y esto mientras inauguraba, la ventana del baño, el lúgubre vacío de la luz de la mañana. Como podría comprobarse allí era, mimetizando el rostro de su angustia, Maldoror un inútil saltarín. De escasos movimientos horrendos animales por su rostro trepaban, llevados todos por la equívoca voluntad de hacer triunfar un imposible reto, pues las manos del héroe querrían figurar garras, o saltar como cóndores sus ojos, o pretender sus sueños la aristocracia de unos actos agudos, pero las formas que, escasamente, la voluntad de Maldoror levantaba, sólo, y en lastimera condición, regar lograban la pequeña acuarela de unos ingenuos monstruos.

La estampa del héroe es, pues, el kilo de una ripiosa mentira, simulando, en imagen reflejada, el engaño de unos trasnochados ojos de águila, o la fábula grotesca de unas inexistentes mejillas de bronce. O es esta estampa alegoría de farsa. O alegoría de movimiento que vanamente gestos heroicos intenta, hasta llegar a traducir el congelado espacio de una fiera canija. Ya que, ¡ay!, para siempre el viejo Maldoror, infiel reflejo de un momento olvidado, en su espejo sólo logrará detener la lamentable superficie de ése, diluído, inútil texto de su hazaña.

Con una advertencia

Casi irreconocibles signos estas noches trazando. Adefesios mudos. Cambiando. Cambiándome siempre.

Casi invisible, pues, entre espacios diminutos. Y, también revolviéndome sin revolver, grotescamente solitario, o lo que no me sueña del sueño de una unidad.

Así confieso estar, siempre, un poco fuera de mis testimonios. Confieso no comprender bien.

Old Maldoror

Like a toothless mouth: a gray opening was that autumn morning. It had lips that munched on the void.

Old, moth-eaten Maldoror was cleaning his teeth while simulating, in the sink's mirror, the stereotyped gesture of the textual shark.

Then he threw his lips out in roulades, but he only attained the peeled particles of a sumptuous, anachronistic engraving, an engraving of a melodramatic sea monster. Or said otherwise: with broken, sterile, sickly metamorphoses, he tried to leap—like a clown trying with a velocipede to leap—among the various skins covering a legion of statues; and this while the bathroom window inaugurated the lugubrious void of the morning light. As could be seen there, Maldoror, mimicking the face of his anguish, was a pointless leaper. With slight horrid movements animals crept up his face, driven by the ambiguous will to make a triumph of an impossible challenge, since the hero's hands wished to feign claws, or his eyes to leap like condors, or his dreams to attempt the aristocracy of a few clever actions, but the forms that, barely, Maldoror's will alone erected, and in pitiful condition, managed to sprinkle the small watercolor of some innocent monsters.

The hero's portrait, then, is a couple of pounds worth of verbose lies, simulating, in a reflected image, the deception of a few haggard eagle eyes, or the grotesque fable of some nonexistent bronze cheeks. Or this portrait is an allegory of a farce. Or an allegory of movement that vainly tries out heroic gestures, until achieving the translation of a puny beast's congealed space. Now, alas! forever will old Maldoror, faithless reflection of a forgotten moment, in his mirror alone manage to hold back the wretched surface of this diluted, useless text of his exploits.

With a Warning

These nights tracing almost unrecognizable signs. Mute motleys. Changing. Always changing myself.

Almost invisible, then, among minute spaces. And tossing and turning without turning as well, grotesquely solitary, or something I can't place in the dream of a unity.

And so I confess to being, always, a little outside my testimonies. I confess not to understand very well.

Texto martiano

Desde una concha electrónica, con la joven quinceañera, Martí desciende bailando. Giran, ahí con el recordatorio alegórico, el punzó descolorido, o el blanco, o el azul desteñido: colores del prisma albino.

Desde una concha electrónica, de mirar y recordar todo el tiempo disponible. ¡Tenemos, todos, el tiempo!

Desde una concha electrónica se aplaude con el silencio. Un punzó descolorido se iza por los rincones. Hay pinos. Y en el sillón del portal el que su vejez desliza.

Desde una concha electrónica ha vuelto la noche albina. Martí ya deja la danza y vuelve a Fundar la Patria. Hay huesos. Hay un parque inexistente. Hay un banco desteñido. Al muerto acuesta Martí. A dormir acuesta al muerto sobre la noche del banco. No se oye. Y un punzó descolorido en el parque inexistente.

Buscándome el vacío

Porque me han seguido los manchones. Porque he comprobado, piezas superponiendo o rostros de esta mañana, que están los desvaídos azules de unas ventanas.

Todo eso quería decir abeto, o el aire; querría decir cielo, o estoy cansado. Aunque como encogiéndose, ensanchándose líneas más del texto, o menos alcanzar nube tamaño de diminuto cisne, ¿dónde estaría mi centro? Pues también debo insistir puse mi mano en un bolsillo y tacto ligero de un vacío logré, aunque realmente no sabía dónde estaba mi mano. ¿Y entonces se trataría de si sólo soy el médium o el ventrílocuo de un texto que no es mío? Por lo que no logro saber cuál es mi nada. Y así, pues, debo volver. Y así me enredo, me insisto, me repito en el no logro tocar, ya que hasta ahora no sé si manchón es mi cuerpo; así como, lo que toco, tampoco puedo llegar a saber si es una sombra.

Ilusión venida a menos

Para el texto estoy persiguiendo abetos y árboles encantados para el texto, como también para el texto la sutil e irónica sonrisa de un congelado vacío. Pero esto, esta labor, sólo llegaría a ser tangible si lograra alcanzar, yo, eso que es superficie de una sibilina astucia verbal.

Martían Text

Martí descends dancing from an electronic shell with the young debutante. They whirl, there, with the allegorical obituary, the discolored scarlet, or the white, or the faded blue: colors of the albino prism.

From an electronic shell, looking and recalling all the available time. We, all of us, have time!

From an electronic shell, applause with silence. A discolored scarlet is hoisted from the corners. There are pine trees. And in the hallway chair, the one whose old age slips by.

From an electronic shell the albino night has returned. Martí leaves the dance now and goes back to Founding the Nation. There are bones. There's a nonexistent park. There's a faded bench. Martí puts the dead man to bed. He puts the dead man to sleep on the bench's night. Inaudible. And a discolored scarlet in the nonexistent park.

Seeking My Void

Because the stains have followed me. Because I've confirmed, superimposing this morning's pieces or faces, that they're the pale blue of some windows.

All this meant fir, or air; it would have meant sky, or I'm tired. Though like shrinking, stretching more lines of the text, or less reaching a cloud the size of a tiny swan, where would my center be? Because I need to emphasize that I put my hand in a pocket and barely touched a void, although really I didn't know where my hand was. So is it a question of whether I'm just the medium or the ventriloquist of a text that isn't mine? Because I can't figure out what my nothingness is. So I have to go back. And thus I get tangled up, insist, repeat the I can't touch, since I still don't know if the stain is my body; I still can't figure out if what I touch is a shadow.

Illusion Come to Naught

For the text I'm pursuing firs and enchanted trees for the text, as also for the text the subtle, ironical smile of a frozen void. But this, this work, would only become tangible if I were able, I, to reach the surface of a sibylline verbal cunning.

Pero, en verdad, no he tomado en cuenta mi cansancio. Por lo que, bien considerada mi actual situación, no me dirigiré hacia mi escritorio, ya que seguiré moviéndome con el rocío real, por entre estos abetos y árboles reales, que he encontrado en el paseo de esta tarde. Así pues, se trata de que como estoy cansado y aunque la melancolía del texto posible me sigue persiguiendo, dudo mucho poder alcanzar, con la palabra, eso como leves chispas, eso en que consiste una ilusión venida a menos.

Arañazo mediúmnico

Cuchillo, filo, faro. ¿Qué más? Y el decorado, filigrana, de una caja de bombones Art Deco.

¿Qué es eso?

Borde donde reaparece el . . . Viejo asunto—todo eso—de la nada. Y en el texto (imposible texto) lo que, con hirsuta fidelidad, bien pudiera perderse.

Pero, confieso que yo tampoco entiendo.

El extraño rigor

Con requerido rigor computarizó el paisaje: la cosa estuvo programada con todos los hierros, alambres, tornillos, etc. ¡Ni una sola imagen sin colocar! ¡Perfecta la acuarela! Por lo que al final, terminada su faena, no cupo duda de que en lo simultáneo del reverso, él no dejó de sacar del horno lo que antes había puesto a calentar: ese juego de sus tantas piezas, perennemente frías.

Colosal olvido

Colosal olvido que ya ni me pertenece, como piedra—¿fulminado?—, y más allá, por supuesto, de cualquier resto de la mirada.

(En los álamos despegos: sus raras cenizas).

Mientras desciendo: sin vocación, ni rumor; tras lo poco—enjuto— de este viento enfermizo.

Se oye el ruido del avión que, sin duda, ahora pasa, no muy lejos de aquí.

But, in truth, I haven't taken my weariness into account. Because of which, given my present situation, I won't head for my desk, I'll keep traveling with the real dew, among these firs and real trees I've come upon in this evening's walk. So it's about how, since I'm tired, and although the melancholy of the possible text keeps pursuing me, I seriously doubt that I can reach, with words, this that's like light sparks, this that illusion come to naught consists of.

Mediumistic Scratch

Knife, edge, beacon. What else? And the decoration, filigree, of an Art Deco box of chocolates.

What's this?

The reappearance at a border of . . . Old matter—all this—of nothingness. And in the text (impossible text) something that, with hirsute fidelity, could well be lost.

But I confess I don't understand either.

Strange Rigor

With requisite rigor he computerized the landscape: the whole thing was programmed, all the chains, wires, screws, etc. Not one image missing! The watercolor—perfect! So that at the end, his task finished, there was no doubt that in the simultaneity of the antithesis, he didn't forget to remove from the oven the thing he was reheating: that game with all its—perennially cold—pieces.

Colossal Oblivion

Colossal oblivion that now no longer belongs to me, stone-like—struck by lightning?—and beyond, of course, whatever remains of the gaze.

(In the indifferent elms: their strange ashes.)

As I descend: without vocation or noise; behind what little there is—and thin—of this unhealthy wind.

The noise of the airplane, which doubtless is passing by now, not very far from here.

Manuscrito para la cajita

Para la cajita. Pudiera decirse que la Transparencia (como, en la pared de la cajita, la foto de aquel pobre diablo que sólo en disfrazarse pensó) cubierta de telarañas. Pero esto, ni mucho menos, es una cajita surrealista. Es—semejante al chabacano dibujo de una hamaca pobre—Como la cosa que traduce a una voz en el ocaso. O más: lo que pudiera parecer más complicado: 1, un discurso que serviría para decir el olvido; o 2, lo desdibujado, en la colisión de un tiempo de mediodía de allá, _____ (HAY, EN EL MANUSCRITO, UN ESPACIO BORRADO) cuando _____ (HAY EN EL MANUSCRITO, TAMBIEN UN ESPACIO EN BLANCO), aquel niño que fui, tomaba el jugo de naranja.

No, vano discurso no es vacío

Blando, pasa: ¿sueño de evaporación desde fijo período de destino? Van por el canal las algas, flotando las cajitas desechadas. Como dado, dativo . . . , donde la humedad podría ser . . . ¿cuál rumbo, cuál discurso? Pero en este mocho canal se puede decir nada de lo que . . . , imprudente (no existe, ni existió); como tampoco de esa agua que, sin ninguna duda, nada más—seco—sabido ha ni ha podido, relatar.

Junto al campo de golf

Esos dos viejos golfistas (¿o son tres golfistas, montados en el carrito añil?). En el campo de los antílopes, en esta tarde antediluviana, cuando con los mandados regreso del *Winn Dixie*. Sosa, tan sosa es la banderita amarilla que ahora ya no se la ve. Pudiera saltar, pero necesariamente camino de prisa como si, absurdamente, fuera a bordar las pesquisas—¿qué pesquisas?—de ese camino levantado—¿cuándo levantado?—sobre lo resbaladizo—¿por qué resbaladizo?—de una quincallería plástica. ¡Vaya Novela de Caballería!

Revisando la visión

Por blanca cal de ese muro del Motel. Del Motel la sonrisa sin gato de la luz neón. Con, bajo ese tubo, la evocación del quirófano en la sombrilla playera. Por lo que como suerte—muerte—bastante escaso el rastrilleo de la piscina sin agua, a la vera de la sombrilla. Pasar, repasar. Soñar, soñar. Ese

Manuscript for the Box

For the box. It could be said to be Transparency (like the photo, on the wall of the box, of that poor fellow who had only wanted to disguise himself) covered with spiderwebs. Far from it—this is a surrealist box. It's like— as is the ordinary drawing of a meager hammock, perhaps—the thing that translates a voice at sunset. Or, still more complicated: 1, a speech that would adequately speak oblivion; or 2, something blurred, in the collision of a noon from over there, _____ (IN THE MANUSCRIPT, THERE IS AN ERASURE) when _____ (IN THE MANUSCRIPT, THERE IS A BLANK SPACE), that boy I was, drank the orange juice.

No, Vain Speech Is Not Empty

Softly, it passes: a dream of evaporation from a fixed period of destiny? Through the canal drift the seaweed, the discarded boxes floating. As if given, dative . . . , where humidity could be . . . what direction, what speech? But in this mutilated canal nothing can be said about . . . , imprudent (it doesn't exist nor has it existed); nor about this water which, without any doubt, nothing more—dry—has known how to nor been able to relate.

By the Golf Course

Those two old golfers (or are there three of them on the purple cart?). In the field of antelopes, in this antediluvian evening, when I return after running errands at the Winn-Dixie. Dull, so dull is the little yellow flag that it's now disappeared from sight. I could jump, but I walk quickly as if, absurdly, I were to perform these investigations—what investigations?—on this raised path—when was it raised?—over the slipperiness—why slippery?—of a plastic hardware store. Some Chivalry Novel!

Revising the Vision

Because of the white lime of this Motel wall. Of the Motel, the grin without a cat of the neon light. With, beneath that tube, the evocation of the operating room in the beach umbrella. Whereby like fate—death—rather scant the raking of the waterless swimming pool, at the edge of the umbrella. Going over and back again. Dreaming, dreaming. This moment—sometimes at

momento—a veces en el crepúsculo—petimetre donde para broma de la foto-
grafía del Motel, ritualmente es como si se quemara la mismísima esquina de
una sucia tarjeta postal, supuestamente en blanco.

Caluroso el día

Una zona de explosión zonza: el día que estúpidamente disiente. Sólo com-
ponen, los sucios cartuchos de papel sobre el sofá abandonado en el terreno
baldío, un no-presagio. Es lo hecho, o es lo no-hecho, para no decir más.
Pero es que, también, con la mirada basta para mantenernos. Soy (aunque
no sé lo que esta pueda significar) una mirada.

Un mandala

Como que se encendió en un circo, pues tiene el esplendor falso de una luz
neón. Me muerdo las uñas para ello, situado en la misma diagonal donde el
pasado, por el lado de una madrugada, fracasó. Así que, también, me limpiaré
de cualquier conjuro, pues sólo el viento, ya híbrido, deberá recorrerse.

Carlos Galindo Lena

Qué hacer si he perdido las llaves . . .

• *A Carmen Sotolongo*

Qué hacer si he perdido las llaves y estoy solo.
Por los techos de la noche oigo los pasos de un animal salvaje.
Gimen los árboles bajo el peso de unas formas
que sirven para clasificar los astros.
Afuera es otoño y alguien llora.
Alguien que conoce el peso de su llanto.
Enmudece la habitación en la que antaño ardía una lámpara de vida.
Yo estoy solo.
Las llaves se han perdido.
Y en las manos surge una flor súbita de sangre.
Padre, oh padre mío, diez primaveras han pasado
sin que el mantel fuera quitado de la mesa.

dusk—a dandy where as a play on the photograph of the Motel, ritually he appears to have burned the exact same corner of a dirty postcard, supposedly blank.

Warm Day

A zone of inane explosion: the day that stupidly dissents. The dirty paper cartridges on the abandoned sofa in the vacant lot merely compose a non-omen. It's what's done, or it's what's not been done, say no more. But it's also that our gaze is enough to keep us going. I am (though I don't know what that could mean) a gaze.

A Mandala

As if she lit herself up in a circus, since she has the false splendor of a neon light. I bite my nails for her, located in the same diagonal where the past, through the side of a dawn, failed. And so I shall also cleanse myself of any spell, since only the wind, already hybrid, should travel through.

Translated by Christopher Winks

Carlos Galindo Lena

What to do if I've lost the keys . . .

+ *To Carmen Sotolongo*

What to do if I've lost the keys and I'm alone.
Along the roofs of the night I hear the steps of a wild beast.
The trees groan beneath the weight of shapes
that serve to classify the stars.
Outside it's fall and someone weeps.
Someone who knows the weight of his tears.
The room where a lamp of life once burned falls silent.
I'm alone.
The keys have been lost.
And in my hands a sudden flower of blood spurts forth.
Father, my father, ten springs have passed
and the tablecloth is still in place.

El pan junto a la jarra,
      y el cuchillo junto a las flores de papel.
Nadie osa decapitar esas flores de antaño,
ni el rostro alucinante que se pudre en su marco.
Las cortinas aún conservan la forma de su llanto.
Pero qué hacer ahora, padre, qué hacer,
      si he perdido las llaves y estoy solo.
Todas las puertas se han cerrado definitivamente,
y el carcelero torpe grita de pie junto a los muros:
"El que ha quedado afuera que se pudra."
Es otoño y alguien llora.
El carcelero arroja las llaves al pozo de la noche.

Siempre es bueno recordar a Tebas . . .

Siempre es bueno recordar a Tebas.
Eteocles no supo distinguir nunca entre la rúbrica de un pájaro en el cielo
y la muerte de un héroe.
Señales siempre existen en el polvo de las sandalias del vencido.
Porque hay una sangre que no debe ser derramada a pesar del deseo de los
      dioses:
la sangre del hermano debe correr libre entre la primavera, el tiempo y la
      esperanza.
No era la hora del rencor y fue la hora del rencor y del odio.
No era la hora de dejar insepultos a los muertos
y Antígona vistió a Polinice con los aromas más sutiles de la tierra.
Mas yo, un hombre de su tierra y de su tiempo, no sabe aún dónde está la
      tumba de la madre.
Por las lágrimas de Antígona sabremos dónde está enterrada Polinice,
porque siempre los sensibles mueren en la séptima puerta.
Pero ¿no es acaso esa la puerta del Paraíso?
Oh dioses, decidme: ¿Eteocles o Polinice?
A mí, oh Antígona, un pedazo de mar me separa del último abrazo de la
      madre.
Pero siempre ha sido así para que se cumplan las nuevas y las viejas
      profecías.
En la cruz murió el hombre un día por el furor y el odio de las almas.
Pero decidme: qué emblema, qué sol, qué cielo puede amparar al que se
      entrega con las manos atadas
o con el corazón ebrio de amor.
Polinice retorna para morir en la séptima puerta.

The bread next to the pitcher,
      the knife next to the paper flowers.
No one dares decapitate those flowers of the past,
nor the hallucinatory face rotting in its frame.
The curtain still keeps the shape of its tears
But what to do now, father, what to do,
     if I've lost the keys and I'm alone.
All the doors have been locked for good and all,
and the sluggish jailor screams by the walls:
"He who has stayed outside can rot."
It's fall and someone weeps.
The jailor flings the keys into the well of night.

It's always good to remember Thebes . . .

It's always good to remember Thebes.
Eteocles never knew how to distinguish between the sign of a bird in the
    sky and the death of a hero.
There are always traces in the dust of the sandals of the defeated.
Because there's a blood that should not be spilled despite the desire of the
    gods:
the blood of a brother should run free amid spring, time and hope.
It was not the moment for bitterness and it was the moment for bitterness
    and hatred.
It was not the moment for leaving the dead unburied
and Antigone dressed Polyneices in the subtlest perfumes of the land.
But I, a man of my land and time, still don't know where my mother is
    buried.
By the tears of Antigone we shall know the grave of Polyneices,
because the sensitive always die in the seventh gateway.
Is it not perhaps the gate of Paradise?
O gods, tell me: Eteocles or Polyneices?
As to me, O Antigone, a stretch of sea separates me from my mother's last
    embrace.
But it has always been thus, that the new and old prophecies may be
    fulfilled.
Because of the rage and hatred of souls the man once died on the cross.
But tell me: what emblem, what sun, what sky can shelter he who
    surrenders, hands tied
or heart drunk with love.
Polyneices returns to die in the seventh gateway.

Yo, hermanos míos, muero porque un pedazo de mar me separa
del último abrazo de la madre.
Sabed que sufro cuando el Corifeo entona su canto de piedad
y Antígona toca con sus manos purísimas el sol.
¿Es así como los muertos entierran a sus muertos?

Ayer el mar era una ausencia

Lo que queda,
lo que quedará de estos cuerpos.
Aquí o allá, nunca
reposará.
GUILLEVIC

Hoy he sabido la verdad.
Mi casa estuvo cerrada
todo el tiempo.
Yo alejado y usted más lejano aún
entre sus sueños.
Al regresar, alguien ha dicho:
"le estuvieron esperando ayer
toda la noche",
y me dieron las señas que a usted
le corresponden.
Más tarde, entre el estupor de la noche
y mi cansancio,
he recibido la noticia
que aún arde entre los vagos lirios
de la frente:
"Su alumno Francisco ha muerto
ayer temprano".
Ayer temprano el mar era una ausencia,
era sólo un pretexto de la cansada tierra.
El cielo germinaba sus palomas,
y las nubes
brillaban como una anunciación.
Mas hoy dejo abierta mi casa
al aire de la noche
para que pueda usted entrar.

I, my brothers, am dying because a stretch of sea separates me
from my mother's last embrace.
Know that I suffer when the leader of the chorus intones his pious song
and Antigone touches the sun with her purest hands.
Is it thus that the dead bury the dead?

Yesterday the Sea Was an Absence

What's left,
what will be left of these bodies.
Here or there, it will never
be at rest.
                    GUILLEVIC

Today I have learned the truth.
My house
was locked.
I far off and you still farther
amid your dreams.
When I returned, someone told me:
"they waited for you yesterday
all night long,"
and the description they gave me
sounded like you.
Later, between the torpor of the night
and my exhaustion,
I received the news
that still burns among the vague irises
of my mind:
"Early yesterday
Francisco your student died."
Early yesterday the sea was an absence,
a merest excuse for the tired earth.
The sky sprouted its doves,
and the clouds
shone like an annunciation.
But today I leave my house open
to the night air
that you may enter.

Translated by Michael Smith

Francisco de Oraá

"Yo no sé cómo voy a no sé donde"

Cuando soy uno que anda por la calle
                                    A dónde voy
Cuando estoy en el sueño a tantos metros encima de mi cuerpo
Cuando gasto como el tonto que soy esta ración de tiempo que me dieron
o me esfuerzo separando la noche para sólo palpar una imagen
o hago con una azada huecos en la tierra para que mi deber sea saciado
Cuando estoy solo o cuando río contigo
o cuando me pregunto: ¿Quién querrá
recoger tanto amor sin uso acumulado
guardarlo en su corazón como en una vasija el rumor de la lluvia?
Porque preguntarán: *"¿Qué hiciste del tiempo que te fue dado a consumir?*
Enterraste tu corazón pero ya no se sabe en qué lugar de la noche"
Cavilarán: *"Era su corazón una botija llena de porquería"*
(Pero lo que me dieron fue este amor a las imágenes del mundo)
Y sé que pesarán tiempo y corazón cumplidos preguntando:
"¿Es esto tu única contribución contra la muerte?
¿para qué aprietas en tu corazón esas imágenes de seres
que ya se te están muriendo
que ya la noche está mordiendo suavemente?"
Y juzgarán *"Éste es quien para huir se emborrachaba con el tiempo"*

          A dónde voy dentro de mí
A dónde voy que nadie ve mis pasos

De cómo fue la muerte hallada dentro de una botija

Esta es la historia de quien halló sólo excrementos
buscando no sabía si era el ojo absoluto
en el podrido callejón de la infancia

(todos sabemos ya que ese lugar mental sólo contiene huesos
que amueblaron el tiempo, bombillas negras y
bolsas de pestilencia)

pensó que el tiempo era tal vez una botija llena de verde lluvia
y el poema tal vez una botija ciega bajo las tablas del tiempo
y la herramienta para machacar los astutos ojillos con que la muerte intenta
    penetrarnos

Francisco de Oraá

I Don't Know How I'm Going I Don't Know Where

When I'm someone walking down the street
                                        Where am I going
When I'm dreaming a few feet above my body
When fool that I am, I waste that bit of time I've been given
or I'm trying hard to divide the night just to stroke an image
or digging holes in the earth with a hoe to fulfill my duty
When I'm alone or when I'm laughing with you
or when I ask myself: Who'd want
to gather up all that unused love
and hold it in her heart like a glass holding the sound of rain?
Because they'll ask: *"What did you do with the time you had to spend?*
You've buried your heart but we don't know in what part of the night"
They'll think: *"His heart was a jar full of filth"*
(But they gave me this love for the world's images)
And I know they'll weigh both time and heart completed, asking:
"Is this your only contribution in the face of death?
Why do you clutch to your heart these images of those
already dying
already gnawed at by night?"
And their verdict will be: *"This one escaped by getting drunk on time"*

        I'm going inside myself
I'm going where no one can see my steps

How Death Was Found Inside a Jar

This is the story of someone who only found excrement
while seeking not knowing if it was the absolute eye
in childhood's rotten alley

(We all know by now that this mental place contains nothing but bones
that were time's furniture, black bulbs and
pockets of pestilence)

he thought that maybe time was a jar filled with green rain
and that maybe the poem was a blind jar beneath the boards of time
and the tool for crushing the sly glances with which death tries to enter us

y halló que tú, Poema, no eres ya un hirviente soñadero
ni el ómnibus en que pasamos despiertos en la noche
ni la venduta donde sopesamos las coles pensativas

(Porque el Echador de Suertes dijo: *"Sabido es que da lo mismo poeta que
    viandero"*)

y al destapar los párpados de la botija verde había dentro
sólo un rumor como la noche,
nada más que la muerte que conservaba su frescura
(que la muerte, esa sola botija llena de tiempo y noche)
porque ya tú, Poema, callejón en el tiempo, no eres
esa fresca botija de donde salen los sueños
sino el parque vacío donde me siento bajo la llovizna

En uso de razón

Pues aspiro a habitar
la mirada geométrica que nunca se corrompe
y hay quienes querrán ser desenterrados
como un par de ojos fósiles la próxima semana;

Procuro en tanto convencerme de haber tenido una infancia
y he deseado sucederme por el amor fallido
de cada día;

       Ya que no alcanzo
el amor nuestro de cada día
ni la alegría semestral,
ni sé qué hacer con mi ofensivo rostro;

Quiero hacer
con materia un objeto más
en el mundo
y para ahogar esta miseria
de cada día, busco
tocar como a una piedra el oscuro propósito
de las imágenes;
desde el ahogo de cada día sube
el oscuro calor del poema,

and he discovered that you, Poem, are no longer a boiling alcove
nor the bus we ride while awake at night
nor the shop where we weigh the pensive cabbages

(Because the Drawer of Lots said: "It's known that poet or grocer, it's all
    the same")

and when the green jar's eyelids were opened
inside there was only a sound like night,
merely death preserving its chill
(death, that single jar filled with time and night)
because you, Poem, alley in time, are not
that cold jar from which dreams emerge
but the empty park where I sit in the rain

Of Sound Mind

I aspire to live therefore
in the geometrical gaze that never goes bad
and there are some who'd like to be dug from the earth
like a pair of fossil eyes the week after;

Meanwhile I'm trying to convince myself that I had a childhood
and I've wished for descendants because of the everyday love
that failed;

            Now that I can't attain
our everyday love
or semiannual joy
and I don't know what to do with my offensive face;

I want to contrive
out of matter
one final object
in the world
and drown this everyday misery
I seek
to touch the dark intention
of images as one would a stone;
from the everyday drowning arises
the poem's dark heat,

descubro la demente mirada de las cosas,
y los llameantes animales
¡ya estaban allí!

Ahora quita el agua y pon el sol

Los áridos de corazón
tierra agrietada al resistero
del tiempo
donde las reses viejas como rocas
pacen la muerte

Felices son las bocas que golpeó el aguacero
Las viejas lluvias nos dejaron
lastimosos ojuelos en el corazón
y por ellos la muy delirante imaginaba los recuerdos
donde el tiempo caía jadeando
Nos dejaron oídos oscuros como el sueño
en los que esa chismosa soplaba cuchicheos
y hacía hervir la noche del amor
La crueldad de los parques de cemento
donde los viejos hablan de amor sudando noche
y entre moco y temblor distraen el tedio
de esperar a la muerte conversando
de cómo cae seco el tiempo que no quiere llover!
"Se han cerrado ya las puertas" "No sé
si era el amor esa agua oscura en que me ahogaba"
Pero sólo la sombra del tiempo que nos cubre
Oír los golpecitos de lluvia en el vacío
"Un vientre que necesita hincharse y deshincharse
Un juego con pelotas de carne—y ¿quién lo gana?"
La indiferencia del jardín en que pasea una vieja su espanto
Esa tinaja seca en que se encuevan las arañas polvorientas del tiempo
Ese sitio del corazón en donde llueve sin parar
"Pero ¿esas barriguitas locas merecer que se sufra por ellas?
Espero que la muerte nos salve del ridículo"

(Me vuelvo hacia la noche como el que ve llover)

I discover the demented gaze of things,
and the flaming animals
were there all along.

Now Take Away the Water and Bring the Sun

Those with parched hearts
earth cracked in time's
hot afternoon
where cattle old as rocks
graze their deaths

Happy the mouths that the cloudburst strikes
The old rains
left in our hearts only remnants of springs
and because of them the delirious woman imagined memories
where time panted
They left us ears as dark as the dream
into which that gossip whispered
and set the night of love to boiling
The cruelty of the cement parks
where old people speak of love sweating night
and between snot and trembling ease the boredom
of waiting for death with talk
about how dry the weather is, it doesn't want to rain!
"They've shut the doors" "I don't know
if that dark water in which I drowned was love"
But only the shadow of time that covers us
hearing the droplets of rain in the void
"A belly that needs to inflate and deflate
A game played with balls of meat, and who's the winner?"
The indifference of the garden where an old woman displays her fright
This dry cistern where time's dusty spiders burrow
This region of the heart where it never stops raining
"But are those crazy tummies worthy of what we suffer for them?
I hope death saves us from that silliness"

(Like someone who watches the rain I turn towards the night)

Vida de niño

1

Pasó ya el tiempo del retrato de familia o del sueño a caballo de cartón y de los pasos en el palomar de la noche; pasó ya la locura de recoger bichitos en el rocío o balancearnos como un soplo sobre el mar. —¿Qué hacen tus ojos calladamente intrusos entre mis papeles, borrando el olor a hierbabruja de mi potro, en cuyos ojos vi el agua por la primera vez? La verdad es tu cuerpo, tus ojos el color de la verdad, tu carne es el silencio de las cosas que en soledad meditan. —Ese soy yo tirado entre astros, peso en la noche; mirando a través del agua, recogiendo las plumas del tiempo en el jardín otra vez niño.

2

Hacia desgracias de vidrio iban los serios cagajones del tiempo. ¡Entierros, nadas prodigiosas! A parsimoniosas muertes conducía el nervioso sigilo de la hormiga. A silencios, a vidrios. Axilas nos cubrían—¡ah, vegetales, noches!— de las hediondas ofensas del tiempo, que desde allí veíamos, ciegos forzados a correr!—En otro mundo crecían los miembros del caballo. Continuamente nos despedíamos.

Ahogado en el serón

El mar que tú no has visto es un azul, díjome el loco, que ha devorado todos los azules. El mar que tú no has visto. Imagina que tienes a la noche dentro de tu serón. Imagina un caballo que está ciego. Imagina que el mar es un serón lleno de pensamientos: te mojará una noche que no has visto y quedarás ahogado en el serón.

Sobre las cosas que, si miras bien, ves en el cielo

En el barril donde guardábamos la lluvia está la noche. Pasan la mula (sanctificada por las moscas) y el carretón de la carbonería. Está aquel "coronel" ido a volina, que nunca el chino de la bodega dio "de contra", el chino con arañas y caracoles en el cuerpo que, dormido, empieza a disparar cohetes. Estoy yo, los cometas (esos locos del cielo) y planetas llovidos hasta el fondo del sueño. Pasa, sobre el hollejo de la luna, la goleta demente que huye de sputniks y discos voladores, implorando irse a pique de una vez a la muerte.

A Boy's Life

I

The time's past for the family portrait or the dream of the cardboard horse and the footsteps on night's dovecote; gone the madness of collecting insects in the dew or swinging like a breath above the sea. "What are your eyes doing silently intruding among my papers, erasing the scent of *hierbabruja* from my colt, in whose eyes I saw water for the first time? Your body is truth; your eyes the color of truth; your flesh the silence of things meditating in solitude." "That's me, cast out among stars, a weight in the night, gazing through the water, collecting the feathers of time in the garden, a child once more."

2

Time's sober turds advanced towards glass misfortunes. Burials, prodigious nothings! The ant's nervous stealth ended in stingy deaths. In silences, in shards of glass. Armpits sheltered us—ah! vegetables, nights!—from time's stinking offenses, which, blind men forced to run, we saw from here! "The horse's limbs grew in another world. We were constantly saying good-bye."

Drowned in the Basket

The sea you've never seen is a bluish color. The madman who'd devoured every blue told me. The sea you've never seen. Imagine you've got the night inside your basket. Imagine a blind horse. Imagine the sea's a basket full of thoughts: a night you've never seen will soak you and you'll drown in the basket.

Concerning the Things That, If You Take a Good Look, You'll See in the Sky

Night's in the barrel where we kept the rain. The mule (sanctified by flies) and the coal wagon pass by. There's that "colonel" gone to pot, to whom the Chinese storekeeper never gave anything extra, the Chinaman with spiders and snails on his body who shoots off rockets while he sleeps. I'm here, the comets (the sky's madmen) and planets that rained into the depths of the dream. The demented schooner fleeing sputniks and flying saucers passes over the moon's husk, begging death to sink for once and all.

Dos sueños con un ave

Nos dirige el sueño la hermana mayor: estamos en la iglesia, en el banco que rige la procesión de sus olas—pero el Muerto no está en ninguna parte—, todos los ojos de la familia conocidos, hasta los más jóvenes, recientemente llagados de la noche. De súbito, el pedante *Gallo* vuela hasta posarse en el altar, donde destroza copas, imágenes, estrellas, morados paños para recoger el tiempo, tejidos celestes, alambres, sogas del gran andamio, planchas de dormido o despierto metal y el silencioso espejo para el Muerto, y ahoga las llamas que callaban como ojos arracimados en un árbol.

2

Visitamos a Mim, esposa de uno de los primos, en las afueras, el barrio de aguas de la luna. Después de los saludos nos presenta, enjaulado, un joven gallo rojo—*"¿Sabían que Ramón está conmigo?"*—a cuya forma nos negamos. Ramón, uno de nuestros más ancianos tíos, suegro de Mim, lejano tanto tiempo de nuestra boca, ausente tanto de nuestros sueños, al tiempo preguntado; llevado, aventurero de la miseria, a fabulosas imágenes; desconocido ya, escondido dictando nuestros sueños, que lo aceptamos con naturalidad: Un "gallo". Pero él nunca ha sido tan joven ni tan rojo.

Aventura entre niños

Larga me fue la noche, breve el tiempo de la conversación atada con pigmeos, no comenzada nunca, cortada con frecuencia por sus oblicuos cuchicheos y su ignorancia del idioma. ¡Pero qué gentes! Mi boca no dejaba su estupor y la elasticidad de mis ojos ya al romperse a causa de sus chillonas costumbres y muy graciosas guerras, su comercio de hormiga por las noches, sus labores sólo alcanzables a distancia o sus pacientes miniaturas. ¡Y qué decir de sus libros de palma, murmullo escrito, chusma de los pájaros! De su futuro a rastras y su horizonte contra el suelo. De sus gordas beldades, incapaces de abandonar el lecho, tullidas ya de recibir tal tropa de homenajes. Y de la absurda geometría supuesta por sus maneras del amor: con alegre criterio distinguían al jinete peor, a los guerreros mas delgados, al ya estúpido anciano. Así, de esta aventura, sólo he ganado una obsesión por esa niña abrumada como un barril, con pezones de vaca pero nalguitas de lactante, insuficiente a su hospital de suegras y de ancianos maridos; y el peso de un instrumento de metal, que supongo automático y cuya utilidad aún desconozco.

Two Dreams of a Bird

1

Our older sister directs our dream: we're in the church, on the bench that rules the procession of its waves—but the Dead Man's nowhere to be found—all known eyes of the family, even the youngest, recently scarred by night. Suddenly, the pedantic *Rooster* flies toward the altar and perches, wrecking goblets, images, stars, purple cloths for gathering time, heavenly fabrics, wires, ropes of the great scaffold, grilles of waking or sleeping metal and a silent mirror for the Dead Man, and quenches the flames that were as silent as eyes clustered in a tree.

2

We're visiting Mim, the wife of one of our cousins, at the edge of town in the neighborhood of lunar waters. After the greetings she shows us a young red rooster in a cage—*"Did you know Ramón's with me?"*—whose shape we refuse to recognize. Ramón, one of our oldest uncles, Mim's father-in-law, so long distant from our lips, so absent from our dreams—time's question mark; poverty's adventurer, drawn toward fabulous images; now unknown, hidden, dictating our dreams—that we accept him as he is. A "rooster." But he had never been so young or so red before.

Adventure Among Children

Long was the night for me, and brief that conversation with pygmies, never begun, frequently cut off by their oblique whisperings and their ignorance of the language. Such people! My mouth hung open and the elasticity of my eyes had reached its breaking point because of their strident manner and amusing wars, their bustling nighttime trade, their labors only approachable from a distance, or their patient miniatures. And what to say of their palm books, written murmurings, rabble of birds! Their struggling futures and their low horizons. Their fat beauties, incapable of getting out of bed, crippled by so great a troop of tributes. And the absurd geometry that their ways of loving assumed: with joyous criteria they distinguish the worst rider, the slimmest warriors, the dimwitted elder. And so, from this adventure, I have only gained an obsession for that girl brimming like a barrel, with nipples like a cow's but the buttocks of an unweaned child, insufficient for her hospital of mothers-in-law and ex-husbands; and the weight of a metal instrument that I suppose is automatic and whose use remains a mystery.

Del pescador

Te haces delgado frente al mar,
te alargas de tendones
en la inentrable desnudez que son las aguas,
pero te encoges bajo el tiempo.
Recibes días como escamas, la noche
como el agua donde el tiempo sucede (y no es posible
decir más de la noche
ni pensar nada del mar que es el vacío del tiempo;
sólo es dable
sentir del tiempo que es una piel que espía aparte).

Siento tu delgado esfuerzo de pez
entrando tiempo como aguas, a echar redes
al tiempo. Pero te secas
en tantas aguas y recibes
la humedad de la muerte
en tanta noche. Quedas seco
pero la copa de tus ojos
es suficiente oído al silencio del mar.

Miras con el silencio de quien tan dulcemente amansa al tiempo
como animal humilde, lo olvida
como un ojo bajo el mar; esperas
con la transparencia que te dio la soledad,
y entras el agua con la lentitud que te cedió el silencio,
pero rompes el tiempo con la desnuda voluntad
de quien ha sido siempre suelto
en el tiempo, despierto entre aguas—como el viento
(el campesino le aprendió los pies al árbol, y eres
huesos del árbol que piensa con estrellas:
no te duermes en tanto azul,
rechazas noche).

Aun con la ciega desnudez del tiempo,
con pobreza de algas y suciedad de mar nocturno,
con los vacíos del que absorbe toda la luz
(y así como el mar los huesos podridos en que duermes)
enjoyas la ceguera de las calles, mojas
el oscuro resentimiento de la ciudad,

Of the Fisherman

You make yourself slender by the sea
your tendons lengthen
in the unenterable nakedness of the waters,
but you shrink beneath time.
You receive days like scales, night
like water where time happens (and there's nothing more
to say about night
or to think about the sea, time's emptiness,
only to feel
that time is a skin observing from afar).

I feel your slender effort like a fish
entering time like the waters, casting nets
toward time. But you dry yourself
in so many waters and receive
the moisture of death
in so much night. You stay dry
but the goblet of your eyes
is enough to hear the silence of the sea.

You gaze with the silence of someone who tames time gently
like a humble animal, forgets it
like an eye beneath the sea, you wait
with the transparency that solitude afforded you,
and enter the water with the slowness silence yielded,
but you shatter time with the naked will
of one who's always been set loose
in time, awake amid waters—like the wind
(the peasant learned about his feet from the tree, and you are
bones of the tree that thinks of stars:
you do not sleep in so much blue,
you reject night).

Even with time's blind nakedness,
with the poverty of seaweed and the filth of a nocturnal sea
with the voids absorbing all the light
(and the sea like the rotten bones in which you sleep)
you bedeck the streets' blindness, moisten
the city's dark bitterness,

con silenciosa luz atruenas
la estupidez de las aceras,
con sartas de absortas llamas, esqueletos
en que se olvida el mar, las agrias joyas
que los ojos del tiempo olvidaron,
las duras luces, las aguas preciosas
que rechazó la noche,
ya tan naturalmente amigas de tus harapos,
de tu opaca sequedad.

De tres fotos de Mella

En casa había una foto de Mella en la pared
como en otras las caras estiradas de los santos.
Entonces yo era un niño tirado en el jardín.
Algo me fascinaba: yo sentía una suave extrañeza al contemplar
aquel perfil voluntarioso
saliéndose de sí, hacia el futuro que comienza en su piel,
de una agresiva seriedad,
quizás hosco, huidizo, displicente para mí
como un árbol reconcentrado en su dureza,
su orgulloso tendón al estallar.

Años después un compañero me dedicó una foto en la que Mella se veía de
    frente
pero en el entrecejo de padre que regaña me parecía oír a Mella
    oscuramente preguntándome:
"¿Qué haces del mundo? ¿Qué haces con tu vida?"
Yo respondí según mi extraño ser lo permitió
—extraño siempre para los demás y ajeno a mi deseo,
de modo que no fui como yo quise
ni viví como quise haber vivido.
Sólo sé que, en el fondo, siempre hubiera querido estar echado en el jardín,
que el jardín se extendiera hasta ser todo el mundo.

¿Habría bastado estar consciente de que jamás podría ponerme ese
    sombrero alón
que usa Mella en la tercera foto, que conocí de los periódicos,
el sombrero del hombre jadeante bajo el sol,
que disminuye el cielo a la cabeza del jinete

with silent light you deafen
the stupidity of sidewalks,
with strings of captivated flames, skeletons
in which the sea is forgotten, the sour jewels
that time's eyes forgot,
the harsh lights, the precious waters
that night rejected,
friends frankly now of your rags,
your opaque dryness.

On Three Photos of Mella

In our home a photo of Mella hung on the wall
as in other homes there hung the gaunt faces of saints.
Back then I was a child lying down in the garden.
It was hypnotic. A gentle astonishment overcame me when I contemplated
that resolute profile
sallying forth, towards the future that began within him,
aggressively serious,
to me perhaps surly, elusive, disdainful
like a tree focused on its own hardness,
his proud sinews strained to bursting.

Years later a comrade inscribed for me a picture of Mella seen from the
    front
but in his reproachful father's brow I seemed to hear Mella's questions:
"What are you doing in the world? What are you doing with your life?"
I answered as my strange self allowed
—strange always to others and alien to my desire,
so that I wasn't what I wanted to be
and I didn't live the way I wished.
I only know that, deep down, I would have wanted to be let loose in the
    garden,
and that the garden would grow and become the whole world.

Would it have been enough to realize that I could never wear the broad-
    brimmed hat
that Mella wears in the third photo, which I first saw in the newspapers,
the hat of the man panting beneath the sun,
which reduces the sky to the rider's head

y es techo fresco del guerrero?
Quizás mi parte fuera sólo estar enamorado de un jardín
creer que mientras tanto esas imágenes de un jardín invertido en el cielo
  aliviarían la desgracia del mundo
y que el mundo echaría a caminar hacia el jardín.

Ahora a veces me avergüenzo de mis cincuenta años,
de tanta vida que perdí.
Pero Mella, que sigue siendo tan joven . . .

11 ENERO 80

Roberto Branly

Atardecer sobre San Anastasio

I

Y allí, lejano, violado, polvoriento,
sobre el herrumbroso paradero, el cielo
se nos encandila, se nos cierra
como flor en celo, entre la música
del tendido eléctrico,
dispersa y grave, encimada tal vez
al templo protestante
donde por descuido te sumergen
en la nada de un bautismo,
y te perforan los ultramontanos,
pero en la farmacia,
en la bodega azul, en la caficola
juegas por un centavo
a ser plateado tomeguín con el refresco,
mientras por el quicio ruedan los faroles,
la calle ondula de adoquines a mansalva,
los negritos corren a los escondidos,
cuentas hasta 40 con Alí Babá,
navegas con la telegrafía sin hilos,
y, al naciente,
alrededor del Pastrana,
surgen las emanaciones bajo el puente
Victoria,

and becomes a cool roof for the warrior?
Perhaps my role was just to be in love with a garden
to believe that meanwhile these images of an inverted garden in the sky
    would relieve the world's misfortune
and that the world would beat a path to the garden.

Now sometimes I am ashamed of my fifty years,
of all that life I lost.
Mella, on the other hand, is still so young . . .

JANUARY 1, 1980

Translated by Christopher Winks

Roberto Branly

Evening Falls on San Anastasio

I

And there, in the distance, desecrated, dust covered,
above the rusty bus stop, we're lit
by the sky, and we close, like careful,
serious flowers, scattered
between the serious, low hum
of power lines, or maybe above the
protestant church where if you're not careful
they'll submerge you in the nothingness
of baptism, your papal convictions
punctured; but at the drug store,
the blue grocery, the candy store, you sip at your penny soda,
pretending to be a wren, while outside the window
lanterns are circling, the street a wave
of loose cobbles, black kids running to hide themselves
while you count to 40 thieves with Ali Baba,
the wireless telegraph guides you, and to the east
around Pastrana the stench erupts
beneath Victoria Bridge,

y el parque, yo no sé por qué,
aún no ha sido inaugurado;
pero, por favor:
que ahora me disfrazo de policía,
y corro delante, veloz, de los ladrones.

2

Sin embargo, estoy solo como siempre,
y el *borinquendeque* canta cuando espera
por la noviecita rubia, retratada
con su traje de banderas en la escuela,
el besito debajo de la lluvia,
la mano contra mano en el paraguas,
y el rojo emblema del *tin* de pelota:
el Paquetero ignora la aritmética,
pero lleva a cabo todos los promedios,
toca el cencerro, muerde las claves,
el otro que recita en las esquinas
—recluta, poeta, guiterista y tranviario—,
conversa con el guitarrero, músico menor,
del conjunto Los Asesinos del Ritmo,
y aquél otro, en su parafernalia,
seminarista, rosacruz, esqueleteado
repunta el tema de la filosofía,
de los deportes, las mujeres y la Vida:
Ah, un tango, por favor, que ya no tengo
con qué condimentar el diálogo,
con qué salpicar estas papitas
que se duelen en el cubilete, en la cerveza,
o, más allá, en la quimbumbia, el coyme,
la mesa verde del billar, en el tapete
entretanto, y hablar como si uno fuera inteligente,
y pasar por comemierda, por alucinado,
por el loco mataperro de las majaderías.

3

Pero, por dentro, es Navidad, y es verde.
Como los muebles, veteados de la infancia,
la luz en sus raudales como nunca,
por la claraboya, las lucetas desoladas,
te despiertan y ya no existen los reyes,

and the park (I don't know why—it isn't
there yet)—but wait,
I'm playing at being a cop now, and I run
so fast I've passed the robbers.

2

But as always I'm alone,
and the nondescript puerto rican sings as he waits
for his blond cutie, dressed for a picture
in her school uniform,
a kiss in the rain,
their hands touching beneath the umbrella,
the red insignia of his baseball team:
the bullshit artist knows no math,
but he's on top of the stats,
he strikes the cowbell, attacks the *clave*
and another, a street-corner orator—
conscript, poet, Guiterista and syndicalist—
chats with the guitar maker, a musician of sorts,
a member of the band called The Rhythm Killers,
and still another, in his getup,
a seminarian, a Rosicrucian, as thin as bones,
turns the talk back to philosophy,
sports, women, Life:
Ah, a tango, please, because I have
no smart answers for this conversation,
nothing to salt these chips
that suffer in the dice cup, this beer,
or, over there, tip cat, the pool hall bouncer,
the green baize of the pool table,
trying to pass for a smartie
but coming off as a jerk, a dreamer,
a pain in the ass.

3

But, actually, it's Christmas, and it's green.
Like the furniture, veined with childhood,
light pours through the skylight
as never before, its desolate rays
wake you and the Three Kings no longer exist,

y Santiclós se fue de picardía;
pierdes el Edén, con la pregunta,
el arbolito está lleno de semillas,
y del nacimiento sólo queda el aserrín.
No: no es verdad. Sí: en el espejo
en declive, la consola timbrea
ante el níquel gastado del teléfono,
con sus tubos plateados de palabras,
chapisteado de victrolas de cuerda
y manigueta,
con la voz en contracampo
de la Mayendía, y un tenor deslustrado
por la nieve.
Antes, fue la cena familiar, como se sabe.
Todos—casi todos—ya cadáveres.
¿Dónde el rioja, el alicante,
las castañas fogueadas de las yemas,
o, en la periferia, el frijol como azabache,
los charoles barnizados del lechón,
el rabanito simple y rojo?
Vamos, vamos. A la mesa los comensales.
Y quizás el gallo en su *ochichornia*.

4

Hablo ahora del cigarro a hurtadillas,
de la cáscara del humo, el bastidor
añejo, el pomo de las cerraduras
y el jazmín.
El jazmín: aparte. En el patio,
lo perfuma el columpio aquél tan triste,
la carriola perdida entre la bruma,
o el perrazo aquel manchado,
con el péndulo del rabo: Danesa
le decían, y el verde siempre, siempre,
que preside, otorga y sueña
en el polvo dorado, su luz piramidal,
en las habitaciones.
Recordemos, además, las peinetas,
el tocador, las fotos patitiesas de la sala,
y el surtidor de nubeazul, nostalgia
de las enredaderas. Por de pronto,
el árbol en la acera abre su abanico,

and Santa has become a joke;
ask the question and you lose Eden,
the tree's full of seeds,
and all that's left of the crèche is sawdust.
No: it can't be true. Yes: reflected in the tarnished
mirror, the telephone box appears to ring
in front of its own spent nickel,
its tubes caked with words,
slapped together like the horns of wind-up
victrolas
that cut between the voices of la Mayendía and a tenor
heard through the scratches.
The family feast was earlier, of course.
All of them—almost all—dead now.
Where are the rioja and the alicante,
the *yema*'s roast chestnuts,
or, on the side, the black beans,
the burnished crackling skin of the pig,
and the plain red radish?
Come on. Come on. Everyone to the table.
Even the rooster with its soppy song.

4

Now I'll tell you about the secret cigarette,
the shell of smoke, the old
bedstead, doorknobs
and jasmine.
Jasmine. It perfumes the sad swing
in the yard, the scooter lost in fog,
the big spotted dog with its tail hanging—Dane,
they called it—and always the green, always,
that grants and presides and dreams
in the golden dust, its light a pyramid,
filling the bedrooms.
And now let's remember the combs,
the vanity, the rigid photographs in the living room
and the cloudblue fountain, a nostalgia
of vines. For the moment
the tree on the sidewalk opens its fan,

la imagen de Bolívar con la espada,
el búcaro color naranja que se fija
bajo un rosal de papel de celofán.
El celofán despierta, bajo la lámpara,
sobre la mesa del centro, ya sabemos,
siempre verde. Y la luz sobre la puerta,
donde las ventanas entornadas, a cal y canto,
el tiempo detienen entre sus postigos.

5

He pronunciado el tiempo y sus constelaciones,
en medio de la puerta, y en la ferretería
las guirnaldas proclaman estas pascuas,
esta alegría de sinsonte,
y ya sobre Reyes, excavada en la erosión
de Pocitos, cerrada por Dolores y Lacret,
digo: entre Concepción y San Francisco,
a cuatro cuadras, simplemente,
de la Calzada, ruedan los tranvías
con sus chispas, los ómnibus repletos
de fotutos, y este delirio tremendo
de estar sobrio,
mientras quedo, tranquilo, presentido,
el sol se hunde por Acosta,
frente a los relámpagos de vidrio
de la Loma del Burro, como un domo,
como un lirio de cometas y chiringas,
allá en la zona perdida, rescatada,
endeble, pálida, de este anochecer
de soledad en vilo.

27–XII–65

Pablo Armando Fernández

Nacimiento de Eggo

Cuentan las bocas muertas que el hombre
vino entre dos luces.

the picture of Bolívar with his sword,
the orange vase beneath a cellophane rosebush.
The cellophane stirs beneath the lamp,
hanging above the table, always green,
as we've come to know. And light comes through
the open windows above the door,
sealed shut,
detaining time between their shutters.

5

I've announced the time and its constellations
in doorway and hardware store,
where garlands proclaim this christmas,
this happiness of songbirds,
and already on Reyes, a great hole
where Pocitos has eroded, closed off by Dolores and Lacret,
there, between Concepción and San Francisco,
four blocks from the avenue, the rumbling trolleys
with their sparks, buses blaring their claxons,
and this tremendous sober
delirium,
while I stay calm and the sun,
as predicted, sinks over Acosta,
igniting flashes of light from the windows
of the dome of Burro Hill,
like an iris of kites, fancy and plain,
in that lost, recovered,
fragile, pallid zone of this evening
of suspended solitude.

DECEMBER 27, 1965

Translated by Todd Ramón Ochoa

Pablo Armando Fernández

Birth of Eggo

The dead mouths say that man
happened between two lights.

La barca era su cuerpo y sus brazos dos poderosos remos.
Solo, en un estrecho de aguas violentas,
el hombre era una luz, dicen los muertos:
antes de la pasada historia, mucho antes
del tiempo porvenir.
Cuentan que iba hacia el monte.
Iba mirando hacia su frente, mirando sus espaldas
y al perfil que para siempre dibujaron
sus manos poderosas. Iba solo,
y era el cristal, el oro que fluía desde su barca,
el torso de todo lo creado,
hasta la hora de su consumación.
En las riberas, borrosa la espesura,
ceniza o carroña humeante; ruinas.
Y el monte, el hombre mismo, dice la historia
de las bocas muertas, nacía sobre las aguas.
Cuando llegó al centro de sí mismo, ya no era un hombre,
era al árbol mayor, sus ramas, múltiples remos,
su tallo, tantas barcas de fortaleza idéntica
y juntos una flor redonda de oro.
Frente a él vió, a sus flancos y espalda
multiplicarse el monte hasta un número exacto,
dividido en fragmentos iguales,
enteros unos y otros, siempre el mismo
que vino entre las aguas y dos luces.

Rendición de Eshu

Avisa a Osain que los hombres vienen,
mientras mi muerte alista,
yerba de mis pesares, alúmamba,
que lo ve todo, desde el lecho del río.
Acompañen de sones
la llegada del dueño único del monte.
Avisa a los Ibeyi, que su cabeza
ya entra en las regiones áureas,
sus bellos ojos más bellos que la lumbre mayor,
y su oloroso aliento, más transparente
que el aire que corona el monte,
dile, flor de mis males,
que ha regresado en victoriosa barca,

His body was a boat and his arms two powerful oars.
Alone, in a channel of violent waters,
man was a light, the dead are saying:
before past history and much before
time yet to come.
They say he went towards the wilderness.
He went, looking forwards and backwards,
and at the profile his hands were etching
forever. He went alone, became
crystal and gold flowing out of his boat,
the trunk of everything created
until his consummation.
Along the shores, thickness of sediment,
ash, steaming carrion; ruins.
And the wilderness, man himself, says history
through these dead mouths, was born upon the waters.
When he reached the center of himself, he did not find a man—
he was the eldest tree, its branches, a fan of oars,
its shoot, so many boats straining together,
a whorl of gold.
Before him he saw, and at his sides and shoulders,
the wilderness multiplying to an exact number,
divided into equal fractions,
complete each one, ever the same,
coming between the waters and two shafts of light.

Surrender of Eshu

Let Osain know that men are coming,
while my death is being prepared,
herb of my sorrows, *alúmamba,*
that sees all from the bed of the river.
Play *sones*
for the arrival of the only lord of the bush.
Tell the Ibeyi that their head now
enters the golden regions,
his beautiful eyes more beautiful than the primal fire,
and his sweet-smelling breath, clearer than air
crowning the bush;
say, flower of my sufferings,
that he has returned in the boat of victory,

él, monte de aguas.
Avisa a Oggún,
que cae mi fortaleza,
entre armas y banderas.
Avisa a Obatalá, que las cadenas
contra las que los dioses no pudieron,
esclavas a su paso se rendían; avisa
a Elegguá
que ni sus llaves ni sus guardias
están seguras.
Acompañen de sones, gentes de Ocha
la llegada del dueño único del monte
mientras mi muerte alista.

de Suite para Maruja

I

La primavera, dices, y escojo madreselvas,
geranios y begonias.
A casa vuelves con los pies mojados,
la falda llena de guizazos ásperos.
Verbenas sin olor en los cabellos
y, entre las manos, romerillo y malvas.

Dices, el aire, y cierro las ventanas,
busco el sillón más próximo a la esquina
donde libros y lámparas me esperan.
Y el aire es la mañana del sol, blanca,
la loca expedición de las hormigas,
pájaros y caguayos de astuta, fina lengua.
Tu canto, por el patio, saliendo del brocal,
los baldes y las piedras.

El sol, dices tranquila, y presuroso escalo
los templos más antiguos. Arenales recorro.
Duermo a la sombra ámbar de un dátil.
Y el sol es la ventana limpia donde te acodas,

he, the tower of waters.
Let Oggún know
that my battlements fall
among weapons and banners.
Tell Obatalá those chains
the gods were powerless against
surrendered to him,
tell Elegguá
nor keys nor sentinels
can be considered safe.
With *sones* celebrate, people of Ocha,
the arrival of the only lord of the bush—
while my death is being prepared.

Translated by Nathaniel Tarn

from Suite for Maruja

I

"Spring," you say, and I harvest honeysuckle
geraniums and begonias.
You reenter the house on damp feet,
your skirt full of coarse weeds,
odorless verbena in your hair
and in your hands rosemary and hollyhock.

"The breeze," you say, and I close the windows,
search out the armchair nearest the corner
where books and lamplight await me.
And the breeze is the sun's white morning,
the crazy expeditions of ants,
birds and turtles with fine, skillful tongues.
Your song, in the yard, emerging
from the well's mouth
and its buckets and stones.

"The sun," you pronounce, and as fast as I can I scale
the oldest temples. I pass through quicksand, I sleep
in the amber shade of a date-palm.
And the sun is the clean window you rest against,

sueltos, la blusa y el cabello,
y es el camino al mar los viernes de la Pascua;
recoger gajos santos que ahuyentan los ciclones;
café que huele a cuaba ardiendo, y sabe a madrugar
de plátanos, anones y ciruelas.
Sin mis brazos ciñendo tu cintura,
sin que lo sepa yo.

Y cuando dices, es la noche, sueño
con países que anduve,
a los que vuelven mis pisadas,
lentas y oscuras, para recobrarte.
Pero la noche no es lo que me pone
el corazón a repartirse en tiempos
que fueron míos, pues la noche es tu voz
conversadora, tu voz que quiere ser
una palabra sola.

    NOV. 3, 1966

II

Cuando anochece, espero
confiarte de una vez todo el espanto
que hay de día en mi pecho.
No es obsesivo gusto por la vida
plena del dios sin tiempo,
ni es el miedo a perder
el poder y la magia del poeta:
miedo a la muerte y al olvido.
Lo que me pone el corazón pequeño,
cuando anochece y estoy contigo, a solas,
es oírme las dóciles palabras
que te ocultan que miento,
cuando te digo: aún no tengo miedo.

    1966

III

Casi siempre, y solos,
en el portal hablamos, claro, los dos,

hair loose and blouse undone,
and it's the path to the sea on Easter Fridays
to gather holy boughs that banish storms,
coffee that smells of burning rue and tastes of morning
bananas, plums and *anones.*
And my arms encircle your waist
without my knowing.

And when you say "It's nighttime," I dream
of landscapes I've walked through
where my path, slow and dark, turns
always towards you.
But it's not the night that divides my heart
between times that were mine, because the night
is your voice
that wants to become
one single word.

    NOV. 3, 1966

II

When night begins to fall I wait
for the moment to confide in you the terror
that I've held in my breast all day.
It's not an obsessive taste for a life
filled with a timeless god,
nor the fear of losing
the power and magic given to poets—
fear of death and oblivion.
What makes my heart shrink
as night begins to fall and I'm alone with you
is to hear the docile words
with which I hide from you that I lie
when I tell you I'm still without fear.

    1966

III

Almost always, and alone, the two of us,
we speak at the doorway

(o en la cocina, que es igual)
de los amigos; sus nombres son palabras
que yo elijo, como quien gusta
de una flor o de un fruto, una joya remota
que tú guardas, amor.
Tú misterio inacabable,
que juntas, hora a hora, mi ser
disperso entre recuerdos que no hemos compartido
Nombres inalcanzables que el niño rememora
en una adolescencia fugaz.
Me desconcierta haberlos olvidado.
Nombres presentes, míos de hoy, huyendo
ruidosos, en silencio,
a nuestra soledad.
¡Nuestra!
Yo me duelo, ¿sabes?: los días nos corroen.
¿A quién hablar? ¿A quién, el corazón,
darle de par en par?
Sufro, hasta que tú remansas mis sospechas
contándome una historia:
de niños malos que resultan buenos,
y niños buenos que la historia infama.

1968

Roberto Fernández Retamar

Un hombre y una mujer

¿Quién ha de ser?
Un hombre y una mujer.
TIRSO

Si un hombre y una mujer atraviesan calles que nadie ve sino ellos,
Calles populares que van a dar al atardecer, al aire,
Con un fondo de paisaje nuevo y antiguo más parecido a una música que a
    un paisaje;
Si un hombre y una mujer hacen salir árboles a su paso,
Y dejan encendidas las paredes,

(or in the kitchen, which is much the same)
of friends; their names words
that I choose as one who desires
a flower or a fruit, a distant jewel
love, that you protect.
You, endless mystery,
that you can bring together, at any hour, my being,
scattered as it is among memories that we haven't shared.
Lost names that the child remembers
in the moment of his adolescence.
I am disconcerted to have lost them.
Current names, those I have now, fleeing noisily
or in silence
to our solitude.
Ours alone!
Did you know that it grieves me? The days eat away at us.
To whom can I speak, to whom
can I open my heart?
I suffer, until you calm my apprehension
by telling me the story
of bad boys who turn out well
and good boys damned by history.

1968

Translated by Mark Weiss

Roberto Fernández Retamar

A Man and a Woman

Who must there be?
A man and a woman.
TIRSO

If a man and a woman happen down streets that no one else notices,
Back streets where night is about to fall and the wind is rising,
The landscape beyond, both new and old, more like music than landscape;
If a man and a woman cause trees to spring up at their step,
And walls to burst into flame,

Y hacen volver las caras como atraídas por un toque de trompeta
O por un desfile multicolor de saltimbanquis;
Si cuando un hombre y una mujer atraviesan se detiene la conversación del
   barrio,
Se refrenan los sillones sobre la acera, caen los llaveros de las esquinas,
Las respiraciones fatigadas se hacen suspiros:
¿Es que el amor cruza tan pocas veces que verlo es motivo
De extrañeza, de sobresalto, de asombro, de nostalgia,
Como oír hablar un idioma que acaso alguna vez se ha sabido
Y del que apenas quedan en las bocas
Murmullos y ruinas de murmullos?

Felices los normales

   ◆ *a Antonia Eiriz*

Felices los normales, esos seres extraños.
Los que no tuvieron una madre loca, un padre borracho, un hijo
   delincuente,
Una casa en ninguna parte, una enfermedad desconocida,
Los que no han sido calcinados por un amor devorante,
Los que vivieron los diecisiete rostros de la sonrisa y un poco más,
Los llenos de zapatos, los arcángeles con sombreros,
Los satisfechos, los gordos, los lindos,
Los rintintín y sus secuaces, los que cómo no, por aquí,
Los que ganan, los que son queridos hasta la empuñadura,
Los flautistas acompañados por ratones,
Los vendedores y sus compradores,
Los caballeros ligeramente sobrehumanos,
Los hombres vestidos de truenos y las mujeres de relámpagos,
Los delicados, los sensatos, los finos,
Los amables, los dulces, los comestibles y los bebestibles.
Felices las aves, el estiércol, las piedras.

Pero que den paso a los que hacen los mundos y los sueños,
Las ilusiones, las sinfonías, las palabras que nos desbaratan
Y nos construyen, los más locos que sus madres, los más borrachos
Que sus padres y más delincuentes que sus hijos
Y más devorados por amores calcinantes.
Que les dejen su sitio en el infierno, y basta.

And make heads turn as if surprised by the sudden blast of a trumpet
Or the gaudy colors of a circus parade;
If when a man and a woman approach the neighborhood chatter falls
    silent,
The sidewalk rocking chairs cease their rocking, corner keychains no
    longer swing,
And tired breath becomes a sigh:
Is it because love so rarely passes by that to see it
Brings wonder, shock, astonishment, nostalgia,
As if one heard a language perhaps once known
Which the tongue scarcely remembers
Except as whispers and the remains of whispers?

Blessèd Are the Normal

    ◆ *for Antonia Eiriz*

Blessèd are the normal, those rare creatures
Who have no crazy mother, drunken father, delinquent child,
Nowhere house, unknown disease,
Who haven't been burnt by devouring love,
Who could live the seventeen faces of the smile and maybe more,
Filled with shoes, archangels in hats,
Satisfied, fat, handsome,
The rintintins and their followers, the ones who grease the wheels,
The winners, the endlessly desired,
Flute players followed by mice,
Vendors and their customers
Knights only slightly superhuman
Men dressed in thunder and women in lightning
The delicate, the prudent, the cunning,
The amiable, the sweet, the edible, the drinkable.
Blessèd are the birds, the dung, the stones.

But let those pass who make worlds, dreams,
Illusions, symphonies, words that confuse
And construct us, those crazier than their mothers, drunker
Than their fathers more delinquent than their children
And more devoured by burning love.
May they descend to their station in hell, and be done with.

Translated by Mark Weiss

Le preguntaron por los persas

• A la imaginación del pintor Matta y, desde luego, a Darío

Su territorio dicen que es enorme, con mares por muchos sitios, desiertos, grandes lagos, el oro y el trigo.

Sus hombres, numerosos, con manchas monótonas y abundantes que se extienden sobre la tierra con mirada de vidrio y ropajes chillones.

Pesan como un fardo sobre la salpicadura de nuestras poblaciones pintorescas y vivaces,

Echadas junto al mar: junto al mar rememorando un pasado en que hablaban con los dioses y les veían las túnicas y las barbas olorosas a ambrosía.

Los persas son potentes y grandes; cuando ellos se estremecen, hay un hondo temblor, un temblor que recorre las vértebras del mundo.

Llevan por todas partes sus carros ruidosos y nuevos, sus tropas intercambiables, sus barcos atestados cuyos velámenes hemos visto en el horizonte.

Arrancan pueblos enteros como si fueran árboles, o los desmigajan con los dedos de una mano, mientras con la otra hacen señas de que prosiga el festín;

O compran hombres nuestros, hombres que eran libres, y los hacen sus siervos, aunque puedan marchar por calles extrañas y adquirir un palacio, vinos y adolescentes:

Porque ¿qué puede ser sino siervo el que ofrece su idioma fragante, y los gestos que sus padres preservaron para él en las entrañas, al bárbaro graznador, como quien entrega el cuello, el flanco de la caricia a un grasiento mercader?

Y nosotros aquí, bajo la luz inteligente hasta el dolor de este cielo en que lo exacto se hace azul y la música de las islas lo envuelve todo;

Frente al mar de olas repetidas que alarmado nos trae noticias de barcos sucios:

Mirando el horizonte alguna vez, pero sobre todo mirando la tierra dura y arbolada, enteramente nuestra,

Being Asked About the Persians

• *To the imagination of the painter Matta and of course to Darío*

It is said that their territory is immense, with seas in many places, deserts, extensive lakes, gold and wheat.

Their numerous people are abundant stains spread monotonously over the earth, with glassy looks and gaudy clothes.

They weigh like a burden on our spattered populations, picturesque and vivacious,

Settled close to the sea: close to the sea remembering a past in which they used to speak with the gods and see their tunics and their beards smelling of ambrosia.

The Persians are powerful and great: when they shake themselves, there is a deep earthquake, an earthquake that runs along the world's spine.

They run all over the place with their brash and noisy chariots, their interchangeable troops, their loaded ships whose rigging we have seen on the horizon.

They wrench whole peoples out as if they were trees, or crumble them in the fingers of one hand, while with the other they make signs that the banquet should continue;

Or they buy men, men who were once free, and make of them slaves, so that they can walk these foreign streets and acquire a palace, or wines, or adolescents:

What for? Who can be anything but a slave who offers his fragrant dialect and the gestures his forefathers kept for him in their entrails to the barbarous croaker; who brings his neck and his sides to the caress of a fat merchant?

And we, here, under the intelligent light as far as the suffering sky in which precision has transformed itself into blue, the island music enveloping everything;

Facing the sea, wave upon wave, afraid of the news it brings of unclean ships;

Looking at the horizon from time to time, but above all at our land, hard and covered with trees, entirely our own,

Aprendiendo unos de otros en la conversación de la plaza pública el lujo necesario de la verdad que salta del diálogo,

Y conocedores de que las cosas todas tienen un orden, y ha sido dado al hombre el privilegio de descubrirlo y exponerlo por la sorprendente palabra,

Conocedores, porque nos lo han enseñado con sus vidas los hombres más altos, de que existen la justicia y el honor, la bondad y la belleza, de los cuales somos a la vez esclavos y custodios,

Sabemos que no sólo nosotros, estos pocos rodeados de un agua enorme y una gloria aún más enorme,

Sino tantos millones de hombres, no hablaremos ese idioma que no es el nuestro, que no puede ser el nuestro.

Y escribimos nuestra protesta—¡oh padre del idioma!—en las alas de las grandes aves que un día dieron cuerpo a Zeus,

Pero además y sobre todo en el bosque de las armas y en la decisión profunda de quedar siempre en esta tierra en que nacimos:

O para contar con nuestra propia boca, de aquí a muchos años, cómo el frágil hombre que venció al león y a la serpiente, y construyó ciudades y cantos, pudo vencer también las fuerzas de criaturas codiciosas y torpes,

O para que otros cuenten, sobre nuestra huesa convertida en cimiento, cómo aquellos antecesores que gustaban de la risa y el baile, hicieron buenas sus palabras y preservaron con su pecho la flor de la vida.

A fin de que los dioses se fijen bien en nosotros, voy a derramar vino y a colocar manjares preciosos en el campo: por ejemplo, frente a la isla de Salamina.

Fayad Jamís

A veces

A veces, en el silencio del pasillo, algo salta,
rompe alguien algún viejo nombre.

Learning one from the other in marketplace conversation the necessary luxury of truth which leaps out of dialogue,

Knowing that all things are held within an order and that man has been granted the privilege of discovering it and expounding it in his surprising speech.

Knowing, for the greatest men have taught us with their lives, that justice and honor do exist, beauty and goodness too, of which we are both the slaves and the custodians,

That not we alone, we few surrounded by this immense body of water and a renown even greater,

But several millions of men shall not speak this tongue which is not ours, which can never be ours.

And we can write down our protest—oh father of language!—in the wings of the great birds which once gave body to Zeus,

But on top of that, and above all, in the forest of weapons, and our fathomless decision to remain always in this land in which we were born:

Or to tell with our own mouths, from now on and for many years, how the fragile being who conquered the lion and the serpent, and built cities and songs, could also beat down the forces of covetous and infamous creatures,

Or so that others tell, over our bones converted into cement, how those ancestors who loved laughing and dancing, made good their word and safeguarded with their own bodies the flower of life.

So that the gods settle themselves among us, trusting us, I am going to pour libations and set out precious foods on the fields—for instance on those that face the isle of Salamis.

Translated by Nathaniel Tarn

Fayad Jamís

Sometimes

Sometimes, in the silence of the hallway, something jumps,
someone smashes some old name.

La mosca enloquecida cruza zumbando, ardiendo,
lejos de la telaraña luminosa.
Esto es así, tan solo, pero tan lleno de sorpresas.
Caserón de fantasmas sin hijos, en que el polvo
hace nuevas ventanas, nuevos muebles y danzas.
No, tú no lo conoces, tú no me has visto mucho las pupilas
y por eso te llenas de lágrimas. Escúchame:
mi casa no se fuga; está lejos siempre.
Por estas escaleras se sube hasta lo negro.
Uno no se cansa de subirlas y jadeando se duerme
sin saber ni los días, ni la fiebre, ni el ruido inmenso
de la ciudad que hierve al fondo.
A veces, en el silencio del pasillo, alguien nace de pronto,
alguien que toca en la puerta sin número y que llama.
No, tú no has estado aquí jamás. No, tú no vengas.
Mi palabra es abrir, pero es que casi siempre
ando de viaje.

Las bodas del hormiguero

¡Fiesta del pino, del panadero y la cigarra recién nacida! Son los gusanos
quienes preparan los toneles de aguardiente. Mi novia canta y baila envuelta
en lo rojizo de la candela. Celebramos las grandes bodas del hormiguero
de mi horcón. Fiesta en la noche interminable, sobre el ardiente pasto del
mundo. ¡Ánimo al cordero que se asusta frente a las llamas sólidas y feroces
que lamen más cielo cuando las ranitas y los limpiabotas echan entre sus
brasas los cuerpos bien lavados del banquerito, el soldadito y el doctorcito!
¡Salud, oh, dichoso, rojo, puro, alegre hormiguero de mi horcón!

Vagabundo del alba

La mañana pálida de París crece sobre mis hombros
después de la noche larga mi amor esta brisa
Las hojas de color de miel del otoño deslizándose por las calles
en las aceras de las hojas del otoño sobre la cabeza de los mendigos
Aún ellos duermen una mujer se ha levantado ha recogido una boina
que había a los pies de un durmiente y le ha cubierto el rostro
La ternura de esa mujer debajo de sus harapos negros
como la flor pálida del día como la paloma
que revolotea sobre el Sena de humo de cristal de plata

The maddened fly buzzes past, seething,
far from the luminous spider web.
This is how it is, alone, but full of surprises.
A big rambling house of ghosts with no children, where the dust
fashions new windows, new furniture and dances.
No, you don't know the place, you haven't really seen my eyes
so you get all weepy. Listen to me:
my house doesn't run away; it's always distant.
We climb these stairs into the dark.
We don't get tired of climbing them, panting we fall asleep
not knowing the days, or fever, or the immense noise
of the city boiling in the background.
Sometimes, in the silence of the hallway, someone is suddenly born,
someone who rings at the numberless door, calling.
No, you have never been here. No, don't come.
My word would open it, but I'm nearly always
traveling somewhere.

The Wedding in the Anthill

Fiesta of the pine tree, the baker and the newborn cicada! It's the worms who
prepare the barrels of moonshine. Wrapped in red firelight, my bride sings
and dances. Let's celebrate the great wedding in the anthill by my hearth.
Fiesta in the endless night, over the burning pasture of the world. Courage
to the lamb that takes fright before the fierce wall of flames licking the sky
ever higher as frogs and bootblacks throw onto the coals the well-washed
bodies of the banker, the soldier and the doctor! To your health, oh lucky,
red, pure, joyous anthill by my hearth!

Wanderer of the Dawn

The pale Paris morning grows over my shoulders
after the long night my love this breeze
Leaves the color of autumn honey gliding through the streets
on the sidewalks the leaves covering the heads of beggars
Still they sleep a woman has risen picked up a beret
by a sleeper's feet and covered his face
The tenderness of that woman under her black rags
like the pale flower of the day like the dove
fluttering over the smoky glassy silvery Seine

Así es que aquí el amanecer yo te lo digo ahora que es otoño
así es el alba la ciudad está muerta sus huesos pueden ser palpados
y nadie dirá nada los policías duermen sus orejas de corcho
las leyes duermen la miseria dormita yo camino camino
primer hombre de este nuevo día como si la ciudad fuera mi mujer
y yo la contemplara dormida desnuda el cielo naciendo de su espalda

Así es París yo te lo digo a veces sueño que recorro un mundo muerto
después de la última bomba muerta hasta la esperanza
Yo no comprendo mucho pero me siento un poco Robinsón Crusoë
Robinsón de esta terrible hermosa grande ciudad que se llama París
Los gatos salen de todas partes buenos días los latones de basura están
     llenos
juguetes rotos frutas podridas trajes papeles desgarrados
papeles donde el olvido ha dejado su oscura cicatriz
El mundo la civilización todo eso ha muerto los gatos y yo sobrevivimos
Frente a uno de estos puentes escogeré mi casa
tal vez aquella de la cortina roja en la ventana
o la otra que avanza como si quisiera saludarme buenos días

Pero no no es verdad detrás de todos esos muros grises hay hombres
que respiran roncan y sueñan
hombres que quizás recuerdan un grito perdido en el valle turquesa de los
     siglos
hombres que acaso están pensando en los nuevos modelos de automóviles
en su trabajo en el amor tal vez en la muerte
Aquella mancha negra que arrastra la corriente es un cartón
creía que era una tortuga creía que era un abogado
y no es más que un cartón a su alrededor flotan tres hojas
como tres corazones de miel tres cifras del otoño
Los árboles salen del río como el humo de los cigarros
Otra paloma revolotea su sombra blanca sobre el agua gris
Los urinarios tienen la belleza astuta de ciertas iglesias de Castilla
voy entrando en ellos para hacer algo mientras pienso
mientras camino mi amor es decir nadie el mundo esas hojas
Los semáforos le dan paso a los gatos a la brisa
en la frente del día pálido estas luces de ámbar

Anoche hablaban de la guerra siempre la guerra
cadáveres espuma de eternidad cadáveres
pero no todos saben cómo es dulce la libertad por ejemplo a estas horas
en que el carro blanco del lechero viene detrás de sus bestias blancas
Una muchacha de Israel me hablaba de la juventud de su país

That's how daybreak is here in autumn I tell you
that's how dawn is the city is dead its bones can be touched
and no one will say anything the police sleep their ears stopped shut
the laws sleep misery dozes I walk I walk
first man in this new day as if the city were my wife
and I watched her sleeping naked the sky rising from her back

That's how Paris is I tell you sometimes I dream that I walk through a dead
    world
after the last bomb even hope dead
I don't understand much but I feel a bit like Robinson Crusoe
the Robinson of this beautiful terrible great city called Paris
Cats emerge from everywhere good morning the garbage bins are full
broken toys rotten fruit suits papers torn apart
papers where oblivion has left its dark scar
The world civilization all that has died the cats and I survive
Facing one of these bridges I shall choose my home
maybe that one with the red curtain in the window
or the other that comes forward as though it wished to greet me good
    morning

But no it's not true behind all those gray walls are men
who breathe snore and dream
men who maybe recall a cry lost in the turquoise valley of the centuries
men who are thinking perhaps about the new models of automobiles
about their work about love maybe about death
That black spot swept along by the current is a cardboard box
I thought it was a tortoise I thought it was a lawyer
and it's nothing more than a cardboard box three leaves floating around it
like three hearts of honey three figures of autumn
The trees emerge from the river like smoke from cigars
Another dove flutters about its white shadow over the gray water
The urinals have the cunning beauty of certain churches in Castile
I enter them to do something while I think
while I walk my love which is to say no one the world those leaves
The traffic signals give the go-ahead to the cats to the breeze
these amber lights on the brow of the pale day

Last night they were talking about the war always the war
corpses foam of eternity corpses
but not everyone knows how sweet is freedom for example at these hours
when the milkman's white wagon follows his white beasts
A girl from Israel was talking to me about her country's youth

ella no tiene religión ella ama a París ella ama al mundo
mañana todos tendremos el mismo rostro de bronce y hablaremos la
    misma lengua
mañana aunque usted no lo quiera señor general señor comerciante señor
    de espejuelos de alambre y ceniza
pronto la nueva vida el hombre nuevo levantarán sus ciudades
encima de vuestros huesos y los míos encima del polvo de Notre-Dame
En la primera panadería que se abra compraré un gran pan
como hacía en mi país sólo que ahora no me acompañan mis amigos
y que ya no tengo veinte años
Entonces hubiera visto todas esas sombras de otro color
hubiera silbado hubiera arrastrado el recuerdo de una muchacha trigueña
En fin todas esas cosas se van quedando atrás
ahora es más importante trabajar para vivir
Algunos pájaros empiezan a cantar las hojas secas caen
Me voy alejando del río de las lanchas de los puentes blancos
parece que estos edificios fueran a caer sobre mi cabeza
se van volviendo gibosos al paso de los siglos
la rue du Chat-qui-Pêche me hace imaginar historias terribles
Pero es mejor continuar es el alba es el alba
las manos en los bolsillos proseguir proseguir
Dos carniceros dan hachazos sobre la mitad de una res
eso no es nada divertido y sin embargo me gusta mirar
mi alma es aún un poco carnicera estamos en 1956
Mañana quizás no será así quizás no habrá carniceros ni verdugos
mi corazón un poco verdugo y un poco ahorcado
tu corazón tu corazón serán polvo agua viento
para los nuevos girasoles
cada semilla como una abeja dormida

El día pálido era blanco ahora amarillea
algunas chimeneas parece que fueron a encenderse
Pasa un soldado con una maleta enorme
rumbo a la Gare de Lyon rumbo a Egipto la muerte
Pasa una mujer en bicicleta ella va a su trabajo
cuando el sol está a la altura de las rodillas como el trigo
todos los días ella va a su trabajo toda la vida
Pasa un camión cargado de vino de estrépito de alba
Ya estoy en el boulevard Saint-Germain miro las vitrinas de las librerías
Algún día compraré un buen diccionario las obras completas de Rimbaud

she has no religion she loves Paris she loves the world
tomorrow we'll all have the same bronze face and speak the same language
tomorrow although you may not want it mister general mister businessman
    mister glasses of wire and ash
soon the new life the new man will build their cities
on top of your bones and mine on top of the dust of Notre-Dame
In the first bakery to open I will buy a large loaf
like I used to in my country except that now my friends are not with me
and I'm no longer twenty
Then I would have seen all those shadows in another color
I would have whistled I would have dragged with me the memory of a
    flaxen-haired girl
In the end all those things are left behind
now it's more important to work to live
Some birds begin to sing the dead leaves fall
I'm going away from the river the boats the white bridges
these buildings look like they might collapse on my head
they're becoming hunchbacked with the passing of the centuries
the Rue du Chat-qui-Pêche inspires terrible stories
But it's better to carry on it's dawn it's dawn
hands in pockets keep going keep going
Two butchers hack with an axe at a side of beef
it's not fun but I like to watch
my soul is still a bit of a butcher it's 1956
Tomorrow maybe it won't be like this maybe there won't be butchers or
    executioners
my heart part executioner and part hanged man
your heart your heart will be dust water wind
for the new sunflowers
each seed like a sleeping bee

The pale day was white now it yellows
some chimneys seem about to catch fire
A soldier passes with an enormous suitcase
on his way to the Gare de Lyon on his way to Egypt death
A woman passes on a bicycle she is going to work
when the sun is knee-high to her like wheat
every day all her life she goes to work
A truck passes loaded with wine with a clatter with dawn
I'm already on the Boulevard Saint-Germain I'm looking in the bookstore
    windows
Someday I'll buy a good dictionary the complete works of Rimbaud

muchos libros mejor es no hablar de eso
Por todas partes hay mendigos durmiendo aquél parece un niño
entre su cabeza y el cemento de la acera no hay más que una lámina helada
Tengo ganas de tomarme café con leche tengo hambre y sed
el alba amarilla tiene un mal sabor en mi boca

París comienza a despertar ya no soy un Robinsón
más bien un extranjero más bien un fantasma
más bien un hombre que no ha dormido
vagabundo de la ciudad el otoño y el alba
mientras mi amor ha de estar mirando las cumbres del Perú
o el cielo esmaltado de China
Yo no lo sé mis pies se cansan eso es todo eso es todo
Después de haber amado vivir el nuevo día
es hermoso
En la ciudad y el corazón arde la misma llama.

Charlot y la luna

• *A la memoria de Escardó*

En los arrabales del Sur Londres o Bayamo
los gatos y la luna juegan en los techos
No falta quien les tire una piedra nunca falta
quien quiera darle cuatro tiros a la luna pero también
hay hombres que al percibirla allá arriba cerca del latón de la basura
bajan corriendo las escaleras hacia el bar de la esquina
a poner un disco en la victrola una pieza un poco nublada
que puede ser la dulzura de la primavera o la ternura de unos ojos perdidos
    para siempre

A veces un mendigo se pasea tambaleándose con un pedazo de luna
sobre la cabeza rodeada por las moscas
Los muchachos del barrio comienzan a gritarle:
"¡Eh Rey hermosa es tu corona de plata!
Vamos a comprarte otra botella"
Y el mendigo
después de bailar un lento vals
se cae al fin sobre el espejo sucio de la acera
Al lado suyo la luna tiembla como una gata friolenta.

lots of books best not to speak of that
Beggars are sleeping everywhere that one looks like a child
between his head and the cement sidewalk there is nothing but a frozen
    sheet of metal
I feel like drinking my breakfast coffee I'm hungry and thirsty
the yellow dawn tastes bad in my mouth

Paris is beginning to awaken I'm not Robinson anymore
just a foreigner a ghost
a man who has not slept
a wanderer in the city the autumn the dawn
while my love must be gazing at the summits of Peru
or the enameled sky of China
I don't know my feet are tired that's all there is
After having loved
to live the new day is beautiful
The same flame burns in the city and the heart.

Charlie and the Moon

> ◆ *In memory of Escardó*

In the slums of South London or Bayamo
the cats and the moon play on the rooftops
There's always someone to throw a stone at them always
someone who wants to take four shots at the moon but also
there are men who noticing it above the garbage bin
run down the stairs to the corner bar
to put a record on the victrola a slightly misty number
that could be the sweetness of spring or the tenderness of eyes forever lost

Sometimes a beggar staggers along with a piece of the moon
on his head surrounded by flies
The local kids shout at him:
"Hey, king, nice silver crown you're wearing!
We're going to buy you another bottle!"
And the beggar
after dancing a slow waltz
falls at last onto the dirty mirror of the sidewalk
At his side the moon shivers like a chilly cat.

En los arrabales del Norte en las playas de Cuba
o en una puerta desvencijada del barrio de Vallecas en Madrid
cuando alguien saca su perrito a orinar o cuando alguien tiende
su única camisa al viento de la noche
la luna aparece sobre un poste eléctrico
y entonces alguien empieza a cantar
"Ya no estoy tan solo
en este mundo . . . "
En una cocina están friendo dos ruedas de pargo
El olor de las cebollas hace volverse al policía que va y viene
por la calle mientras espera que el primer ladrón
con sus ojillos melancólicos
surja con su enorme saco bajo una ventana apagada

Los bigotitos de Charlot saltan como dos mosquitos furiosos
pero el amo del pargo no lo dejará pasar
Todas esas paredes todos esos pasillos
escaleras hacia el polvo y la noche
están llenos de seres humanos que quieren comer y vivir
a pesar de las telarañas o el cuchillazo por la espalda
quieren vivir
Hasta los huesos retorcidos de los ancianos
quieren vivir
llamas anaranjadas sobre el pasto ríos amarillos del otoño
Ahora mismo la luna resbala por la frente de los miserables
y un avión pasa zumbando hacia otros continentes o hacia las playas del
        vacío

Sobre una botella vacía saltan los niños
sobre una muñeca de trapo sobre el rostro
bermejo de todos los tiranos del mundo saltan los niños
pajaritos de la llovizna pajaritos del sol
Ellos que son capaces de ir hasta Saturno
sobre el cuello de una jirafa
Ellos que saben construir una ciudad
con unos pedacitos de vidrio y de barro
Los capitanes de los solares yermos los conquistadores
de las grandes bestias prehistóricas
Los que guardan a veces en sus cofres
todo cuanto es preciso para comprar un helado
Charlot está ahí soñando entre los niños
Sus zapatos tropiezan en todas partes

In the slums of the North on the beaches of Cuba
or in a ramshackle doorway in the Vallecas district in Madrid
when someone takes his little dog to pee or when someone hangs out
his only shirt in the night wind
the moon appears over an electrical pole
and then someone begins to sing
"I'm no longer so alone
in this world . . . "
In a kitchen two slices of fish are frying
The smell of onions makes the police turn round coming and going
through the street while they wait for the first
melancholy-eyed thief to emerge
from a dark window with his enormous sack

Charlie's whiskers twitch like two furious mosquitoes
but the owner of the fish won't let him pass
All those walls all those corridors
stairways rising toward the dust and the night
are full of human beings who want to eat and live
in spite of the spiderwebs or the knife in the back
they want to live
Even the twisted bones of the old folks
they want to live
orange flames over the grass yellow rivers of autumn
Right now the moon slips down over the heads of the wretched
and a plane zooms past toward other continents or toward the beaches of
    emptiness

The children are jumping on an empty bottle
on a rag doll on the bright red
face of all the tyrants in the world the children are jumping
little birds of the drizzle birds of the sun
They who could go as far as Saturn
on the neck of a giraffe
They who know how to build a city
out of pieces of glass and clay
The captains of empty lots the conquerors
of great prehistoric beasts
Those who sometimes keep in their coffers
all that is needed to buy an ice cream
Charlie is there dreaming among the children
His shoes stumble in every direction

Charlot está ahí los grillos han dejado de chillar
De la luna salen doce palomas
que vienen a revolotear sobre el coro de los que juegan
hasta que una se posa en el pie izquierdo de Charlot
"¡Viva la noche del traspatio vivan las palomitas de cristal!
¡Viva el olor de los árboles vivan los helados de fresa!"

A ése lo van a enterrar en un potrero
a ese otro lo van a coronar
a aquel de los ojos de granos de maíz
lo van a sentar en una silla eléctrica
Esto ya está repartido
y el que sólo se alimenta de sombra no es el que tiene diez fábricas
trabajando para su alegría
y el que nació con la nariz muy grande
no es el que va escondido detrás de la llama blanca de una mujer
Allá arriba están los gatos olfateando
los latones de basura
Las chimeneas no despiden ningún humo
el tocadiscos de la esquina va a reventar
igual que un sapo gigantesco
mientras una garganta de madera antigua
dice que todo todo va a volver a empezar
¿Y el loco de la casa de enfrente?
¿y las muchachas de cuello de vía láctea?
¿y mi cigarro que arde sin cesar?
Charlot aparece allá abajo de nuevo
y se pone a bailar al son de un mambo
mientras de su sombrero sale la luna la lámpara dulce del arrabal

Por esta libertad

Por esta libertad de canción bajo la lluvia
habrá que darlo todo
Por esta libertad de estar estrechamente atados
a la firme y dulce entraña del pueblo
habrá que darlo todo
Por esta libertad de girasol abierto en el alba de fábricas encendidas y
    escuelas iluminadas
y de tierra que cruje y niño que despierta
habrá que darlo todo

Charlie is there the crickets have stopped their screeching
Twelve doves fly out of the moon
and flutter above the chorus of playing children
until one settles on Charlie's left foot
"Hurray for nights in the backyard hurray for the crystal doves!
Hurray for the smell of the trees hurray for strawberry ice cream!"

They're going to bury him in a pasture
that other fellow they're going to crown
him over there with eyes like grains of corn
they're going to sit him in an electric chair
It's already divvied up
and the man who only feeds on shadow is not the man who has ten factories
working for his joy
and the man who was born with an enormous nose
is not the man who hides behind the white flame of a woman
Up there cats sniff
the garbage bins
The chimneys send out no smoke
the record player on the corner is going to burst
like a giant toad
while an old wooden throat
says that everything everything's going to start again
And the madman in the house across the street?
and the girls with necks like the milky way?
and my cigar that won't stop burning?
Charlie shows up down there again
and begins to dance to the sound of a mambo
while the moon sweet lamp of the slums emerges from his hat

For This Freedom

        For this freedom of a song in the rain
we must give everything
For this freedom of being firmly tied
to the strong and gentle core of the people
we must give everything
For this freedom of a sunflower open in the dawn of busy factories and
    schools lit up
and creaking earth and a child awakening
we must give everything

No hay alternativa sino la libertad
No hay más camino que la libertad
No hay otra patria que la libertad
No habrá más poema sin la violenta música de la libertad

    Por esta libertad que es el terror
de los que siempre la violaron
en nombre de fastuosas miserias
Por esta libertad que es la noche de los opresores
y el alba definitiva de todo el pueblo ya invencible
Por esta libertad que alumbra las pupilas hundidas
        los pies descalzos
        los techos agujereados
        y los ojos de los niños que
            deambulaban en el polvo

    Por esta libertad que es el imperio de la juventud
Por esta libertad
bella como la vida
habrá que darlo todo
si fuere necesario
hasta la sombra
y nunca será suficiente.

Heberto Padilla

En tiempos difíciles

A aquel hombre le pidieron su tiempo
para que lo juntara al tiempo de la Historia.
Le pidieron las manos,
porque para una época difícil
nada hay mejor que un par de buenas manos.
Le pidieron los ojos
que alguna vez tuvieron lágrimas
para que contemplara el lado claro
(especialmente el lado claro de la vida)
porque para el horror basta un ojo de asombro.
Le pidieron sus labios

There is no alternative to freedom
There is no path except for freedom
There is no other homeland but freedom
There will be no more poems without the violent music of freedom

     For this freedom that is the terror
of those who've always violated it
in the name of opulent miseries
For this freedom that is the night of the oppressors
and the definitive dawn of the entire people now invincible
For this freedom that lights sunken eyes
         shoeless feet
         roofs with holes
         and the eyes of children who
            wandered in the dust

     For this freedom that is the empire of youth
For this freedom
beautiful as life
if called upon
we must give everything
even our shadow
and it will never be enough.

Translated by Jason Weiss

Heberto Padilla

In Difficult Times

They asked the man for his time
so that he might add it to the time of History.
They asked him for his hands,
because in a difficult era
there's nothing better than a pair of good hands.
They asked him for his eyes
that once held tears
so that he might contemplate the bright side
(especially the bright side of life)
because one astonished eye is enough for the horror.
They asked for his dry, cracked lips

resecos y cuarteados para afirmar,
para erigir, con cada afirmación, un sueño
(el-alto-sueño);
le pidieron las piernas,
duras y nudosas,
(sus viejas piernas andariegas)
porque en tiempos difíciles
¿algo hay mejor que un par de piernas
para la construcción o la trinchera?
Le pidieron el bosque que lo nutrió de niño,
con su árbol obediente.
Le pidieron el pecho, el corazón, los hombros.
Le dijeron
que eso era estrictamente necesario.
Le explicaron después
que toda esta donación resultaría inútil
sin entregar la lengua,
porque en tiempos difíciles
nada es tan útil para atajar el odio o la mentira.
Y finalmente le rogaron
que, por favor, echase a andar,
porque en tiempos difíciles
esta es, sin duda, la prueba decisiva.

El discurso del método

Si después que termina el bombardeo,
andando sobre la hierba que puede crecer lo mismo
entre las ruinas
        que en el sombrero de tu Obispo,
eres capaz de imaginar que no estás viendo
lo que se va a plantar irremediablemente delante de tus ojos,
        o que no estás oyendo
lo que tendrás que oír durante mucho tiempo todavía:
        o (lo que es peor)
piensas que será suficiente la astucia o el buen juicio
para evitar que un día, al entrar en tu casa,
sólo encuentres un sillón destruido, con un montón
        de libros rotos,
        yo te aconsejo que corras enseguida,
        que busques un pasaporte,

to affirm,
to build, with each affirmation, a dream
(the-noble-dream);
they asked for his legs,
hard and sinewy,
(his old roving legs)
because in difficult times
is there anything better than a pair of legs
for construction or the foxhole?
They asked for the forest that nourished him as a child,
with its obedient tree.
They asked for his chest, his heart, his shoulders.
They told him
it was strictly necessary.
They explained to him afterwards
that this whole donation would be useless
unless he gave his tongue,
because in difficult times
nothing is so useful for stopping hate or lies.
And finally they implored him
please, take a walk,
because in difficult times
this is, no doubt, the decisive test.

Discourse on Method

If after the bombing is over,
walking on the grass that can grow just as well
among the ruins
        as in the hat on your bishop's head,
you can imagine that you're not seeing
what's going to be right before your eyes,
        or that you're not hearing
what you'll have to hear for a long time yet:
        or (still worse)
you think that cleverness or good judgment will be enough
to keep you from finding
only a demolished rocking chair and a heap of broken books
        when you come home one day,
        I advise you to run at once,
        to look for a passport,

alguna contraseña,
    un hijo enclenque, cualquier cosa
que puedan justificarte ante una policía por el momento torpe
        (porque ahora está formada
        de campesinos y peones)
y que te largues de una vez y para siempre.
Huye por la escalera del jardín
        (que no te vea nadie).
No cojas nada.
                No servirán de nada
ni un abrigo, ni un guante, ni un apellido,
ni un lingote de oro, ni un título borroso.
No pierdas tiempo
                        enterrando joyas en las paredes
        (las van a descubrir de cualquier modo).
No te pongas a guardar escrituras en los sótanos
        (las localizarán después los milicianos).

Ten desconfianza de la mejor criada.
No le entregues las llaves del chofer, no le confíes
la perra al jardinero.
No te ilusiones con las noticias de onda corta.

Párate ante el espejo más alto de la sala, tranquilamente,
        y contempla tu vida,
        y contémplate ahora como eres
        porque ésta será la última vez.

Ya están quitando las barricadas de los parques.
Ya los asaltadores del poder están subiendo a la tribuna.
Ya el perro, el jardinero, el chofer, la criada
        están allí aplaudiendo.

Oración para el fin de siglo

Nosotros que hemos mirado siempre con ironía e indulgencia
        los objetos abigarrados del fin de siglo: las construcciones,
        y las criaturas
        trabadas en oscuras levitas.
Nosotros para quienes el fin de siglo fue a lo sumo
        un grabado y una oración francesa.

some countersign,
       a sickly child, anything
that could give you an alibi for a sluggish police force
       (because it's all
       peasants and farmhands now)
and to get away once and for all.
Escape by the back stairs
       (so that no one will see you).
Don't take anything.
                It'll be of no use—
not an overcoat, or a glove, or a family name,
not a bar of gold, or a vague title.
Don't waste time
                hiding jewelry in the walls
       (they'll find it anyway).
Don't start keeping manuscripts in the cellar
       (the military will find them later).

Be wary of the most loyal maid.
Don't hand the keys to the chauffeur, don't entrust
the gardener with the dog.
Don't fool yourself with news from the shortwave radio.

Stop before the tallest mirror in the living room, calmly,
             and contemplate your life,
             look at yourself as you are now
             because this will be the last time.

Now they're taking the barricades from the parks.
Now the assailants of power are mounting the podium.
Now the dog, the gardener, the chauffeur, the maid
             are in the crowd applauding.

Prayer for the Turn of the Century

We who have always glanced with irony and indulgence
       at the motley collection of things from the turn of the century: the
             buildings,
       and the children
       fettered in dark suits.
We for whom the turn of the century was at most
       an engraving and a French prayer.

Nosotros que creíamos que al final de cien años sólo había
      un pájaro negro que levantaba la cofia de una abuela.
Nosotros que hemos visto el derrumbe de los parlamentos
      y el culo remendado del liberalismo.
Nosotros que aprendimos a desconfiar de los mitos ilustres
      y a quienes nos parece absolutamente imposible
      (inhabitable)
      una sala de candelabros
      una cortina
      y una silla Luis XV.
Nosotros, hijos y nietos ya de terroristas melancólicos
      y de científicos supersticiosos,
      que sabemos que en el día de hoy está el error
      que alguien habrá de condenar mañana.
Nosotros, que estamos viviendo los últimos años
      de este siglo,
      deambulamos, incapaces de improvisar un movimiento
      que no haya sido concertado;
      gesticulamos en un espacio más restringido
      que el de las líneas de un grabado;
      nos ponemos las oscuras levitas
      como si fuéramos a asistir a un parlamento,
      mientras los candelabros saltan por la cornisa
      y los pájaros negros
      rompen la cofia de esta muchacha de voz ronca.

Los poetas cubanos ya no sueñan

Los poetas cubanos ya no sueñan
            (ni siquiera en la noche).

Van a cerrar la puerta para escribir a solas
cuando cruje, de pronto, la madera;
el viento los empuja al garete;
unas manos los cogen por los hombros,
los voltean,
      los ponen frente a frente a otras caras

(hundidas en pantanos ardiendo en el napalm)
y el mundo encima de sus bocas fluye
y está obligado el ojo a ver, a ver, a ver.

We who believed that after a hundred years what was left was
    a black bird holding a grandmother's hairnet.
We who have seen the collapse of parliaments
    and the patched-up ass of liberalism.
We who learned to distrust famous myths
    and to whom the idea of a parlor with candelabras
    a curtain
    and a Louis XV chair
    seems absolutely impossible
    (uninhabitable).
We, children and grandchildren now of melancholy terrorists
    and superstitious scientists,
    we who know that today we commit the error
    that someone else will condemn tomorrow.
We, living the final years
    of this century,
    stroll about, incapable of improvising an unplanned
    movement;
    gesticulate in a space more restricted
    than the space in an engraving;
    put on dark suits
    as if we were going to attend a parliament,
    while the candelabras flare in the cornice
    and the black birds
    break the hairnet of this girl with their hoarse voices.

Cuban Poets Don't Dream Anymore

Cuban poets don't dream anymore
        (not even at night).

They get up to close the door so they can write alone
when suddenly the wood creaks;
the wind pushes them adrift;
some hands catch them by the shoulders,
turn them around,
        set them face to face with other faces

(sunk in swamps burning with napalm)
and the world flows above their mouths
and the eye is obliged to see, to see, to see.

Para aconsejar a una dama

¿Y si empezara por aceptar algunos hechos
como ha aceptado—es un ejemplo—a ese negro becado
que mea desafiante en su jardín?

Ah, mi señora: por más que baje las cortinas; por más
que oculte la cara solterona; por más que llene
de perras y de gatas esa recalcitrante soledad; por más
que corte los hilos del teléfono
que resuena espantoso en la casa vacía;
por más que sueñe y rabie
no podrá usted borrar la realidad.

Atrévase
Abra las ventanas de par en par. Quítese el maquillaje
y la bata de dormir y quédese en cueros
como vino usted al mundo.
Echese ahí, gata de la penumbra, recelosa, a esperar.
Aúlle con todos los pulmones.
La cerca es corta; es fácil saltar,
y en los albergues duermen los estudiantes.
Despiértelos.
Quémese en el proceso, gata o alción; no importa.
Meta a un becado en la cama.
Que sus muslos ilustren la lucha de contrarios.
Que su lengua sea más hábil que toda la dialéctica.
Salga usted vencedora de esta lucha de clases.

Poética

Di la verdad.
Di, al menos, tu verdad.
Y después
deja que cualquier cosa ocurra:
que te rompan la página querida,
que te tumben a pedradas la puerta,
que la gente
se amontone delante de tu cuerpo
como si fueras
un prodigio o un muerto.

To Advise a Lady

And if she were to begin by accepting certain facts
as she has accepted—for example—that black scholarship student
pissing defiantly in her garden?

Ah, my lady: however much you lower the curtains; however much
you hide your spinster face; however much you fill
that recalcitrant solitude with dogs and cats; however much
you cut the wires of the telephone
that rings frightfully through the empty house;
however much you dream and rave
you cannot erase reality.

Take a risk.
Open the windows wide. Remove makeup
and bathrobe and stand as naked
as you came into the world.
Wait there, apprehensive cat of the shadows.
Howl your lungs out.
The fence is short; it's an easy jump,
and the students are sleeping in their lodgings.
Wake them up.
Burn yourself in the process, cat or kingfisher, it doesn't matter.
Put a scholarship student in your bed.
Let your thighs illustrate the struggle of contraries.
Let your tongue be more agile than all dialectics.
Emerge as the victor in this class warfare.

Poetics

Tell the truth.
At least tell your truth.
And after
let anything happen:
let them tear up your beloved page,
let them knock down your door,
let people
crowd around your body
as if you were
a miracle or a corpse.

Paisajes

Se pueden ver a lo largo de toda Cuba.
Verdes o rojos o amarillos, descascarándose con el agua
y el sol, verdaderos paisajes de estos tiempos
de guerra.
El viento arranca los letreros de Coca-Cola.
Los relojes cortesía de Canada Dry están parados en la hora vieja.
Chisporrotean, rotos, bajo la lluvia, los anuncios de neón.
Uno de Standard Oil Company queda así como
          S   O   Compa y
y encima hay unas letras toscas
con que alguien ha escrito PATRIA O MUERTE.

El lugar del amor

Siempre, más allá de tus hombros veo al mundo.
Chispea bajo los temporales.
Es un pedazo de madera podrida, un farol viejo
que alguien menea como a contracorriente.
El mundo que nuestros cuerpos
(que nuestra soledad) no pueden abolir,
un siglo de zapadores y hombres
ranas debajo de tu almohada,
en el lugar en que tus hombros
se hacen más tibios y más frágiles.
Siempre, más allá de tus hombros
(es algo que ya nunca podremos evitar)
hay una lista de desaparecidos,
hay una aldea destruida,
hay un niño que tiembla.

Landscapes

They can be seen throughout Cuba.
Green or red or yellow, peeling off the walls because of water
and sun, the actual landscapes in these times
of war.
The wind tears loose the Coca-Cola posters.
The clocks courtesy of Canada Dry are stopped at the old hour.
Broken, the neon signs sputter in the rain.
A Standard Oil sign becomes something like
        S   O   Compa y
and above in crude letters
someone has written PATRIA O MUERTE.

The Place of Love

Always, past your shoulders I see the world.
It sparkles beneath the storm clouds.
It's a piece of rotted wood, an old lantern
swaying as if against the current.
The world that our bodies
(our solitude) can't abolish,
a century of sappers and frogmen
under your pillow,
in the place where your shoulders
become softer, more fragile.
Always, past your shoulders
(we can never avoid it now)
there is a list of the missing,
a village destroyed,
a child trembling.

Translated by Jason Weiss

José Álvarez Baragaño

Los distritos sonoros

Donner un sens plus pur aux mots de la tribu
MALLARMÉ

Un mar de gracia constante está en la rosa,
su bahía absoluta detiene mis rumores,
no me cambia la vida ni esa música anciana.

Mi viaje al infinito tiene palabra de honor,
para que se gasten los espejos, no oiga mi voz,
Laura otoñal, llegaré intacto, pleno de trayectos,
aún reside esta floja mar en mis entrañas.

Aunque me vista de distancia yo estaré muy cerca,
los barrios pobres de la luz arderán en sueños,
no habrá tierra en mi carne que haya sido tocada,
cada cosa en su sitio, mi palabra en tu boca.

Amada, mi ser no es mental, doy frescura a mi piel
con agua de existencia, la calle es como un río de fragancia,
como un metro humano, océano de vida, sinfonía de cuerpos;
déjame vagabundear por tu palabra arcana,
y ser vago en tu mundo ya romero-arból
y rosa cartesiana,
cuando el misterio te ponga en mis brazos,
qué hará mi persona, piel impertinente, lumbre gozadora,
en tu figura como un mar de gracia.

Yo oscuro

Bajo mis lámparas escribo
Heráclito oscuro vino en la botella
El yo fino como la niebla
Oculta el ser escarpado
Las sonoras banderas las tormentas
Él me hablaba
    Junto a los puertos y las islas
de Cuba centro doloroso y la desgracia
Bajo lámparas fuego cenizas rosas

José Álvarez Baragaño

Sonorous Districts

Donner un sens plus pur aux mots de la tribu
MALLARMÉ

A sea of constant grace is in the rose,
its absolute bay detains my murmurs,
not even that ancient music changes my life.

My journey to the infinite has its word of honor,
so that mirrors may wear away, it doesn't hear my voice,
autumnal Laura, I'll arrive intact, filled with byways,
this weak sea still dwells within me.

Though I clothe myself with distance I will be quite near,
light's shantytowns will burn in dreams,
no earth on my flesh will be touched,
everything in its space, my word in your mouth.

Beloved, my being's not mental, I make my skin fresh
with water of existence, the street's like a river of fragrance,
like a human subway, ocean of life, symphony of bodies;
a vagabond, let me wander through your arcane word
become a tramp in your world just turned to rosemary-tree
and cartesian rose,
when mystery puts you in my arms,
what will my persona do, impertinent skin, pleasure-loving light,
in your figure like a sea of grace.

Dark Self

Beneath my lamps I write
Dark Heraclitus came in the bottle
Self delicate as fog
Steep being hides
The sonorous flags the storms
He spoke to me
                By the ports and islands
of Cuba painful center and disgrace
Beneath lamps fire ashes roses

Las manos escriben
Lo que no pueden decir
Levitando como la niebla sobre el río
¿Por qué no desciendo los números colores
Azul negra azul
Con el impacto del acto del amor
Sobre un enjambre de linternas?
Por último
Bajo mis lámparas alucinadas
Morirán mis años como mariposas
Fuego agua viento labios
Digo lo que digo
Mis años arden al sol de mis palabras.

Los muertos

Yo estaba lejos,
Leyendo en el frío de Europa
Mi nombre coagulado en el fango.
No pude hacer nada para salvarlos.
No pude hacer nada
No hice, digo, nada.
Ahora me gritan
                    Y
Nos gritan
Desde esa multitud
Que siente al futuro pasearse entre sus brazos
Que agarran los fusiles.
Nos gritan y nos llaman
Con un alarido que no es del terror,
Ni del sueño,
Ni del hambre;
Con el alarido de su mano arrancando
La hoja roja que apoyan
Sobre la espalda blanca del sol
Como un gran monstruo conmovido.
Entre la multitud y yo
Palpitan millones de corazones;
Palpitan las entrañas blancas de la aurora
Y siento algo que habla

Hands write
What they cannot say
Rising like fog over the river
Why don't I descend the blue black blue
Numbers
With the impact of lovemaking
On a cluster of lanterns?
And finally
Beneath my hallucinated lamps
My years will die like butterflies
Fire water wind lips
I say what I say
My years burn in the sun of my words.

The Dead

I was far away
Reading in the cold of Europe
My name frozen in the mud.
I could do nothing to save them.
I could do nothing
I mean, I did nothing.
Now they shout
                To me, to us
From that multitude
That feels the future entering its arms
That clutches the rifles.
They shout to us, they call us
With a shriek not of terror,
Nor sleep,
Nor hunger;
With the shriek of their hand tearing off
The red page that they lean
On the white back of the sun
Like a huge tender monster.
Between me and the multitude
Millions of hearts are beating
The white heart of dawn is beating
And I feel something speaking

Con una voz caliente:
Es el pueblo que habla.
Mi mano no se paraliza, prosigue

En la mano del canto
Del porvenir marchando con el pueblo.
Entre mi nacimiento
Y mi edad
Se deslizan los muertos
De Alemania
España,
Polonia,
Oradour,
      Stalingrado.
Pero
      Hablan ahora
Cantan ahora
Desde el corazón de la multitud.
El poema se destruye
Para dar nacimiento a la acción;
La palabra de nuevo
Que es la palabra
Hablando por los que murieron y los que nacen
Sobre América y el mundo.
La mano de la multitud
Me agarra: es una mano conmovida
La mano de la multitud
Se hace transparente en mi corazón;
La mano de la multitud:
Millones de lenguas gargantas dientes;
Habla, actúa, me dice
En esta gran aurora del hombre
En cualquier plaza de Cuba.

Revolución color de libertad

I

HABLAN LOS MUERTOS

Estamos fijos como las palabras en un poema: nosotros que roturábamos la
   tierra, el humo, el carbón y el lecho de los vientos y las lluvias;

In a fervid voice:
It's the people speaking.
My hand isn't paralyzed, it carries on

In the hand of song
Of the future marching with the people.
Between my birth
And my present age
The dead flow on
From Germany
Spain,
Poland,
Oradour,
      Stalingrad.
But
      Now they speak
Now they sing
From the heart of the multitude.
The poem is destroyed
To give birth to action;
The word once again
Which is the word
Speaking for those who died and for those who are born
About America and the world.
The hand of the multitude
Grasps me: it's a tender hand
The hand of the multitude
Becomes transparent in my heart;
The hand of the multitude:
Millions of tongues throats teeth;
It speaks, it acts, it speaks to me
In this great dawn of mankind
In any public square in Cuba.

Revolution, the Color of Freedom

I

THE DEAD SPEAK

We are set like the words in a poem: we who ploughed the earth, the
    smoke, the coal, and the beds of winds and rains;

Fijos en el archipiélago del pueblo que nos habla con la voz abierta de la
    violencia;
La muerte es nuestro blasón en la pradera de coral del último exilio;
    Quemamos nuestra vida como el tungsteno del ser en la gran lámpara
    dc la libertad;
Cuba, tu geometría de cuerpo y órganos maltratados
Sube y desciende.
¿Quien nos dio la muerte conocía la muerte?
Sólo nosotros la sabemos en nuestra tranquila aristocracia,
Cenizas de la historia aventadas por el labio purísimo del pueblo;
Sólo nosotros la sabemos y la poseemos la muerte
Creciendo como un río en el verano de los trópicos;
Sus insectos, sus mensajes, sus manos de delicia,
Nos consumen en este estar sin ser
Perdidos en el espejo de la historia
Para que nunca más
Ese mundo de tortura, de miedo y de asco
En su vacío se repita;
Para que nunca más
Los ángeles envenenados ensucien nuestro cielo
Nosotros mantenemos esta lucha de gigantes invisibles
Junto al mar, junto a los jardines de la reina, atacados y devorados por los
    asesinos.
¿Quiénes éramos? Teníamos un nombre que nos fue arrancado con nuestro
    cuerpo, mordido por la noche titilante del trópico que todo lo consume.
Oye Cuba, te lo decimos al oído
En la gran noche del alma que es la muerte,
Combatimos y combatiremos,
Anónimos como el himno de los astros,
Porque ese sol que todo lo atraviesa,
Muros de cal y muerte, muebles de dolor y lámparas de desesperación
Sea y al final de los tiempos
El que vemos sol bastión de libertad.

II

HABLAN LOS COMBATIENTES

Hoy las tierras y los ríos,
Las paredes del alba, los salvajes alientos de nuestras banderas,
Porque la muerte o la libertad se abre como un abanico en nuestras manos.
Rompimos la tierra, viajábamos de noche por el mundo,
Cuando los traidores envilecían, corrompían y asesinaban el pueblo,

Set in the archipelago of the people who speak to us with the open voice of
     violence;
Death is our coat of arms in the coral meadow of final exile; We burn our
     lives like the tungsten of being in the great lamp of freedom;
Cuba, your geometry of battered body and organs
Rises and falls.
Did he who put us to death know of death?
We alone know it in our peaceful aristocracy,
Ashes of history blown by the people's purest lips;
We alone know and possess death
Swelling like a river in the tropical summer;
Its insects, its messages, its hands of delight,
Consume us in this becoming without being
Lost in history's mirror
So that this world in its void
Of torture, fear, and disgust
May never come again;
So that poisoned angels
May never soil our sky again
We continue this struggle of invisible giants
By the sea, by the queen's gardens, attacked and devoured by assassins.
Who were we? We had a name torn away from our bodies, bitten by the
     flickering all-consuming tropical night.
Listen, Cuba, we're whispering in your ear
In the great night of the soul that is death,
That we fought and will fight,
Anonymous as the hymn that the stars sing,
Because this sun that pierces through everything,
Walls of whitewash and death, furniture of pain and lamps of despair
Now and until the end of time may it be
The sun that we see, the bastion of freedom.

II

THE FIGHTERS SPEAK

Today the earth and rivers,
The walls of dawn, our flags' wild breathing,
Because death or freedom opens like a fan in our hands.
We broke the earth, we traveled by night through the world,
When traitors debased, corrupted, and slaughtered the people,

Nuestra palabra encendida como el vuelo de los gavilanes en el espacio
Nace de las fuentes centrales de la pureza.
Éramos la verdad, el encuentro del pueblo y su destino,
Nuestro pueblo de minerales, de tierras rojas, de tambores incansables, nos
    lo pedía.
La noche fue nuestro testigo y nuestro homenaje,
Cuando La Habana, cuando Santiago,
Cuando la extensión de nuestras provincias era corrompida por el llanto y
    el miedo,
Nuestros pechos de fuego fueron las flechas de la aurora, dijeron:
Despierta amada tierra, somos tus señores libertarios, el rojo y negro de las
    revoluciones viene por el ínclito mundo de la libertad,
Empujamos el ancho surco de la historia, somos su apellido, su razón de ser.
Con nuestras voces de agua, de humo, de diamantes,
Elementales conquistadores de la verdad,
Respondíamos a los minerales de la tierra, a sus águilas, a sus bestias de
    amor.
Fuimos como las flechas que antaño atravesaron la luz,
Subíamos nuestra tierra escogida por la revolución,
Nuestras rosas de invierno se abrieron transparentes,
Y en nuestro fuego se consumieron los traidores.

Nuestro nombre no está escrito . . .

Nuestro nombre no está escrito en los arcos de triunfo ni en los cielos
    letales,
Nuestros nombres sin forma agregan, materia al infinito,
Desalojamos de las aguas los triunfos fraternales
Recorrimos las cimas del viento y del zafiro
Al golpe de nuestros disparos
La extensión se estremecía,
Oh gargantas del hombre
Quemadas por el fósforo
Oh manos del hombre
Por la pólvora honradas
Oh pechos del hombre
En silencio partidos
Oh gran patria del hombre
Recuerda nuestros pasos.

Our words aflame like the flight of sparrow hawks through space
Are born from the springs of purity.
We were truth, the encounter of the people and its destiny,
Our people of minerals, red earth, tireless drums, asked it of us.
Night was our witness and homage,
When Havana, when Santiago,
When all of our provinces were corrupted by tears and terror,
Our fiery breasts were the arrows of dawn, and they said:
Awake, beloved earth, we are your liberating lords, the red and black of
    revolutions is coming through freedom's illustrious world,
We are ploughing history's broad furrow, we are its surname, its reason for
    being.
With our voices of water, smoke, diamonds,
Elemental conquerors of truth,
We answered the minerals of the earth, its eagles, its beasts of love.
We were like the arrows that once pierced the light,
Chosen by revolution we ascended our land,
Our winter roses opened transparent,
And in our fire the traitors were consumed.

Our name is unwritten . . .

Our name is unwritten in the triumphal arches and the lethal heavens,
Our unformed names add matter to infinity,
We dislodge fraternal triumphs from the waters
We walk the heights of wind and breeze
At the thunder of our shots
All around us shudders,
Oh throats of man
Burned by phosphorus
Oh hands of man
Honored by gunpowder
Oh breasts of man
Shattered into silence
Oh great fatherland of man
Remember our passing.

Translated by Christopher Winks

César López

Como en cualquier ciudad . . .

Como en cualquier ciudad que se respete, sitio elegido, plaza
fuerte, así, de esa manera casi sorprendente para los incrédulos,
comenzaron a aparecer los ángeles.
No se trataba de esas rubicundas e infantiles criaturas, alas
y batas de colores claros, que salen en las procesiones o en las veladas de los
   protestantes.
Fue que la ciudad se iba poblando de misterios, seres predominantemente
   nocturnos.
Hay mariposas diurnas, pero las hay nocturnas.
¡Extraña cosa esto de los ángeles! Las órdenes angélicas mostraban
obsesivas y determinadas predilecciones. Y no era el caso
determinar su sexo, su número en la punta de una aguja:
La ciudad nunca conoció el medioevo. Aquella temporada
ofreció toda suerte de devociones, éxtasis y desmayos. Con precisión
nadie recuerda el sitio ni el momento de la aparición del primero,
del ángel que brindó las señales iniciales de estar en posesión de la ciudad.
Pero se sospecha que aparecieron a la caída de la tarde. (Hora
tradicionalmente romántica y ya llena de sombras provechosas),
cuando varias jovencitas, excitadas por alguna incompleta y masculina
caricia del jardín o pasillo, salían apresuradas de la Escuela Normal.
El deslumbramiento cortó la respiración de muchas de ellas, lo que no
   impidió
la más desatinada carrera loma abajo (no hay que olvidar que entonces
se trataba de vírgenes tan orgullosas como inexpertas). A partir
de ese momento, los ángeles se fueron multiplicando como si fueran
conejos o moscas; aparecían, o mejor dicho dejaban su indudable rastro
en todas partes, preferiblemente en aquéllas bien habitadas. Ya se sabe
que *todo ángel es terrible* (algunos jóvenes estaban altamente influidos
por Rilke en ese tiempo) y *que lo bello no es más que el inicio de lo terrible
que todavía podemos soportar* y entonces era lógico: *Quién si yo gritase
me oiría desde las órdenes angélicas.* Por lo tanto
las jovencitas (que en esto los ángeles no tenían vacilación alguna)
lo que más atinaban era a echarse a correr, primero, siempre a cerrar
los ojos según los cánones de la belleza angélica, y luego, en la mayoría
de los casos, caían desmadejadas en brazos de los ángeles.
Pero claro está, ante estos conceptos metafísicos de interpretación, surgió

César López

As in any respectable city . . .

As in any respectable city, at a chosen site, a secure
plaza, just like that, in a way almost surprising to the incredulous,
angels began to appear.
Not those rosy childish creatures, pastel wings
and gowns, that sally forth in religious processions or to the evening
    meetings of Protestants.
The city was being populated with mysteries, predominantly nocturnal
    beings.
There are diurnal butterflies, but these are nocturnal.
This strange business of the angels! The angelic orders exhibited
obsessive and precise habits. And it wasn't a question of
determining their sex, their numbers on the head of a pin:
The city knew nothing of the Middle Ages. That time
that had afforded every chance of devotions, ecstasies, and fainting spells.
    No one remembers
the precise location or moment when he first appeared,
the angel who first announced possession of the city.
But it was suspected that they appeared at sunset (which according to
    tradition
is romantic and full of useful shadows)
when various young women, excited by some incomplete masculine
caress in garden or hallway, rushed forth from the teachers college.
The dazzling light was breathtaking to many of them, which didn't slow down
their reckless downhill race (it ought not be forgotten that these
were virgins, as proud as they were inexperienced). From that
moment on, the angels multiplied
like rabbits or flies; they appeared, or rather, left a definite trace
everywhere, especially in the most populated areas. It's well known
that *every angel is terrible* (some of the young were highly influenced
by Rilke then) and *that what is beautiful is only the incitement of the terrible
that we can yet endure,* and then logically: *Who if I cry out
will hear me among the angelic orders.* Therefore
the girls (and the angels never hesitated)
who were most sure began to run, eyes closed
according to the law of angelic beauty, then falling,
most of them, exhausted into the angels' arms.
But clearly, preceding these metaphysical concepts of interpretation,

la tesis opuesta (un profesor de literatura, bastante ingenioso,
señaló la lectura conceptual de cierto libro de Rafael Alberti):
Y surgieron las admiradoras de los ángeles traviesos
con todas sus posibles consecuencias. Se habló inclusive de ángeles neuróticos.
Lo sorprendente fue la multiplicación estruendosa de los ángeles. En todas sus
    variantes.
Ya en las noches nadie osaba sin miedo desandar por las calles.
Los ángeles, brillantes, relucientes, con sus rostros hermosos e imposibles
(es un decir, pues nadie les vio con propiedad las caras) se lanzaban
audaces delante de los automóviles, gritaban maravillosamente, tomaban
la leche que repartían los lecheros madrugadores o asustaban
a la noctámbula comadrona, que iba afanosa a sus quehaceres propios.
Así que disminuyó el abasto de la leche y el nacimiento se realizó
rigurosamente en hospitales y clínicas. La ciudad se vio libre
de vehículos nocturnos. La nocturnidad, no así la alevosía, se transformó en
    angélica.

Otras cosas diversas sucedían.

Los católicos trataban de adorarlos y los soberbios protestantes,
desde el púlpito, se fatigaban para encontrar la interpretación de estos hechos.
"La ciudad de Sodoma había sido visitada por los santos varones en vísperas
de su destrucción; y el buen Jacob había luchado, nada menos que toda la
    noche
con el ángel." (Sépase que ni Jacob ni el ángel boxeador eran homosexuales.)
Las gallinas seguían poniendo huevos. Pero los ángeles muy bien se
    alimentaban.
Unas niñas de sociedad, un tanto heterodoxas, organizaron
un "Welcome Nice Angel's party". El éxito estuvo asegurado de antemano,
sólo que por un ligero error de cálculo el sarao no pudo celebrarse.
Los señores del gobierno, preocupados, celosos más bien,
habían hecho traer de cierto lugar cercano un rígido capitán de policía
que si bien no tenía demasiada experiencia en su trato con ángeles,
había hecho desaparecer otras diferentes plagas molestas a la autoridad.
Los ángeles fueron naturalmente acusados de comunistas.

Mientras, los ángeles exquisitos, e incongruentes, mantenían sus reiterados
    gustos
por las más bellas y despampanantes mujeres de la ciudad.
Y el ángel del señor anunció a María. En realidad no fue la anunciación
hecha a María, sino a toda joven hermosa que hubiese bien topado con un
    ángel.

the opposite thesis had also emerged (a professor of literature ingeniously cited
a theoretical reading in a certain book by Rafael Alberti).
And the admirers of the naughty angels
brought forth every possible theoretical consequence. Even the possibility
that the angels were neurotic was touted. It was their noisy multiplication
    that was surprising. In all their variants.
Now no one dared go home through the streets at night without fear.
The angels, gleaming, shining, with their handsome and impossible faces
(as it's said, for no one actually sees their faces) flung themselves
audaciously in front of automobiles, cried out marvelously, drank
the milk that the morning milkmen distribute, or frightened
the midwives walking at night to their anxious labors.
So the supply of milk was diminished and being born was strictly relegated
to hospitals and clinics. The city found itself free
of nocturnal vehicles. Nighttime, without premeditation, became angelic.

Other things followed.

The Catholics tried to worship them and the proud Protestants,
from the pulpit, wore themselves out trying to interpret these acts.
"The city of Sodom was visited by saints on the eve
of its destruction; and the good Jacob wrestled with the angel
all night long." (It was of course understood neither Jacob nor the angelic
    boxer were homosexuals.)
The hens continued to roost. But it was the angels who ate the eggs.
A few debutantes, a bit heterodox, organized
a "Welcome Nice Angels party." Its success was assured,
and it was only a slight miscalculation that kept it from happening.
The government leaders, worried, and also jealous,
had brought in from a certain nearby place a strict police chief
who although he didn't have much experience with angels,
had made other plagues that had threatened authority disappear.
Naturally, the angels were accused of being communists.

Meanwhile, the exquisite illogical angels maintained their taste
for the most beautiful, the most stunning women of the city.
And the angel of the Lord came to Mary. It wasn't in fact the annunciation
made to Mary, but to every beautiful girl who happened to run into an
    angel.

Eduviges Almánzaga, la solterona, se paseaba furtiva e insistente
vestida en un fino y provocativo camisón de dormir por los jardines
de su antigua casa. Pero nunca fue visitada por los ángeles.
Algunas muchachas salían embarazadas, otras tuvieron
estrepitosos ataques de nervios o hemorragias.
Discreta la ciudad, pensó en la gracia. Y los comentarios y apuestas
le fueron dados por añadidura.
Mas el poderoso capitán de la policía decidió acabar con los ángeles.
Salió a la calle. Fuertemente armado y con escoltas
se dedicó a perseguirlos. ¡Cuántos pensaron
en la provocación y la herejía! Difícil de explicar es todo esto.
Pero los ángeles desaparecieron. Hubo heridos y presos.

Y un elegante yate que estaba anclado en la bahía zarpó rápidamente.
Sus tripulantes eran media docena de apuestos jóvenes belgas
que celebraban su reciente graduación en la Universidad de Lovaina
con un alegre viaje alrededor del mundo. Los acompañaba
una famosa bailarina persa de inclinaciones sexuales un tanto amplias y
    equívocas.

¡Qué silencio de ángeles en la ciudad entonces! El capitán, soberbio, quedó
    por algún tiempo dueño de la ciudad.

El poeta en la ciudad

Recosta'o en el quicio (¿de la mancebía?)
más flaco que la tradicional e inexistente
vara de tumbar gatos, miraba *encenderse las noches*
de mayo, como si astros y luceros
no se alumbraran siempre, no estuvieron
a la disposición de los que observan y escudriñan
con atención en la ciudad reciente,
y a la vez eterna, la inmensidad de su cielo estrellado.

El muro paradójico la ensancha, no la limita,
vuelve con tantos años, es el tiempo
que no sabe descifrar ese poeta arrogante y humillado:
Juega con cuentas de colores, tiraflechas
y un incipiente arcoiris lo lastima;
algo pidió prestado a sus vecinos que ahora

Eduviges Almánzaga, the spinster, paraded furtively and persistently
dressed in a fine and provocative nightgown through the gardens
of her ancient home. But the angels never came to her.
Some girls became pregnant, others had noisy
attacks of nerves or nosebleeds.
The city soberly thought of grace. And commentaries and wagers
were thrown in as a bonus.
But the powerful police chief decided to put an end to the angels.
He went into the street. Armed to the teeth and surrounded by
  bodyguards,
he dedicated himself to their pursuit. The provocation and the heresy
had gone too far! All of this is difficult to explain.
But the angels disappeared. Some were wounded and imprisoned.

And an elegant yacht that was anchored in the bay quickly sailed off.
Its crew was a half dozen dashing young Belgians
celebrating their recent graduation from the University of Louvain
with a joyous circumnavigation of the globe. They were accompanied
by a famous Persian dancer whose sexual tastes were both ample and
  ambiguous.

What a silence of angels in the city then! The proud police chief remained
  for some time in control of the city.

The Poet in the City

Leaning against the doorway (of the brothel?)
skinnier than
Jack Sprat, he *watched the nights of May*
in flame, as if the stars and planets
weren't always lit, weren't always
available to those who carefully observe and investigate
in the new and also eternal
city the immensity of the star-filled sky.

Paradoxically, the wall doesn't enclose, but opens it,
it returns with so many years, it's time itself
that the arrogant and humiliated poet doesn't know how to make sense of.
He plays with colored beads, a slingshot
and an incipient rainbow that comes back to haunt him;
something borrowed from his neighbors who now

exigen su devolución y su ganancia.
Es como si nunca, como si siempre,
como si la vida inmóvil hubiera permanecido allí,
en el calor y la falsa frescura del anhelado invierno.

A ese hombre le tiemblan las manos
por su torpe quehacer de levantar ladrillos
para sólo llevarlos tontamente de un lado a otro,
sin siquiera lograr construir una torre, una escalera,
en la repetición de estrofas y sílabas contadas.
Aunque sea un tejadillo para evitar el viento.

Vio tantas cosas, imaginó las lágrimas, fingió
la risa y hasta el mismo entusiasmo
y quiso ser; se desgarró en tremendo desafío. Astuto
en la carencia del padre y los abuelos
se fue inventando una inquietante galería de retratos
y acomodó la voz desafinada, sin darse cuenta
de lo turbio, lo inútil y de *la soledad,*
la lluvia, los caminos. La ronda,
no lo sabe (o tal vez lo sabía),
era imaginaria. Voces, chasquidos, chispas
que saltan de los cascos del caballo,
cabriola y desespero. Sordo para la música.
No se atrevió al asalto de los campos hermosos.
Las muchachas de entonces despreciaban sus dientes y sus pelos,
mientras que los hombres *contados y furiosos* codiciaban su sexo no
    estrenado,
adivinaban prodigios, se insinuaban. Y el alma del poeta
sin comprender, *sorda a los ayes, insensible*
al ruego, desconocía lúbricas cataratas,
estremecimientos, suspiros secretos, charquitos de agua sucia.
Ahora regresa como si en realidad alguna vez
hubiera partido, como si fuera cierto;
y al paso de las gentes se descubre
falsamente impasible, displicente, caduco.
Ajusta su dicción, su palabra
que presume impecable aunque conoce
y afirma, no sin un trazo de coquetería,
la *quiebra de la perfección*; espera aplausos,
al menos algún gesto comedido de aceptación;
un reguilete. Peregrino sentado, se pregunta

demand its return, with interest.
It's as if never, as if always,
as if unchanging life might still be there, in some other place,
in the heat and the deceptive coolness of a yearned-for winter.

His hands shake
with the stupefying labor of lifting bricks
only to carry them from one side to the other,
never managing to build a tower, a staircase,
out of the repetition of stanzas and counted syllables.
Although it might be a shack to protect him from the wind.

He has seen many things, imagined tears, feigned
laughter and even enthusiasm
and wished it so. And a terrible defiance broke his heart. Shrewd,
lacking a father and grandfathers
he invented a disturbing gallery of portraits
and took on an off-key voice, unaware of
the muddy, the useless, and *solitude,*
rain, roads. The patrol—
he didn't know (or perhaps he did)
that he'd imagined it. Voices, cracks of the whip, sparks
that fly from the hooves
of the skittish, despairing cavalry. Deaf to the music.
Its boldness failed in the assault on the beautiful fields.
The girls of that time despised his teeth and skin,
while the men, *upstanding and furious,* coveted his untried genitals—
they imagined, hinted at, prodigies. And the soul of the poet
uncomprehending, *deaf to sighs, insensible*
to pleas, refused to recognize lubricious waterfalls,
trembling, secret sighs, puddles of filthy water.
Now he returns as if he really had departed,
once again, as if it were true;
and the people flowing by find him
falsely impassive, disdainful, obsolete.
He adjusts his diction, his language
that he presumes impeccable even though he knows
and admits, not without a hint of coquetry,
the collapse of perfection; he waits for applause
or at least some gesture of polite acceptance;
a pinwheel. A sedentary pilgrim, he wonders

de qué sirven los barcos, los aviones, medallas
o ataúdes y los nombres pomposos de las calles.
No hubo besos robados, ni fruteros, ni acaso
caracolas rosadas o rozadas, aventuras ecuestres.

Un cura, un pastor, una santera
y los chinos vendedores de hortalizas, pescados y mariscos
se enredan en el desfile militar sin brillo.
Trastruecan la memoria y el recuerdo
—¡Señor, tenga cuidado, en la ciudad
la lluvia es peligrosa . . . y a su edad
no es conveniente resfriarse! ¡Evite las fracturas!

¡Ah, qué preocupada y distante es esta gente
que ya no reconoce al niño o al jovencito,
al hombre aquel que, mozo, rompía los espejos!
Los cines han cerrado sus puertas, la banda
de música municipal ya no toca en el parque
sus melodías y ritmos aburridos, sus imaginarias
y bailables disonancias. Ni siquiera hay hastío.
Y el poeta intenta tararear, mas desentona.
No es posible para él otra cosa que rumiar en silencio
todo lo que no fue. Lo que se escapa
o se fugó veloz por las ventanas rotas
de la ciudad. Por claraboyas. Por los cortejos
hacia el cementerio. Desdibujado en la ambición ilusa.
¡Qué puede hacer entonces recostado
al quicio antiguo y cursi (¿de la mancebía?)!

—¡El señor está loco o es un bobo, babieca
o bucólico actor que nunca supo
su papel y se ha quedado *mudo y absorto y de rodillas!*

Petrificado. Sordo. Tal vez ciego. En calzoncillos.
No importa. *Entra y sale un perro triste.*
Canta allá dentro una voz.
Sí importa. Lo que cuenta es el tiempo
aunque no lo comprende. Los años
se han perdido sin lustre y están resquebrajados.
El hueco en la memoria. El sudor y el salitre.

¡Si tuviera un espejo! O al menos una grabadora
que acumulara el olvido y el paso de los meses

what boats, planes, medals
or coffins and the pompous names of the streets are for.
There were no stolen kisses, nor bowls of fruit, nor perhaps
snails rosy or worn, equestrian adventures.

A priest, a pastor, a *santera*
and the Chinese vendors of vegetables, fish and shellfish
become entangled in the dull parade of soldiers.
They confuse memory and remembrance:
"Take care, sir, in the city
rain is dangerous . . . and at your age
it's risky to catch a cold. Watch for cracks in the sidewalk!"

Ah, how preoccupied and distant these people
who no longer see the child or youth,
the man whose beauty, in his day, broke mirrors!
The movie theaters have closed, and the municipal band
is no longer filling the square with its boring tunes
and rhythms, its fanciful
and danceable dissonance. Even tedium is missing.
And the poet tries to hum, but out of tune.
All that's left for him is to think in silence
of all that he was not. All that escapes
or flew from the broken windows
of the city. Through skylights. Through funeral processions
toward the cemetery. Blurred by naive ambition.
So why is he leaning
against the tacky old doorway (*of the brothel?*)!

—He's nuts or a fool, a simple-minded
hayseed actor who never learned
his part and has remained *mute and distracted and on his knees!*

Petrified. Deaf. Blind, maybe. In underpants.
It doesn't matter. *A sad dog comes and goes.*
Over there, within, a voice is singing.
It does matter. What counts is time
although he doesn't understand it. The years
are lost, lusterless, crackled.
The gap in memory. The sweat and sea-spray.

If he owned a mirror! Or at least a tape recorder
that would gather the forgotten and the passage of months

más allá de las calles y de las novias muertas.
Como no puede girar siquiera el cuello rígido
y contemplar la casa que no le pertenece
sólo le queda reconstruir a tientas
lo que no pudo ser: —*Y aún guardo las dos blancas azucenas*
que me diste, que me diste
al despedirme de ti. Ciudad, ciudad, ciudad,
remordimiento aparte, repite, recostado,
rememora y recuerda roncamente,
que me diste, que me diste
al despedirme de ti.

Antón Arrufat

de Repaso final

I

Mi familia muerta está sentada en la sala
y conversa de las cosas del día.

Por esta calle arrastran muertos
—dice mi madre donde está ahora—
viendo pasar los muertos y las coronas.

Mi familia muerta está sentada en la sala.

Mi tía con sus largos brazos,
el pelo teñido, recordando.
Juan dijo que vendría a buscarla
y nunca volvió. Ella lo vio
con otra mujer y con el niño.
Juan dijo que vendría a buscarla
—repitió la familia.

La mesa con el búcaro y las flores
de papel, el radio viejo y el bastón.

beyond the streets and the dead sweethearts.
He can't even turn his stiff neck
to look at the house that doesn't belong to him,
all that's left is rebuilding blindly
what couldn't be. —*And still I keep the two white lilies*
that you gave me, that you gave me
when you said goodbye. City, city, city
putting remorse aside, leaning, he repeats,
in a hoarse voice, remembers and recalls
that you gave me, that you gave me
when you said goodbye.

Translated by Rebecca Seiferle

Antón Arrufat

from Final Revision

I

My dead family sits in the living room
chatting about the everyday.

The biers of the dead pass down this street—
my mother says from her present place—
watching the passage of the dead and their wreaths.

My dead family sits in the living room.

My aunt with her long arms,
her dyed hair, remembering.
Juan said he'd come for her
but he never came. She saw him
with another woman and a child.
Juan said he'd come for her,
the family repeats.

The table, its vase and paper
flowers, the old radio and the cane.

Dios de la vida, exclama mi padre,
y recoge los restos del día.
Quisimos hacer nuestra vida
a golpes, mientras sonaba
el reloj del comedor.

Mi familia muerta está sentada en la sala.

¿No irás al cine esta tarde,
antes de la comida?
Al cine, mirando sus vidas,
sin que puedan cambiarlas,
con los ojos vacíos,
en la vigilia, cuando
crecen las uñas y el pelo de mi madre
es una cabellera sobre los huesos apagados.

Yo pienso en ella y no sé si llorar.
Si las imágenes alcanzaran la resurrección.

Sombras mías, ruinas que no podré rescatar,
manos sin huesos, pies que no caminan
y dejan olvidados los zapatos.

Sombras que no necesitan la oscuridad.
Aparecen bajo el sol, en las tardes,
sin que las invoque, cuando me levanto
despierto en medio de las luces.

Escucha, mi familia:
estoy aquí donde no hay nadie, viviendo
por ustedes, arrastrando los muertos,
y los miro entrar con las puertas cerradas.

Escuchen, sombras mías: en los sillones
que no encuentro, la noche viene
para apagar los trajes y las begonias.

5

El gallo que canta en el patio,
el otro que responde, es el mismo
que oyó Martí cuando vino a la Isla.
Anuncia, ave solar,

God of life, exclaims my father,
and gathers up what's left of the day.
We wanted our life to happen
in a single stroke, while the clock
in the dining room tolled.

My dead family sits in the living room.

Will you go to the movies this afternoon,
before dinner?
To the movies, watching its lives that can't be changed,
their empty eyes,
sleepless, as
nails grow and my mother's tresses
are hair upon extinguished bones.

I think of her and don't know whether to cry.
Whether the images will be enough for resurrection.

My shades, ruins that I won't be able to redeem,
hands without bones, feet that no longer walk
and whose shoes are forgotten.

Shades that need no darkness.
They appear beneath the sun, in the afternoons,
without any invocation, when I get up
awake in the midst of light.

Listen, my family:
I am here where there's no one, living
for you, pulling the biers of the dead,
and I see them pass through closed doors.

Listen, my shades: in the rocking chairs
that I don't find, night comes
to extinguish suits and dresses and begonias.

5

The rooster that sings in the yard,
the other that answers, is the one
that Martí heard when he came to the Island.
Announce, solar bird,

el día distinto, el amanecer del monte.
Están en él los dioses esperando
que el hombre cumpla.

El gallo rojo, plumas mojadas en alcohol,
la sangre sobre mis espaldas opacas.

Él regresa, se golpea
el pecho con los puños, canta,
besa la tierra.

El monte se ilumina
como si guardias invisibles
se pasaran las luces.

La Isla arde en virtud de la sangre.

Volvemos a decir piña,
majagua, cedros,
yagrumas de la melancolía.

Tantos muertos
hablan por nuestras bocas.
¿Cómo no siento horror
ante la mancha de sangre en el camino?
Oh, cabeza enterrada con pañuelos.

Aquí en el polvo presiento
los huesos del castigado,
el jarrito y la yunta.
Noche, sol del triste, que nos recibes
cuando el bote se aleja,
líbrame, eterna noche, del verdugo.
Aquí en el polvo tropiezo
con la fusta, con los grillos de hierro.
Los huesos, apenas enterrados,
lanzan clamores. Que mis labios
hereden las órdenes proféticas.

A lo largo de los rieles
desfilan los entierros.
Despídelos, hijo. Estos muertos
son nuestros muertos y el monte los aguarda.
Sobre los árboles estarán sus cabezas,

the bright new day, the dawn of the forest.
The gods are there, waiting for man
to obey.

The red rooster, feathers wet with alcohol,
the blood upon my gloomy shoulders.

He returns, strikes his chest
with his fists, sings,
kisses the earth.

The forest is lit
as if by invisible watchmen
passing their lanterns.

The Island burns by the power of blood.

We return to invoking pine,
linden, cedars,
yagrumas of melancholy.

So many dead
speak through our mouths.
How can I not feel the horror
of the blood stain in the road?
Oh, head buried beneath scraps of cloth.

Here in the dust, I sense
the bones of the punished,
the jug and the yoke.
Night, sun of the sorrowing, that receives us
when the boat recedes,
free me, eternal night, from the hangman.
Here in the dust, I stumble upon
riding crop, shackles.
The fresh bones
shout. May my lips
inherit the prophetic order.

Along the length of the rails
the funerals file by.
Bid them farewell, my son. Those dead
are our dead and the forest awaits them.
Their heads will soar above the trees,

los párpados abiertos,
porque nada es efímero.
Despídelos, hijo. El día se acerca.
Cada muerto bajo la tierra
prepara la primavera.

Nuestra sangre
dejará llegar el bien a la casa.

LA HABANA, 1962

José Kozer

Te acuerdas, Sylvia

Te acuerdas, Sylvia, cómo trabajaban las mujeres en casa.
Parecía que papá no hacía nada.
Llevaba las manos a la espalda inclinándose como un rabino fumando una
  cachimba corta de abedul, las volutas de humo le daban un
  aire misterioso,
comienzo a sospechar que papá tendría algo de asiático.
Quizás fuera un señor de Besarabia que redimió a sus siervos en épocas del
  Zar,
o quizás acostumbrara a reposar en los campos de avena y somnoliento
  a la hora de la criba se sentara encorvado bondadosamente en
  un sitio húmedo entre los helechos con su antigua casaca algo
  deshilachada.
Es probable que quedara absorto al descubrir en la estepa una manzana.
Nada sabía del mar.
Seguro se afanaba con la imagen de la espuma y confundía las anémonas y
  el cielo.
Creo que la llorosa muchedumbre de las hojas de los eucaliptos lo asustaba.
Figúrate qué sintió cuando Rosa Luxemburgo se presentó con un
  opúsculo entre las manos ante los jueces del Zar.
Tendría que emigrar pobre papá de Odesa a Viena, Roma, Estambul,
  Quebec, Ottawa, Nueva York.
Llegaría a La Habana como un documento y cinco pasaportes, me lo
  imagino algo maltrecho del viaje.

their eyelids open,
because nothing is ephemeral.
Bid them farewell, my son. Day approaches.
Each death beneath the earth
readies the spring.

Our blood
will allow the good to come home.

HAVANA, 1962

Translated by Rebecca Seiferle

José Kozer

Sylvia, Do You Remember

Sylvia, do you remember the women of the house, how hard they worked.
It always seemed that father did nothing.
Smoking his short birch pipe hands clasped behind him he paced like a
      rabbi, mysterious in a cloud of smoke.
Looking back it seems to me there was something asiatic about him.
Maybe he had been a lord of Bessarabia who had freed his serfs in the days
      of the Czar,
or perhaps he would rest in the oat fields and at threshing-time sleepily
      would sit bent forward in his threadbare coat in a damp
      place among the ferns.
I imagine he'd become transfixed upon discovering on the steppe an apple.
He who knew nothing of the sea.
Doubtless he would struggle with the image of foam, confusing anemones
      with sky.
Even the weeping mass of eucalyptus leaves would have frightened him.
Imagine then what he must have felt when Rosa Luxemburg, tract in
      hand, appeared before the Czar's court.
Forced to emigrate from Odessa to Vienna, Rome, Istanbul, Quebec,
      Ottawa, New York.
Weary of traveling poor father would arrive in Havana like one document
      and five passports.

Recuerdas, Sylvia, cuando papá llegaba de los almacenes de la calle
      Muralla y todas las mujeres de la casa Uds. se alborotaban.
Juro que entraba por la puerta de la sala, zapatos de dos tonos, el traje azul
      a rayas, la corbata de óvalos finita
y parecía que papá no hacía nunca nada.

Rebrote de Franz Kafka

Es una casa pequeña a dos niveles no muy lejos del río en un callejón de
      Praga. En la madrugada
del once
al doce noviembre tuvo un sobresalto, bajó a la cocinilla con la mesa
      redonda y la silla de tilo, el anafe y la llama azul de metileno.
      Prendió

la hornilla
y el fuego verdeció a la vez (tres) llamas en los tres cristales de la ventana:
      olía a azufre. Quiso

pasar
a la salita comedor a beber una tisana de boldo y miel, corrió la silla y se
      acomodó delante de una taza de barro siena que había colo-
      cado no se sabe hace cuánto sobre el portavasos de mimbre a
      seis colores, obsequio
de Felicia: y una vez más
apareció Felicia con la raya al medio, las dos trenzas y un resplandor de
      velas en el óvalo blanco de aquel rostro ávido de harinas y
      panes de la consagración, rostro

tres veces
una llamarada en el cristal de la ventana: apareció. Y era una vez más la
      niña tres veces de sus muertos, acudían

al golpe
del triángulo unos músicos de cámara y al golpe de la esquila (las tres) en
      el alto campanario no muy lejos del río: se arrellanaron, diez

tazas, diez
sillas en la inmensa casona de las mansardas, la casa en que los miradores y
      las cristaleras (establos y galpones) se abrían día y noche, el
      agua

Do you remember his return from the Muralla Street stores, the women of
    the house quivering with excitement.
I swear to you that when he entered through the living room door in
    two-toned shoes a striped blue suit and a thin tie decorated
    with ovals
it would seem that papa had never done anything.

Kafka Reborn

It's a modest two-story house not far from the river on a narrow street in
    Prague. In the early morning
between the 11th
and 12th of November he awoke with a start and descended the stairs to
    the small kitchen with its round table and lindenwood chair,
    its portable stove and methyl-blue flame. He lit

the burner
and the fire became at once (three) flames reflected in the window's three
    panes: smell of sulphur. He wished

to go
to the dining nook to drink a medicinal tea of honey and boldo leaves, he
    moved the chair and settled in before a sienna-colored clay
    bowl which he had placed, he'd forgotten when, on the six-
    colored wicker tray,
Felicia's
gift; and once again
Felicia appeared her hair in braids and the radiance of candles reflected on
    the white oval of that face greedy for consecrated loaves and
    cakes, that face

three times
a burst of flames in the window pane: she appeared and was again three
    times the child of her dead, a few chamber players

responded to the stroke
of a triangle and the stroke of a bell (at three) in the high belfry not far
    from the river: they took their ease, ten

cups, ten
chairs in the immense country house with its mansard roofs, the house in
    which bay windows and glass doors (barns and sheds) were
    open day and night, the water

y las esponjas
relucían. Pues, sí: era otra época y un coro de muchachas vigilaba las
    teteras (bullir) los eucaliptos (bullir) la mejorana y un agua
    digestiva (mentas) aguas
de la respiración: todo
tranquilo (por fin) todo tranquilo, subió los escalones y vio que se tendía en
    el cristal de la ventana (por fin) sin una aglomeración de pájaros
en la ventana.

La dádiva

Nací en la casa del moribundo; su cadáver está extenuado: no lo sacudo
    más, se apaciguó.

Yace, con los pies hacia Oriente.

Son enormes; tronchos, consanguíneos: aún, destilan desde allá lejos en
    aquel otro país sus volutas de aroma a camomilas; ovaladas: el
    óvalo de su cabeza rapada se aja todavía sobre una almohada;
    y ved, en la funda bosquejaron un pez de escamas gualdas la
    saeta de un pájaro diagonal: absorto, ora en el lino de la funda;
    dista, del blanco sitio del lino: y por piedad se encarama sobre
    el pez simularon las bordadoras un estallido; del lúpulo.

Sus estambres gualdas reavivaron la escama de los peces.

Yo, las conozco: en sus sillas de majagua con la lira en el respaldar,
    bordando; por cada muerto una túnica de arpillera que huele
    a sudor o espliego, un pez un pájaro para reposar la cabeza
    en el légamo: las bordadoras, liman; la cabeza del muerto
    está lustrosa, lustrosos sus pies: seda, es la túnica; blandísima
    arpillera, el lino de la funda.

Un batracio antiquísimo, el cadáver.

No está mermado: las moscas lo mordisquean, intacto. Un enjambre de
    supuración intacto reluce en sus poros, lino abierto: todo
    lo que vuela, es suyo; quieta crisálida. Todo lo que vuela es
    extirpado de sus senos cada vez más recónditos, rebosantes:
    las bordadoras sacan el hilván amarillo de la hez de esos fon-
    dos, sacuden la oruga.

and the sponges

shone. Yes: it was another time, and a chorus of girls tended the teapots
(boiling) the eucalyptus (boiling), the marjoram and a diges-
tive water (mint leaves) respiratory

waters: at peace
at peace (at last), he climbed the stairs and saw himself stretched out in the
window pane (at last) no crowd of birds

in the window.

The Offering

I was born in the house of the dying man; I no longer shake his exhausted
corpse, he rests in peace now.

He is laid out, his feet face eastward.

They are enormous; two stems of the same bloodline: from them in that
far-off country the scent of chamomile rises in spirals; ovoid:
the oval of his shaved head withered rests as ever upon a
pillow; look, they have limned on the pillowcase a fish with
golden scales the arrow's-flight of a diagonal bird: entranced,
it prays on the linen of the pillowcase; it is far from the white
space of the linen; its piety empowers it to soar above the fish
the seamstresses have simulated an outburst: of hops.

The scales brought back to life by their golden yarn.

I know them well: they sit to their embroidery on lyre-backed mahogany
chairs, for each corpse a burlap robe smelling of sweat or lav-
ender, a fish a bird for the head's repose in the mud: the seam-
stresses do their touch-up; the head of the corpse is luminous,
luminous its feet: the robe silk, soft beyond softness the cloth
of the pillowcase.

The corpse of an old toad.

It has not shrunk: flies nibble at an intact body. An intact mass of
suppuration glows from its pores, an open-work cloth: all
things that fly are his; the quiet chrysalis. All things that fly
come forth overflowing from ever more hidden cavities: from
those depths the seamstresses pull the yellow basting of the
dregs, they shake the larva.

Exudan, un filamento de vidrio.

Concavidad, sin cronologías: boceto. Y sobre la cama, no muere: lo
aderezan. Es nuevo; con una camisa de felpa roja anchos
pantalones beige, estrujados: en las trenzas que cuelgan sobre
su pecho entrelazaron guirnaldas en flor de las leguminosas:
imparcial.

Se incorpora; lo han ayudado.

Sus grandes pies desnudos segregan el orín de los clavos que liban en su
agujero las hormigas: los pétalos que bajan por sus ropas for-
jan un insaciable avispero amoratado a sus plantas; pájaros de
hez peces de lino se apresuran, a anegarse: sonríe.

Reconoce en las hormas del espacio, una puerta.

Soles, por Levante: los plateros de la comunidad huelen a cardamomo las
nigromantes, se desperezan: lo sitúan. Y sacan las artesas
colmadas en la oval cernida de la harina, hacia las plazas: las
bandadas picotean en la miga de pan que refulge entre sus
brazos en alto.

Jerusalén celeste

La mariposa blanca rozó mis prados, un domingo: prados en que estoy
implicado, llenos de amargón. A la derecha

la laguna que aún me convoca y yo me niego; he de vivir: engordar y reír,
enrojecer como

un burgomaestre cachetudo, Hals. Qué vi a la izquierda: tráfico. La
automotriz irrealidad de las ciudades, yo

por mí

me cambié y vi plumones: qué felices que fuimos cuando descubrí el
domingo de los amargones y cocinaste

al aire libre un pernil grande que tenía la forma de un huso, lo adornaste a
base

de clavo y maíz,

papas hermosas de Idaho; jugaron al salto de la suiza nuestras hijas: eran dos

They exude a filament of glass.

Timeless concavity: a sketch. And on the bed he is not dead: they dress
      him. He is renewed: a red plush shirt, wide, wrinkled beige
      pants; they have woven garlands of leguminous flowers
      through the braids hanging above his chest: impartial.

He sits up; they have helped him.

His large bare feet secrete the rust of nails that ants sip in their holes;
      the petals that fall from his clothing amass in an insatiable
      empurpled wasp's nest at his feet; birds of the dregs linen fish
      rush to submerge themselves: he smiles.

He sees in the shoetrees of space a door.

Levantine suns: the local silversmiths smell of cardamom, the necromancers,
      resuming their work, position him. And they carry to the
      plaza troughs abundant with ovals of sifted flour: flocks of
      birds peck at the crumbs refulgent between his lifted arms.

The Heavenly Jerusalem

On a Sunday the white butterfly skims across my meadows: dandelion-
      filled meadows of my imagining. To the right

is the lake that calls to me, but I refuse it; I shall live: grow fat, laugh, turn
      rubicund,

Hals, as any plump-cheeked burgomeister. To the left: traffic. The
      automotive unreality of cities, and I,

I turn and see soft down: how happy we were when we found that Sunday
      of dandelions and you cooked outdoors

an enormous ham shaped like a spindle, garnished it

with cloves and corn

and beautiful potatoes; our daughters played jump rope: there were two,

las mariposas celestiales y si fueran tres hubiera dado igual que fueran
        cuatro, trenzas y cabellos al caracolillo hilvanados de azul

y amarillo

en toda la brotación de mis prados: a la comba, nuestras hijas subieron
        altísimamente

a nuestra primera gran convocatoria que fue en el cielo, amada: de la
        cintura te agarré y me provocó

subir

contigo al árbol de cuatro troncos añosos, no hubo manera: qué lindo,
        fracasamos. Reíste de la cintura

para abajo y me dejé llevar por tus anchas pasarelas japonesas, tu viejo
        puente español de argamasa

y piedra, nos picó una hormiga: sonreímos; la hinchazón y aquel timbre a
        músicas lejanas nos amedrentó

como si hubieran caminado las niñas sobre las aguas de la laguna a la
        derecha

y por la izquierda

de pronto hubiera rezongado el destructor de la ciudad

tachonada.

Última voluntad

La pura verdad sólo me interesan las palabras, no todas las palabras (no me
        interesa la palabra palabra, es la pura verdad) nieve no es una
        palabra que me interese (no me interesa pasar frío, y la nieve,
        quiero decir la nieve lírica, ya está muy vista) he ahí una pala-
        bra de menos: por la n habrá otras más. Muchas. Nabab, que
        es una palabra exótica, no habrá la menor oportunidad de
        utilizarla, sonora palabra, mas sobran palabras sonoras, pode-
        mos descartarla: qué queda. La imagen pasajera de cualquier
        palabra, a falta de imagen queda un concepto (retoza, en la
        cabeza) se deshace: la pura verdad no me interesa nada de la
        palabra nada, las abstracciones me resbalan, tibio tibio las abs-
        tracciones: yo quiero ver, y tocar (sobre todo tocar); yo quiero

those heavenly butterflies, and if they had been three they could be four,
    braids and curly tresses arranged in blue

and yellow

in all the flowery growth of my meadows: at jump-rope our daughters
    climbed high up

all the way to our first great gathering which was in the heavens, my love: I
    grabbed you by the waist and was moved

to climb

with you onto the tree with four old trunks, but there was no way to do it:
    how nice, we failed. You laughed from the waist

down and I let myself be carried across your wide Japanese bridges, your
    old Spanish masonry bridge, an ant

bit us: we smiled; the swelling, and the distant chime of music terrified us

as if the girls had walked across the surface of the lake and back again

and the spangled destroyer of the city

grumbled.

Last Will and Testament

The truth is I only care about words, not every word (I don't care for the
    word word, if truth be told) snow isn't a word I care for (I don't
    care to be cold, and snow—I mean to say lyric snow—has
    become so commonplace) one less word now: and for the let-
    ter n there are others. A multitude. Nabob, an exotic word—
    not the least chance to use it, a sonorous word, but there's an
    overabundance of sonorous words, we can discard it: what's
    left? The fugitive image of any word, lacking an image leaves
    a concept (leaping inside us) it crumbles: in truth I care not at
    all for the word nothing, abstractions leave me limp with bore-
    dom, tepid tepid abstractions: I want to see and touch (above
    all touch); I want to sniff the spoor of the word buckwheat, my

oler el olor de la palabra alforfón, madre mía, cuántas combinaciones: aspas en rotación las palabras: veleta rota en sílabas cualquier palabra; y al borde, lo moribundo, qué dice. *Mará, mará*: ¿eso es lo que dice? Acerco el oído, puras interferencias; y gusto, mastico por el paladar el tallo de la verdolaga, mas nada se aclara ni nada ya me dice: aquí al borde, maná, mojiganga son las demás palabras, hacia atrás, o hacia adelante hasta aquí, al borde: qué, a qué hablar con palabras: óigame, el pan que coloco sobre la mesa se abre por el centro de su yagua, brota ceniza (hormigas de nuevo brotaron): entonces, qué. Están las cosas entenebrecidas de tanto repensarlas, tanto clasificar y describir, describir no vuelve camaleón al camaleón, no vuelve la madre, nada se nos devuelve, abramos paso que ya se va la jacaranda de esta vida, soy *jómet* (la lagartija): nada. Verde que perdió el rabo. Mojiganga a la que se le cayó el antifaz, ved ahora cráneo del rostro, esqueleto del cuerpo, pelado gólgota: peleón que fui, ahora me siento y resbalo hacia adentro: un lindo día allá afuera. Eufrates. Mucha distancia. Un dios de níquel o zinc no da abasto con la gente, me ha bastado el nitrógeno para estar vivo. Espurio pero vivo. Con un habla cualquiera pero no todas las palabras. Capulí nada me dice ni nada tiene que ver conmigo; moribundo, a ver, a su azar no me puedo adaptar: ni al diccionario, después de todo, demasiado extenso. Para la hora señalada cualquier palabra es buena; a su señal, lino, por ejemplo: el arca al hombro, pan sobre la mesa, la mano a la cabeza, y en el punto de trascendencia de la cabeza, sea trigal la palabra que escuche, por ejemplo, en un cruce amarillo de ejes: o sea por omisión, pan. Y vea yo recompuestas todas las cosas desmigajadas.

Ánima

En Ecbatana el arco iris sólo es visible en santidad.

La floresta a mano derecha entre las ruinas se ha cuajado de acianos.

En cada flor desaparece otra estrella otro corpúsculo azul de Dios.

Antares (blanca) Alfa del Centauro (negra) Régulo (púrpura) Aldebarán
    (azul) (su azul aún no es verdadero): anaranjado (Arturo)
    argenta (Altair) oro (Vega).

god, how many combinations: the words are mill-stones turn-
ing; whatever word a mill vane broken into syllables; and at the
edge the dying, what does it say. *Marah, marah*: is that what
it says? I listen closely, nothing but interference; and I taste, I
crush a stem of purslane against my palate, but it clarifies or
tells me nothing now: here on the edge, manna, masquerade
are the remaining words, backward, or forward to this place,
at the edge: what, to what to speak with words: listen to me,
the bread that I've put on the table parts, down to the center of
its husk, brings forth ash (ants brought forth once more): and
then, what. Things are obscured by so much thought, classifica-
tion and description, description doesn't bring the chameleon
back to the chameleon, doesn't bring back the mother, doesn't
bring anything back to us, let's clear the way for the jacaranda
of this life, I am *homet* (the lizard): nothing. A green thing
that lost its tail. The masquerade of her whose veil is dropped,
see the face's skull, the body's bones, skin of golgotha peeled
away now: the donnybrook I was once, now I sit down and
slide inwards: outside a lovely day. Euphrates. Much distance.
A god of nickel or zinc can't cope with people, nitrogen has
been enough to keep me alive. Spurious, but alive. With some
or another word but not with every word. The word *capulí* tells
me nothing, it has nothing to do with me; dying, for instance,
I can't adjust to its destiny: nor, finally, to the dictionary—too
vast. At the final moment any word will do; linen, for instance,
at that moment: the ark on one's shoulder, bread on the table,
hand on head, and at the head's point of transcendence, be
it the word wheatfield that I hear, for instance, in the yellow
crossing of axles: or be it bread, by omission. And might I see
made whole all crumbled things.

Anima

In Ecbatana the rainbow is only visible in a state of holiness.

The grove to the right among the ruins is clogged with corn flowers.

Within each flower is lost another star another blue corpuscle of God.

Antares (white) Alpha Centauri (black) Regulus (purple) Aldebaran (blue)
(even now its blue not true-blue); orange (Arcturus) silver
(Altair) gold (Vega).

De Vega el azul en potencia es más intenso: su corpúsculo ya estría el oro
  ya se reconfigura a mano derecha en la floresta una última
  secuencia de acianos.

El nombre de la estrella oscurece todavía uno de los apellidos de Beatriz
  oscurece (lapislázuli, retenido) la figura de Guadalupe encinta,
  todavía: desconoce la estatua de sal (al fondo). La azul inten-
  sidad del corpúsculo en la mirada de Guadalupe (guía) mano
  derecha a la floresta.

A mano izquierda (al fondo) la sal se desmorona (la estatua fue reconocida):
  un charco verdinegro refleja la intensidad bajo el sol del
  mediodía de un arrayán.

Guíame, arrayán, a los campos de aciano (guíame) tras la columna de sal
  al ojo lapislázuli de Guadalupe a la esfera imperecedera de la
  estrella en ruinas (Beatriz) ya en alto a la izquierda (Guada-
  lupe) a la derecha (al fondo) guiadme del jaspe a la amatista
  al pie del resplandor.

Reino

Comíamos anón mirábamos el gomero: la cinta métrica en la blanca pared,
  llena de libros: saco el libro (brújula) de santidad (en voz
  alta). Básculas, en la hora de la alimentación. Colgadas a
  orear (secarse) las toallas, una segunda muda la ropa blanca
  de cama. Tu escorzo (maja, desnuda; adormilada) sobre el
  edredón (albo) (espliego) orientación sur: se posó la garza; la
  melliza de la garza se posó a su encuentro en el aspa hierática
  de su sombra sobre el (níveo) edredón: ¿ya duermes? ¿Otra
  vez, ya duermes? Borneo, lento, el gerifalte: y vio la inmóvil
  pantomima de la garza en la copa del anchuroso gomero al
  pie del jardín, se abalanzó a su sombra, sobre la cama: una
  sopa de acelgas, chayotes, papas; un vaso de vino blanco (frío)
  pese al frío, exterior: Vivaldi. Maestoso, maestoso y largo
  Vivaldi: el libro abierto en 2 Samuel 18, completo, léase, y
  donde el etíope habla, sellemos nuestra voz a su silencio: éste
  es un día, en este incomprensible lugar el río Chíllar, su seco
  cauce desciende hasta su puerto, desemboca, y su agua viva
  se desprende, Jordán: loma Gólgota la pelada, lago reseco
  vuelto a su caudal, riberas de Galilea. ¿Hay más señales? Alza
  la vista, garza boba; atención: frac y alpargatas, siete polleras

Vega's blue is more intense perhaps: its corpuscle now scores the gold reshapes to the right a last clump of corn flowers in the grove.

The name of that star still darkens one of Beatrice's family names, still darkens (lapis lazuli, remembered) Guadalupe's pregnant body: it doesn't (at bottom) acknowledge the statue of salt. The blue intensity of the corpuscle in Guadalupe's gaze (guides) to the right side of the grove.

To the left (at bottom) the salt is crumbling (the statue noticed): beneath the midday sun a dark green pool reflects the intensity of the myrtle.

Lead me, myrtle, to fields of corn flowers (lead me) past the pillar of salt to Guadalupe's lapis lazuli eye to the imperishable sphere (Beatrice) of the star in the ruins now overhead to the left (Guadalupe) to the right (at bottom) lead me from jasper to amethyst to the foot of the hill of splendor.

Dominion

We would eat *anón* and gaze at the rubber tree: the tape measure on the book-lined white wall: I pull out the (compass) book of holiness (aloud). The scales of judgment, at the hour of nourishment. The towels airing (drying) a second set of white linens. You, foreshortened (maja, naked; dozing), on the (alabaster) (lavender) eiderdown facing south: the heron alighted there; her twin alighted at their meeting on the hieratic cross her shadow cast on the (snowy) eiderdown: are you sleeping? Once again, are you sleeping? Slow tack of the gyrfalcon: and saw the heron's still pantomime in the crown of the stout rubber tree at the foot of the garden, flung itself at its shadow on the bed: a soup of chard, chayote, potatoes; a glass of (cold) white wine, despite the cold: Vivaldi. Maestoso, maestoso and largo Vivaldi: the book open to 2 Samuel 18, all of it, that it be read, and where the Ethiopean speaks, may we seal our voice to his silence: it's a day, in this incomprehensible place the Chíllar River, its dry bed, descends to its port, empties, and its living waters separate, Jordan: naked skull of Golgotha, dry lake returned to its channel, the shores of Galilee. Are there still more portents? Raise your gaze, you silly heron; pay attention: tailcoats and espadrilles, seven

revueltas gruesos calcetines de algodón blanco, se nos puso la carne de gallina. Jerusalén, Jerusalén de andamios, Celeste. Quién vive. Qué escafandras, necesitamos. Yo no lo sé. Falló el pulmón, viva la gloria; falló el ventrículo, aleluya por los horóscopos, el Sitio. Somos (enteros). Dos. Facsímiles, en coincidencia. Derecha interpretación de la carne: lo demás, huelga. Huelgan nuestras manos entrelazadas, ya estamos en vínculo. Idénticos, en vejez perpetua se nos recibe. Esa vejez, un estado mayor. ¿Y qué se come? Ah que el alma fornique. El resplandor, un cuenco hondo de arroz hervido, grano suelto: eternidad (la palabrucha) llevarse algo a la boca, sentarse entre helechos y sombras, ojo lector. Y por repetición del hambre, otro salmo otro pez, ropas blancas.

La casa de enfrente

Me encaramo al perímetro circunscrito de una sombra que aparenta un
cierto árbol de un cierto patio en la casa de enfrente, aparento
(entreabriendo los ojos) (puertas entornadas) (visillos) (espio-
naje, la siesta) aparento una entrada lateral (por el pasillo, sube
por el pasillo) a mis espaldas (reconozco) la casa de enfrente,
espejo la casa de la centenaria ceiba del patio cuarteado, can-
teros (estrechos) alrededor, rosa de los vientos, cuatro esta-
ciones, la cardinal hormiga, sur, sur, desagües (alrededor) la
ceiba en el centro: reja circular de hierro forjado pintada de
negro, pura apariencia de herrumbre, desbarajuste de pájaros
a la tarde, fogueo, se oyó un disparo, Red Ryder, municiones,
una pistola de aire, aljabas y denuestos, perdigones, salvas
triunfales, todo cabe en el embozo de una sábana, la aguja del
mediodía traspuso la siesta, seis de la tarde, hace un par de
lustros que están muertos. Todos toiticos todos. Ni una mota.
Ni astilla, óseo resto, recto descarnado, ni un punto de carde-
nillo: polvo, todo sometido al embozo de la sábana. Rabo de
lagartija. Escarabajo boca arriba, hormigas enloquecidas a la
carga del totí desventrado: todo un orden. Fui yo. No que le
di yo. Le di en el ojo, certero. Niños aciagos. Terminamos de
discutir. Toca a dos muertos por cabeza, comebolas, papana-
tas (la voz dictamina desde lo alto de una fronda). Voz haz pus
pez negra: hoz. La espantada. Todos a una. Cada cual arre-
bujado en su embozo. Aquélla, aquélla, inseñalable. Tajante.
Indiscriminado tragante. Cruces de ramas secas al pie de la

disheveled heavy skirts white cotton socks, it gives us goose flesh. Jerusalem, heavenly Jerusalem of scaffolds. Who goes there? What casque for diving do we need? I have no answer. Lungs gone, the glory lives; ventricles gone, hallelujah for horoscopes, the Place. We remain (intact). Two. Facsimiles, coinciding. Straightforward interpretation of flesh: the rest, obvious. Our hands entwined, of course, we are bonded now. Identical, entered into endless age. Old age an exalted state. And what's to eat? May the soul fornicate. The splendor, a deep bowl of boiled rice, loose grains: eternity (that cliché) for bringing something to the mouth, for sitting down among ferns and shadows, the reading eye. And to rehearse hunger, another psalm another fish, white linens.

The House Across the Way

I climb to the closed perimeter of a shadow that resembles a particular tree in a particular yard of the house across the way, I become (opening my eyes a slit) (doors half-ajar) (lace curtains) (siesta espionage) I become a side door (through the hallway, climb through the hallway) at my back (I recognize) the house across the way, a mirror, the house of the ancient ceiba surrounded by cracked concrete, a circle of (narrow) flowerbeds, windrose, four seasons, the cardinal ant, south, south, drains (encircling) the ceiba in its center, circular wrought iron grating painted black, the obvious appearance of rust, a panic of birds in the afternoon, fired at, a shot rang out, Red Ryder, ammunition, an air gun, insults and arrowcases, beebees, triumphal salvos, all contained in the fold of a counterpane, the needle of noon passes over siesta, six in the evening, they've been dead for a decade. All of them, the whole shebang. Not a speck. Nor a splinter. The rest bone, fleshless rectum, not even a dot of verdigris: dust, everything contained by the fold of a counterpane. Tail of a lizard. Beetle on its back, a tumult of ants attacking the disemboweled blackbird: an entire structure. "I did it." "No, it was me—I hit it right in the eye." Children as destiny. End of the argument. We each bag two, "dummy, dimwit" (the voice of judgment descends from a frond). Voice beam pus tar: sickle. General panic. All of us. Each hidden beneath his own hood. That woman, impossible to show her. Cut and dried. A drain that makes no judgments.

ceiba por cada pájaro. Diecinueve, aquel mes. Eres un exagerao. Te digo que fueron diecinueve. 19. Paquetero. Nueve, y como mucho dos. Concedido. Míos. Fui yo. ¿Nieva? Culata de arma de fuego al hombro, calibro, mirilla, calimbo, cayó. ¿Viste? No vi nada. Míralo, malherido o fulminado. En el ojo, certero. En el pescuezo. ¿Dónde? Ni sombra del totí muerto o herido. Aquí no hay nada. Son rápidas las hormigas (negras) (coloradas) de este patio. No me digas. ¿Ventisca? ¿Aguanieve? Avefrías y colimbos jaraneando a la altura de las cumbres nevadas. Ése que oye vaciar la carga de municiones, cuerpo de pájaro, ya escuchó el disparo primordial, no puede aseverarse que lo suscitó. No presta ya atención. Está ido. Ya escuchó. Que hagan lo que quieran. Que disputen. La Tajante tiene setecientos nombres (nombretes) y la sartén por el mango: Dios a lo sumo tiene un par de apodos, unos atributos. Volvamos al pasado, nonatos. Volver a empezar. ¿Cuál era tu rostro antes de nacer? Comequeque koan. Sigue nevando. El totí se extravió. Mocharon la ceiba. La hormiga colorada se comió las demás. Acabo de cumplir sesenta y cinco años, me poso en el ribete inexistente de un árbol, truena, el saltimbanqui cae, acera o patio de hospital rural, batas blancas esplendentes, Primera o Segunda Guerra Mundial: he disparado, emigró mi abuelo, a mis tíos se los cargaron como al totí en los campos (de concentración) y cuando lo del bombardeo de Dresde, qué decir, hubo en casa una cierta euforia, no sé qué pasó en la casa de enfrente, mi padre me agarró por los hombros, a trompicones me metió en un cuarto, aquel fue sin duda el día más feliz de mi vida, la penumbra.

Danzonete

Mi tío es pecoso, con el pelo rojo como la candela conflagrada.

Mi tía tiene la piel blanca leche de burra, la cabellera ensortijada, castaña con visos grana, los ojos negros.

En la Plaza de Armas se reunió el pueblo a festejar la efeméride patria. La retreta toca un danzonete antañón, de sombrero de paja y pañuelo de encaje, desde una glorieta.

El pueblo le abrió hueco a mis tíos ejecutando aquel largo, interminable danzonete; el pueblo corea "yo quiero bailar contigo, al compás del danzonete."

Crosses of dry branches at the foot of the ceiba, one for each bird. "I bagged 19 that month." "You're making it up." "It was nineteen. 19." "You're lying." "OK, nine." "Two at most." "OK. Mine. It was me." It's snowing? Rifle butt at my shoulder, I take aim, sight, contact, and it's down. "Did you see it?" "I saw nothing. "Look at it, wounded, struck down. Right in the eye. In the neck." "Where?" Not a trace of a dead or wounded blackbird. Nothing here. "The (black) (red) ants in this yard are very fast." "You don't say." Blizzard? Sleet? Lapwings and loons sport among snowy peaks. He who marked the discharging guns, body of a bird, had already heard the primordial shot, no one could say that he made it happen. He no longer bothers with it. He's distracted. He's heard it before. Who cares? Let them argue if they want. Death the Slasher has seven hundred names (nicknames) and all the marbles· God has at best a pair of nicknames, and a few attributes. Let us return unborn to the past. Let us begin again. What was your face before you were born? A dumb koan. It's still snowing. The blackbird went missing. They hacked at the ceiba. The red ant ate the rest. I've just turned 65, I perch on the nonexistent edge of a tree, it thunders, the acrobat falls, sidewalk or yard of a rural hospital, resplendent white labcoats, the First or Second World War: I fired, my grandfather emigrated, like a blackbird my uncles were slaughtered in the (concentration) camps, and when they bombed Dresden, believe it or not, there was joy in our house, I have no idea what happened in the house across the way, my father grabbed me by the shoulders and shoved me into a room, that was the happiest day of my life, the twilight shadows.

Danzonete

My uncle is freckled, his hair is red, flame upon flame.

My aunt is as pale as donkey's milk, her hair in ringlets, chestnut with glints of red, her eyes black.

The crowd gathers in the Plaza de Armas to celebrate the national holiday. In the bandstand the musicians play a danzonete of other days, the days of lace and boater hats.

The crowd opens a space as my aunt and uncle execute a long, an endless danzonete. In chorus the crowd sings, "I want to dance with you to the beat of the danzonete."

A la verdad, nadie baila mejor que la pareja de los polacos. Jamás trivializa la elegancia, jamás hace gala de donaire: la perfección es comedimiento, exactitud. El paso, al paso.

Airosa, tía viste pantalón de dril y guayabera, sombrero de pajilla, zapatos blancos. Ha de ser el sol del mediodía que aún relumbra al atardecer, ese sol de Jericó, padre de alucinaciones.

Cómo si no explicar la ropa de hombre de mi tía. Cómo si no explicar la vuelta maja y desenvuelta que acaba de dar, se vio girar el ruedo inabarcable de una falda alrededor de un punto fijo de compás, tía chapada a la antigua con su ropa de hombre.

Se puso el sol, mis tíos forman en el aire la aguja de una catedral al juntar las manos, unir las yemas de sus dedos.

El vuelo de la falda quedó suspenso con el último acorde de la banda municipal, fijo en los ojos de mi tía el cadáver óseo de su marido.

Miguel Barnet

Así, la muerte

Muere El Gordo que inflaba con sus pulmones
las llantas de bicicleta
el que se emborrachaba frente al Castillo de la Punta
huyéndole al día

Muere Patricio con sus manitos secas
y el último billete de lotería en el pecho

Muere en su camastro de paja Tente el de Palmira,
pobre santero tan viejo . . .

Murió a las 12 de la noche, cuando derramaba aguardiente
para su santo protector, Oggún Arere
Yo no sé por qué me da tanta pena con Tente

Muere Israel, que vendía telas al por mayor
y me decía con nostalgia ¡Quiero que vaya a Polonia para que coma higos!

Muere Susanita, la vieja del Hotel, cansada de llorar
en el sillón del patio
sus llaves al cinto y su naríz gorda . . . Susanita

No one dances better than these two yids. They never take elegance lightly, they never pretend to charm: perfection is restraint, exactitude. Step after step.

My graceful aunt is dressed in cotton pants and guayabera, boater hat, white shoes. The midday sun must still be brightening evening, that Jericho sun, father of all hallucinations.

How else account for my aunt in men's clothing. How else explain the gay twirl and counter-twirl she's just completed, the endless hem of a skirt her compass point, my aunt in her old-fashioned men's clothing.

The sun has set, my aunt and uncle make of their hands in the air a cathedral's steeple, fingertips joined.

At the band's last chord the twirling skirt remained suspended, and in my aunt's glance was fixed her husband's bony corpse.

Translated by Mark Weiss

Miguel Barnet

Death's Like That

Fatso has died who could inflate
bicycle tires with his lungs
he used to get drunk across from the Castillo de la Punta
escaping the day.

Patricio has died his small dry hands
clasping a last lottery ticket to his breast.

Tente, from Palmira, has died in his filthy bed of straw
poor old santero

He died at midnight while pouring aguardiente
for Oggún Arere his protector.
I don't know why I'm so sad about Tente.

Israel has died who sold cloth wholesale
and told me, filled with nostalgia, "I'd like you to go to Poland to eat figs."

Susanita has died, the old hotel keeper, worn out from weeping
in the rocker in the yard
her keys dangling at her waist, her thick nose . . . ah, Susanita!

Muere, no recuerdo sus ojos, el muchacho aquel que
se recostaba horas
al poste cubierto de serpentinas
del Paseo del Prado

Muere, pero más lento, Oscar el banquero
impregnado de violetas hasta las sienes
y con toda la carga de un hombre hueco

Ha muerto el gitano de la filarmónica
que con su mono en la cintura giraba tierno en la ciudad

Ha muerto también Lucía o Lucrecia
la costurera de mi madre
empeñando su máquina de coser para saciar a Humberto
su marido hasta siempre
Los ojos de ella le corren por el cuerpo

Ha muerto, yo quisiera terminar, Jesús
—el mulato de la Biblioteca
Me han dicho que de tanto leer. ¡No sé!

Ha muerto Picasso colgado
de una barra de chocolate
                              ¡Ay! ¡Este Picasso
                                  hacía maravillas
                                      en el circo!

Ha muerto ¡Qué serio es esto!
                              Dios

Una vez más no sé por qué lo digo

Quisiera seguir la corriente de los ríos

Suite cubana

Un estruendo de hojas silbantes
llena mi vida
Las flores del jardín de mi Comité de Defensa
estallan en colores pequeñitos

Henchido por el yodo y la voluptuosidad
un negro de diente de oro se abanica

The hustler died—I can't remember his eyes—
who used to lounge for hours
against the post with the streamers
on the Paseo del Prado

Oscar the bookie has died, but more slowly,
soaked to the ears in violet water
at the end light as a husk

The gypsy organ grinder is dead
whose monkey danced its tender dance
at the end of its leash all over town

Lucía, or was it Lucrecia, is also dead
my mother's seamstress
who sweated day and night over her sewing machine
to support Humberto, her eternal husband
Her eyes pierce his body now

Jesús is dead—I wish this was over—
the *mulato* from the library
They say that too much reading killed him. I don't know!

Picasso's dead, hung
from a bar of chocolate
                     That Picasso
                          did amazing things
                               at the circus!

Dead. This is awful
                     God

Once again I don't know why I say that name

I could have wished to flow away like a river

Cuban Suite

My life is filled with the din of whistling leaves
The tiny flowers in the garden of my local Committee of Defense
burst into color

High on iodine and voluptuousness
a black man with a gold tooth fans himself

a estilo de los años cincuenta
y exhibe su camiseta entalcada
Mi vecina Flor
llora con películas argentinas
y escribe a máquina poemas lunáticos
En una confabulación de notas estridentes
dos novios entonan un bolero de Orlando de la Rosa
Ajenas al blue jeans y la Streisand
las mujeres urbanas se contonean untadas de salitre
La tristeza es una simple desesperanza
de miradas perdidas y labios carmín
Si pudiera bailaba un danzón de Valenzuela
con Mariana Gamborino
porque yo también soy el trópico
y me muero por cantar a la puerta de todos los enamorados

Ahora que las sílabas de mi corazón
han amanecido en mi casa
reparto mi voz a los cuatro puntos cardinales
Con marímbula y tambor
proclamo que vivo locamente enamorado de mi país.

Caminando la ciudad

Yo también soy un privilegiado
de esta época
Crecí sobre los muros altos
y filosos
Fui un niño triste, eso sí,
por encima del gusto por los zapatos charolados
y las lágrimas de Deborah Kerr y Cary Grant
Mis ojos se licuaron en silencio
junto a los rincones sombreados del Vedado
En mi calesa de celuloide
soñé con imágenes inconfesables,
quiero decir con negras desnudas
sobre un paisaje espumoso
Yo mismo inventé todas las historias de la ciudad
Y sobre la urdimbre de sus chinas pelonas
edifiqué mis castillos de miedo
Si toqué a la puerta de los iluminados

as they did in the 50s
showing off his bright white undershirt
My neighbor Flor
weeps over Argentine films
and types crazy poems
In a conspiracy of shrill notes
two newlyweds sing a bolero by Orlando de la Rosa
Big-city women strut down the Malecón
their faces salty with sea-spray
not for them blue jeans or Streisand
This sadness is an everyday hopelessness
of red lips and lost glances
If only I could have danced a danzón by Valenzuela
with Mariana Gamborino,
because I too am of the tropics
and would give my life to sing at the gates of every lover

Now that the syllables of my heart
have dawned in this house
I raise my voice to the four cardinal points
and proclaim with marimbula and drum
how madly in love I am with my country

Walking the City

I, too, am among the privileged
of the age.
I was nurtured on high, slender walls,
a melancholy child,
in spite of a taste for shiny shoes
and the tears of Deborah Kerr and Cary Grant.
My eyes would melt in silence
in Vedado's shady places.
In my celluloid seat
I dreamed unspeakable things,
black women, naked
in a foamy landscape.
I myself invented all the stories of the city
and I built my castles of fear
upon the schemes of the penniless Chinese.
If I knocked at the doors of the great

no fue para pedir un mendrugo o una estrella
sino para dejar una flor abierta y perfumada
Créanme, he sido un hombre privilegiado de mi época,
sin tiempo para lamentar mis penas personales
Hay cosas que me miran con un brillo roído
y yo las miro
¡Qué se va a hacer!
Yo debo caminar estas calles
sin temor a que algo de improviso
salte y me sorprenda ensimismado
Como un animal de sueños
voy a tocar las cuerdas de mi invención
y que venga luego el juglar con su guitarra
Yo seguiré caminando la ciudad
que palpita en mi piel
y si por casualidad toco a tu puerta,
no temas, Lezama, no soy el fantasma
de un poema de Baudelaire
ni estoy mudo para decirte que estás aún entre nosotros,
con todos los que te rodeamos,
como a un árbol de oscuras señales,
como a una fuente de peces esmaltados
Si escribo todo esto es únicamente
para decirte que mis pies no se cansan
de andar por estas calles que fueron de barro,
por estos palacios que Julián del Casal
vio cubiertos de nieve
y que no llevo piedras en los bolsillos
sino los sones de Teodora Ginés
para repartir entre los andariegos solitarios
y los dormidos de los parques

Me recuesto al Malecón
ansioso de pulpos venenosos y botellas azules
Cruza un camión sonoro frente a mis ojos
Va cargado de hombres y mujeres
hacia el trabajo voluntario
No sé por qué me recuerda un coro de vihuelas medievales
Expongo mi corázon al viento
y al salitre
He traspasado el umbral de mi casa de sombras
Ahora sé que soy mi semejante

it wasn't to beg for a crust or a star,
but to leave an open, perfumed flower.
Believe me, I have been among the privileged of my time,
without time to lament my personal sorrows.
There are things that watch me with a rusty sheen
and I watch them—
there's nothing to be done!
I must walk these streets
without fear of whatever unforeseen
may lunge at me when I'm lost in thought.
Child of the minstrel and his guitar,
like a dream beast
I will pluck the strings of my invention.
I continue walking the city,
it throbs in my skin,
and if by accident I knock at your door,
fear not, Lezama, that I'm the ghost
of a poem by Baudelaire
nor will I refrain from telling you that you are still among us,
among the crowd of us who surround you,
like a tree of dark signals,
a fountain of enameled fish.
I write this only
to tell you that my feet have not wearied
of going through these streets that were once mud,
through these palaces that Julián del Casal
saw covered with snow
and that I carry in my pockets not stones
but the *sones* of Teodora Ginés
to distribute among solitary wanderers
and sleepers in the parks

I lean against the Malecón
nervous about poisonous octopi and toxic jellyfish.
A noisy truck passes
carrying men and women
volunteers for the harvest.
Why am I reminded of a chorus of medieval lutes.
I expose my heart to wind and spray.
I have crossed the threshold of my house of shadows
And I know now that I've become my own reflection.

Con pies de gato

El viento ha quemado mi pelo,
el viento frío, arrasador
Con pies de gato camino en lo oscuro
Cautelosamente, como una fiera prevenida,
me acerco a tu corazón
El olfato y la noche son mi brújula
Como no sabes que existo te expones
al desamparo y al susto
Después de todo eres más frágil
que el estambre
y no sabes huir
Entre tú y yo se cierne sólo la lluvia
que espejea tus brazos
No puedes verme porque voy cubierto de árboles
La noche, pródiga de mis sueños, me juega de nuevo
una mala pasada
Feroz, bebo de tu desnudez hasta que mis labios
se sequen o se olviden
Ojalá que una flecha te atraviese el corazón
para rehacerte a mi imagen, para resucitarte
No culpo a la noche de tu aparición
sino a sus duendes

Memorándum XIV

Estoy en mi cama frente al televisor
Ella va a asesinar a un hombre
No he seguido la trama
pero creo que es a un traidor
En sus ojos, los de ella, claro está,
hay láminas de fuego y cascadas ojerosas
Siempre me duermo ante el televisor
Pero este filme tiene algo de desván
y me desvelo
Hay autos que vuelan sobre los techos
de pizarra californiana
y policías negros que van a la caza del traidor,
o quién sabe, de la persona que va a ser asesinada
Ella lleva un arma de fuego plateadísima

On Cat's Feet

The wind has scorched my fur
the cold wind, the leveler
On cat's feet I glide through the dark.
Carefully, with a wild beast's caution,
I approach your heart,
your scent and the night my compass.
Since you don't know that I exist you expose yourself
to helplessness and fright.
After all you are weaker
than a ball of yarn
and you haven't learned to run away.
Only the rain silvering your arms
hovers between us.
You can't see me, my path hidden beneath trees
The night, prodigal with dreams, plays again
its dirty trick on me.
Fiercely I drink your nakedness until my lips
dry out or forget.
God grant that an arrow pierce your heart
to remake you in my image, to revive you.
It's not the night that I blame for your apparition
but its ghosts.

Memorandum XIV

I'm lying in bed watching TV
She's going to kill some guy
I haven't been following the plot
but I think he's betrayed her
In her eyes
are sheets of flame and hollow cascades
The TV always puts me under
But this film has something of attics about it
and I stay alert
There are cars flying over the slate roofs
of California
and black cops hunting the betrayer
(at any rate, the guy who's about to get killed)
Her gun is very shiny

y es rubia como aquella muchacha de Avon
que nunca he olvidado
Ahora tengo miedo y me cala el frío
de mi aire acondicionado BK 1500
Te espero en mi cama anfiteatro
mientras ella salta con su pistola de plata
por muros celestiales
Si no llegas antes del disparo
te aseguro que la víctima seré yo

En el barrio chino

Yo te espero
bajo los signos rotos
del cine cantonés
Yo te espero
en el humo amanillo
de una estirpe deshecha

Yo te espero
en la zanja donde navegan
ideogramas negros
que ya no dicen nada

Yo te espero a las puertas
de un restaurante
en un set de la Paramount
para una película que se filma a diario

Dejo que la lluvia me cubra
con sus raíles de punta
mientras presiento tu llegada

En compañía de un coro de eunucos,
junto al violín de una sola cuerda
de Li Tai Po,
yo te espero

Pero no vengas
porque lo que yo quiero realmente
es esperarte

and she's as blond as the Avon Lady
that I've never forgotten
I'm terrified now and my BK 1500 air conditioner
is giving me the chills
I wait for you in the theater of my bed while
silver gun in hand she leaps
through celestial walls
If you don't get here before she shoots
I'll be a goner.

In Chinatown

I wait for you
beneath the wrecked marquee
of the Chinese movie
in the yellow smoke
of an extinct dynasty

I wait for you
by the gutter
where black ideograms
that no longer say anything
float

I wait for you at the door
of a restaurant
on the Paramount lot
where they shoot the same film every day

Anticipating your arrival
I allow the rain to cover me
with its broken lines

Accompanied by a choir of eunuchs
and Li Tai Po's
violin with just one string
I wait for you

But don't ever come
what I really want
is to wait for you

Translated by Mark Weiss

Belkis Cuza Malé

Las cenicientas

Somos las cenicientas.
El señor Botticelli pintó para nosotras
las tres hadas madrinas.
No somos inocentes.
El Príncipe nunca nos ha besado.
No hemos pisado su recámara,
ni lamido su vientre.
Vivimos en la cocina,
nuestra luna es el fuego.
Nuestros pies son enormes;
un largo baño no nos vendría mal.
Andamos con sayas rotas,
con las greñas al aire
y comemos pan duro.
No somos inocentes.
Por negritas, por feas y por putas
fuimos chifladas en el certamen de Miss Universo.
Pero gritamos (las deslenguadas)
¡merde! al culo del rey
y ¡merde! a sus ministros,
aunque ellos rabien con nuestra peste.

La fuente de plata

Esta tarde he traído conmigo una fuente de plata.
No sé para qué ha de servirme
pues nunca he tenido fuente de plata.
Vivimos sin estos lujos y tú me preguntas:
"¿Se venden aún esas cosas?"

Nadie te exige ahora que tengas una fuente de plata.
Ni siquiera de segunda mano.
¿Quién podría exigirte semejante lujo en estos tiempos?
Será suficiente con los buenos modales a la mesa
y la pulcritud de las uñas.
Pasadas están de moda, por ejemplo, las gracias al Señor.

Belkis Cuza Malé

The Cinderellas

We are the cinderellas.
Mister Botticelli painted the three
fairy godmothers for us.
We are not innocent.
The Prince has never kissed us.
We have not set foot in his chamber,
nor licked his belly.
We live in the kitchen,
our moon is the fire.
Our feet are enormous;
a long bath would suit us nicely.
We go around in ragged skirts,
our hair disheveled
and we eat stale bread.
We are not innocent.
Because we were black, ugly and whores
they booed us at the Miss Universe pageant.
But we (the foulmouthed) cry out
merde! to the king's ass
and *merde!* to his ministers,
though they rage at our stench.

The Silver Platter

This evening I've brought a silver platter with me.
I don't know what good it'll do me
since I've never had a silver platter.
We live without these luxuries and you ask me:
"Do they still sell those things?"

No one requires you now to have a silver platter.
Not even second hand.
Who could require such a luxury in these times?
It's enough to have good table manners
and well-trimmed nails.
Saying grace, for example, is out of fashion.

Será mejor que vivas sin esos lujos
y no quieras nunca servir la ensalada del pobre
en una fuente de plata.

Caja de Pandora

La calle es el peligro, pero avanzas sin rumbo
y te sorprendes junto a la mano de bronce
de las altas puertas. Y cuando estás a punto de ser escuchado
de cometer una torpeza,
una ráfaga de aire te detiene un instante,
te hace volver el rostro y descubres a la vieja
parada junto a ti
con su pesada jaba de yarey, donde brilla, escondida,
su caja de Pandora.
Desconfías de la imaginación, no cedes
y dejas pasar
                  los argumentos del tiempo
y la sola idea del amor.

Ella continúa su paso.
Fue sólo la tentación de ofrecértelo todo.
¿Por qué no te picó el milagro de la curiosidad?

Crítica a la razón impura

Abre la puerta de su casa y entra
como un desconocido,
como si penetrara en el mundo
por la puerta de atrás.
En las paredes navega el barco
que grabó su hija,
la cuenta de la lavandería
cuelga del palo mayor.
Sus vecinos han decidido casarse hoy
y pedirle por un rato los muebles.
Entra en su casa y comienza a escribir,
necesita arreglar el mundo de algún modo,
crear un hombre para ella,
una niñera para su hija
y un poco de vida para los gatos que no tiene.

It's better to live without those luxuries
you don't ever want to serve a pauper's salad
on a silver platter.

Pandora's Box

The street is the danger, but you wander forth
and surprise yourself beside the bronze knocker
of the tall doors. And when you're about to be heard
committing a gaffe,
a gust of air stops you for an instant,
makes you turn your face and you discover the old woman
standing beside you
with her heavy wicker basket, where her hidden
Pandora's box sparkles.
You distrust your imagination, you don't give in
making way for
                  time's arguments
and the mere idea of love.

She continues on her way.
It was only the temptation to offer you everything.
Why were you not tempted by the miracle of curiosity?

Critique of Impure Reason

She opens the door to her house and enters
like a stranger,
as if she were entering the world
by the back door.
On the walls the ship
drawn by her daughter sails,
the laundry bill
hangs from the mainmast.
Her neighbors have decided to get married today
and to borrow her furniture for a while.
She enters her house and starts to write,
she needs to arrange the world somehow,
to create a man for herself,
a nanny for her daughter
and a bit of life for the cats she doesn't have.

Ella empieza a escribir,
como si estuviera delante de un jurado,
saca sus heroínas de papel,
porque ella es una muchacha que vive sola,
que duerme sola,
que baila sola.

Ella es la muchacha
que ustedes necesitan destruir
para sentirse más firmes.

El ombligo del mundo

En el vientre de una muchacha
hay mordiscos y grandes cicatrices,
carneros que el tiempo casi borra.
Hay huesos y letreros y hebras de cabelleras masculinas
y señales de tránsito;
hay pastillas esterilizadoras
y bombas de reloj, pistolas, dientes de leche,
fuego por napalm,
hojas y mariposas,
tiestos de flores y anillos de compromiso.
Los grandes crímenes,
los divorcios,
los desahucios,
se hacen en el vientre de una muchacha.
El ombligo del mundo
es el vientre de una muchacha.

Buscadores de oro,
reyes alquilados,
soldados de chocolate,
mentirosos,
violadores,
profesores de estética,
presidentes de Estados Unidos,
violinistas,
cuatreros,
hombres casados,
curas de aldeas,
tramposos,

She begins to write,
as if she were before a jury,
she takes out her paper heroines,
because she is a girl who lives alone,
who sleeps alone,
who dances alone.

She is the girl
you need to destroy
in order to feel stronger.

The Navel of the World

In a girl's belly
there are bites and big scars,
sheep that time has almost erased.
There are bones and posters and strands of men's hair
and traffic signs;
there are sterilizing pills
and time bombs, pistols, baby teeth,
napalm fire,
leaves and butterflies,
pots of flowers and engagement rings.
The great crimes,
the divorces,
the evictions,
ripen in a girl's belly.
The navel of the world
is a girl's belly.

Prospectors,
kings for hire,
chocolate soldiers,
liars,
rapists,
professors of aesthetics,
United States presidents,
violinists,
horse thieves,
married men,
village priests,
swindlers,

provocadores,
científicos,
médicos,
trotamundos,
jueces,
proletarios,
caníbales,
parlanchines,
borrachos,
rescabuchadores,
no hurguen más en el vientre de las muchachas.

Nancy Morejón

Parque Central, alguna gente (3:00 P.M.)

el que atraviesa un parque en La Habana grande y floreciente
con mucha luz blanca mucha luz blanca
que hubiera enloquecido el girasol de aquel Van Gogh
con luz blanca que llena los ojos de los chinos de los chinos fotógrafos

el que atraviesa un parque y no comprende esa luz blanca se repite casi
el que no entiende de esas horas
da todos los rodeos innecesarios y todas vueltas
alrededor del parque central de La Habana
el que atraviesa un parque con árboles sagrados
el que pasa con los ojos abiertos y cerrados
amando el golpe de la Revolución en los ojos
el golpe que se lleva en los ojos y en la cintura
el que se sostiene de esa luz puede que sepa de la noche y el vino

porque en los parques y en este que es central el de La Habana
los viejos se sientan en un banco encienden un tabaco se miran y conversan
de la Revolución y de Fidel
los viejos que ahora permanecen en un banco y toman
el sol y toman el sol y toman el sol
para nadie es secreto
allá van dos hombres y una cartera vieja destartalada

provocateurs,
scientists,
doctors,
globetrotters,
judges,
proletarians,
cannibals,
chatterboxes,
drunks,
voyeurs,
stop poking around girls' bellies.

Translated by Jason Weiss

Nancy Morejón

Some People/Central Park/3:00 P.M.

He who walks through a park in La Habana great and flourishing
with a lot of white light a lot of white light
that would have driven mad this Van Gogh's sunflower
the white light filling the eyes of the chinese of chinese photographers

he who walks through a park and fails to understand this white light
   which repeats itself almost
who fails to understand these hours
makes all the unnecessary trips through and all the side-trips round
the central park of La Habana
he who walks through a park with sacred trees
who passes with his eyes open and closed
loving the Revolution's beat in the eyes
the beat one carries in the eyes and wears at one's belt
he who leans on that light maybe he knows about night and wine

for in the parks and in this one which is central this of La Habana
the old sit on a bench and light a cigar and look at each other talking about
the Revolution and Fidel
the old who sit on benches now and take
the sun and take the sun and take the sun
it's a secret for no one
there go two men with a shabby old briefcase

una mano regordeta un grito con un sombrero gris
los viejos que se ven al lado de una estatua
del apóstol Martí en 1966 en diciembre de 1966 acabándose el año y
    esperando
"el aniversario de la libertad y rindiendo homenaje a los mártires"
sí
a todos los hombres que murieron del pueblo y su sangre
para tomar el sol de la tarde en La Habana Cuba territorio libre de América
el que atraviesa en esa forma el parque este mundo la vejiga de la
    Revolución
tiene que suspirar
y andar despacio y respirar
y andar ligero y suspirar y respirar y andar despacio
y dar toda la vida

rabiosamente
        compañeros

    16 DE DICIEMBRE DE 1966

Luis Rogelio Nogueras

Mujer saliendo del armario

> • *a Diony María Durán, por toda defensa*

Estoy en mi cuarto, mirando hace horas el armario.
Cuando salga esta mujer ¿qué voy a responderle?
¿Me comeré las uñas? ¿Le hablaré de Blake?
Ella me dirá que no quiere saber nada del infierno.
Estoy hace horas en el cuarto, chiflando,
mirando de reojo el armario, estrujando el sombrero
entre las manos. Cuando salga esta mujer,
levantaré la cortina, señalaré hacia el balcón,
diré que más allá está ardiendo un sol
que no quiere morir,
pero ella me dirá que no quiere asunto con los astros.
Tengo el corazón pálido esta vez, las manos frías,

a plump hand a cry in a gray hat
the old people one sees beside a statue
of the apostle Martí in 1966 in December 1966 the year ending and in the
    hope
of "liberty's anniversary and an homage to the martyrs"
yes
to all men who died among the people and to their blood
to take the sun of afternoon in La Habana Cuba free territory of America
he who walks through the park this way this world the bladder of the
    Revolution
must sigh
and walk slowly and breathe
and walk lightly and sigh and breathe and walk slowly
and give up his whole life

like with rage
            comrades

DECEMBER 16, 1966

Translated by Nathaniel Tarn

Luis Rogelio Nogueras

Woman Emerging from the Closet

  • *To Diony María Durán, my only protector*

I am in my room, watching the closet for hours.
When this woman emerges, how will I answer her?
Will I chew my nails? Speak to her of Blake?
She will tell me that she's not interested in hell.
I have been in the room for hours, whistling,
watching the closet out of the corner of my eye, crushing my hat
between my hands. When she emerges
I will raise the curtain, point to the balcony,
tell her that farther off a sun is burning
that doesn't want to die,
but she will tell me that she has no wish to quarrel with the stars.
My heart is pale now, my hands are cold,

la mirada fija en el armario.
Cuando salga esta mujer,
me haré pasar por manzana, por mano suave,
por levita en el perchero,
pero ella me dirá que no quiere saber nada de mis libros.
Esta noche saldrá esa mujer del armario,
a pedirme el corazón nuevamente, a cobrar sus honorarios,
a preguntarme.

Un tesoro

• *para Felicia Cortiñas*

Entre las flores del patio
que crecen en macetas rajadas o en latas
de conserva que han perdido el color
mi hija está jugando a encontrar
un fabuloso cofre de monedas de oro,
enterrado quién sabe por qué pirata de su imaginación.
Atareada, no me siente llegar
a las puertas de su mínimo universo.
La llamo
y sorprendida me mira, y sonríe.

Ayer, 12 de septiembre, fue su cumpleaños.
Ayer, mientras los patriotas chilenos
eran asesinados en las calles de Santiago.
Quién pudiera
lejos de la furia del mal, lejos
de la venganza y el odio y la sangre y el lodo
de este momento
bajar año por año al fondo de su edad
y ayudarla a buscar
el tesoro.

Canta

Canta, amigo mío, la canción de mañana. Mira
el crepúsculo, escucha el viento
que barre la gran plaza asoleada donde anoche nos reunimos

my gaze fixed on the closet.
When she emerges
I will make myself pass for an apple, a soft hand,
a coat on a hanger,
but she will say that she's not interested in my books.
Tonight she will emerge from the closet
once more she will request my heart, request her fee,
she will ask me.

A Treasure

• *For Felicia Cortiñas*

Among the flowers in the yard
growing in cracked flowerpots or tin cans
that have lost their color
my daughter pretends to find
a fabulous chest of gold coins,
buried who knows when by whatever pirate of her imagination.
Preoccupied, she doesn't sense my arrival
at the gates of her tiny universe.
I call her;
surprised, she looks at me and smiles.

Yesterday, September 12th, was her birthday.
Yesterday, while Chilean patriots
were being murdered in the streets of Santiago.
Who
far from the fury of evil,
far from the vengeance, hatred blood and muck
of this moment
would be able to descend year by year
to the depth of his years
to help her search
for her treasure.

Sing

Sing, friend, the song of morning. See
the dawn, hear the wind
sweeping the great sunny space of the plaza where we gathered

para oír los más hermosos discursos.
Ven, canta una canción que se escuche en el confín del mundo;
una canción que sea al mismo tiempo
un canto de guerra y un canto de cuna,
un himno y un íntimo, delicado canto de amor.
Amigo mío, ven y canta el instante en que la mañana
más hermosa de la vida calienta los corazones;
canta al mar, a la Revolución,
al rostro de esa muchacha que hunde los dedos en la tierra de tu alma y
    siembra una semilla.
Canta a la noche y canta a los martillos
que cuando amanece comienzan a golpear el hierro al rojo vivo para
    moldearlo
a nuestra imagen y semejanza.
Canta al coraje, al álgebra, al amor, al trabajo, a la dialéctica.
Firma todas las libretas escolares
y endurece tus manos hombro con hombro con el fuego.
Escribe el verso de este tiempo, amigo mío,
para que seas un poco el humo que anuncia en lo distante
las grandes siderurgias,
los grandes complejos industriales,
los grandes incendios.

Don't look back, lonesome boy

Unas aguas que se agotan
ZENEA

Pausada, pacientemente lo hemos olvidado todo.
Cuando sobre la cama hacíamos temblar los clavos
Y tú subías murmurando, gimiendo como una espuma dulce
Y sonaba la guitarra en el radio, por debajo de las voces,
Creíamos (al menos yo creía) en las fuerzas de nuestros brazos,
En la minuciosa precisión a toda prueba de nuestras vacilantes, líquidas
    memorias,
En el poder absoluto de los poemas que escribí,
Cuando brincaba descalzo de la cama y a tientas,
Mientras tú dormías,
Garabateaba cualquier papel, en un libro.
Cuántas palabras hermosas, graves, urgentes quedaron olvidadas.
Entonces yo creía que sólo bastaba escribir, ruda, impúdicamente,
Amarte,

last night to hear the most beautiful speeches.
Come, sing a song that may be heard to the ends of the earth;
at once a song
of war and a lullaby,
hymn and intimate, delicate love song.
Friend, come and sing the moment at which life's loveliest
morning warms all hearts;
sing of the sea, the Revolution,
the face of that girl who sinks her fingers into the soil of your soul and
    plants a seed.
Sing of the night and of the hammers
that at dawn begin to strike the red-hot iron to mold it
into our image and likeness.
Sing of courage, algebra, love, labor, dialectic.
Leave the classroom
and harden your hands shoulder to shoulder with the fire.
Write the poetry of this time, my friend,
so that you may become a wisp of smoke announcing in the distance
steel mills,
industrial complexes,
conflagrations.

Don't Look Back, Lonesome Boy

Some springs that are exhausted
ZENEA

Deliberate, patient, we have forgotten everything.
When we made the bed tremble
And you rose whispering, moaning like a gentle wave
And on the radio the guitar played beneath the singers,
We believed (at least I did) in the strength of our arms,
In the meticulous precision worthy of our flickering, liquid memories,
In the absolute power of the poems that I wrote,
When I leapt barefoot from bed and groped about,
While you slept,
Scribbling on whatever scrap of paper, or in a book.
How many lovely, grave, urgent words were lost.
In those days I thought it enough to write, crudely, shamelessly,
To love you,

Que las cosas eran así, que serían así mientras tú estuvieras dormida, desnuda,
Mientras yo tuviera a mano un pedazo de papel, la pared del cuarto,
Cualquier rincón en blanco del planeta;
Entonces creíamos que la guitarra, la maldita guitarra continuaría tocando aún.
Esta noche he visto lo poco que pagan por la vida,
Y tú y yo lo ignorábamos.
Esta noche una sombra, cualquier sombra
Basta para apagar aquel fuego fuerte, indestructible, eterno,
Cualquier viento del sur bastaría para apagar mi voz.
La memoria es un agua que se agota
Y no podemos (al menos, yo no puedo)
Recordar, por ejemplo, aquella otra noche
Que nos pareció particularmente habitada sólo por ti y por mí y las palabras.
(¿Llovía? ¿Teníamos qué? ¿Cuánto nos dijimos?)
Ciega mirada la del hombre que vuelve su rostro hacia el pasado
Porque olvida dos veces;
Qué patético es el que intenta mirar con amor las cenizas del amor;
Tan patético como esos payasos que, enloquecidos, en la noche,
En medio de la carpa desierta,
Contorsionan su cuerpo
Y lanzan su voz estridente contra las gradas vacías.

SANTIAGO DE CUBA, 19, XI, 69

(Yambos interrumpidos)

Te amo. La Revolución asciende
JEAN SÉNAC

Ah, si el poema fuera
suficiente para decir: te amo,
muchacha, compañera.
Si te pudiera regalar un ramo
de flores y tomarte
simplemente de la mano y caminar;
si pudiera besarte
bajo la noche húmeda, junto al mar
Ah, si con un poema
yo pudiera decirte cuánto te amo,
muchacha, compañera

That that's how things were, how they would be while you slept, naked,
While I grabbed a piece of paper, the wall of the room,
Any blank corner of the planet;
In those days we thought that the guitar, the damned guitar would still be
    playing.
Tonight I have seen how little life is worth,
And you and I had no idea.
Tonight a shadow, any shadow
Is enough to smother that strong, indestructible, eternal flame,
Any wind from the south would be enough to smother my voice.
Memory is an exhausted spring
And we can't (I can't, at any rate)
Remember, for example, that other night
That seemed to us especially inhabited by you and me and words alone.
(It rained? We had what? How much did we tell each other?)
Blind gaze of the man who turns his face to the past
Because he forgets twice;
Pathetic to look with love at the ashes of love;
As pathetic as clowns who, lost in madness, at night,
In the empty circus tent,
Contort their bodies
And hurl their shrill voices against the empty bleachers.

SANTIAGO DE CUBA, NOVEMBER 19, 1969

(Interrupted Iambs)

I love you. The Revolution is coming.
            JEAN SÉNAC

Ah, if the poem were
enough to say: I love you,
        my girl, my comrade.
If I could give you a bouquet
        of flowers and just
walk hand in hand with you;
        if I could kiss you
in the damp night by the seaside
        Ah, if I could tell you
with a poem how much I love you,
        my girl, my comrade

Pero no.
Éste es el tiempo pleno de la belleza
y tú sabes que te amo, sin noches húmedas, sin mar,
sin flores, sin poemas. El amor respira
y canta en todas partes; las luces del porvenir
pueden verse a lo lejos, en ciertos días claros;
el amor es íntimo y plural,
tuyo, mío y de todos.
Por eso, qué importa que el poema no pueda
decir lo que tú sabes hoy 19 de algún mes:
que yo te amo
en este tiempo hermoso que es ya
el pasado del futuro;
que yo te amo,
muchacha, compañera

Pérdida del poema de amor llamado "Niebla"

♦ *para Luis Marré*

Ayer he escrito un poema magnífico
lástima
lo he perdido no sé dónde
ahora no puedo recordarlo
pera era estupendo
decía más o menos
que estaba enamorado
claro lo decía de otra forma
ya les digo era excelente
pero ella amaba a otro
y entonces venía una parte
realmente bella donde hablaba de
los árboles el viento y luego
más adelante explicaba algo acerca de la muerte
naturalmente no decía muerte decía
oscura garra o algo así
y luego venían unos versos extraordinarios
y hacia el final
contaba cómo me había ido caminando
por una calle desierta
convencido de que la vida comienza de nuevo

But no.
This is a time filled with beauty
and you know that I love you, without damp nights or ocean
or flowers or poems. Everywhere love breathes
and sings; on clear days we can see
the lights of the future in the distance;
love is private and plural,
ours, mine, everyone's.
So it makes no difference that the poem
can't say what you already know on this 19th day
of whatever month: that I love you
in this beautiful time that is already
the future's past;
that I love you,
my girl, my comrade

Loss of the Love Poem Called "Mist"

♦ *For Luis Marré*

Yesterday I wrote a magnificent poem
sadly
I lost it somewhere
and now I can't remember it
but it was great
it said more or less
that I was in love
it said it, of course, in another way—
it was really good—
but she was in love with another guy
and then there was a really beautiful part about
the trees the wind and then
it said something about death it didn't
say death, of course, it said
dark claw or something like that
then there were some extraordinary lines
and toward the end
it told how I walked
through an empty street
convinced that life would begin again

en cualquier esquina
por supuesto no decía esa cursilería
era bueno el poema
lástima de pérdida
lástima de memoria.

Oración por el hijo que nunca va a nacer

Éramos tan pobres, oh hijo mío, tan pobres
que hasta las ratas nos tenían compasión.
Cada mañana tu padre iba a la ciudad
para ver si algún poderoso lo empleaba
—aunque tan sólo fuera para limpiar los establos
a cambio de un poco de arroz—.
Pero los poderosos
pasaban de largo sin oír quejas
ni ruegos.
Y tu padre volvía en la noche,
pálido y tan delgado bajo sus ropas raídas
que yo me ponía a llorar
y le pedía a Jizo,
dios de las mujeres encintas y de la fecundidad,
que no te trajera al mundo, hijo mío,
que te librara del hambre y la humillación.
Y el buen dios me complacía.
Así fueron pasando años sin alma.
Mis pechos se secaron,
y al cabo tu padre murió
y yo envejecí.
Ahora sólo espero el fin,
como espera el ocaso a la noche
que habrá de echarle en los ojos su negro manto.
Pero al menos,
gracias al buen Jizo,
tú escapaste del látigo de los señores
y de esta cruel existencia de perros.
Nada ni nadie te hará sufrir.
Las penas del mundo no te alcanzarán jamás,
como no alcanza la artera flecha
al lejano halcón.

on some corner
of course it didn't say it that pretentiously
it was a good poem
sad loss
sad memory

Prayer for the Son Who Will Never Be Born

We were so poor, my son, so poor
that even the rats felt sorry for us.
Every morning your father would go to the city
to see if someone powerful would hire him
—even if only to clean the stables
for a handful of rice.
But the powerful
would pass by without stopping, hearing neither groans
nor entreaties.
And at night your father would return
pale, and so thin beneath his shabby clothes
that I would weep,
and I begged of Jizo,
god of pregnant women and fertility,
not to bring you into the world, my son,
to deliver you from hunger and humiliation.
And the kind god granted my prayer.
So the years passed soullessly.
My breasts dried up,
your father died,
and I grew old.
Now I wait only for the end,
as sunset waits for night
to throw its black cloak over its eyes.
But at least,
thanks to Jizo,
you escaped the whip of the masters
and this cruel dog's life.
Nothing and nobody will make you suffer.
As the skillful arrow fails to reach
the distant hawk
the sorrows of the world will never reach you.

Un poema

En el vórtice de la lucha de clases
escribió un poema de amor

Acosado por el hambre de justicia
escribió un poema de amor

Entre la muerte y la tortura
escribió un poema de amor

Entre la sangre y las balas
escribió un poema de amor

Un poema de amor para nadie
para una mujer que no existía

Y ahora
amado hasta el fondo de su sombra
por esta muchacha que besa sus heridas
ahora
que en la helada noche ella lo cubre con su cuerpo
desnudo
se arma de papel y lápiz
salta de la cama
y sin estorbar el sueño de su amada
escribe un poema social
un poema estremecido por huelgas y batallas
un poema por cuyos versos cruzan
pidiendo justicia
las masas obreras y campesinas

El último caso del inspector

El lugar del crimen
no es aún el lugar del crimen:
es sólo un cuarto en penumbras
donde dos sombras desnudas se besan.

El asesino
no es aún el asesino:
es sólo un hombre cansado
que va llegando a su casa un día antes de lo previsto,
después de un largo viaje.

A Poem

In the vortex of class warfare
he wrote a love poem

Confronted by the hunger for justice
he wrote a love poem

Surrounded by death and torture
he wrote a love poem

Among blood and bullets
he wrote a love poem

A poem for no one
for a love who didn't exist

And now,
loved to the depth of his shadow
by this girl who kisses his wounds
now
that in the chill of night she covers him
with her naked body
he arms himself with pen and paper
leaves the bed
and without disturbing his lover's dream
writes a political poem
a poem shaken by strikes and battles.

The Detective's Last Case

The crime scene
isn't the crime scene yet:
it's just a half-lit room
where two naked shadows kiss.

The killer
isn't the killer yet:
he's just a tired man
who's about to return from a long trip
a day early.

La víctima
no es aún la víctima:
es sólo una mujer ardiendo
en otros brazos.

El testigo de excepción
no es aún el testigo de excepción:
es sólo un inspector osado
que goza de la mujer del prójimo
sobre el lecho del prójimo.

El arma del crimen
no es aún el arma del crimen:
es tan sólo una lámpara de bronce apagada,
tranquila, inocente
sobre una mesa de caoba.

Una muchacha

En la misma calle,
pero en distintas casas,
un filósofo,
un poeta,
un guerrero
y un alquimista
tejían y destejían los enigmas del Universo.
El filósofo meditaba sobre el Ser,
se preguntaba una y otra vez
por qué existe lo que existe
y por qué existe de este modo y no de otro.
El alquimista molía lentamente en su mortero de mármol
polvos que quizás lograrían engañar a la muerte,
buscaba en su retorta un elixir
para preservar al cuerpo de su fatal corrupción.
El guerrero trazaba sobre un mapa
los esquemas de relampagueantes ofensivas,
movía sus ejércitos invisibles,
trataba de adivinar el flanco débil del próximo enemigo.
Y el poeta emborronaba incontables cuartillas,
desgranaba las palabras del idioma
en busca de un verso muy nuevo

The victim
isn't the victim yet:
she's just a wife burning
in another's arms.

The special witness
isn't the special witness yet:
he's just a daring detective
enjoying his neighbor's wife
on his neighbor's bed.

The murder weapon
isn't the murder weapon yet:
it's just an unlit bronze lamp,
peaceful, innocent
on a mahogany table.

A Girl

In the same street,
but in different houses,
a philosopher,
a poet,
a soldier
and an alchemist
wove and unwove the riddles of the Universe.
The philosopher meditated on Being,
asking himself over and over again
why that which exists exists
and why in this manner and not another.
The alchemist slowly crushed in his marble mortar
powders that perhaps would deceive death,
he would search his retort for an elixir
to preserve the body from its fatal corruption.
The warrior traced on a map
plans for lightning offensives,
moved his invisible armies,
guessing which flank of the approaching enemy was weaker.
And the poet smudged uncountable sheets of paper,
uncovering the words of the language
in search of new verse

que tratase de asuntos muy viejos
como el amor, la verdad y el mañana.

Por fin venció el cansancio.
Y en distintas ventanas
de la misma calle
asomaron cuatro hombres fatigados,
que intercambiaron un leve saludo
desde sus mundos distantes.

Y cada uno permaneció en sí mismo
hasta que pasó aquella muchacha hacia el mercado,
con una cesta de coles frescas bajo el brazo.
Entonces,
como se acallan los instrumentos de la orquesta
cuando el director baja con gesto decidido la batuta;
como desaparece el paisaje cuando caen los párpados,
se acallaron, desaparecieron
alejandrinos y marchas forzadas,
razones vitales y pócimas,
y ocho ojos fijos
siguieron el leve temblor
de los senos puntiagudos
de aquella muchacha
que caminaba sin prisa hacia el mercado.

Viaje

Raudo el tren sobre raíles semihundidos en la nieve,
bajo la noche de tinta.
Mamá Claudia lee a Nekrasov;
Larisa come una manzana mientras observa nada
a través del cristal empañado de la ventanilla;
yo escribo lo que veo, lo que oigo, lo que puedo:
poketá, poketá, poketá,
monótona canción de las ruedas
sobre el duro camino de hierro;
poketá, poketá, poketá,
angustiado silbido del tren
en el corazón de la tiniebla;
poketá, poketá, poketá,
la zorra astuta sigue las huellas

about old themes
like love, truth, and the future.

Finally exhaustion triumphed.
And from different windows
on the same street
four tired men leaned out
exchanging a casual greeting
from their distant worlds.

And each of them stayed in place
until a girl passed on the way to market,
a basket of fresh cabbage
dangling from her arm.
Then,
as when the instruments of the orchestra fall silent
when the conductor definitively lowers the baton;
as when the landscape disappears at the lowering of eyelids,
alexandrines and forced marches, vital reasons and potions
fell silent, disappeared,
and eight rapt eyes
followed the slight tremble
of the pointed breasts of that girl
walking slowly to market.

Voyage

The train runs swiftly on rails half sunk in snow,
in the ink-black night.
Mother Claudia reads to Nekrazov;
Larisa eats an apple while observing nothing
through the steamy glass of the window;
I write what I see, what I hear, what I can:
poketa poketa poketa,
the monotonous song of the rails
on the hard iron path;
poketa poketa poketa,
the train's anxious whistle
in the heart of the darkness;
poketa poketa poketa,
the smart vixen follows the tracks

del pequeño conejo que huye;
poketá, poketá, poketá,
y los dientecillos de Larisa
se clavan en la roja manzana;
poketá, poketá, poketá,
los viejos ojos de mamá Claudia
luchan con el sueño y la fatiga;
poketá, poketá, poketá;
yo trato de escribir lo que veo,
poketá.
Lo que oigo,
poketá.
Lo que puedo,
poketá.
¿Por qué tan de prisa
va el tren hacia su destino?
¿Por qué tan de prisa
va la vida hacia la muerte?

MOSCÚ, RIGA, NOV., 1978

Lina de Feria

Poema para la mujer que habla sola en el Parque de Calzada

en tu sombrilla de huecos no se comprende ningún rumor
se cuentan las historias de todas las ciudades que perdieron el mar
de los sitios donde no se pudieron levantar más que ruinas
donde a veces nada valió la pena
y deseabas tantas manos improbables
que terminaste siendo un gajo contra el suelo.
hablabas para creer
y ahora incrédula de los parques
incrédula de los hombres
incrédula de ti misma
creces de la incoherencia como un golpe humano
como algo ante lo que uno tiene que quitarse la mirada
o sentir como un enrojecimiento ante la falta de tradición

of the tiny fleeing rabbit;
poketa poketa poketa,
and Larisa's tiny teeth
are plunged into the red apple;
poketa poketa poketa,
Mother Claudia's old eyes
struggle with sleep and fatigue;
poketa poketa poketa;
I try to write what I see,
poketa.
What I hear,
poketa.
What I can,
poketa.
Why does the train rush so fast
to its final stop?
Why does life rush so fast
towards death?

MOSCOW, RIGA, NOV. 1978

Translated by Mark Weiss

Lina de Feria

Poem for the Woman Who Talks to Herself in Calzada Park

within your parasol of holes no sound is understood
stories are told of all the cities that lost the sea
of places where only ruins could be built
where sometimes nothing was worth the effort
and you wished for so many improbable hands
that in the end you had become a broken branch on the ground.
you spoke to believe
and now disbelieving in parks
disbelieving in men
disbelieving in yourself
you spring from incoherence like a human blow
like something from which one averts one's gaze
or blushes before the loss of tradition

ante el nada que dejar
alguien descarriló tus márgenes
y ahora nos arrancas de tu tiempo
para dejarnos en la categoría de sombras que no respetas
desclasados del cuerpo frente a ti
bien que tienes tu razón
y apenas si la crítica vale
si la denuncia mía no es otra cosa
que el instinto de sentirte animal nuestro
        especie nuestra
                posibilidad y término nuestro.
(que eras como cualquier ser lógico y ahora la soledad te abruma
y nadie te detiene y nadie podría detenerte)
¿qué serías en el antes,
la madre, la concertista, la prostituta,
la que tenía el tedio, la alienada, la del amor platónico,
la asexual, la torpe, la que no tuvo continuación?
eres patética y extraordinaria
si mientes mientes con tu verdad
y así te vemos algunos con tu banco con tu sombrilla
con tus labios pintados por fuera con una línea de temblor
haciendo tus cuentos que nadie recuerda
                y eterna como un retrato
estoy segura que sabrían oírme si digo que eres
un personaje de antonioni o de buñuel
que serías un absoluto para dostoyevski
y que tus manos son para chagall
estás cercana a ellos de alguna manera
como lo estás de mí en algún sitio común de la vida
mujer que habla como a martillazos
nadie hablará de ti pero te quedas
vergüenza que repite su canción
fuera de moda es cierto
frente al teatro de calzada y d.

No es necesario ir a los andenes

No es necesario ir a los andenes
A buscar el farol que marca la salida
Para saber que la tristeza
Puede estar cómodamente instalada

before the nothingness that remains
someone derailed your margins
and now you expunge us from your time
reducing us to the category of shadows beneath your notice
banished from the bodies before you
even if you're right
and if the criticism scarcely matters
if my denunciation is nothing more
than the instinctual feeling that you're our animal
   our species
        our possibility and end.
(that you were a logical being now overwhelmed by solitude
and no one stops you and no one could stop you)
what might you have been before,
mother, performer, prostitute,
one who was bored, who was deranged, who loved platonically,
asexual, awkward, without sequel?
you are pathetic and extraordinary
if you lie it's with your truth that you lie
some of us see you thus with your bench and your parasol
your lips outlined by a shaky hand
making up stories that no one remembers
        and as unchanging as a portrait
I'm sure they would understand if I said that you're
a character out of antonioni or buñuel
that you might be a perfect dostoyevski
and that your hands are signature chagall
you are close to them in some way
as you are to me in some common place of life
a woman who speaks like hammer-strokes
no one will speak of you but you remain
a shameful thing repeating its unfashionable song
across from the theater at the corner of calzada and d.

You Don't Have to Go onto the Platform

You don't have to go onto the platform
To figure out how to leave the station
To know that sadness
Can be conveniently installed

En el adiós de una gente de pueblo
O en la muchacha que va a alcanzar
La muerte de su padre con un telegrama
Que le brinda un asiento sin número.

A veces lo más triste
Puede estar en la expresión de la mujer
Vendiendo el boleto tras la reja
Y que mecánicamente poncha el pedazo de cartón
Como si lo supiera todo del viaje
O como si no supiera nada
Y le pide al que hace fila con mi hombro
Que nos desplace rápido
Porque ya es tiempo de continuar.

Y es que no hay nada peor
        Que una cara sin rostro.

Preámbulo

el venado se azora
ante la fuente de la costumbre
y detiene su acto de beber.
ha recorrido el mismo camino de la tarde
pero no hay pájaros bebiendo ni hay bosques
usurpando la piedra milagrosa ni hay hongos
comestibles para los seres que se arrastran.

el venado se azora ante el enigma
y con las astas tensas en el aviso del otoño
se pregunta qué es lo que ha sucedido
bajo su vientre de animal que siempre estuvo
paciente como una nave que bojea al mundo
tocando los acantilados agudos de la orilla.

el venado hembra patea la imagen de su infancia
en que miró de reojo tras el arbusto débil
la tertulia de los lobos sangrientos.
el venado patea y espera que el venado
le traiga la rama entre los ojos.

In the townspeople's farewell
Or in the girl who's going to overtake
The death of her father with a telegram
That offers her an unnumbered seat.

Sometimes the saddest thing
Can be found on the face of a woman
Selling the ticket behind the grille
Who mechanically punctures the piece of cardboard
As if she knew the whole journey
Or as if she knew nothing
And tells the man next to me in line
That we should get a move on
Because it's already time to leave.

Because there's nothing worse
      Than an expressionless face.

Preamble

the deer is anxious
before the usual fountain
and stops its drinking.
it has traversed the afternoon's habitual path
but no birds drink nor are there groves
usurping the miraculous stone nor the edible
mushrooms for crawling things.

the deer is anxious before the enigma
its antlers tense before the precursors of fall
it asks itself what's happened beneath its animal belly that was always
as patient as a ship coasting the world
and touching at the shoreline's sharp cliffs.

the female deer stamps on the imprint of its childhood
when it saw out of the corner of its eye
the gathering of bloody wolves
behind the fragile shrub.
the deer stamps and hopes the deer
will bring it the branch between its eyes.

Translated by Michael Smith

Delfín Prats

No vuelvas a los lugares donde fuiste feliz

No vuelvas a los lugares donde fuiste feliz
a la isla que con él recorriste
como Adriano los dominios de su imperio
con el muchacho de Bitinia
(ese mar de las arenas negras
donde sus ojos se abrieron al asombro
fue solo una invención de tu nostalgia)

Extraviado en medio de la noche
no puedes recordar
has perdido los senderos del sueño
y despiertas buscándolo en el ocio
y el juego de los soldados y su lengua
extraña a tus oídos había sido para él
un descubrimiento en ese día hecho
para crecer en la memoria de ambos
como las montañas que entonces los rodearon

Di adiós a los paisajes donde fuiste feliz
vive la plenitud de la soledad
en el primer instante
en que asumes la separación
como si ya su estatua
en ti elevada por el amor
para la eternidad fuera esculpida
contra el cielo de aquella isla
contra sus ojos más grandes
y más pavorosos que el silencio

Para festejar el ascenso de Ícaro

Te veo ascender en el espacio: un sueño. "Para él—me digo—la tierra es azul-azul: una naranja, allá." Ícaro, tan lejos de mis bosques. Mi infancia, espléndido contén contra la náusea. Ciudades, alimentadas por la niebla. Oyes, como todo descubridor, pasar bandadas ¿de pájaros? Manantiales, desde la roca. Por la voz de los hombres antiguos, en el acto de dar nombre a las cosas, conoces su mensaje: fiesta del recordar. Dibujarás los remotos

Delfín Prats

Never Return to the Scenes of Your Happiness

Never return to the scenes of your happiness
to the island you and he crossed together
like Hadrian visiting his domains
with the Bithynian boy
(that sea with its black sand beaches
where his eyes would widen in astonishment
was just the invention of nostalgia)

Misplaced in a midnight
you can't recall
you have lost the dream's pathways
and you awaken seeking it
in the games and pastimes of soldiers and their speech
strange to your ears had been for him
that day a discovery
that was to grow in both your memories as tall
as the mountains that encircled you then

Say goodbye to the landscapes where you were happy
live the fullness of the solitude
in that first moment
when you assumed separation into yourself
as if now his statue
raised up by love within you
were sculpted for eternity
against the sky of that island
against his eyes that are larger
and more terrible than silence

In Celebration of the Ascent of Icarus

I watch you ascend into space: a dream. "For him," I tell myself, "the earth is
a deep blue: over there, an orange." Icarus, so far from my forests. My child-
hood a splendid protection from nausea. Cities nurtured by clouds. Like
every explorer you hear the passing of flocks. Birds? Fountains, bursting
from the rock. You have learned your message from the voices of old men
giving names to all things: it is the celebration of memory. You will draw the

bisontes, el oráculo y la lira del dios en los espacios del nuevo cielo, niebla a ti semejante. Veo cómo asciendes. Te elevas hacia estrellas que ardieron sobre el Etna ¿cuántos siglos atrás? "Su esfuerzo es inútil—me digo—, el sol derretirá sus alas." Y quizás no, Ícaro, quizás, al otro lado de tu empeño, descubras colibríes, la Ítaca celeste, los frutos del granado en el lluvioso patio, y nos convenzas, a nosotros, escépticos, que vacilamos en seguirte, de que tú (únicamente tú), Ícaro, estabas en lo cierto.

Fábula del cazador y el ciervo

El ciervo escapa, lejos del cazador que lo persigue
como el juglar al verso que entre nieblas discurre
Cercana la infancia, distantes las montañas
que azulean a lo lejos, al borde del abismo
por donde cruzan, trémulas, las manos del juglar
Toda la expectativa por el futuro incierto está en sus ojos
La yerba fresca, la espesura del bosque
el borde tímido del agua
no pueden ser la obra del azar
como tampoco pueden serlo los amorosos cantos
que el cazador dispone como una trenzada red para atraparlo
Lejos de la mirada del juglar el ciervo escapa
por la linde del bosque. El universo:
inocente metáfora de Dios que al unísono copian
las pupilas del ciervo y el canto del juglar
Y cuando finalmente es atrapado, disuelto en el discurso
ardiendo en el abrazo, que el vino y las palabras enardecen
el ciervo nuevamente escapa
lejos del cazador que lo contempla
ahora en los contextos de la fábula

Viento de Patmos

Tiempo de higos verdes
Tiempo de higos verdes
Cada mañana atisbo más allá del muro
que me separa del Jardín de vedados espejismos
y repito la apremiante consigna:
Este es un tiempo de higos verdes.
Amanezco con esta convicción

distant bison, and the oracle and lyre of the gods, in the expanse of new sky, a mist that resembles you. I watch your ascent. You rise toward the stars that burn over Aetna, how long ago? "Your attempt is useless," I tell myself, "the earth will melt your wings." And maybe not, maybe, Icarus, beyond your efforts you have found hummingbirds, the celestial Ithaca, pomegranates in the rain-drenched yard, and you convince us, skeptics that we are, who hesitate to follow you, that you (and you only) were right.

Fable of the Hunter and the Stag

The stag escapes, far from the hunter who pursues him
like the jester chasing a verse that flows off into mist
Childhood is close, the mountains are far
blue in the distance, at the edge of the abyss
through which the jester's trembling hands cross
All of his hopes for an uncertain future are in his eyes
The fresh grass, the dense forest
the timid edge of the water
can't be merely the work of chance
any more than the love songs
that the hunter lays out like a braided net to catch it
Far from the jester's gaze the stag escapes
through the edge of the forest. The universe:
God's innocent metaphor that the stag's eyes and the jester's song
copy in unison. And when it's trapped at last, dissolved in
the warm discourse and embrace that wine and words ignite
the stag once more escapes
far from the hunter who understands it now
within the context of the fable.

Wind Out of Patmos

Season of green figs
Season of green figs
Each morning I see farther beyond the wall
that separates me from the Garden of forbidden illusions
and repeat the urgent slogan:
It's a season of green figs.
I wake up with this conviction

paso por ella la jornada ardua
estregado a la estulticia, a lo inútil
y a la hora del anhelado encuentro
la comparto contigo
en lugares condenados a la devastación
rigurosamente sustraídos al afecto de Dios.
Este es el tiempo de los higos verdes.
Los animales parecen intuirlo
toman una distancia cautelosa
se apartan de quienes permanecemos a la espera.
Para la amorosa amistad
también es este el tiempo de los higos verdes.
He visto demasiado para cruzar los brazos.
El viento de Patmos mueve mis queridos papeles
se cierne sobre la casa de mis padres
está amenazando los lugares, que tú y yo,
juntos, intentamos salvar de la devastación y el caos.
He visto demasiado para esperar en calma
que se produzca la revelación.
Civitas Dei, tu llamada en la zarza, tu señal
en el arco tendido como un único signo de supervivencia.

Excilia Saldaña

La mujer que ríe y llora

• *A Jorge Berroa, la música*

El estanque transparente se burla del mar.

Tiempo de llanto y tiempo de risa y tiempo:
la perfección del dolor
                    se muestra en la reincidencia.

Tiempo de risa y tiempo de llanto y tiempo:
la risa es la finitud del dolor,
su más alta prueba. Su prueba de fuego.

it stays with me through the difficult day
buffeted by stupidity and uselessness
and at the hour of the yearned-for meeting
I share it with you
in places condemned to ruin
strictly separated from God's affection.
This is the season of green figs.
The animals appear to sense it
they keep a cautious distance
they stray from whoever we continue to wait for.
For amorous friendship
it's also the season of green figs.
I have seen too much to do nothing.
The wind out of Patmos moves my beloved papers
hovers above my parents' house
it's threatening the places that you and I,
together, are trying to save from chaos and ruin.
I have seen too much to wait calmly
for the revelation to happen.
Civitas Dei, your cry in the wilderness, your sign
in the rainbow displayed as an only token of survival

Translated by Mark Weiss

Excilia Saldaña

The Woman Who Laughs and Cries

• *To the musician Jorge Berroa*

The pond mocks the sea.

Time of tears and time of laughter and time:
the perfection of sorrow
                    appears in the repetition of a mistake.

Time of tears and time of laughter and time:
laughter is the limit of sorrow,
its toughest trial. Its trial by fire.

La risa es la sombra del dolor.
El dolor, el sitio silencioso de la risa.
Ambos, el cuerpo del tiempo.

Y el tiempo
        es el agua y la flor danzando en la noche
        el misterio lunático del fuego.

En el lugar donde se dan cita la perplejidad
de la porcelana
                        y la orfandad
de los junquillos
        allí
la casa es como una fuente
y el ojo líquido del amor embebe el pañuelo
de las constelaciones.

Un mundo acaba de rodar como una naranja transparente,
su ruido ensordece el espacio y sólo queda el tiempo
de la risa y del llanto hermanados. Y el tiempo.

Cante la guitarra lo que no cantan las venas:

> *Una vez quise ser pluma*
> *otra vez quise ser reja*
> *pero el vuelo nunca quiso*
> *enredarse en mi pobreza*

Cante la guitarra lo que no cantan las venas:

> *Una vez fui jardín*
> *otra vez panal de cera*
> *pero el pecho de la miel*
> *recuerda sólo a la abeja*

Cante la guitarra lo que no cantan las venas:

> *Una vez quise ser ola*
> *otra vez barca velera*
> *pero el mar ay nunca quiso*
> *ser el potro de esta hembra*

Cante la guitarra lo que no cantan las venas:

> *Una vez yo fui la herida*
> *otra vez la vaina vieja*

Laughter is the shade of sorrow.
Sorrow is laughter's silent abode.
Both are the body of time.

And time
is the nighttime dance of water and flower
the crazy mystery of fire.

In the place appointed for the meeting of the perplexity
of porcelain
and the orphanhood
of jonquils
there where
the house is like a spring
and the liquid eye of love imbibes the cloth
of the constellations.

A world stops spinning like a transparent orange,
its sound deafens space and all that's left is the time
of laughter and tears together. And time itself.

May the guitar sing what veins don't sing:

Once I wished to be a feather
another time a cage
but flight never wished
to be trapped in my poverty

May the guitar sing what veins don't sing:

Once I was a garden
another time a honeycomb
but only the bee remembers
the honey's heart

May the guitar sing what veins don't sing:

Once I wished to be a wave
another time a sailing ship
but oh! the sea never wished
to be this mare's foal

May the guitar sing what veins don't sing:

Once I was the wound
another time the old scabbard

siempre el cuchillo ignoró
que su casa era mi pena

Cante la guitarra el romance de mi espera.

Ni llanto ni risa. Sólo el tiempo
como un río interminable
entre las manos de amasar estrellas y recuerdos.

Porque el olvido no existe,
                            no es ni pájaro,
                                    ni viento,
                                    ni iglesia.

Lo que existe es la angustia.
Lo que existe es la tierra seca de la angustia.
Su cuerpo limpio sin árboles ni bestias.
Lo que existe es la sed de la angustia.
Capa de agraz, boca curtida.

Lo que existe es la espera

en el tiempo de la risa y en el tiempo del llanto
y en el aleteo del delfín
y en la vigilancia silenciosa
        de la cola del pavorreal
y en la piedra caída en el estanque
y en el círculo que se cierra.

La naranja lentamente se hace amarilla,
sacrifica su belleza a la sed.
La boca espera la frescura o el veneno.
El tiempo asume la perfección del dolor,
                            su finitud,
su presencia. Ampara la risa.
Justifica el tiempo, todo el tiempo
que como pez se escapa, ríe y llora.

El estanque transparente se burla del mar.

the knife never knew
that its home was my pain

May the guitar sing the romance of my longing.

Neither tears nor laughter. Only time
like an endless river
gathering stars and memories in its hands.

Because forgetting doesn't exist,
                              it's neither bird,
                                  nor wind,
                                  nor church.

What exists is anguish.
What exists is the parched earth of anguish.
Its body cleansed of trees and beasts.
What exists is the thirst of anguish.
A layer of bitter grapes, a weathered mouth.

What exists is longing

in the time of laughter and the time of tears
and in the dolphin's flapping
and the silent watchfulness
                        of a peacock's tail
and the stone that fell in the pond
and the circle that's closed.

Slowly the orange turns yellow,
its beauty sacrificed to thirst.
The mouth awaits either freshness or poison.
Time takes on the perfection of sorrow,
                                  its limit,
its presence. It protects laughter.
Time, all of time, that escapes
like a fish, justifies, laughs and cries.

The clear pond mocks the sea.

Translated by Mark Weiss

Raúl Hernández Novás

Quién seré sino el tonto

But the fool on the hill
sees the sun going down
and the eyes in his head
see the world spinning round
LENNON Y McCARTNEY

Quién seré sino el tonto que en la agria colina
miraba el sol poniente como un viejo achacoso,
miraba el sol muriente como un rey destronado,
el tonto que miraba girar el mundo,
guardando en su rostro las huellas de la noche.
Quién seré sino el tonto de siempre atraído por el mar,
aquel que en el mar feroz dejó su nombre.
Quién sino el tonto que lloraba
y lloraba por el mar, las flores, las muchachas, la esbelta luna sonriendo.
Sobre la colina está solo *and nobody seems to like him*,
pero él ve el mundo moverse a su alrededor,
el sol rebotar como una pelota roja
en el horizonte. El sol tragado por el mar, frío entre los peces.
Quién seré sino aquel que ya no mira,
no oye, no palpa, absorto, esas tierras astrales, esos frutos,
las viñas de la realidad, airoso manto.
El que ve la noche descender como un cuerpo
inapresable, el que siente la luna caer sobre sus hombros
como una tela delicada, aquel que en la marisma
jugaba a rey, a payaso, a rey, a oscuro caballo.
Absorto, solo, en la colina, gritando
como loco, bajo los pájaros que emigran
señalando un carcomido rumbo. Yo,
el loco, el tonto que siempre he sido, girando en la burla,
torpe bufón de florida pirueta, riendo,
con dientes podridos, la realidad inapresable
como implacable cuerpo, a nuestro lado, descansando en las hierbas
brotadas de los muertos, entre sonrisas de nocturnas flores.
Quién seré, Dios mío, sino el loco tonto, el oso bronco, el jorobado torpe,

Raúl Hernández Novás

Who Would I Be If Not the Fool

But the fool on the hill
sees the sun going down
and the eyes in his head
see the world spinning round
LENNON AND McCARTNEY

Who would I be if not the fool who from the rough hill
beheld the sun in the west like a sick old man,
beheld the dying sun like a king dethroned,
the fool who saw the world spinning,
preserving in his face the traces of night.
Who would I be if not the fool forever drawn to the sea,
who abandoned his name in the ferocious sea.
Who but the fool who wept
and wept for the sea, the flowers, girls, the smiling, slender moon.
He is alone on the hill *and nobody seems to like him,*
but he sees the world stir around him
the sun rebounding against the horizon
like a red ball. Swallowed by the sea, cold among the fish.
Who would I be if not the one who, lost in thought, no longer observes
hears or feels those starry lands, those fruits,
the vineyards of the real, the airy mantle.
Who sees night fall
like a body that can't be caught, who feels slipping through his fingers
the moon falling like a delicate cloth
upon his shoulders, who on the moor
played the king, the jester, the king, the jack of spades.
Lost in thought, alone, on the hill, howling
like a madman, beneath the birds
migrating along their worn path. I,
the madman, the fool I have always been, spinning in mockery,
clumsy buffoon of florid gestures, laughing,
teeth rotted, reality that can't be caught
like an unappeasable body beside us relaxing on grass
that sprouts from the dead among smiles of nocturnal flowers.
Who, God help me, would I be if not the crazy fool, the rough bear,

bufón bailando, reuniendo rumbos entre sus brazos, flores
para una mujer que no existe, quien mira al sol dormirse cual tembloroso
   viejo
y al mundo girar en burla alrededor de sus hombros destronados.

Sobre el nido del cuco

> *Ellos tienen unas vitrinas y usan unos zapatos.*
> *En esas vitrinas alternan el maniquí con el quebrantahuesos disecado,*
> *y todo lo que ha pasado por la frente del hastío del búfalo solitario.*
> *Si no miramos la vitrina, charlan*
> *de nuestra insuficiente desnudez que no vale una estatuilla de Nápoles.*
> *Si la atravesamos y no rompemos los cristales . . .*
>   JOSÉ LEZAMA LIMA, "PENSAMIENTOS EN LA HABANA"

I

En estas tardes medrosas
en que no llama nadie a la puerta
y no suenan los timbres y la casa
es un gran frigorífico lleno de silencio
en estas tardes que gravitan sobre los parques
impidiendo la vida y los juegos
—tardes que pesan como un fardo hiriente
sobre los hombros de la estatua inmóvil—
en medio de esta lluvia que no cae y moja
los huesos tan desnudos en la ausencia de voces
sin nadie en mi experiencia I think of you Billy
yo ta también pienso en ti Bi Billy
reconstruyendo mis memorias de piedra
tan pesadas como fuente de sangre
y no tengo nada que decirte porque no llama nadie
y no hay nadie en mi experiencia

Quizás jugamos en el mismo parque
un teléfono mudo entre nosotros
un eléctrico hilo que devana temblando
trabajando en la blanca rueca de la distancia
la senda en cuyo fin cae una nieve triste
un vuelo de pájaro callado
un empeño de ave que emigra

the clumsy hunchback, the dancing clown, gathering pathways in his
 arms, flowers
for a woman who doesn't exist, observing the sun bed down like a
 trembling old man,
the world spinning in mockery around his dethroned shoulders.

Over the Cuckoo's Nest

They have some show-windows and wear some shoes.
In those show windows they alternate the mannequin with the stuffed ossifrage,
and everything that has passed through the forehead of the lonesome buffalo's boredom.
If we don't look at the show-window, they chat
about our insufficient nakedness that isn't worth a figurine from Naples.
If we go through it and don't break the glass . . .
JOSÉ LEZAMA LIMA, "THOUGHTS IN HAVANA"

I

In those fearful evenings
when no one calls at the door
and the doorbells don't ring and the house
is a large refrigerator stuffed with silence
in those evenings that weigh upon the parks
interfering with life and games
—evenings that press like a cruel burden
upon the shoulders of the unmoving statue—
in the midst of a rain that doesn't fall but soaks
bones naked in the absence of voices
having no one in my experience *I think of you Billy*
I al also think of you Bi Billy
rebuilding my memories in stone
memories heavy as a fountain of blood
and I have nothing to say to you because no one calls
and there's no one in my experience

Maybe we play in the same park
a mute telephone between us
an electric cord coiled vibrating
working in the white curve of distance
the path at whose end a sad snow falls
the flight of a silent bird
a migratory bird's promise

viste con tierra de Wisconsin mis huesos al garete
un telegrama que las aves llevan y entre nosotros
no más una vitrina luminosa
que yo atravieso sin romper los vidrios.

II

Qué gaviota de azúcar rozó las olas
de aquellos mares de Virginia
donde viaja la barca de los locos
con todos nosotros Billy con todos nosotros
Dios mío somos nada más unos pendejos
somos unos locos en un barco que gira
y echamos velas y anclas y gobernalle al mar
y echamos a suerte el viento enemigo y estamos esperando
esperando a Jaws y Jaws no viene
y no hunde el barco y la ballena blanca
como una tumba de cristal no viene
Mac Mac Mac Dónde te has metido
me has dejado al timón y yo no sé
gobernar esta nave y te escondiste te escondiste with candies
pero en vez de ocultarte riendo estabas triste
Por qué dime te escondes con tu dulce
luminoso en los labios y nos dejaste solos por qué hermano
por qué padre nos has dejado solos en esta barca de los locos
que no sé gobernar
                          denme el cuaderno
de bitácora que han repasado las sirenas
con esas manos verdes como nubes
con sus manos de algas y jacintos
Y en el cuaderno de bitácora
tras la noche estéril sin dulces y sin juegos
tras el juego soñado without candies
sin la estrella de azúcar en la boca
vacía la piñata de los cielos
y el garrote tierno en nuestras manos el garrote
con que hemos de golpearnos a ciegas sin dar con la piñata
poniéndonos el rabo vergonzoso y las orejas del indecible burro
sin dar con la pelota redonda como el mundo en el vacío estadio
después del halloween lluvioso y de puertas cerradas
(han envenenado los dulces han enterrado agujas en las manzanas)
y mudas calabazas sin luz las calabazas de ella

seen with the soil of Wisconsin my bones gone to pot
a telegram carried by birds and between us
nothing but a shining window
that I pass through without breaking the glass.

II

What sugary gull skimmed the waves
of those Virginia seas
where the ship of fools sails with all of us aboard
with all of us Billy with all of us
my god we're just a bunch of cowards
a bunch of crazies on a spinning boat
and we toss sails and anchors and rudder into the sea
and we let the enemy wind take us and we wait
we await Jaws and Jaws doesn't come
and the ship doesn't sink and the whale white
as a crystal tomb doesn't come
Mac Mac Mac Where have you gone
you've left me at the helm and I don't know how
to steer this ship and you hid you hid *with candies*
but instead of laughing you were sad
tell me why you hide with the gloss
of candy on your lips and left us alone why brother
why father have you left us alone on this ship of fools
that I don't know how to steer
                                        give me the logbook
that the sirens thumbed
with those green cloudlike hands
those hands of seaweed and hyacinth
And in the logbook
after the sterile night without sweets or games
after the dreamed-of game *without candies*
no sugar star in the mouth
the heavenly piñata empty
and the tender club in our hands the club
with which we strike blindly without hitting the piñata
pinning the shameful tail and ears on the unspeakable donkey
without finding the ball that's as round as the world in the empty stadium
after the rainy Halloween of closed doors
(they've poisoned the candy hid needles in the apples)
and mute unlit pumpkins her pumpkins

junto a un cuerpo de estrella parpadeante
en el cuaderno en blanco de bitácora
Billy yo escribo *rien* como el monarca
tras la noche vacía de sus bodas

III

     You know
     If you break my heart I'll go
     But I'll be back again

"Y le llevé las flores y así le dije Would you
marry me anyway? Would you have my baby?
y ella sonrió con labios de caramelo con
sus colmillos de azúcar el ángel vigilaba
el telón de las hojas del jardín soñoliento
y yo le dije quieres compartir esta suerte
la barca sin estrella mar hiel enamorada"

     no es usted a quien aman
        compréndalo
     renuncie gentilmente

"Le llevaba unas flores al retablo vacío
descorrían las hojas su telón soñoliento
una escena una escena el carnaval del mundo
en medio de la turba de feos monigotes
una estrella riendo como un ángel de azúcar
tan sólo un torbellino que la dejara a ella
ángel y marioneta en el jardín del sueño"

     no es usted a quien aman

"El tablero vacío seguiría aplaudiendo
las luces se apagaron me quedo sin embargo
siempre hay algo que ver se hizo lo oscuro ahora
vendrán caras extrañas sobre el tablado a ciegas
compréndalo las hojas del telón se cerraron
y cerraron las puertas de la ciudad hiriente"

     renuncie gentilmente

"Que la siga leal en extramuros
el perro de la casa es un consuelo
ser gozque de su falda el halloween lluvioso

next to the body of a twinkling star
in the white logbook Billy I write
rien as the king did
after his empty wedding-night

III

> *You know*
> *If you break my heart I'll go*
> *But I'll be back again*

"And I brought her flowers and I asked *Would you*
marry me anyway? Would you have my baby?
and she smiled with caramel lips with
sugar teeth the angel watched over
the curtain of leaves in the sleepy garden
and I asked do you wish to share this destiny with me
the ship without a star a sea bitterness smitten"

     it's not you they love
       understand
     give it up quietly

"I brought some flowers for her empty altarpiece
the leaves stripped off their sleepy curtain
a play a play the carnival of the world
in the midst of the crowd of ugly puppets
a star laughing like a sugar angel
alone a whirlwind that drops her
angel and marionette in the dream's garden"

     it's not you they love

"The empty stage would keep applauding
the lights were turned off but I'm still here
there's always something to see it's dark now
strange faces will mount the stage blindly
understand that the leaves of the curtain were closed
and the gates of the painful city as well"

     give it up quietly

"Let me follow her faithfully outside the city walls
the dog of the house is a delight
yapping around her skirt this rainy Halloween

por los lejanos pueblos que la siga llevando
la cántara de flores junto al jardín dormido
velado por el ángel con su espada de fuego
ante el telón cerrado junto al jardín me dijo"

>no es usted a quien aman
> compréndalo
> renuncie gentilmente

"Lleva el cántaro al río trae el cántaro a casa
llénalo de tu leche la leche de tu piel
las olas de tu pecho hondos cielos de leche
los hilos de tu entraña filamentos de nube
muñeca descosida alada marioneta
escucha esta vasija sus latidos de barro
trae el cántaro a casa lleva el cántaro al río"

>"la lecherita ciega
> quebró mi corazón"
> . . . but I'll be back again

IV

I never lost as much but twice
and that was in the sod
EMILY DICKINSON

Cerré la puerta y dejé el mundo afuera
me recluí intramuros de mí misma
y no había nadie en mi experiencia
y no se lo dije a mi madre
y no se lo dije a mi padre
Cuando cerré la puerta a la tarde vacía de Amherst
y me quedé intramuros los ángeles llegaban recibía
la visita de Walt con sus barbas de nieve
su pecho tormentoso sus regalos
de blanca navidad yo estaba sola
y había perdido y ganado dos veces
todo ocurrió en la tierra y en el césped
sólo llevaba pequeños presentes
a los graves vecinos a mi dueño
dulces pequeñas estrellas de azúcar
y fui dos veces dueña del tesoro
y no se lo dije a mi madre

through distant towns I follow her bearing
the pitcher of flowers next to the sleeping garden
guarded by the angel with his fiery sword
in front of the closed curtain next to the garden she told me"

        it's not you they love
           understand
        give it up quietly

"Carry the pitcher to the river bring it home
fill it with milk the milk of your skin
waves of your skin deep skies of milk
the threads of your heart the filaments of clouds
disjointed doll winged marionette
listen to this vessel its clay throbbing
bring the pitcher home carry it to the river"

        "The blind milkmaid
        has broken my heart"
        . . . but I'll be back again

IV
   I never lost as much but twice
   And that was in the sod
    EMILY DICKINSON

I shut the door and left the world outside
I became a recluse within the walls of myself
and I had no one in my experience
and I didn't tell my mother
and I didn't tell my father
When I shut the door in the empty Amherst evening
and stayed indoors the angels came I received
a visit from Walt with his snowy beard
his turbulent breast his white
Christmas presents I was alone
and had lost and gained twice
everything happened in the earth and the grass
I only carried small gifts
to my solemn neighbors to my master
sweet sugar stars
and twice I was the owner of the treasure
and I didn't tell my mother

y no se lo dije a mi padre
y me encerré a morir entre los muros
para guardar avara mi tesoro
sedosos intramuros de mí misma
                              Padre
estoy llamando tirándote la puerta

mira mis dedos aún vacíos
de los anillos de la felicidad

y yo gritaba ¡despierta!

     burglar banker father
     I am poor once more!

v

     Someone is knocking at the door
     Somebody is ringing the bell

     Someone is knocking at the door
     Somebody is ringing the bell

     Open the door

     Let them in

Billy I have long dreamed without candies
la estrella de azúcar *et rien*
et rien nada ha pasado
que no lo sepa el padre que no lo sepa la madre
ni el maestro y su mujer la señorita
las personas mayores
estoy en la habitación vacía
en el viaje vacío de los locos
en el hueco oscuro del árbol que cruje
como un frigorífico de silencio
Billy crece la sombra
como una marea sin estrellas
y ya está muy oscuro
hello darkness my old friend

Billy yo estoy contigo
¿Vendrá el doctor Noel con sus barbas de nieve
a dejar caramelos en las habitaciones
a abrir los corazones y restañar los cántaros deshechos?

and I didn't tell my father
and I shut myself in to die within the walls
to hoard my treasure
the silken walls of myself
                    Father
I'm calling I'm pounding at your door

look the rings of happiness
are still missing from my fingers

and I screamed: wake up!

    burglar banker father
    I am poor once more!

v

    Someone is knocking at the door
    Somebody is ringing the bell

    Someone is knocking at the door
    Somebody is ringing the bell

    Open the door

    Let them in

Billy I have long dreamed without candies
the sugar star *et rien*
et rien nothing's happened
that father doesn't know that mother doesn't know
nor the teacher and his wife the young lady
the elderly
I'm in the empty room
in the empty voyage of the crazies
in the dark hollow of the tree that creaks
like a refrigerator of silence
Billy the shadow is growing
like a starless tide
and it's very dark now
hello darkness my old friend

Billy I'm with you
Will Doctor Noël come with his beards of snow
to leave caramels in the rooms
to open hearts and stanch the bleeding of broken pitchers?

¿Vendrá a despertar al niño muerto
al que durmió a tu lado without candies?
No hallo las indicaciones señorita enfermera
miss Ratched la enfermera está hablando con su lengua de fuego
y de su boca salía una espada aguda de dos filos
una espada de fuego para guardar el camino del árbol

Billy yo estoy contigo
Déjenlo que entre let him in
a la terraza donde están dormidos
a los dormidos los cuidará quejoso
se agrupará la mañana helada en terrones de azúcar

        Let the sunshine
        Let the sunshine in
            the sunshine in

Alguien está tocando a la puerta
a la puerta cubierto de rocío
pasa las noches del invierno
Open the door
Let him in

Billy un teléfono mudo entre nosotros
estás sangrando en el manicomio helado
Let it be Let it bleed
déjenlo déjenlo que sangre
y que su sangre abrigue al mundo
Let him bleed que hable su corazón por la herida
con sílabas de sangre
con que ha de convencer al mundo
y ha de vencer al mundo
y mellar la espada del ángel
la espada de la boca de miss Ratched
Let it be   let him bleed

Billy yo estoy contigo
tú estás bajo la nieve yo en mi cuarto
yo estoy con los dormidos without candies
ruedan mis ojos por la nieve
es una blanca estepa ¿se da cuenta?
allí vi a un conocido y lo detuve
            gritándole ¡Hernández!
rueda la nieve en pelotas que no hemos de golpear

Will he come to awaken the dead child
who slept at your side without candies?
I don't find the indications nurse
Miss Ratched the nurse spoke with her tongue of fire
and from her mouth came forth a two-edged sword
a sword of fire to guard the tree's path

Billy I'm with you
Déjenlo que entre let him in
to the terrace where they're sleeping
grumbling he will tend to the sleepers
they will be clumped together in the frozen morning into lumps of sugar

> Let the sunshine
> Let the sunshine in
>   the sunshine in

Someone is knocking at the door
at the door covered with dew
the winter nights pass
Open the door
Let him in

Billy a mute telephone between us
you're bleeding in the frozen asylum
Let it be Let it bleed
let it let it bleed
and may your blood protect the world
Let him bleed that his heart may speak through his wound
in syllables of blood
with which the world must be convinced
and conquered
and the sword of the angel dented
the sword in the mouth of Miss Ratched
Let it be   let him bleed

Billy I'm with you
you're in the snow and I in my room
I'm among the sleepers without candies
my eyes roll through the snow
it's a white plain, do you know that?
I saw an acquaintance there and stopped him,
              shouting, Hernández!
the snow rolls into balls that we don't have to hit

muñeca de la nieve como blanca mujer
en pelotas que no hemos de acertar
que no hemos de acertar con nuestros leños
en este juego en el vacío estadio
las pelotas fantásticas de nieve
blancas esferas de algodón dulce
y no podremos romper la piñata del cielo
para que caigan las estrellas de azúcar

Billy yo estoy contigo
en la tarde medrosa y vacía donde no suenan timbres
en el juego vacío donde no acude nadie
en el cuarto vacío donde todos dormimos sin dulces con pastillas
en la barca vacía de los locos que gira como el mundo
en la noche vacía de las bodas del rey
en la casa callada como un gran frigorífico vacío
en el parque vacío donde la tarde abruma los hombros de la estatua
Billy yo estoy contigo yo estoy contigo madre
padre yo estoy contigo

                  río manzanares

yo estoy contigo
señorita Ratched

             déjame pasar

entremos todos juntos

             let us in

    Alguien está tocando a la puerta
    Alguien está sonando el timbre

    Alguien está tocando a la puerta
    Alguien está sonando el timbre

    Abran la puerta

    Déjenlos entrar

VI
    Como sueñan humillarnos,
    repitiendo día y noche con el ritmo de la tortuga
    que oculta el tiempo en su espaldar:
    ustedes no decidieron que el ser habitase en el hombre;
    (. . .)
    Como quieren humillarnos le decimos
    the chief of the tribe descended the staircase.
    (. . .)

snow puppet like a pale woman
into balls that we don't have to hit squarely
that we don't have to hit squarely with our sticks
in this game in the empty stadium
imaginary snowballs
white spheres of cotton candy
and we won't be able to break the sky piñata
that the sugar stars may fall

Billy I'm with you
in the frightening, empty evening when bells don't ring
in the empty game where no one comes
in the empty room where we all sleep without sweets with pills
in the empty ship of fools that spins like the world
in the king's empty wedding night
in the house still as an enormous empty refrigerator
in the empty park where evening bears down on the statue's shoulders
Billy I'm with you I'm with you mother
father I'm with you
                         manzanares river
I'm with you
Miss Ratched
                         let me cross over
let's all go in together
                         Let us in
         Someone is knocking at the door
         Somebody is ringing the bell

         Someone is knocking at the door
         Somebody is ringing the bell

         Open the door

         Let them in

VI
Since they dream of humiliating us,
repeating day and night with the rhythm of the tortoise
that conceals time on its back:
you didn't decide that being should dwell in man;
(. . .)
Since they want to humiliate us we say to them:
The chief of the tribe descended the staircase.
(. . .)

Ellos que cargan con sus maniquíes a todos los puertos
y que hunden en sus baúles un chirriar
de vultúridos disecados.
Ellos no quieren saber que trepamos por las raíces húmedas del helecho
(. . .)
y que aunque mastiquemos su estilo,
we don't choose our shoes in a show-window.
JOSÉ LEZAMA LIMA: "PENSAMIENTOS EN LA HABANA"

Let us enter the tree
Let us enter the room
Let us enter the garden

Romped la sórdida vitrina
Quitad al ángel de la puerta
con su espada flamígera
          la tierra será el paraíso
el guardián a la puerta de la ley
poned en su lugar al cherokee de roble
con la frente de hastío del búfalo diezmado
          y vio en sueños una escala
el jefe de la tribu descenderá la escala
porque no entre el ángel de exterminio
con su lengua neutrónica de fuego
que crezca el Gran Teatro de Oklahoma
para cubrir para abrigar al mundo
como la sangre cálida del tonto en la colina
y en la muralla china otra torre de Babel
para escalar el árbol de la vida
para tocar las barbas de nieve del cielo
como el pecho finísimo de Walt
la hierba perfumada de los muertos
Venga Noel a repartir regalos
dulces de miel a las habitaciones
a reparar los viejos corazones
de hiriente maquinaria enmohecida
y a restañar los cántaros deshechos
Somos los humillados los pendejos
Los abalorios que nos han regalado
han fortalecido nuestra propia miseria
Somos los parias íngrimos del mundo
      ah look at all the lonely people
los descosidos los amarrados los ateridos

They who carry their mannequins to all the ports
and who push down into their trunks a screeching
of stuffed vultures.
They don't want to know that we climb up along the damp roots of the fern
(. . .)
and that though we may chew their style,
we don't choose our shoes in a show-window.
                    JOSÉ LEZAMA LIMA, "THOUGHTS IN HAVANA"

    Let us enter the tree
    Let us enter the room
    Let us enter the garden

Break the filthy window
Dismiss from the gate the angel
with his flaming sword
          the world will be paradise
the guardian of the gate of the law
replace him with the wooden indian
wearing the weary expression of the slaughtered buffalo
          and he saw in his dreams a stairway
the chief of the tribe will descend it
that the exterminating angel may not enter
with his neutronic tongue of fire
that the Great Theater of Oklahoma may grow
to cover to shelter the world
like the warm blood of the fool on the hill
and on the great wall of China that other Tower of Babel
for scaling the tree of life
for touching the snowy beards of the sky
like Walt's most delicate breast
the fragrant grass of the dead
Noël comes to distribute presents
honey candies to the rooms
to fix the jagged machinery
of old hearts
and stanch the bleeding of broken pitchers
We are the humiliated the cowards
the trinkets they gave us
have increased our misery
We are the pariahs that the world has abandoned
      ah look at all the lonely people
the ragged the shackled the cold

trepamos por las raíces del helecho
no escogemos nuestros zapatos en una vitrina
nuestra alma no está en un cenicero
aquí estamos los negros y los indios
a la puerta cubiertos de rocío
allí vi a un conocido y lo detuve
                    gritándole ¡Billy!
somos un tal chatterjee un tal hernández
somos un tal zuzuki un tal kuusinen
un tal jones un tal müller un tal nguyen
Aquí estamos todos los negros
que no venimos a rogar
                    Estamos
llamando tirándote la puerta

                y yo gritaba ¡despierta!

    Let us in
                Let us in
                    Don't worry
                    Billy
        Te enviaré un telegrama con las
aves
viajeras:
            Romperemos la piñata
        del cielo
            Y habrá estrellas para todos

7 DE NOVIEMBRE DE 1982

Amando Fernández

Descenso de la agonía

Tú nada puedes dar pues nada tienes:
ni trozo de pan blanco para el hambre ni un sitio junto al fuego que
    caliente la carne
del que avanza en el frío de la noche,

we creep through roots of bracken
we don't choose our shoes in a show-window
our souls are not in an ashtray
here we are blacks and indians
covered with dew at the door
I saw an acquaintance there and stopped him,
                shouting: Billy!
we are called chatterjee hernández
suzuki kuusinen
jones müller nguyen
Here we are all blacks
and we don't come to pray
             We're
calling pounding at your door

       and I screamed: wake up!

  Let us in
        Let us in
              Don't worry
              Billy
  I'll send you a telegram by way of the
migrating
birds
    We'll break the sky
piñata
    And there'll be stars for everyone

NOVEMBER 7, 1982

Translated by Mark Weiss

Amando Fernández

Deathwatch

You have nothing to give because you have nothing:
not a scrap of white bread to keep hunger at bay, nor a place by the fire to
    warm the flesh
of the one who approaches through the cold of night,

ni agua fresca que calme la otra sed,
ni flores que hagan olvidar el aire espeso y corrompido del hombre que se
   muere.
Tu verdad está próxima y quisieras ofrecer un incruento sacrificio, un
   íntimo holocausto,
al Dios que te vigila los minutos.
Tu tierra se ha quedado en el silencio del abrojo:
ni el más bajo reptil, ni indeseables alimañas, hacen nido. No esperes el
milagro de la lluvia oportuna

El capitán

Estás perdido en una gran ciudad.
Caminas hacia el centro.
Y no sabes por qué.

Llegas a una calle cerrada.
Buscas una salida pero no la hay.

Vuelves sobre tus pasos. Sales de la calle
a una avenida silenciosa
que da a una bahía, y a un puerto.
Tienes la sensación de haber estado ahí;
pero no sabes cuándo.

Alrededor hay montañas cubiertas de nieve.
El aire frío.

Bajas hacia los muelles.
Sólo ves algunos barcos viejos, de carga.
En uno de ellos hay un hombre
que te saluda agitando una mano.

Te acercas a la escalerilla.
Desde allí le preguntas
si te permite subir. Parece el capitán.

Con un gesto te indica que subas.
Tú lo haces.
Al llegar a bordo te abraza.

no cool, fresh water to assuage that other thirst,
nor flowers to perfume the thick, rotten air of the dying man with
    oblivion.
Your truth is at hand and you'd like to offer up a bloodless sacrifice, an
    intimate holocaust,
to the God watching over your minutes.
Your world left behind in the thistle's silence:
not the lowliest reptile, nor hateful vermin
will nest. Do not expect
the miracle of an opportune rain.

The Captain

You are lost in a great city.
You walk toward the center.
And you don't know why.

You come to a dead end.
You look for a way out but there is none.

You retrace your steps. You leave the street
for a silent avenue
that leads to a bay and a port.
You feel that you've been there before;
but you don't know when.

Snow-capped mountains on all sides.
Cold air.

You go down to the docks.
All you see are a few old freighters.
There's a man in one of them
who greets you, waving his hand.

You approach the Jacob's ladder.
You ask for permission
to come aboard. He seems to be the captain.

He beckons for you to climb up.
And you do.
On board he embraces you.

El viento se levanta fuerte.
Vas vestido con ropa muy ligera.
Pero no sientes frío.

El capitán señala al interior del barco.
Antes de entrar se vuelve a ti;
con emoción—ahora sabes quién es—te dice:
"Entra. Zarpamos mañana, muy temprano."

La estatua

Estás solo en la casa.

Hace tiempo que estás sentado en esa silla
en un rincón oscuro del cuarto,
y te resistes a moverte.

Estás sentado rígido.
Sientes la tensión que crece en tus caderas,
en los músculos del cuello, en la espalda.

Respiras. Te mantienes
en esa misma posición—¿desde cuándo?—
Y no es posible cambiarla.

Sabes que algo en ti depende
de esa persistencia;
de un sometimiento extraño
a una única postura,
a una asumida decisión.

Estás solo en la casa
Y estás sentado rígido. Respiras.

No te mueves. Sabes que si te mueves
caerás roto en pedazos—mil pedazos—
como una estatua de yeso.

A strong wind picks up.
Your clothes are thin.
But you don't feel cold.

The captain points to the ship's interior.
Before going in he turns to you;
with emotion—you know who he is now—he bids you:
"Enter. We sail tomorrow, at first light."

The Statue

You're alone in the house.

You've been sitting in that chair for a long time
in a dark corner of the room,
determined not to move.

You sit stiffly.
You feel the tension growing in your hips,
in the muscles of your neck, in your back.

You breathe. You've held
that same pose, for how long?
And you can't change it.

You know that something in you depends
on that persistence;
on a strange submission
to a single posture,
a steadfast resolve.

You're alone in the house
And you sit stiffly. You breathe.

You don't move. You know that if you move
you will fall and break into pieces, a thousand pieces,
like a plaster statue.

Translated by Cindy Schuster

Soleida Ríos

Pájaro de La Bruja

♦ *a Joel James*

El pájaro nació del filo de un machete.
Nada tiene que ver con el sinsonte
el choncholí o la torcaza triste.
Nació del filo de un machete
no de la hueva blanca de una pájara vieja.

Ni alondra ni quetzal
ni el aura ansiosa tras las últimas huellas.
Vive en el canto de La Bruja. Allí es su nido.
Canta como los pájaros del mar y los del monte.
Arrea las mulas. Y en mal tiempo
vuela implacable sobre los guanos de un bohío
y entonces alguien tiene que morir.

De marzo a octubre el pájaro es culpable.
Si cae un rayo en medio de la palma
si se desborda el río
si una décima viene lejanísima
con el aroma del último café
siempre—de marzo a octubre—
el pájaro es culpable.

2

Dicen que como fiesta mágica hace tiempo
unos compadres se vieron una noche
cerca del canto de La Bruja.
Que allí sacaron la enorme botijuela
que era un secreto de los dos
en nombre de los hijos.
Dicen que algo se puso en el lugar
donde la hombría se rompe, no se sabe.
Que halaron los machetes.

Soleida Ríos

The Witch's Bird

♦ *to Joel James*

The bird was born of a machete's blade
It's nothing like mockingbird
blackbird or mournful dove:
it was born of a machete's blade
not from some old bird's white egg.

Neither skylark nor quetzal
nor the buzzard that anxiously tracks last footsteps,
it lives in The Witch's song. It makes its nest there,
and it sings like the birds of sea and forest.
It goads the mules. Implacable, in foul weather
it flies above a hut's palm thatch
and someone must die.

From March to October it's the bird's fault:
if lightning strikes the midst of a palm tree
if the river floods
if a verse comes infinitely slowly
bearing the aroma of the last of the coffee
in every case—from March to October—
it's the bird's fault.

2

They say that once a pair of friends
found themselves in the night
near the Witch's song, where they had gathered
for a bout of magic,
and that they brought forth the enormous urn
of amulets and bones that had been till then
the secret they held
in trust for believers.
They say that something came among them
in that place where the bonds of the human
are broken; but no one really knows.
And that machetes were drawn.

3

El pájaro nació en el último escalón
violento del corazón dentro del pecho.
Nadie lo puede ver
pero ha volado por todas las lomas
de la Sierra.

Maleva y los niños en el paraíso

• *a Carolina, a Estela y Chiqui*

Los únicos paraísos no vedados al hombre
son los paraísos perdidos
J. L. BORGES

En el jardín
y más al fondo, en los ojos de Maleva
los niños se tiran de los árboles.

Aquellos niños puros que ya fuimos
cubiertos por pañales blanquecinos
se tiran de los árboles.
Pero se tiran a morir
a que nos olvidemos.
Y se tiran riendo
porque disfrutan de antemano
la pena que vendrá
la desesperación en que más tarde
o más temprano
sucumbiremos todos.

La muerte de los niños no está escrita,
Ellos la prefiguran en la rareza de sus juegos.
Ayer, si no es que hace un instante
o hace doscientos siglos
los niños figuraban ciertos juegos
como en una nostalgia de niños anteriores.

(Los primeros, los últimos que vuelven
a comenzar las filas
ya no figuran nada, gritan
carne de momia carne de momia
queremos la *cabeza del escudo*.)

3

The bird was born on the last violent rung
of the heart hidden deep within the breast.
No one can see it
though it has flown over all the heights
of the mountains.

Maleva and the Children in Paradise

• to Carolina, Estela, and Chiqui

*The only paradises not forbidden to man
are those that are lost.*
J. L. BORGES

In the garden,
further back, Maleva sees
children falling from the trees.

Those innocent children that we once were
diapered in white
fall from the trees.
But they fall to their deaths
so that we may forget.
And they laugh as they fall
because they enjoy in advance
the sorrow to come
the despair that
soon or late
we all succumb to.

The death of these children is not predestined.
They prefigure it in the oddness of their games.
Before, whether an instant or
two hundred centuries ago,
the children invented games
as if nostalgic for earlier children.

(The first, the last that return
to begin the lines
now invent nothing, they shout
mummymeat mummymeat we want
the head on the shield.)

Quiénes simulan ser los últimos.
Quiénes son los primeros.

Los niños
hace un instante o hace doscientos siglos
entraron al jardín con papeles marcados.
Se tiran de los árboles.
Se tiran.

El texto sucio

I

¿Accederé a un castillo sólo porque estoy viendo sus paredes y escalones de piedra, porque he sentido (presentido) aquel olor a viejo, lo húmedo fuerte que me corta la respiración? Si no hay en verdad puente, foso, torre o pabellón . . .

Doy este paso que me instala obligatoriamente en el Lugar, el Sitio. Y, como después recordaré, no sé moverme. Ya sucedió otra vez. Otra vez. Voy dando tumbos. Más bien rodeo, hago eses largas, anchas. O pregunto.

Preguntaré si es que no fueran falsas las mujeres que veo al final del salón, recortadas en la pared de piedra, como postales, como preciosas miniaturas. Trajes del Medioevo, largos, amplios. Rojos y azules vivos. Mujeres de *Le Roman d'Athis et Prophilias.* Salen de la pared de piedra, se ocupan de algo que no puedo saber. Y sale de entre esas mujeres la que llaman el Pollo, esposa de Walter L. (W.L., Jefe de una Oficina, ya se verá). Ella, el Pollo, tan vistosa como siempre, arrastra un traje azul, su largo pelo en trenzas amarillas, se acerca.

> El Pollo. Ah, Soledad, ¿tú aquí . . . ?
> Contesto "así es".
> El Pollo. ¿Y Mario?
> Contesto "allá".
> El Pollo. ¡Ah!

Extrañamente, aun para mí misma, sin meditarlo, sin venir al caso, digo "nosotros no sabemos vivir". (Un *nosotros* sin límites. Un *no* definitivo, lapidario. Un presente ¿simple? Quitar el lapidario *no* quizás resolvería el escalofrío de esa frase pero la inscribiría en la Mentira o en la Burla.) Pongo mi propio ejemplo, me oigo decir "si me soltaran en un País, como a Mario, ¿podría yo vivir?, ¿sabría vivir?"

> El Pollo. ¡Ah!

Who pretend to be the last.
Who are the first.

The children
whether an instant or two hundred centuries ago
came into the garden with roles assigned.
They fall from the trees.
They fall.

Dirty Text

I

Must I enter a castle because I see before me its stone walls and stairs and smell the scent (presentiment) of age, its heavy suffocating dankness? Even if in fact there is no bridge, moat, tower, or pavilion?

I take the step which situates me irrevocably within the Place, the Site. Only later will I remember that I don't know how to move. It's happened once before. Once before. I stagger, or better, I walk in circles. I trace long, fat S's. Or I question.

I ask myself whether the women I see at the far end of the great hall, etched into the stone wall like postcards or pretty miniatures, are real. Long, voluminous medieval gowns. Lush reds and blues. Women out of a romance of courtly love. They detach themselves from the wall to attend to some business or other that I don't understand. The one we call the Chicken emerges from the crowd—Walter L's wife (W.L., department head, that Walter). Overdressed as usual, she approaches, dragging the train of her blue gown behind her, her long hair in yellow braids.

> The Chicken: Soledad? You're here . . . ?
> I answer: That's right.
> The Chicken: Where's Mario?
> I answer: There.
> The Chicken: Ah!

Oddly, even for me, without a moment's hesitation and apropos of nothing, I respond, "no, we don't know how to live." (A *we* without limits. The *no* absolute, lapidary. Present indicative? Removing that lapidary *no* might dissipate the terrible chill of the phrase, but that would implicate it instead in The Lie or The Joke.) I offer my own example; I hear myself say, "if, like Mario, they suddenly let me loose in whatever Country, could I survive? Would I know how to live?"

> The Chicken: Ah!

El asunto era, es que nosotros (nosotros, ¿quiénes? ¿Los del castillo, a los que nunca he visto? ¿Las mujeres del Medioevo? ¿Todos? Todos, ¿quiénes?) con tanta vida organizada, no hemos aprendido a vivir. No habíamos aprendido, decía, en lo individual. No sabíamos (insisto, ni que me hubieran dado cuerda) resolvernos la vida personalmente. Sin la Intervención, sin Una Decisión Ajena.

El Pollo. (Se pasa por la nariz el pañuelito bordado con finísimos hilos de oro y plata.) Así es.

"Mario sí" le digo al Pollo. "Mario ha sido capaz de abrirse paso y sobrevivir dignamente en Buenos Aires". Y cuento todo lo que sé de la vida de Mario allá en Buenos Aires. Mis propios recuerdos. El Pollo asiente, "así es".

II (INTERLUDIO)

Seis o siete escalones. Puras piedras oscuras, igual que en la pared. Bajo. Observo. Salón pequeño. Se representa una escena para que sea fotografiada. O era representada con alguna intención que desconozco. Dos hombres. Una mujer. Un sofá. Una pequeña mesa baja. La mujer, una muchacha, es de las medievales. Está frente a los hombres, de pie, a una distancia prudencial, la punta de la zapatilla apoyada en la mesa. Veo las espaldas de los hombres. Claro, bajo los escalones.

El hombre sentado en la derecha del sofá me pareció conocido. Al finalizar los escalones me apoyo en su espalda. Apoyé la mano para sujetarme. Eso parecía. Luego, viendo que realmente no lo conozco, me apoyo con más fuerza. Gesto impertinente. Hice que el hombre de la derecha del sofá a quien no conocía, se doble con mi peso. Total impunidad. O ningún peso y es por ello que el hombre no reacciona. Bajo. Doy unos pasos.

La muchacha medieval se contorsiona, hace como si fuera a elevarse del suelo, se agita (cuelgan telas livianas, sueltas, transparentes), muestra el cuerpo (ceñido hasta el tobillo en un leotard verde brillante), lo ofrece. El hombre de la derecha, sobre el que me apoyé, ayuda, participa. Él o la mesa sirven de sostén. La muchacha medieval se eleva en una sacudida (el cuerpo hace un ángulo agudo con el piso), mueve un brazo, la mano. Toda ella se mueve, convulsa, pero pone ahora una intención en su brazo convulso, la mano convulsa y el hombre de la derecha se dobla, muerde la pelvis de la muchacha medieval, pasa la lengua, traga, da otra mordida, traga, recorre lentamente la costura, el pliegue hondo del leotard verde brillante, ennegrecido, traga, se dobla más, encaja las mandíbulas, sostiene él solo el cuerpo en el aire. El cuerpo, el ángulo agudo que hace un instante era sacudido brutalmente, reduce la fuerza de impulsión, empieza a palpitar, a moverse en tiempos regulares, tic tac tic tac. Como un corazón, un hígado. En la boca del hombre.

"The important thing was (we? who? Those from the castle, those I've never seen? The medieval women? All of these? All, who?)—is—that leading such regimented lives we haven't learned how to live. We haven't learned it." I go on—I can't stop myself: "We don't know how to solve the problems of our own lives. Without Divine Intervention, without A Decision from Above."

The Chicken (she wipes her nose with a handkerchief embroidered in gold and silver): That's right.

"But Mario does," I tell her. "He's been able to make his own way. He's doing well in Buenos Aires." And I tell her what I know about Mario's life in Buenos Aires. Everything I remember. The Chicken nods, "That's right."

II (INTERLUDE)

Six or seven stairs. The same dark stone as the wall. I descend. I look around. A small chamber. A scene is being performed for the camera. Or for some other reason. Two men. A woman. A sofa. A petite table, low to the ground. The woman, a girl, is one of those dressed in medieval clothing. She stands, facing the men from a safe distance, the toe of her slipper balanced on the table's edge. I can see the men's backs. I descend the stairs.

The man sitting on the right side of the sofa seems familiar. As I approach the bottom of the stairs I rest my weight on his back, supporting myself with my hand. Or so it seems. And when I realize that I don't know him at all, I press down still harder. Impertinent gesture. I force this unknown man—the one on the right, on the sofa—to bend beneath my weight. With total impunity. Or perhaps he doesn't react because I'm weightless. I finish my descent and take a few steps forward.

The medieval girl begins to writhe. It's as though she were about to float. She stirs (they drape her in diaphanous veils) displays her body (swathed to the ankles in skin-tight bright green) and offers herself. The man on the right, the one I'd used for support, does his part, assists her. He or the table support her. With a lurch, she rises, her body describing an acute angle to the floor. An arm moves, a hand moves. She is quivering, vibrating, she tenses her twisted arm and hand, and the man bends over, bites her pelvis, licks at her, swallows, bites again, swallows, lingers at the seam, the deep pleat of her bright green garment (now darkened), swallows, bends still further, and thrusts his jaws into her, holding her aloft. Her body, which moments before had been shaking violently, relaxes, subsides into a regular beat. Tick tock tick tock. Like a heart, a liver. Held aloft by the man's mouth.

Fue el clímax. Lo que buscaban. Lo sentí. Sentí una profunda excitación, una excitación que me elevó del suelo. Se lo digo a Teresa Lavandero mientras camino los pasillos de piedra buscando salir del Sitio, del Lugar. Le digo "con algunos hombres no tuve nunca una excitación así". Grandiosa. Sorprendente.

III

Paredes sólidas. Piedras. Aberturas que seguro van a dar al vacío. Sara Esquivel trajina en la cocina de su casa. Arrastra el traje azul. Se mueven con cierta nerviosidad las finas cintas de su tocado azul-plateado. Mientras trajina sostenemos una larga conversación. Hablaba de un cristal, de una inscripción en un cristal. De pronto digo "qué sueño más bonito he tenido". (Son las palabras de Sara Esquivel, no mis palabras. Siento eso.) Y hablo de Mario. Cuento todo lo que son mis recuerdos de la vida de Mario en Buenos Aires.

—Él ha podido . . . Él ha sabido . . .
—Así es— concuerda Sara Esquivel.

Y le refiero mi conversación con el Pollo. Minuciosamente. Pero nos enzarzamos en La Misma Conversación. Yo subrayo, doy peso, exagero el sentido de mis palabras. Digo ". . . y ese miedo a los extranjeros, como si nosotros no estuviéramos *perdidos*".

Digo ahora *perdidos*. Fue la segunda palabra que utilicé, la palabra que me socorre. Porque la otra, la primera que quise decir, se me traba en la boca. Ya no la puedo recordar. Esa palabra, con todo su peso específico, con todo su volumen, me equivoca la expresión, se hace una bola rara, de trapo, sucia, se hace un mascón entre mis dientes. Y no sale. No puedo pronunciarla. Ni bien ni mal. Digo ". . . como si nosotros no estuviéramos *perdidos*". Y perdidos sale obligada, empujada, cae delante de mí, extraña, en La Conversación. Sara Esquivel no se da por aludida, no se percata de la dificultad, del atolladero en que me pone la negación (¿mi negación?) de una palabra que sustituyo sólo a fuerza por perdidos. Será por eso que va a una de las aberturas de la pared de piedra, a la mayor de las aberturas, echa una mirada rápida, se vira y dice:

—¡Ah!, yo lo sabía. No quise decirte . . . (Aquí, en orden: gravedad, aire de misterio, conjunto de gestos que se sintetizan o resumen en: mueca habitual: cara de animal asustado. Luego cesa. Mejor, se atenúa) . . . Él me preguntó a mí.

Él me preguntó a mí. *Él* me preguntó a mí. La Nimiedad se torna espesa. Crea El Reino de la Confusión. Él, ¿quién? ¿Qué pregunta? ¿Cuándo?
Inquirir me devolvería de inmediato a la Realidad. Por tanto:

The climax. What they were seeking. I feel an extraordinary excitement. It lifts me off the ground. I tell this to Teresa Lavandero as we search the stone hallways looking for an exit from the Site, the Place. I say to her, "There are men with whom I've never experienced that much excitement." Enormous. Astonishing.

III

Solid walls. Stone. Openings that surely lead nowhere. Sara Esquivel busies herself in the kitchen. She drags the train of her blue gown behind her. The delicate ribbons in her silver-blue coif flutter nervously. While she works we are engaged in a long conversation. She has been talking about a mirror, an inscription on a mirror. All of a sudden I exclaim, "what a great dream I had." (But they feel like Sara's words.) And I talk about Mario. I tell her everything I remember about his life in Buenos Aires.

"He was able to . . . He knew how to . . . "
"That's right," she agrees.

Then I repeat in minute detail my conversation with The Chicken. But we're still embroiled in The Same Conversation. I underline, emphasize, exaggerate the meaning of my words. I say ". . . and this fear of foreigners, as though we weren't *lost*."

I actually say it: *lost*. But it's my second choice, the word that saves me. The first—the one I would have preferred—sticks in my throat. I can no longer remember it. That word, with all its heft, its specificity, its volume— I can't remember it—becomes a bolus of filthy rags, a wad of stuff stuck between my teeth. It won't come out. I can't pronounce it. I repeat ". . . as though we weren't *lost*." The word *lost* bursts forth, expelled, falls awkwardly into The Conversation. Sara doesn't notice, isn't even aware of my problem, the mess I've fallen into because of the denial (my denial?) of the word for which I have substituted *lost*. Is that why she walks to the widest opening in the stone wall, glances out, turns to me again, and says:

"I knew it! I knew it all along! I didn't want to tell you . . . (and then, one after another: seriousness, a mysterious air, and a series of expressions synthesized from or subsumed beneath her habitual grimace and the look of a frightened animal. It stops then, or rather, diminishes . . .) . . . It was his request . . . "

It was *his* request! *His* request! This Trifle is suddenly less amusing. It creates The Kingdom of Confusion. His! Whose? What's he asking? When?
With these questions I return abruptly to Reality. Therefore:

Sara Esquivel se aleja. La veo recortada en la pared de piedra. Una postal, una preciosa miniatura. Altísimo tocado. Azul. La crispación del meñique derecho la descubre.

La muchacha medieval se acerca al público (al Vacío), hace una reverencia.

El hombre de la derecha, sobre el que me apoyé, El Detonante de la Excitación (es pintor, fotógrafo, cineasta) se acerca, deja que se le caiga la cabeza.

El otro hombre del sofá saluda sin pararse.

El Pollo se sujeta con gracia el largo traje azul, sonríe (dientes raros, sin crecimiento, amarillos), ladea la cabeza.

Mario está Allá, no comparece.

Teresa Lavandero mira al Vacío, rumia "el texto sucio, ¿adónde vamos a parar?"

Yo me acerco estornudo ya dije presentir estornudo el olor viejo que me corta la estornudo.

22 DE JULIO DE 1990
Y 1–2 DE DICIEMBRE DE 1995

Recogí limones

I

Pocos, pero espléndidos, verdes y robustos. Cinco o seis limones descomunales que, extrañamente, formaban un racimo colgado de un tallo frágil de la planta. Ya nos íbamos. Era el momento en que partíamos después de una parada momentánea. Entramos a una casa. No sé porqué, no sé a ver qué o a quién. Alguien, entre los que partíamos, mandaba. Al pasar veo un cartucho colocado en una esquina fuera de la casa. Fui allí, vacié el cartucho con apuro. Había frijoles negros, arroz y como un polvo claro. Lo vacié todo en algún recipiente o sobre un muro. El polvo claro se ve al final, cuando sale y se expande. En el cartucho vacío puse los limones y alguien que no era El Que Mandaba, desaprobó lo que hice. Yo estaba satisfecha.

II

Antes hacíamos una comida con vegetales. Pequeños retoños y frutos. Se iba juntando todo, escogiendo y luego pasabas en una fila para que Otro revisara. Ese otro era Alguien Que Sabía, Alguien que podía decidir.

Mis plantas estaban en una fuente llana, pero era menester hervirlo todo. El Que Mandaba lo había dicho "falta hervirlo". También era preciso escoger entre una rama y otra que se le parecía. Una era mala, podía estropear la comida o, a lo mejor, era dañina. Yo observaba, me detenía en esas dos ramitas. Ambas tenían frutos, como cerezas, como los frutos de un árbol que

Sara Esquivel recedes into the distance. She is etched into the stone wall. A postcard, a pretty miniature. Big hair. Blue. Identified by the curl of the little finger of her right hand.

The medieval girl approaches the audience (the Void), bows.

The man I had leaned upon, the man on the right, The Detonator of Excitement (painter, photographer, cinéaste) steps forward, nods.

The other man on the sofa waves without rising.

Gracefully The Chicken holds the train of her blue gown, smiles (odd teeth, stunted, yellow), and wags her head.

Mario is Away, he won't be appearing.

Teresa Lavandero peers into the Void, mumbles "dirty text, where will it end?"

I come forward I sneeze I have said it presentiment I sneeze that suffocating smell I sneeze.

JULY 22, 1990
AND DECEMBER 1–2, 1995

Gathering Lemons

I

Just a few, but gorgeous, green and plump. A bunch of five or six unusually large lemons that, oddly, hang from a single fragile stem. We're just leaving after a brief stop. We enter a house. I don't know why, or who or what we wish to see. Someone—a member of our group—is in charge. As we're entering, I notice a small cardboard box that's been left at curbside. I promptly empty it. Inside there are black beans, rice and a sort of translucent powder. I pour it all into another container or against a wall. The translucent powder is the last to empty. I place the lemons in the box. Someone else, not He Who Is In Charge, disapproves. This pleases me.

II

Earlier we had been preparing vegetables for a meal. Tiny shoots and fruit. We would chop and clean everything, then stand in line for the Other to inspect our work. This was Someone Who Knows, Someone whose judgment counted.

My vegetables were on a simple platter, but everything had to be boiled. He Who Is In Charge had said "it's necessary to boil everything." It was also necessary to choose between one sprig and another very like it. One was rotten, it could ruin the whole meal, or worse, it could be fatal. I studied those two little sprigs for a long time. Both were studded with a fruit like a white

hubo en el patio de mi casa, que eran blancos y sabían áspero y tenían un jugo pegajoso. La otra ramita se distinguiría igualmente por el fruto aunque la diferencia, de haberla, era sutil. Bien bien ya no puedo saber. Tenía mucho verde mi bandeja y había que hervirlo todo. Lo verde.

III

Veo desde una ventana o allá en una ventana, a una mujer. Digamos el ojo de una mujer. Veía como a distancia a esa mujer encuadrada en el marco de una ventana, supongamos que en un cuarto. La visión era estrecha, limitada, en blanco y negro. Sólo aquella mujer. Pero no puedo asegurar si la ventana era el punto desde el cual yo veía o si era el otro, el que vi. A través de esa mujer, de su ojo, se ve otra mujer. La visión real da otra imagen y pasa como por una lupa, da esa sensación incómoda, de grosor artificial, esa molestia.*

Después es este grupo en camino que no identifico, esta guagua pequeña . . . Nos mandan a bajar. Bajamos . . . Y encuentro ese racimo de limones que, decía, son pocos pero espléndidos.

19 DE NOVIEMBRE DE 1991

---

*Y anoche estábamos mirándonos la boca con una lupa. Caín y yo. Nos mirábamos el labio superior porque los dos sentíamos una molestia. Sucedió también que Aníbal J., mi venerado amigo, vituperó a su gusto por teléfono y amenaza con no poner un pie en el Asteroido mientras esté Caín. Otra molestia. Y el día anterior V. J., mi amiga, la réplica femenina y en pequeño de Aníbal J., habíase ido, horrorizada por el hecho de que yo viva con "semejante personaje".

El camino del cementerio

Había mucho movimiento y podría ser festivo porque me veo andar con un muchacho yendo y viniendo entre edificios muy iluminados. El muchacho es alto y delgado, no creo que lo conozca. No es Gigi. No es aniñado ni lacio como Gigi. Sin embargo, tenemos un acercamiento, hay entre nosotros una sensación de espera de lo que va a venir, un cierto grado de calor que yo he sentido erótico y no existe con Gigi. Ese movimiento nos reúne con otras personas. Parece que es festivo aunque, pensándolo bien, puede haber otras razones. Pero nada de esto es lo que me interesa.

Por la mañana, como en un semisueño, hago por recordar lo que había visto antes, lo que en verdad me interesaba. Esforzándome para recordar, de pronto, salto en la cama. Un ratoncito me cruzó por encima o me rozó, o vi que iba a rozarme. Salté en la cama, no es que soñara que saltaba. Salté y

cherry, like the fruit on a tree that grows in my courtyard, bitter, and sticky with juice. The other sprig was distinguished by the same fruit, and the difference, if there was one, was very subtle. I may never know. There were so many vegetables on my platter and all of them had to be boiled. All of them.

III

Out the window, or framed by it, I see a woman. Or at least a woman's eye. I see her as if from afar, outlined by the window frame, probably inside a room. The scene is narrow, cramped, in black and white. Just that woman. But I can't be sure if I watch her from a window or if it's the other way around, and I'm looking toward it. Beyond this woman, beyond her eye, I see another. It's as though I'm watching the entire scene through a magnifying glass. It bothers me, this uncomfortable sensation of artificial magnification.*

Then there's this other group of travelers that I can't identify, going somewhere in a small bus.

They tell us to get out. We do, and I find that bunch of lemons that, as I've said, are few, but gorgeous.

NOVEMBER 19, 1991

---

*Last night Cain and I were examining each other's mouths with a magnifying glass. We each had some sort of irritation on our upper lip. Another annoyance: Aníbal J., my esteemed friend, spit venom through the phone, threatening not to set one foot inside the Asteroide as long as Cain was there. And the day before, V.J., another friend, an exact replica in miniature of Aníbal J., but female, had walked out suddenly, horrified that I lived with "someone like that."

The Road to the Cemetery

A lot of coming and going. Perhaps it's a holiday because I see myself strolling with a young man between brightly lit buildings. The young man is tall and slender, and I don't think I know him. It's not Gigi. He's not childish or languid like Gigi. Nevertheless, we feel an affinity for each other. There's a feeling of waiting for what comes next between us, a certain degree of heat that I interpret as erotic and that doesn't exist between Gigi and me. All the coming and going brings us into contact with others. It's like a holiday, but it occurs to me that there could be other explanations. But this isn't really what concerns me.

In the morning, still half dreaming, I try to remember what I've seen, what has originally caught my attention. Suddenly, while trying to remember, I leap up. A small mouse has scurried across me or brushed against me, or was about to. I leap up in bed—I didn't just dream this. I leap up, and then I

pude recordar. Lo que había visto antes era un grupo de personas que iban por el agua, por un río, para el cementerio. Caminaban en el agua rumbo al cementerio. Yo los veía de espaldas, veía el boscaje, los árboles, no el verde de los árboles, y el agua y los pies en el agua. Yo no iba. Y se lo comenté a alguien, ése que no era Gigi, "no voy al cementerio". Parece que había que ir al cementerio, masivamente. No me interesaba ir al cementerio y además no quería tomarme el trabajo de ir por dentro del agua. La otra persona, que no es Gigi pero ahora sé que tampoco es el muchacho de la espera, me responde que yo tendría que ir alguna vez y yo insisto que no.

—Nunca.

El Camino del cementerio antes era otro. Eso lo sabía, lo tengo claro, y la persona con la que hablo también lo tiene claro. El Camino anterior era otro, por tierra, como debe ser, y lo han utilizado para otras cuestiones. Esa persona me hace ver, con excesivos argumentos, que el cambio de Camino obedece a una necesidad y, como ya es un hecho el camino a través del agua, dice que yo tendría forzosamente que ir también por ahí, igual que los demás. Pienso, o le digo, que a mí lo que me molesta, lo que me hace trinar no es ir al cementerio sino ir obligatoriamente y por un camino que no es el Camino del cementerio.

CALLE CONCORDIA, DOMINGO, 12 DE AGOSTO DE 1990

Lourdes Gil

Desvelo de los pájaros anoche

Dichosos los que miran como piedras,
más elocuentes que una piedra. . . .
HEBERTO PADILLA

Toda la noche los oímos volar:
su vuelo era el dibujo orbicular de los presagios,
la simiente derramándose en lo oscuro.
Durante noches infinitas desvelados
no supimos leer en la penumbra el aleteo.
Nada enseñaba ya San Juan después de tantos siglos,
ni oscuridad sonora ni cena que lograra
enamorarnos. Somos los abandonados de la fe,

remember. What I had seen before was a group of people in the water; they were in the river, walking through it, on their way to the cemetery. I had seen them from behind. I saw the woods, the trees, but not the foliage, and the water and the feet in the water. I'm not going with them. I tell this to someone, whoever it is who isn't Gigi, "I'm not going to the cemetery." It appears that we are expected to go to the cemetery en masse, but I'm not interested in going to the cemetery, and besides, I don't want the trouble of trudging through the water. The other person, who isn't Gigi but isn't the young man I had walked with either, tells me I should really go sometime, but I insist:

"Never."

The Road to the cemetery used to be a different road. I know that. I'm absolutely certain of this and so is the person I'm talking to. The Road used to follow another route, on solid ground, as it should, and now that Road is used for something else. The person in question rationalizes the change, protesting much too emphatically that the change in the Road follows some inner logic; moreover, since the route through the water exists in fact now, I too will eventually end up taking it, like the others. I think, or I say aloud, that it's not going to the cemetery that rankles, but being forced to go, and on a road that's not really the Road to the cemetery.

CALLE CONCORDIA, SUNDAY, AUGUST 12, 1990

Translated by Mark Weiss

Lourdes Gil

The Birds' Insomnia Last Night

Happy are those who gaze like rocks,
more eloquent than a rock . . .
HEBERTO PADILLA

All night we heard them circling:
their flight was an orbicular drawing of omens,
a seed spilling in the darkness.
Through interminable wakeful nights
in the dim light we didn't know how to read their fluttering.
After all those centuries Saint John of the Cross had taught us nothing,
neither sonorous darkness nor a supper
that managed to charm us. We are those whom faith has deserted,

los sumidos de álgida alegría y rechinar de dientes.
Cómo advertir las lides del amor, los mensajes
de las calandrias en la sombra
sin festines de San Juan ni recreo de los sentidos,
con nuestras conjeturas habituales
desvaneciéndose en el aire.
Si se inundaba de pétalos la noche y no
nos enterábamos.
Se colmaba de juncos amarillos cada hebra abierta
del otoño, de besos desbordantes,
de la ternura que ahora se vuelca compartida
y que creímos se había perdido para siempre.
No veíamos ninguna de estas cosas.
No entendimos lo que el sueño traía a diario
en su arpillera. No comprendimos
la fábula que iba depositándose en furias
y poemas
sobre el párpado. Ni los nenúfares
que enrojecían a la luz y perforábanse de arpegios
si se juntaban nuestras manos.
No asumimos la asfixia del deseo
alojado en su arco interminable de inocencia.
Era un vuelo de aves lo que oímos pasar,
un alvéolo de estrellas que hace miles de años
están muertas y fosforescen todavía.
Ah, fuga de los dioses, abandono, torrentes
de la lluvia, gritos de cimarrón, de profecías
incumplidas en los montes. Himnos vedas himnos
pánicos, misterio inasible del amor,
anclaje vegetal de una pasión, su anillo de oro,
celo ensordecedor de la cigarra,
la verde seducción de su quejido, de su vientre
al temblor de la corteza de los arces.
Descorre los visillos. Que nos visiten
el cuello arqueado de la anémona,
el sibilante ruego del país perdido,
los coros de aves cubiertas de guirnaldas.
Desde el coral los canes mudos del cronista
anuncian el regreso de los dioses.
Hinchan de almizcle las vasijas con sus fértiles
danzas. Desasidos de todo van cayendo exhaustos
sobre nuestros cuerpos dormidos, desnudos.

those who, overwhelmed by chilly happiness, grind their teeth.
How to understand the ways of love, the messages
of the larks in the shadows,
without the feasts of Saint John
or the pleasures of the senses,
our habitual conjectures
evaporating into the air.
As if the night were drowned with petals and we couldn't understand.
It was filled with yellow reeds, each a split
autumnal thread overflowing with kisses,
with a shared tenderness now capsized
that we thought was lost forever.
But we saw none of these things.
We didn't understand what sleep brought back daily
in its rucksack. We didn't comprehend
the fable that was about to rest on the eyelid
in rages and poems.
Or the water lilies
that reddened in the light and were pierced with arpeggios
if our hands entwined.
We didn't assume that the asphyxiation of desire
is lodged in its endless arch of innocence.
It was a flight of birds we heard passing,
an alveolus of stars that for thousands of years
had been dead but still glittered.
Ah, the flight of the gods, abandonment, torrents
of rain, the cries of fugitive slaves, of unfulfilled
prophecies in the wastelands. Forbidden hymns
the hymns of Pan, the ungraspable mystery of love,
the vegetal anchorage of a passion, its ring of gold,
the deafening zeal of the cicada, the green
seduction of its moan, of its womb
on the trembling bark of the maples.
Open the curtains. May they visit us,
the arched neck of the anemone,
the sibilant prayers of a lost land,
the choirs of birds covered with garlands.
And from the reef, the mute dogs of the chronicler
announce the return of the gods.
With their fertile dances they swell the cups
with musk. Freed of everything, they fall, exhausted,
on our naked, sleeping bodies.

Fata Morgana

• *A Jesús Díaz*

Si lo que dijo Kafka fuera cierto
—que algunos han logrado sobrevivir el canto de las sirenas
pero que nadie ha sobrevivido a su silencio—
entonces debo estar agradecida a las deidades que nos rigen.

Pues a pesar de haber abandonado tierra firme
de haber zafado las cuerdas del almácigo en el puerto
para lanzarme en pos de los clamores de sus voces
(remolinos ubicuos que ensordecen en la noche
y no parecen brotar de sus gargantas)
a pesar
de haber perseguido los blancos brazos espectrales
de Loreleis desmelenadas en lo alto de las rocas
entre marinos vendavales
a pesar
de haber flotado a la deriva en la negrura del océano
haber visto apagarse el resplandor del coro
y cómo cesaba el aleteo de sus manos.

He sobrevivido al canto de tu amor.

Y quizás (como afirmara Kafka)
no habría sobrevivido
al silencio del cielo
al del mar sin magias y sin aves
sin destino.

Reina María Rodríguez

Ellas escriben cartas de amor

escriben hasta que apague la luz
hasta que se acabe la llamita.
escriben en los baños   en   las oficinas
escondidas de los maestros y de las ratas.

Fata Morgana

 • *To Jesús Díaz*

If what Kafka said was true
—that some have managed to survive the songs of the sirens
but none have survived their silence—
I should be grateful to the gods who govern us.

So, though I have abandoned terra firma,
cast the lines from the mooring-post
and launched myself towards the sounds of their voices
(ubiquitous whirlwinds that deafen us at night
and seem not to flow from their throats)
and though I've pursued
the pale spectral arms
of the wild Lorelei on crags
amidst oceanic gales
though I've weltered
in the black troughs of tides
and seen the splendor of the chorus drift away
and their hands stop fluttering.

I have survived the song of your love.

And perhaps (as Kafka said)
I would not have survived
the silence of the sky
or of the sea without magic, or birds,
or destiny.

Translated by Gabriel Gudding

Reina María Rodríguez

Women Write Love Letters

they write until the light burns out
until the shrinking flame is extinguished.
they write in bathrooms   in   offices
hidden from teachers and rats.

escriben todavía sin descanso
para echar en el fondo de los baúles
cositas muertas   las letras pegadas al papel
la sofisticación de las palabras
que quisieron hacer
alguna travesía nunca exacta.
ellas escriben cartas de amor con preámbulos
papelitos puestos una y otra vez
de manera diferente.
lanzados desde el globo de la astucia
desde el hospital   desde el castillo
donde aparecen los sueños que no pudieron asirse.
con tanto temor como bajar de un pedestal húmedo
sonámbulas ellas escriben
sin otra técnica que un corazón ligeramente corrompido
por las feroces garras de los años
por la tinta azul petrificada en las noches de espera
ellas escriben para convencer a alguien
para convencer a una sola persona
que tal vez no ha venido
o se ha perdido definitivamente
entre la multitud.

Una mujer se desnuda frente a un profesor estupefacto

• *Zoe*

no supe desnudarme en el cementerio romano
delante de los ojos del profesor
y de aquellos dioses de mármol
para salir después tranquilamente y vestirme
como si todo hubiera sucedido
como si nada fuera a suceder
más allá de ese grito
roto al caer sobre mi piel
larguirucha y perdida en el remoto bosque
sin un rostro sensual ni el valor de un rostro sensual
y los estupefactos dedos impacientes del profesor
que se quedaron quietos
sin una historia contra los muertos
del cementerio donde uno puede ser como cualquiera

still they write, ceaselessly,
to throw little dead things
into the depths of the trunks   the letters stuck to the paper
the sophistication of the words
that attempted
some imprecise crossing.
they write love letters with preambles
little papers with phrases written over and over
in different ways.
launched from a shrewd world
from the hospital   from the castle
where dreams surface that they have never grasped.
somnambulant, they write
with as much fear as if descending from a wet pedestal
with no technique other than the heart slightly tainted
with the years' ferocious claws
with blue ink gone hard during nights of longing
they write to convince someone
to convince one single someone
who perhaps has not arrived
or who has become definitively lost
in the crowd.

A Woman Undresses in Front of a Stupefied Professor

• *Zoe*

I couldn't figure out how to undress in the roman cemetery
in front of the professor's eyes
and those marble gods,
how to leave calmly afterwards and put my clothes back on
as if everything had happened
as if nothing were going to happen
beyond that cry
broken when it hit my skin
lanky and lost in the remote forest
without a sensual face or the courage of a sensual face
and the professor's stupefied impatient fingers
that remained motionless
without a story to wield against the dead
in the cemetery where you can be like
anyone

con el temor de aparecer desnuda todavía
y jugar a ser niños y serpientes en la nieve
pero ella tuvo otros juegos de la infancia
que no comprendí
la libertad de atreverse a competir con las estatuas
y dejarse acariciar dejarse acariciar
en la noche   en el frío   entre losas mojadas.

Una muchacha loca como los pájaros

> . . . *una extraña ha venido a compartir*
> *mi cuarto en esta casa . . . una muchacha*
> *loca como los pájaros*
>
> DYLAN THOMAS

espacio de mi puerta
una muchacha loca entra en mi cuarto
ya no soy yo
le presto esta cabeza
una cabeza oscurecida en el estanque del espejo.
es ella la que llega?
con un cambio de sombrero rozará el ala
su calma   su tristeza.
espacio de mi puerta
entre el laberinto y voltearme estaba sola.
por eso tuve que inventarla
ponerle estos zapatos
hacerla caminar sobre mí.
una imagen de la que uno nace es la única manera
de nacer dos veces.
alguien vendrá después y la apartará?
saltará del fondo donde se esconde la que vuelve
a sobrevivir
la que ha llegado y no sabe dónde está?
la muchacha que empezó adentro
ha terminado el tiempo de su fin:
esa cámara oscura   ese instante en que detrás del lente
o entre ese lente y yo
estaba su ojo   jamás la realidad ni la certeza

afraid of still appearing in the nude
and of pretending to be children and serpents in the snow.
but she had other childhood games
that I didn't understand
the freedom of daring to compete with the statues
and stroking herself   stroking herself
in the night   in the cold   among wet tombstones.

A Girl Mad as Birds

*. . . a stranger has come
to share my room in this house . . .
a girl mad as birds . . .*
DYLAN THOMAS

space of my door
a mad girl enters my room
now I'm not me
I lend her this head
a head tarnished in the mirror's pondwater.
is she the woman who's coming?
with a change of hat her calm   her sadness
will scrape against the frame.
space of my door
between the labyrinth and the changing of my mind, I was alone.
that's why I had to invent her
put these shoes on her
make her walk over me.
the only way to be born twice
is for an image to give birth.
will someone come along later and take her away?
will she jump out of the background, where she's hiding, she who
    continues
to survive?
she who has arrived and doesn't know where she is?
the girl who began inside
has lived out her purpose:
that *camera obscura*   behind the lens in that instant
or between that lens and me
was her eye   never reality or certainty

sólo ese ángel muerto que no es ya la visión ni la experiencia
por eso tuve que inventarla
sin saber   sin querer.
espacio de mi puerta
tengo los dedos ásperos de tanto andar contra el agua
apoyando lo que quema y arde
vendrá por fin? modelaré este invento
para sentar otra vez frente a mis pájaros
a otra muchacha loca en el espejo.
dejémosla fingir
se mueve   me convence
déjenla correr ya muerta su sombra contra el río
que ella crea que aparece y se va
me llevará hasta el fin?
se ha quedado dormida sobre el rodillo y su fábula
es así. me toparé en el sitio encontrado
con el vestido que dejó vacío
y la devolveré
sin mí   sin la que fui.
espacio de mi puerta
laberinto prestado. yo casco nueces con los pies.
devuélvela señor y que parezca
esa misma que quise cuando yo me inventaba.

Pescadores (crudo)

• *para J. A. Miralles*

No es láudano lo que van a sacar
del fondo ocre de tu espera
en el muro.
Bajo, muy abajo, al fondo,
se descompone y fracciona el pensamiento.
Cadáveres de peces, sombras de luces
que antes fueron perfiles de barcos
—hierros fundidos de la imaginación
que la costa salvaje ha reducido
a esa miseria de contaminación
sin ser ya nada,
chatarra para depredadores.

that's why I had to invent her
unknowingly   unintentionally.
space of my door
my toes calloused from walking so long against the water's flow
supporting a body that burns and is consumed
will she arrive at last? I will shape this creation,
I'll sit down again facing my birds
facing another mad girl in the mirror.
we should allow her to pretend
that she moves   she convinces me
let her run, already dead, her shadow on the river
she creates, it appears and disappears
will she take me to the river's end?
she has fallen asleep on my rolling pin and that's her
story. I'll bump into myself in the space
found inside the dress she left empty
and I'll return her
without me   without the woman I was.
space of my door
loaned labyrinth. I crack nuts with my feet.
give her back, so maybe she'll appear
the same woman I intended when I invented myself.

Translated by Kristin Dykstra and Nancy Gates Madsen

Fishermen (Rough)

• *for J. A. Miralles*

It's not laudanum that they'll pull out
of the ochreous depths of your patience
waiting on the wall.
Deeper, much deeper, at the bottom,
thought decomposes and breaks apart.
Fish corpses, shadows of lights
that once marked ships' profiles
—shackles forged from the imagination
reduced by the wild coast
to the wretchedness of pollution
not being anything anymore,
scrap iron for scavengers.

Busco el movimiento del hilo de nylon
porque quiero recuperar la historia hundida y así,
los veo halar algo que fue inconstante,
desde el potro del muro con su pesar a flote.
Pero a flote no viene otra vez la vida en su barco,
y no se ha pescado suficiente para atravesar esta calma chicha
que engaña con su lapso a la tempestad.
Cuando la tarde se va de tu visión de hacerla
contra el rostro de esos pescadores
de camisas casi pardas,
recordándonos
que algo salvaje y especial
con pellejo lustroso al sol
no pescarán.

Abilio Estévez

Las pequeñas cosas

• *para Antón Arrufat*

Mi amigo anda en busca de cosas pequeñas: un dedal, caracoles partidos, la tira de un encaje, una llave con la que abrir el cofre imaginario. Me muestra un alfiler y de pronto, gracias a ese insignificante objeto, puede explicarme el temor y el temblor de un pobre filósofo. Un puñado de arena en la mano le sirve para entender la caída de un imperio; el botón de una camisa para imaginar cómo era el silencio en las ciudades medievales.

Contra toda lógica, mi amigo no está loco. Ocurrió con demasiada simpleza. Una tarde, en la esquina de San Miguel y Soledad, encontró un pedazo de cristal y tuvo la pueril idea de mirar a través de él. Vio una amplia llanura en donde ocurría una batalla, vio a un poeta al que una carcajada le rompía el pecho, vio al perro indefenso de una reina que acababan de decapitar. Sorprendido, mi amigo regresó con su pedazo de cristal y lo guardó en una caja.

Desde esa tarde, todo lo pequeño que encuentra lo guarda allí. Su casa está tan llena de nimiedades que simula un museo de cosas inservibles. Su único dilema es que las pequeñeces, evocadoras de tantas grandezas, ya no lo dejan vivir cómodamente. Cada vez necesita una casa más grande.

I watch for movement in the nylon line
because I want to recover sunken history and so
I see them haul out something changeable,
the fishermen like horsemen, riding the wall of the Malecón,
their heavy grief afloat.
And there hasn't been enough fishing to navigate this dead calm
that deceives us by lapsing into storms.
Then the afternoon vacates the vision you were creating of it
against the faces of those fishermen
in their browned shirts,
reminding us
that they can't fish out
a wild and special something
with a hide that would shine in sunlight.

Translated by Kristin Dykstra

Abilio Estévez

Small Things

    • *for Antón Arrufat*

My friend goes about looking for small things: a thimble, broken conch shells, a fragment of clay tile, a key with which to open an imaginary chest. He shows me a needle and suddenly, thanks to that insignificant object, he can explain to me the fear and trembling of a poor philosopher. A fistful of sand helps him comprehend the fall of an empire; a shirt button to imagine what silence was like in medieval cities.

Against all logic, my friend is not crazy. It all began very simply. One afternoon, on the corner of San Miguel and Soledad, he found a piece of glass and had the childish notion of looking through it. He saw a wide plain where a battle was going on, he saw a poet with his chest split by loud laughter, he saw a defenseless dog that had just been decapitated by his mistress, the queen. Surprised, my friend took his piece of glass home and put it in a box.

Since that day, he keeps all small things he finds. His house is so full of trifles it resembles a museum of useless objects. His only dilemma is that the tiny things that conjure up so many great events no longer allow him to live in comfort. He's always needing a bigger house.

Frente al río

Me han dicho que no es un sueño, pero veo un puente y por debajo el río limpio y azul, y una sombra que no es una sombra, sino una luz diferente. Veo a una mujer que pasa sonriente y luego a un hombre que también sonríe. Ambos me miran y tienden las manos hacia mí.

Me han dicho que no es un sueño, pero veo a miles de hombres y mujeres sobre el puente que de pronto es un magnífico arco de cristal. Y yo miro al río y veo las piedras de su fondo, los peces con el color del fuego, y comprendo que debo continuar mirándolo, porque es un río limpio y azul que deja, a cada instante, de ser él mismo.

Me han dicho que no es un sueño.

Visita del abuelo

Llegaba de noche, siempre muy tarde, cuando mamá era sólo aquel canto, una voz, nada, y la lucecita trémula espantaba a los espíritus. Papá se iba, nos dejaba con el silencio, tantas cosas de verdad que iban pasando por el muro: un animal, una sombra, un grito. La casa simulaba una gigantesca pecera vacía, y en medio de los cristales, mamá y yo únicos entre un eco y un murmullo.

Abuelo llegaba, un esfuerzo tras otro, cansado el paso. Se perdía por el pasillo donde los juguetes se olvidaban y había alas de murciélagos, murciélagos de verdad que llenaban el techo de sombras. Era tanto el espacio y tan poco a la vez, tan pequeño el patio inmenso donde nos perdíamos para recibirlo.

Sin palabras, ocupaba el sillón. Su presencia comenzaba por un silencio sombrío. Y lo veíamos balancearse. Y el tabaco, su brillo, nos ayudaba; conocíamos por él los caminos secretos de la casa: un rincón, la estrella polar, un faro, la casuarina inmensa hasta el cielo.

Mamá pedía silencio. Lo miraba y me miraba, muda. Pedía que yo me acercara más, un tanto más en busca de sus ojos, cristales que devolvían el mundo de otra forma. Recuerdo sus manos: relámpagos: abrían la noche en dos reflejos. Las paredes caían destruidas y huían los murciélagos espantados, y el espacio era su simple palabra. Antorchas, sus ojos encendidos.

Yo preguntaba: "Mamá, ¿qué dice?"

"Cállate, hijo." Un gesto, una brusca orden pedían atención. Mutismo y miedo se unían en una palabra sola.

De pie, altísimo, abuelo nos rodeaba, y se escuchaba su voz. Decía que el infierno era una espera permanente. "El látigo de una espera alivia la culpa",

Facing the River

I've been told it's not a dream, but I see a bridge and below it a blue and limpid river, also a shadow that is not a shadow but a different light. I see a woman who passes smiling and then a man who's also smiling. Both look at me and stretch their hands out to me.

I've been told it's not a dream, but I see thousands of men and women on the bridge that suddenly becomes a magnificent crystal arch. And I look at the river and see stones on the bottom, fish the color of fire, and I understand that I must keep looking at it because it is a blue and limpid river that at each instant ceases to be itself.

I've been told it's not a dream.

Grandfather's Visit

He would arrive at night, always very late when Mama was only a song, a voice, nothing, and the flickering light was scaring off the ghosts. Papa left us, he left us with the silence, so many things that were truly passing through the wall: an animal, a shadow, a shout. The house resembled a giant empty fish bowl, and in the middle of the glass walls, only Mama and I between an echo and a murmur.

Grandfather arrived with great effort, his step weary. He disappeared down the corridor past forgotten toys and bat wings, real bats that filled the ceiling with shadows. The space was so large and so small at the same time, the vast patio so small where we went to welcome him.

He sat down in the rocking chair without speaking. His presence began with a melancholy silence. And we saw him rocking. And the cigar, its gleam, helped us. From him we learned of secret passages of the house: a corner, the polar star, a street lamp, the casuarina tree reaching up to the sky.

Mama called for silence. Mute, she looked at him and at me. She asked me to come closer, still closer, to look into his eyes, crystals that would return the world in another form. I remember his hands: lightning bolts that opened the world into two reflections. The walls collapsed and the bats fled terrified and the space was his simple word. Torches, his eyes flamed.

"Mama," I asked, "what is he saying?"

"Quiet, my child." A gesture, a brusque order demanded attention, muteness and fear joined in a single word.

Erect, very tall, Grandfather surrounded us, and he spoke aloud. He said that hell meant waiting forever. "The lash of waiting lessens guilt," he went

repetía. Se enrojecían más sus ojos. En la espalda, alas enormes. En la boca, lenguas de fuego para cada sílaba.

Y yo quería huir, aunque la mano me retenía y quedaba a sus pies, absorto, confundido.

Yo preguntaba otra vez: "Mamá, ¿qué dice?"

"Cállate, hijo."

Pero yo entendía e iba repitiendo: "El infierno es esta casa con sus muebles y sus estampas adorables, esta dulce paz en que papá nos deja cada crepúsculo, y tu voz, mamá, tu canto también es el infierno. Yo mismo, que voy entrando por esa puerta, esa pared, y pierdo los límites del sueño como quien pierde una prenda, una flor. Yo soy el infierno y me pongo los zapatos. Desaparezco para siempre en abrazos y besos de despedida. Dime, mamá, ¿es esto lo que dice?"

Entonces, no sé por qué, el sillón de abuelo quedaba solo, meciéndose vacío. El patio y el tabaco, un simple recuerdo.

"Mamá, ¿tú crees que abuelo vuelva?"

Y ella también desaparecía, desaparecía asintiendo.

"Sí, hijo, espéralo, espéralo siempre. La misma ausencia anuncia los regresos."

Iraida Iturralde

Claroscuro

Turbulento el mar en el recuerdo,
no el larguísimo espolón
que circunda y pertrecha el mural de la bahía.
Allí los peces se asoman a la calma,
al extraño estupor de una manigua,
no al placer vertiginoso
de su límpida ciudad distante.
Se entrampa entonces la memoria entre las algas,
en el baile sincopado de las olas
sobre el leve crespar de la menguante.
Y hay también en la memoria el estelar perenne,
el antigua resplandor sobre las aguas.

on. His eyes turned redder still. On his shoulders enormous wings. In his mouth, a tongue of fire for each syllable.

I wanted to flee, but his hand held me and I stayed at his feet, engrossed, confused.

I asked again: "Mama, what is he saying?"

"Quiet, Son."

But I had understood and I kept repeating: "Hell is this house with its furniture and charming engravings, that sweet peace in which Papa left us at each twilight, and your voice, Mama, your song also is hell. And me too who keep entering through that door, that wall, and I lose the outline of the dream as someone loses a token, a flower. I am hell and I put on my shoes. I disappear forever amidst farewell embraces and kisses. Tell me, Mama, is that what he's saying?"

Then, I don't know why, Grandfather's rocker was left abandoned, empty, rocking back and forth on its own. The patio and the cigar, a mere memory.

"Mama, do you think Grandfather will return?"

And she also disappeared, disappeared agreeing.

"Yes, my child, wait for him, wait for him forever. Absence itself portends return."

Translated by Cola Franzen

Iraida Iturralde

Chiaroscuro

In memory a stormy sea,
not the long seawall
that surrounds and supplies the wall of the bay.
There the fish can be seen in the calm,
in the strange stupor of swamps,
not in the frantic pleasure of its distant, clean city.
So memory is ensnared in the seaweed,
in the syncopated dancing of waves
above the ebb tide's slight curl.
And memory also retains the fixed star,
the ancient radiance on the water.

Esta tarde se levantan los nuevos héroes
de antaño.
Secuestradas a lo lejos dos hermanas,
Irina y Alexandra,
descifran la armadura de un crustáceo.
¿Tendrá sus nombres grabados en la espalda
como su historia, allá en el tronco,
guarda la ceiba sabia?
¿Sabrá decirles si la arena en la otra orilla
esconde los secretos de su andar descalzo,
o si ellas son costal de un alegre cocodrilo
atrapado por el mangle
oscuro y mustio de un ocaso?

La palma, alada y alta,
les salpica la frente a las hermanas,
les da la brisa transparente que gira dócil
en el cuello de su colosal penacho.
El sol las sorprende mojadas
por el enrejado de espuma.

El rostro de la nación

Andando entre los vuelos
de una madre ajena,
se enreda la lengua
al pronunciar su nombre.
De báculo sirve la memoria
el marinero errante que
a la puerta asoma.

Que detenga la represa
el líquido del suelo,
repleto de aforismos.
Que se pudra adentro
el ícono insolente,
su carga de mendrugos que
en la noche apesta.

Ahora griten,
que allá los andantes

The new heroes of the past awake this evening.
Two sisters, Irina and Alexandra,
kidnapped far away,
decipher the shell of a crustacean.
Will their names be etched on its back
like their story, preserved on its trunk
by the wise ceiba?
Can it tell them if the sand on the other shore
hides the secrets of their barefoot wanderings,
or if they are the bag in the form of a happy crocodile
captured in the dark and wilted mangrove of a sunset?

The palm, winged and tall,
splashes the faces of the sisters,
gives them the transparent breeze
that twists in the neck of its enormous crest.
The sun surprises them, drenched
by the lattice of foam.

The Face of the Nation

Lost in the flounces of a foreign mother
the tongue becomes twisted,
pronouncing its name.
Memory is the prop, the mariner
who in his wandering
arrives at our door.

Let the dam hold back
the water from that soil
filled with aphorisms.
Let that insolent icon
rot from within,
its burden of shards
a stink in the night.

Cry out now:
those who wander there

se han quedado mudos.
Pendientes del mar,
se alejan.

Exilio, la sien

La cáscara del pez
de algún modo se aproxima,
despide el rumor salobre
que la piel esconde.
Su aroma no es estéril,
es la conciencia unida
que de algún modo nos deshoja.
La sien es el espejo:
adentro nos desgarra,
afuera, aislados de la isla,
nos derrota.
Lejos los frutos, muy lejos,
erguidos e invisibles nos imploran.
El alma, atónita, se encoge.
Sólo la música nos redime,
de algún modo nos consuela.

Ruth Behar

Carta

• *para Dulce María Loynaz*

Mi querida amiga:

Yo tengo las hojas del otoño. Tú tienes el azul del mar.

Yo tengo las carreteras más anchas y espantosas del mundo. Tú tienes las calles derrumbadas de nuestra isla llorona.

Yo tengo el miedo de un cordero en una madriguera de lobos. Tú tienes el valor de un guerrero samurai.

have fallen mute.
Intent on the sea,
they flee.

Exile, the Brow

The husk of the fish
brings it closer somehow,
exudes the brackish murmur
that the skin hides.
Its odor matters,
it's our shared awareness
that somehow strips us bare.
The brow is our mirror:
it rends us within,
and defeats us without,
separated as we are from the island.
From afar, from a long way off,
insistent and invisible the fruit beckons.
Thunderstruck, the soul shrinks back.
Only music redeems us,
consoles us somehow.

Translated by Mark Weiss

Ruth Behar

Letter

• *for Dulce María Loynaz*

Dear friend:

Mine are the leaves of autumn and yours the sea's blue.

Mine the world's widest, fiercest highways, yours the broken streets of our weeping island.

Mine the lamb's fear in a den of wolves, yours the courage of a samurai.

Yo tengo la plata y el acero; tengo una casa demasiado grande para mí y un calendario donde están marcados los días que no estaré; tengo mañana y mañana, lo tengo todo.

Tú tienes la mirada de tus ojos . . .

Ofrenda

Hace unos meses por poco te abandono.

Te digo que ya iba a cerrar la puerta sin mirar para atrás.

Te digo que no pensaba tocarte otra vez.

Te digo que me había olvidado cómo besarte.

Eso fue en el invierno, y en el invierno me desespero. Ventanas cerradas, puertas bajo llave, días como sombras, y recuerdos de una isla a la que nunca voy a volver.

Perdóname, perdí un país, en mí no se puede confiar. Así que toma esta ofrenda. Préndeme como incienso. Mírame arder.

Hacerme ceniza.

El mundo

En un parqueo vacío en Michigan me senté a llorar. De repente vino una gaviota, desde un mar lejano. Se paró frente a mis pies, perdida también.

Amé al mundo más que mi propia vida.

Un deseo para el año que viene

¿Recuerdas el vino raro que nuestro amigo Teófilo nos dio de regalo de bodas? ¿Por qué nunca lo tomamos?

Este año, te digo, compraré mi pastel yo misma, gracias.

En la dulcería me preguntan: ¿tiene velas? ¿Es para un cumpleaños? Sí, les contesto, el mío. No quiero velas.

Este año no quiero velas.

I have silver and steel, too large a house, and a calendar where days I'll be away are marked; all the tomorrows, everything, is mine.

And you, you have your gaze . . .

Offering

A few months ago I almost left you.

Let me tell you, I was ready to shut the door and not look back.

Let me tell you, I didn't think I would ever touch you again.

Let me tell you, I had forgotten how to kiss you.

That was in winter, and in winter I fall into despair. Windows shut, doors locked, days like shadows, and memories of an island I will never return to.

I have lost a country, you can never trust me. Take then this offering. Light me as you would incense and watch me burn.

Reduce me to ashes.

The World

In an empty parking lot in Michigan I found myself weeping. Suddenly a gull arrived from a distant sea. It appeared at my feet, also lost.

At that moment I loved the world more than my very life.

A New Year's Wish

Do you remember the rare wine that our friend Teófilo gave us for our wedding? Why did we never drink it?

This year, I tell you, I will buy my own cake.

In the bakery they ask me: do you have candles? it's for a birthday? Yes, I answer, my own. And I don't want candles.

This year I don't want candles.

Pero de todas maneras pido algo: la próxima vez, por favor, déjame tomar todo el vino que se nos da para celebrar.

La próxima vez, déjame no temer la embriaguez.

La próxima vez, déjame amar la flor más que la arcilla.

Déjame recordarme de regar mi jardín.

Ángel Escobar

Las puertas

A todas las puertas les duelen las espaldas.
Y más les duelen, más, cuando guardan refranes
en casas muy alegres.
El Ajeno lo sabe y no se acerca.
Se sienta lejos de ellas meditando:
"En el costado izquierdo las bisagras
atornillando el giro de las puertas,
que siempre sólo un pie les queda libre.
Si te hicieran pasar eso sería
dando un pasito alante,
el empeine apuntando a la cocina
y la espalda explayándose en tu frente.
Solo si ya estás dentro
y la puerta le ofreciera el cogote a cualquier otro
podrás verle la cara, y más abajo el pecho
atravesado por un ojo de cíclope lampiño.
Tienen un cinturón con hebilla
casi siempre importada. Sólo una llave
tiene la contraseña para estas cajas fuertes
de estos bancos
que en vez de guardar oro guardan gentes.
Les cuelgan leontinas para entregarse a medias,
y un hueso defectuoso que le llaman pestillo
decide abrir o no,
aunque el que llegue se sepa el santo y seña.

Nevertheless I ask you, let me drink the wine they give us next time, all of it.

Next time let me not fear intoxication.

Next time let me love the flower more than the clay.

And let me remember to water my garden.

Translated by Mark Weiss

Ángel Escobar

Doors

The backs of all doors ache.
And they ache even more when they're keeping sayings
inside happy homes.
The Stranger knows it and doesn't come near them.
He sits at a distance and thinks:
"On their left side joints
hinge the swinging of doors
and they only leave one foot free to move about.
If they made you go in it would be
one little step at a time,
their insteps pointing to the kitchen
and backs reaching out to your forehead.
Only if you're already in
and the door offered its nape to anyone else
could you see its face, and, below, its chest
split by the eye of a hairless Cyclops.
They wear a belt whose buckle
is almost always imported. Only one key
has the pass code for the safes
of these banks
holding people not gold.
They dangle from watch chains to half surrender themselves,
and a defective bone known as the latch
decides whether or not to open,
even if he who comes knows the door inside-out.

Y por eso me dicen transeúnte, porque siempre las puertas
me dan con el trasero en pleno rostro.
Mañana tendré yo también alguna
que me cuide este llanto de huérfano abollado
por pedradas que lanza la intemperie,
o pasado mañana no habrá puertas."

El Ajeno se para y ve cómo la noche
sube con una vara sus cordeles
y se mecen chorreando anchas sábanas negras.

Se echa a andar ensartando palabrotas,
y ve que alguien con frac se está riendo
asomado a la puerta de la casa de enfrente.

El pulgar y el índice

El llanto de un niño en lo oscuro no implica
a las librerías de tomos usados ni a los edificios
múltiples de oficinas. El llanto de un niño
espera. Los demás se dan vuelta. Sentados a la mesa,
de uno en uno, aferrados a su color sin nombre,
todos comprenden el delirio. Yo acaso soy la mesa,
soy lo que está servido. Y lloro. Pónganse de pie,
y opinen. Opinen. Yo no soy el malvado, nadie me convierte,
nadie me condecora. Es inútil mi esfuerzo
como inútil es toda correspondencia ajena. Dicen:
"Quedémonos afuera". Y se preguntan: "Acaso somos tontos".
"Quémalo, quémalo", gritan, "quemémoslo, quemémoslo".
—A este otro capaz que hasta lo degollemos—, dicen.
(Ya pasó. No hay vuelta. Está el colgado.) El golpe—
el zoquete pide la comprensión y el pie
le da en el medio. Buena presa para el convite
también tú quedas lejos, hablando
de la mampostería. Atragántate y cállate.
Hay un niño que llora y una mesa entreabierta.
(La cabeza pequeña da en el muro. Y la grande
también.) "La espuma esa que cae, el sol
aquel que aúlla". Por qué habría de envidiar
yo la elocuencia ajena. Nadie como yo

Me they call a passer-by, because doors are always
shoving their behinds in my face.
I'll have my own tomorrow,
to care for my sobs of an orphan stoned
by the rocks that the open air tosses,
or else on the following day there will be no doors."

The Stranger gets up and sees the night
lifting its strings with a rod;
swaying, they drip thick black sheets.

He sets out, muttering curse words,
and notices that someone in a tux is laughing,
peering out the door of the house across the street.

The Thumb and the Index Finger

The crying of a child in the dark involves
neither used bookstores nor office
parks. The crying of a child
waits. Others turn their backs. Seated at the table,
one by one, clinging to their nameless color,
all understand the delirium. I could be the table,
could be what is served. And I cry. Stand, stand
and speak. Speak. I'm not the evil one, no one converts me,
no one awards me medals. My effort is as useless
as other folks' reciprocity. They say:
"Let's stay outside." And ask themselves: "Are we stupid?"
"Burn him, burn him," they scream, "let's burn him, yes."
—And maybe we'll even behead that other one, they say.
(It's over now. There's no going back. The hanging man is here.)
The blow—
the knucklehead asks for understanding and gets kicked
in the gut. A good prey for the banquet,
you also stay away, speaking of
the stonework. Stuff yourself and shut up.
There's a child who cries and a half-open table.
(The small head pounds on the wall. And so does the big one.)
"That falling foam, that
howling sun." Why would I envy
another's eloquence. No one like me

para sonreír, a veces, llorando, como un niño
en lo oscuro, sin implicar los libros,
los edificios múltiples de oficinas,
las calles por donde, aun así cabizbajo,
otro se regocija.

Hospitales

Yo vi a Rimbaud amarrado en una cama
y al Papá Protagónico amarrándolo duro,
y su piyama, soltándolo—gritaban y se soltaron
los huesitos vírgenes con doctores soplando
el fagot roto,
se quebraron los vasos, las persianas, los símbolos
y luego a cada cual según su síntoma
le entregaron su píldora, sus ojos, su cuaresma.
Era el año bisiesto de estos días de marzo y vi
cómo se ahorcaba el chivo en un pedrusco.
El choncholí explotando su cercado, y él sentado
mirando por arriba—
responsabilidad y culpa a los teléfonos,
a los viejos modales de los jueces
y a sus hijos. Yo vi a Rimbaud escupiendo
en una cesta de ojos bien templados,
y sanos como agujas. Lo vi. "No me
arrepiento". Estoy tranquilo, soy
el escriba, el buey
que no ha tenido nada. Estoy tranquilo.

Los cuatro cuentos

"Tú y yo nos vamos a morir temprano.
Tú y yo nos vamos a morir mañana.
No mañana, hoy. Quizás ya estemos muertos."
Me dijo con cansado paso y gestos
que remedaban lo que dirá el verso
último de mi sueño. Al descampado
dos sombras (ya no son inusitadas
puesto que tú las ves y las vio el claro

to smile, sometimes, while crying, like a child
in the dark, without involving books,
office parks,
the streets where, even when downcast,
another rejoices.

Hospitals

I saw Rimbaud bound to a bed
Protagonist Papa binding him fast,
and his pajamas also, releasing him—they were screaming and the small
   virgin
bones broke loose while doctors blew
into a cracked bassoon,
the glasses shattered, the blinds, the symbols,
and then they delivered to each, as their symptom called for,
their pill, their eyes, their Lent.
It was March of a leap year then, and I saw
how the goat was strangled on a boulder.
The blackbird taking advantage of its enclosure, and he, seated,
watching from above—
holding the phones accountable and to blame,
as well as the timeless manner of judges
and their children. I saw Rimbaud spitting
into a basket of eyes that were well-tuned
and healthy as needles. I saw him. "No
regrets." I am at peace, I am
the scribe, the bull
who has never had anything. I am at peace.

The Four Tales

"You and I will die early.
You and I will die tomorrow.
Not tomorrow, today. We could even be dead already."
He told me this with his tired gait and grimaces
that mimicked what the last line
of my dream will say. Outdoors
two shadows (no longer surprising
since you can see them and the clear

ojo de esta patraña que no acaba).
Dos sombras—al envés del argumento:
a diario salen miles de los Metros—
éramos. Él me hablaba como un preso
le habla a otro preso sin hablar: retazos
que mi prolijo olvido, esa otra araña,
borró cumpliéndose a sí mismo un pacto.
Sólo a ese olvido la memoria alcanza.
(Te dejo a ti, lector, en zona franca.
Y al que nunca verá, su franja blanca:
$\qquad$).
Fatiga ser dos sombras. Menos cierto
no es el agobio que le dan al cuerpo
del que ambulando se harta de reflejos
en una ciega habitación, y en vano
grita, sonriendo a su inconstante Habana,
como un rey de ajedrez: "Ya yo estoy muerto".

Otro

Si yo no fuera un cuchillo
podría conversar con alguien que anda por ahí.
Le diría que su horror es mi horror,
pero desde otro lado—
lo atroz no tiene nunca una sola cara.
O quizá todo sería silencio.
Mi balbuceo no alcanza a formar juicios.
Si ese, de quien me despido sin ver,
no fuera a su vez un cuchillo,
la conversación no sería ya la leche derramada,
o la doncella descuartizada en su aposento.
Él viene de un mundo que a mí me está prohibido,
donde una moneda se iguala a la vigilia
y la pesadilla sólo engendra dos cuervos
que, paulatinamente, le han sacado los ojos,
por lo que ya no podrá verme, aunque quisiera.
A mí me taponearon los ojos con el miedo—
tampoco podría verlo aunque quisiera.
Yo vengo de un mundo que a él le está vedado,
donde el sueño es lo estéril que añora una cigarra,

eye of this unending sham has also seen them),
two shadows—the reverse of the argument:
every day thousands emerge from the subways—
we were two shadows. He who spoke to me as a prisoner
speaks now unspeaking to another prisoner: shreds
that my meticulous oblivion, that other spider,
erased so as to fulfill its pact with itself.
That oblivion is the only thing that memory attains.
(I'll leave you, reader, in a tax-free place
And leave to whom will never see a blank space:
).
It's exhausting to be two shadows. The burden on the body
of one who tires of reflections pacing
in a blind bedroom is just as real. In vain
he shouts, smiling like a chessboard king
at his inconstant Havana: "I'm no longer dead."

Another

If I weren't a knife
I could talk to someone walking by.
I would tell him that his horror is my horror,
but from another angle—
the atrocious always has more than one face.
Or maybe everything would be silence.
My babbling can't take the form of judgments.
If he to whom I bid a careless farewell
weren't also a knife,
the conversation would cease to be spilt milk,
or the damsel torn to pieces in her chamber.
He comes from a world that, to me, is forbidden,
where a coin equals wakefulness
and the nightmare gives birth to two crows
which, gradually, have pulled out his eyes,
so that even if he wished, he couldn't see me.
They plugged up my eyes with fear—
even if I wished, I couldn't see him either.
I come from a world that is banned to him,
where sleep is the barrenness a locust longs for

y un atardecer casi lila dice que esta es la tierra
que nos dieron, donde sería bonito remontar
sin más un papalote, y arrimarle un ramito
de albahaca al próximo suicida.

La sombra del decir

Manto cuidado a polvo retenido,
no fuga el sol ni el dos se decapita.
Roza la yerba el pie, y no hay escala
que en vuelo llegue donde tú te inmolas.
Y no hay más fe que límite y aguanta.
Toca mi corazón verbo de estrella—
número, solsticio, maratón. Corro a ponerme
a resguardo del tiempo. Ni un tilín
para misa. El cruzado me mira. El cruzado
soy yo—ven a mi vera, ausculta.
Ay, rastrojo que exhalo, mira, mira
cómo se va: pie, dolmen, bulla—sólo escucha
la música. Y este dolor que mata a mi costado.
Es de ti, yo lo sé. No hay aquí neorromanticismo
ortopédico. Sólo el alma me embulla:
dónde pongo la cara, rocío verde, llamarada.
Doy de mí, me saben mis iguales, y apabulla
ese decir, el artilugio, el soplo. Quiero estar
donde no hoy, ni joyas ni desplante ciego.
Verás cómo me inmolo en pos del decir
la sombra, madre, a maquinal desidia
y alas rotas. Cómo llega la máscara, ceniza
del hablar. Pon fuera, y que no acompañe
mi pequeña voz, Dios que me anega:
déjome solo, y allá el palacio exhibe sus caireles.
Voy y me planto, planta ante el sol y árbol
que no admite el desliz. Nada, nadie suplanta
esta caída, este revoltijo de nervios. Viaje
no. Estoy sentado en el suplicio. No hay
ni yo ni tú que pueda hablar así.
Decir, decir qué; sólo el silencio, hollín
que me atortola. Y sólo la mirada, el dos—
y trinidad que adoras. Creen que quiero
ver avecillas, columnas, ceremonias. El monte

and an almost lavender sunset says that this is the land
we were given, where it would be nice to simply fly
a kite, and to bring a sprig of basil
to the next suicide.

The Shadow of Speech

Blanket cared for by retained dust,
the sun doesn't flee nor is the number two beheaded.
Grass brushes against the foot, no stopover
in flight may reach the place where you immolate yourself.
And there's no faith left than limit and endure.
Touch my heart, stellar verb—
number, solstice, marathon. I run to take shelter
from time. Not even a tinkling bell
for church. The crusader stares at me. I am
the crusader—come to my side, feel me.
Oh, residue that I exhale, see, see
how it escapes: foot, dolmen, clatter—only listen
to the music. And this pain that's killing my side.
It's yours, I know. There's no orthopedic
Neo-Romanticism here. Only my soul stimulates me:
where I put my face, green dew, a blaze.
I give from myself, my equals know me, and it crushes me,
that speech, the ploy, the blow. I want to be
where not today, nor gems nor blind outburst.
You'll see how I immolate myself so as to speak
the shadow, mother, all the way to machine-like neglect
and broken wings. How the mask arrives, ash
of speech. Exclude it, let it not accompany
my small voice, God overwhelming me:
he left me alone, and there the palace shows off its curls.
I go there and plant myself, a plant before the sun and tree
intolerant of missteps. Nothing, nobody displaces
this fall, this jumble of nerves. Not
a voyage. I sit on the torment. There's not
an I or a you that can speak like this.
Say, say what; only silence, soot
befuddling me. And only the gaze, the two—
and the trinity you adore. They think I want
to see little birdies, columns, ceremonies. The wilderness

puede ser, la ciudad soy: no más subterfugios—
toda la creación, colmillo de jabalí a mi muslo.

Y ver y ser el agua, lo que aguarda. Me tienen
entre sospechas, y el duro pecho cae sobre ti,
divierte, ojo puesto al espanto rumbo a ti.
No creas: soy la confirmación de lo que existe,
y de lo que no. Mi sí fecunda la tierra, y ella es,
y ella es: me acoge, palabra esperma que la cubre,
me cubre. No la dejo: oro al suplicio no, sólo
la piedra en que ponerme, atrás la danza—
montaña que cargo, llano, valle contrito,
he aquí el garabato que todo significa.

La guardería infantil

Nos han puesto a dormir,
y aquí dormimos.
Nos dicen que vendrá un aya rusa,
una nodriza inglesa,
o una buena hada eficiente, coreana o japonesa.
Nos han metido en cunas,
en camas y camastros,
y en sacos de dormir importados—:
lo importante, dicen, es que durmamos
esto que no es ni el sueño eterno.
Lo quieren, y lo hacemos—
como niños contentos—:
no somos marmotas,
ni estamos en los Alpes altos;
somos, entre otras cosas, adultos ya—
pero otros son los guardadores:
ellos, también adultos, son
los que nos cantan qué seremos—
algo así como alguaciles,
o ediles o serenos o magos—
o es que abogados o enfermeros;
o economistas en este carrusel
bonito del dinero—; y otros son los que fungen
de tutores; pero ellos están en otra parte,
donde nos dicen que está la vida—
la muy púdica siempre estará afuera—;

could be, I am the city: no more subterfuges—
all creation, the tusk of a wild boar at my thigh.

And to see and be water, what awaits. They're
suspicious of me, and my hard chest falls on top of you,
it diverts, an eye on the scare toward you.
Don't be so sure: I am proof of what exists,
of what doesn't. My yes impregnates the earth, and it is,
it is: it takes me in, sperm word covers it,
it covers me. I don't leave it: gold to the torment, no, only
the boulder on which to sit, the dance left behind—
a mountain I carry, plains, contrite valley,
herein the scrawl that signifies everything.

Daycare Center

They've put us to sleep,
and here we sleep.
They tell us that a Russian governess,
an English wet nurse,
or a good efficient Korean or Japanese fairy will be coming.
They've put us in cribs,
beds, cots,
and imported sleeping bags:
that we sleep, even if this is not the eternal sleep,
is what matters, they say.
They wish it and we obey
like happy children:
we're not marmots,
and we're not atop the Alps;
we are, among other things, adults—
but others are our keepers:
they, too, are adults
who sing to us what we'll become—
constables of sorts,
councilmen or night watchmen or magicians—
or maybe even lawyers or nurses,
or economists in this nice carousel
of money; it's others
who function as tutors; but they're elsewhere,
where they tell us life is—
which must be shy it's always outside;

y no sabemos cómo estarán, así, siendo tutores:
presumimos, un momento antes de dormirnos,
que la que hace de Gran Mamá estará viendo teleseries,
o haciéndole bolillos al Obispo—
siempre hay un obispo y una puta en el aburrimiento—;
y el que hace de Gran Papá estará en su oficina—
dictando algún decreto que resumirá,
para siempre, El Noticiero de las Nueve,
y lustrando una pistola única—
siempre hay una pistola y un cuchillo en el aburrimiento—;
o, a lo mejor, ellos están, también,
aquí durmiendo—; así no seremos
ni siquiera motivo de una fotografía borrosa,
menos de un video clip que embulle a algún frenético.

Nadie nos mira; Dios no está; no hay Homero.

Nos han puesto a dormir,
y en verdad que por siempre dormiremos.

Quién le teme a Franz Kafka

Los lógicos nos metieron en esta habitación.
No es un laberinto ni un túnel ni una cloaca;
es simplemente una habitación.
No hay minotauros ni ciegos ni ratas.
Los lógicos no nos dicen cómo nos metieron en ella.
Menos aún nos dicen cómo podremos salir.
No podemos estar dentro ni afuera,
según aseguran los lógicos; pero lo cierto
es que la habitación es real,
y una de las dos cosas debería suceder—
siempre según los lógicos—,
pero ninguna de las dos cosas sucede.

Frente frío

Tengo eczema en el alma.
La regaría con ácido muriático,
con un poco de seconal o de paciencia.

we don't know how they're doing, our tutors:
we suppose, for a moment before falling asleep,
that she who plays Big Mama is watching soap operas
or baking buns for the Bishop—
in boredom there's always a bishop and a whore—
and that he who plays Big Papa might be at the office,
dictating a decree that will summarize,
once and for all, the Nine O'Clock News,
and cleaning his only gun—
in boredom there's always a gun and a knife;
but maybe they, too,
are sleeping here; and we won't even get to be
subjects of a fuzzy photograph,
not to mention a video clip arousing the over-excited.

No one watches over us; God is not in; there is no Homer.

They've put us to sleep,
and it's true that we'll be asleep forever.

Who's Afraid of Franz Kafka

The logicians put us in this room.
It is neither a labyrinth nor tunnel nor sewer;
it is simply a room:
No minotaurs nor blind people nor rats.
The logicians aren't saying how they got us here.
They're saying how we can get out even less.
We can't be in or out,
the logicians claim; what is true
is that the room is real,
and one of two things should happen—
the logicians always tell us—
but none of them ever does.

Cold Front

I've got eczema in my soul.
I would drench it with muriatic acid,
some seconal or patience.

No quiero que sea de nailon,
ni que me la pongan a bailar
entre un billar y otro. No que se me escurra.
Así podrida la quiero.
Que se me pegue al cuerpo.
Quizá yo pueda ver un paisaje, un día.
Lloro despacio; pero una lluvia de enero
añoro: sí, sí, que borre mi tristeza—
un manto, un paño para taparme el rostro.
No tengo megáfono ni coturnos;
no puedo ser una máscara.
Se me sacude el cuerpo; tiemblo,
me mortifico. Qué es esto que viene por mí—
me anega en lágrimas pardas cual el fango
y dice: "Todavía, todavía". Soy
acaso un mono trágico—
eso es: soy sólo un mono trágico
que no tendría que ver con la gramática.

Ramón Fernández Larrea

Poema transitorio

• *A Victor Rodríguez Núñez*

Es difícil vivir sobre los puentes

Atrás quedó la negra boca el odio
y no aparece el esplendor
esto es también el esplendor
pero tampoco

La cegadora luz siempre estará más adelante
La cegadora luz siempre estará
su nido está en la punta
hacia allí van tus pasos. No te detengas
no te detengas no
o el vértigo hundirá su temblor en tus ojos

I don't want it to be made of nylon,
nor do I want them to set it dancing
between two billiard balls. I don't want it to drip.
I prefer it rotten like this.
That it may stick to my body.
Perhaps I'll be able to see a landscape, one day.
I cry slowly; but I long for some January
rain: yes, to wash my sadness away—
a blanket, a cloth to cover my face.
I have neither a megaphone nor stilts;
I can't be a mask.
My body shakes; I tremble,
torment myself. What is this that comes for me—
drowns me in dark tears as would mud
and says: "Still, still." Perhaps
I am a tragic monkey—
that's it: a tragic monkey
that has nothing to do with grammar.

Translated by Mónica de la Torre

Ramón Fernández Larrea

Transitory Poem

♦ *To Victor Rodríguez Núñez*

It's difficult to live on bridges

They left behind the black mouth the hatred
and the splendor makes no appearance
this is also splendor
but less so

The blinding light will always be further along
The blinding light will always be
its nest is on the headland
your steps go towards it. Don't stop
don't stop don't
or vertigo will sink its trembling in your eyes

la cegadora luz siempre estará ante ti
hacia allí va tu sangre pero no la verás

Es difícil vivir sobre los puentes.

Cantando con mi abuelita sobre las piernas

La pobre vieja ya no se conmueve con nada

El polvo sigue polvo tras su débil adiós
la pobre abuela desolada
ni la más honda catástrofe puede sacarla de la tierra

Recuerdo un limonero
que la tribu ayudaba a crecer
chorros y chorros de familiar orine le sabotearon cada noche
alánimo qué temible aventura la fuente se rompió
la vieja respiraba sin decir ni esta boca es mía

Toda esa gente solitaria de dónde viene
Toda esa gente solitaria de dónde son

Cualquier noche que quieras podrás ver las estrellas
las lucecitas remotas que ofrece el turístico cielo
mínima bendición que recibimos siempre siempre
aparten ese humo que no nos deja distinguir
ese humo ciudad ese humo turbio irresponsable
ahora la abuela está encerrada en dos metros de lodo
ya no toca los búcaros con temblorosa resignación
con arrugada abulia con mirada de asombro
para saber si la pared respira
apartemos el humo la sangre de la guerra
con aquellos manteles que conocieron tantas manos
con la cuchara lívida que era casi habitual.

II

La vieja en ocasiones salía a vivir en su portal
buenos días mujer noticias de la casa
o se encerraba en su cigarro
un baño humeante por no ser regañada
pero mamá pero mamá *toda esa gente solitaria*
vive dios
de dónde son toda esa gente solitaria ajena a la pérdida

the blinding light will always be before you
your blood flows towards it but you don't see it

It's difficult to live on bridges.

Singing with My Grandmother on My Lap

Nothing makes the poor old woman move now

Dust to dust after her feeble goodbye
poor grandmother desolate now
not even the deepest catastrophe can pull her from the earth

I remember a lemon tree
that the whole tribe nurtured
sabotaged each night with buckets and buckets of family piss
to arms to arms what a mess the well's run dry
the old woman breathed without muttering a word.

All the lonely people where do they all come from
All the lonely people where do they all belong

Any night when you wish you could see the stars
distant lights that fill the touristy sky
the little blessing that we always always receive
take away that smoke that keeps us from seeing ourselves
that smoke city that irresponsible murky smoke
now my grandmother is buried in six feet of mud
now she doesn't stroke the flower pots with trembling resignation
with wrinkled apathy with an astonished gaze
to find out if their sides breathed
Take away the smoke the blood of war
with those table cloths that so many hands have known
with the trowel that was almost habitual.

II

The old woman sometimes lived in her doorway
good day woman what's the news of the house
or she would lock herself in the smoky bathroom
with her cigarette so that she wouldn't be scolded
but mama but mama *all the lonely people*
good god
where are all the lonely people from unaware of the loss

de tus dientes
pero mamá *de dónde viene*
El limonero augusto con su pequeña obligación
de ayudar al bisté a mejorarse y al pescado
Las tablas se mantienen como siempre podridas
El mundo roe y roe con su clamor las fibras
Ahora la pobre vieja no está ni en la memoria
no está ni en el alánimo sólo el polvo responde
Cuando llueve o brilla el sol
eso no es más que el estado del alma

Estamos todos a punto de morir
todos bajo una lluvia de hirviente gelatina
la pobrecita vieja se refugió la refugiamos
en esa tierra roja alegre como pocas
el siglo veinte escapa sobre una flor de sangre
la tribu anda dispersa *toda esa gente solitaria*
toda esa gente solitaria de dónde viene poca cosa
hay el mismo portal el mismo oscuro y trabajoso silencio
el limonero cumple año tras año tras año su función

El único muchacho que parece salvarse.

El país de los elfos

posiblemente nunca respires
tienes una mano en el vientre no respires
posiblemente no sueñas
no puedas dormir
con la mano en la ingle no duermes
no respires
posiblemente no haya nunca
raíz dorada ni rama ni tierra para revolcarte
el país de los elfos te espera
el país aguarda por ti
eres pequeñito no respires no sueñes
porque los ogros te descubrirán

el país se siente desgraciado sin tus pies

me llamo ramón
desgraciadamente me llamo ramón
tengo un país pequeñito a mis pies

of your teeth
but mama *where do they come from*
The stately lemon tree with its small obligation
to flavor the steak to improve the fish
the boards as always remain rotted
The world gnaws and gnaws at the fibers with its noise
Now the poor old lady isn't even remembered
she isn't even in the call to arms only the dust answers
When it rains and shines
it's just a state of mind

We're all about to die
all of us in a rain of boiling gelatin
the poor old lady was sheltered we shelter her
in that red earth happy as few are
the twentieth century slips away on a flower of blood
the tribe walks away disperses *all the lonely people*
all the lonely people where do they all come from nothing much
there's the same doorway the same dark and laborious silence
the lemon tree performs its duty year after year after year

The only boy who seems to save himself.

The Land of Elves

maybe you'll never breathe
your hand is on your belly don't breathe
maybe you're not dreaming
you may not sleep
with your hand in your groin you're not asleep
don't breathe
maybe there's never been
a golden root or branch or earth for you to wallow in
the land of elves awaits you
the land prepares your coming
you are tiny don't breathe don't dream
because the ogres could find you

the land feels wretched without your feet on it

my name is ramón
unfortunately my name is ramón
at my feet is a tiny land

soy un gnomo el elfo sin alas
no respiro no hay dios de mi talla
me llamo ramón en el país de los elfos
el día tiene veinticuatro horas
el día es una especie de país
me llamo ramón no sueño
ni invento otro país debajo de mi vientre
las alas siempre me faltarán
el país estará siempre lejano

como un sueño como un vientre como el país de los elfos

cojones.

Roberto Méndez

Fábula peligrosa

No está más la libélula
en esa hoja,
menos duró la gota
que la historia se ha bebido.
Ahora, dentro de un satisfecho lagarto
reposa.
Sólo un instante, de verde a verde, tuvo;
lástima de oro y negro sutil,
lástima de lagarto que se ha dormido
y no dejan enseñanza
más que la gota.
Cuidado con decirlo a los niños.

Ensayo sobre la tristeza

Michel Eyquem, señor de Montaigne,
está escribiendo,
amo de siervas y lebreles, la pluma
rechina en los ensayos, su vida
va sacando de un frasco oscuro.

I am a gnome a wingless elf
I'm not breathing there's no god as small as me
in the land of elves my name is ramón
there are 24 hours in a day
the day is a kind of land
my name is ramón I'm not dreaming
and I don't invent another land beneath my belly
I'm always wingless
the land will always be far away

like a dream like a belly like the land of elves

damn.

Translated by Mark Weiss

Roberto Méndez

Dangerous Fable

The dragonfly's no longer
on this leaf,
the drop that was drunk by history
lasted still less.
Now it rests
inside a sated lizard.
It lived but an instant from green to green;
a pity its subtle gold and green,
a pity the lizard that slept
and they left no education
beyond the drop.
Take care how you tell this to children.

Essay on Sorrow

Michel Eyquem, sieur de Montaigne,
writes,
I love my servant-girls and hounds, the quill
squeaks across his essays, his life
will be drawn from a dark bottle.

La tristeza, dice,
es el campo cuando los lobos vienen,
el fin del hombre constante,
débil mano buscando la sombra.
Yo, que sólo reino en un parque,
con una muchacha gris
y un gato,
he visto partir al otoño
sin más mensajes,
puedo decir que la tristeza
es un lugar casi tibio
para cobijar los pájaros de la memoria.
Una mano enguantada
echa, uno por uno,
los reyes al fuego,
todos reos de melancolía;
voy en pos de la última calle
que los vientos dejaron,
señor de mí mismo,
dueño de la tristeza.

Lo estelar

Son los cómicos que trabajan en una ermita dormida, mientras a su lado un pintor trabaja el signo [. . .] En esas ruinas falta el techo, pero el pintor se aprovecha para precisar lo estelar . . .

JOSÉ LEZAMA LIMA

Después de las ruinas no hay un cuarto de espejos,
ni siquiera un espejo para situar el tercer árbol,
las ruinas son sólo columnas destechadas,
la flauta cruza libremente entre ellas, no tienen más fe
que considerar el pasado como un agua indivisible,
¿cuál es el sitio de la contemplación?
¿dónde abrir la puerta por la posición exacta?
Dos hombres que se dan la espalda pueden ser invisibles,
mas la noche sigue picoteando los manteles,
escoriando los parlamentos hasta sólo dejar
vacíos sombreros, máscaras, una cena deshecha;
entre los comediantes que parten y el pintor
precisando en un mínimo espacio el astro
sólo está lo estelar como una carcajada;

Sorrow, he says,
is the field when wolves arrive,
the end of the persistent man,
a weak hand in search of shade.
I, lord only of a park,
with a gray girl
and a cat,
I've seen the departure of autumn
and it left no messages,
and I can say that sorrow
is an almost tepid place
in which to shelter birds of memory.
One by one a gloved hand
launches kings
into the fire,
guilty, every one, of melancholy;
I'm off in pursuit of the last street
that the winds leave,
lord of myself,
master of sorrow

The Stellar

They are the actors who work in a sleeping hermitage, while at their side a painter paints a sign [. . .] The roof is missing from those ruins, but the painter uses this to help him fix the stellar . . .

JOSÉ LEZAMA LIMA

After the ruins there is no chamber of mirrors,
not even a mirror for finding the third tree,
the ruins are nothing but roofless columns,
the flute floats freely among them, but their only faith is
to think the past an indivisible water,
what is the place of contemplation?
where should the door be opened precisely so?
Two men back to back can be invisible,
but night keeps pecking at the tablecloths,
flaying the conversations until there's nothing left
but empty hats, masks, a disrupted supper;
among the actors who leave and the painter
fixing the star in a tiny space
it's the stellar alone like explosive laughter;

paso, repaso el camino de los árboles,
¿sabes por qué un pino es tan distinto a la memoria?
bajo sus mantos podrían descubrirse cuerpos hermosos,
si se deslizaran en las aguas toda palabra les sería permitida
pero la madrugada sólo admite sus danzas
y él reprocha calladamente su escasa música
¿cuánto darás por esa mancha?,
unos vidrios deshechos, el agua mercurial que cabe en un pañuelo.
Repito para el Sordo: todo espacio puede precisarse en un signo,
el pincel redondea con piedad y asco sus contornos,
entre un espejo y otro, el amanecer y los ángeles que desayunan;
hijos de hombres, ¿creeréis en la muerte anunciada como una flauta?,
la fe sólo puede estar sobre las columnas sin techo,
es triste ser invisibles pero un gesto errante nos identifica
¿y la máscara?, sobre las colinas hay un relámpago,
concluyo los parlamentos, está puesta la mesa para los espíritus
¿y la máscara?, tras el caballete comienza el laberinto:
él sólo ve una ermita abandonada y la noche,
la risa de los cómicos no basta.

Rolando Sánchez Mejías

Cálculo de lindes

1

Entre las partes
y el todo—ninguna
relación.

       Sin embargo
se movía, astuto, *aquello,* a
ras de tierra interpretando
el Libro de Instrucciones.

2

La imposibilidad de moverse
en el vector de la vida: el bosque

I cross and recross the wooded path,
do you know why a pine tree is remembered so clearly?
beautiful bodies can be found beneath their cloaks,
if they glide through the water every word may be granted them
but it's dawn alone that allows their dances
and he quietly reproaches their scant music
how much will you give for that stain?
a few broken windows, mercurial water that fits in a handkerchief
I repeat for the Deaf Man: all of space can be fixed in a sign,
between one and another mirror with piety and disgust the brush traces
the shapes of dawn and the breakfasting angels;
sons of men, do you believe in death announced like a flute?
nothing but faith can exist above roofless columns,
to be invisible is sad but a wandering gesture identifies us
and the mask? over the hills there's a flash of lightning,
I end the conversations, the table is set for the spirits
and the mask? beyond the ridge the labyrinth begins:
he alone sees an abandoned hermitage and the night,
the laughter of the actors is not enough.

Translated by Mark Weiss

Rolando Sánchez Mejías

A Calculus of Boundaries

1

No relationship
between the parts
and the whole.

　　　　　Nonetheless
that one was persuasive, astute,
interpreting the Book of Instructions
at the most basic level.

2

The impossibility of moving aside
on life's vector: the woods

resultó abrupto, inexplicable, sin espesor
los árboles en la cuadrícula del córtex
y en la cuadrícula del territorio
también sin espesor.

3

Primo: elegir
por azar
del anaquel
un cerebro de circunvoluciones mondas ad usum

Segundo: cocer
la cínica cabeza del caimán
(cocer y cantar, incluso bailar)
con hilo y pegolín.

Tercio: ajustar
el sistema
a las variedades del inconsciente.

Así circuló por entre nuestras mujeres:
con la ferocidad del dinero. Muñeco,
no ángel: somos gente sencilla
y hemos visto rodar
desde el cielo
estirpe semejante,
otros lelos
de frente trepanada
por el rodillo de la Naturaleza.

4

Operaciones básicas:

   a) Errar.

   b) Mirar la luna.

   c) Mugir (como una vaca en celo).

5

De las marionetas conservaría la inespecífica atracción por el vacío: series des-
concentradas prolongándose en una maraña de modus operandi. Su umwelt,
como el de las arañas: pura virtualidad.

turned out to be rugged, inexplicable, the trees
in the checkerboard of the cortex without density
and in the checkerboard of the territory
without density as well.

3

First: select
by chance
from the shelf
a brain whose convolutions
have been stripped bare ad usum

Second: stew (and sew)
the cynical head of the crocodile
(stewing and singing, also dancing)
with thread and paste.

Third: adjust
the system
to the diversity of the unconscious.

In this manner he made his way among our wives:
with the ferocity of money. A doll,
not an angel: we are simple folk
and we have seen
a similar breed descend
from the sky,
other dimwits
their foreheads crushed
by Nature's rolling pin.

4

Basic operations:

  a) Wander.

  b) Look at the moon.

  c) Low (like a rutting cow).

5

He would retain the marionette's nonspecific attraction for the void: a dis-
oriented series continuing in a thicket of modus operandi. Its umwelt, like
a spider's: pure virtuality.

6

en
una rápida volición

con
el puño abierto

casi sin
sentido

pescar

en
el

aire

7

vio
en el pasto
conjuntos discretos de vacas

extensiones vacías
de conceptos
en el pasto (pensó)

(no obstante
finalmente
vacas) pensó

mientras se borraba el pasto

8

Migrañas, etc.

9

Abrir
claros en el bosque.

Encima
negra nube de anófeles y abajo
—inter castaños—quebrar
gaznates de jabatos,
que husmean zurrones,

6

with
a quick volition

open-
fisted

almost
unconsciously

fishing

in

air

7

he saw
in the field
discrete groups of cows

empty extensions
of concepts
in the field (he thought)

(nevertheless
in the end
they were cows) he thought

as he erased the field.

8

Migraines, etc.

9

Opening
clearings in the woods.

Above
a black cloud of anopheles mosquitoes and below
—inter chestnut trees—breaking
the windpipes of young boars
that sniff the game-bags,

que muerden bellotas,
como él.

Entrambos—máquina y cerdo—una
solución para el cálculo de lindes
en tiempo de Movilización Total.

Visto de golpe, el asunto: empresas
de la Razón. O mejor dicho
visto el bosque
de conjunto: un
Dichtung.

Y en detalle
(intra bellota rota):
¡partículas de luz!

10
(coro de niños)

no partí
yo la nuca
del occiso
en cuestión

ya chillaba

ya la luna
alta y blanca
en la fronda
lo enfriaba

y en el fondo
sombras densas
y no menos
inhumanas

ya fugaban

11

Nada brilló
en la borrosa constancia de la realidad.

bite acorns,
like him.

Both—machine and pig—a
solution for the boundary calculus
in a time of Total Mobilization.

Seen in a flash, the theme: Reason's
businesses. Or better,
the forest
seen as a whole: a
Dichtung.

And in detail
(intra a broken acorn):
particles of light!

10

(boys' chorus)

I didn't separate
the nape
from the victim
in question

I already screamed

the moon
high and white
in the foliage
already chilled it

and at the bottom
shadows dense and
no less
human

had already run away

11

Nothing shone
in the blurred constancy of reality.

Translated by Mark Weiss

Rogelio Saunders

Vater Pound

Vater Pound escribía sus instrucciones sobre la Poesía
sentado junto al fuego del hogar en un Medio Oeste ya sólo imaginado,
en la cabaña de troncos rodeada de abetos o de pinos,
con una manta escocesa sobre las piernas quebradas.
Le debo el fantasma inocente de Sexto Empírico
y silenciosos desplazamientos de alejandrinos licenciosos.
La luna blanca y el búho sobre el pico del abeto.
Fragilidad, tu nombre es Mr. Pound.
Un niño convencido de la justeza del Universo
y equivocándose siempre, sin embargo,
como una rosa bebiendo entre las dunas.
Pecoso y luego greñudo. Pecoso y luego.
       Infinitamente greñudo.
Un viejo salvaje y frágil.
La importante distribución de los lados y la altura.
El búho blanco y la luna sobre la rama del abeto.
La barba circundando un rostro como un mar circundando una isla,
como un bosque sepultando una casa.
Pelos. Pelos. Pelos.
La dificultad de transmitir un conocimiento.
La dificultad de hablar en nombre de los otros.
La imposibilidad de ser hasta el fin uno mismo.
La imposibilidad. Oh la imposibilidad.
Siempre la imposibilidad, la sinusoide del trigrama.

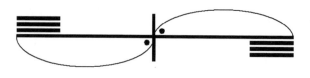

Abeto	Luna
Casa	Búho
Anciano	Hoja pintada
Mono	Arroyo

Rogelio Saunders

Vater Pound

Vater Pound would write his instructions on Poetry
seated next to the fireplace in an only imagined Midwest,
in the log cabin surrounded by firs or pines,
with a Scottish shawl over his broken legs.
I owe him the innocent ghost of Sextus Empiricus
and silent shiftings of licentious alexandrines.
The white moon and the owl on the tip of the fir tree.
Fragility, your name is Mr. Pound.
A boy convinced of the correctness of the Universe,
and yet always wrong,
like a rose drinking among the dunes.
Freckled and then disheveled. Freckled and then.
       Infinitely disheveled.
A savage and fragile old man.
The important distribution of sides and height.
The white owl and moon on the fir branch.
The beard encircling a face like an ocean encircling an island,
like a forest hiding a house.
Hairs. Hairs. Hairs.
The difficulty of conveying something known.
The difficulty of speaking in the name of others.
Impossibility of being oneself to the very end.
Impossibility. Oh, the impossibility.
Always the impossibility, the trigram's sinuosity.

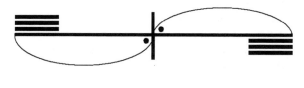

Fir	Moon
House	Owl
Old man	Painted leaf
Monkey	Stream

No Mussolini	No Adams	No Gesell	No Confucio
No Cavalcanti	No Dante	No Ovidio	No Homero
No _____	No _____	No _____	No _____

Y entonces, de pronto, por así decirlo, Mr. Pound desaparece.
Mr. Pound disappears.

Haciendo honor a su nombre se hundió en el marasmo inextricable de la
    Oikonomía.
Inextricable, inexplicable.
¿Es así como uno se vuelve loco?
¿Es así como uno se vuelve loco?
¿Loco, loco, loco, loco?
¿Y por qué todo es tan frágil, tan disperso, tan híbrido?
¿Cómo cortar de una vez la cabeza verdadera de la hidra?
Mr. Pound paseándose por una calle de Londres.
Mr. Pound subido sobre el pretil de un puente.
Mr. Pound haciendo cabriolas en una ventana de Pisa.
Mr. Pound en su celda: un ideograma trazado rápidamente sobre la cal.
Mr. Pound un poco antes: colgado de una rama y chillando a la luz de la
luna. Chillando de terror, balanceándose entre el follaje, una risa extraña, hi,
hi, hi, hi, hi, advirtiendo a los que pasan, a lo lejos, por el cruce de caminos,
brillando las hojas plateadas, los ojos saltando como ranas en el arroyo.

He aquí al Poeta.

¿O sea que la locura tiene al fin un nombre?
¿O sea que este discurso es acaparable como los granos de trigo?
¿O sea que ya pueden alzarse los párpados hinchados y gritar en el viento:
    «Dios proveerá»?
El viento que es todo y que se lo lleva todo.
Dunas. Dunas. Dunas. Dunas.
Lo que fulmina, lo que mata, lo que paraliza, ¿es esto?
Lo que dispersa, lo que rasga, lo que divide, lo que enajena.
Tengo la clara certeza de estar loco mientras me balanceo en esta rama de
    abeto.
Soy un búho, soy una hoja pintada, soy la luna.
Y equivocándose siempre, sin embargo.
Instrucciones, resoluciones. Pálido diccionario.
Almanaque de las cosas, lista infinita. *Infero.*
Pero sólo entonces, sin embargo, la realidad del ínfero.
O mejor dicho: realidad es ínfero.
O mejor dicho todavía: sólo lo real puede ser infernal.

Not Mussolini	Not Adams	Not Gesell	Not Confucius
Not Cavalcanti	Not Dante	Not Ovid	Not Homer
Not _____	Not _____	Not _____	Not _____

And then, suddenly, so to speak, Mr. Pound disappears.
Mr. Pound desaparece.

Doing honor to his name, he plunged into the inextricable swamp of
   Oikonomia.
Inextricable, unexplainable.
Is this how one goes crazy?
Is this how one goes crazy?
Crazy, crazy, crazy, crazy?
And why everything is so fragile, so dispersed, so mixed?
How finally to cut off the true hydra head?
Mr. Pound strolling down a London street.
Mr. Pound atop the railing of a bridge.
Mr. Pound cutting capers in a Pisan window.
Mr. Pound in his cell: an ideogram rapidly traced in the whitewash.
Mr. Pound a little before: hanging from a branch and howling to the moon-
light. Howling with fear, swinging among the foliage, a strange smile, hi, hi,
hi, hi, hi, warning those passing, from a distance, through the crossroads,
the silvery leaves shining, eyes jumping like frogs in the stream.

This is the Poet.

Or is it that finally madness has a name?
Or that this discourse can be hoarded like grains of wheat?
Or that the squinting eyelids already can rise and cry in the wind: "God
   will provide"?
The wind that is everything and that carries everything away.
Dunes. Dunes. Dunes. Dunes.
What strikes dead, what kills, what paralyzes, is this it?
What disperses, what slashes, what divides, what drives mad.
I have the clear certainty of being crazy while I swing on this fir branch.
I'm an owl, I'm a painted leaf, I'm the moon.
Yet always wrong.
Instructions, resolutions. A pale dictionary.
An almanac of things, an infinite list. *Inferus.*
Or better, the reality of the inferus.
Or still better: reality is the inferus.
Or even better said: only the real can be infernal.

Felipe el Hermoso: he ahí el Infierno.

Alguien lo descubrió rápidamente y sacó provecho.

Ejem. Dicho sea con sus propias palabras: *un crimen americano.*

Eliminando la *residua* y colocándolo en el centro del círculo:

> UN CRIMEN

De modo que como decía era éste el gesto de danzar sobre los escalones.

No bajar ni subir, simplemente danzar sobre los escalones.

Porque los escalones, como sabía Piranesi, no están encima ni debajo: *están en todas partes.*

Esta era la locura de Piranesi.

La multiplicación de los escalones.

La proliferación de las lilas en la primavera.

La fiesta de la muerte.

El mundo crece para la soledad, *mundus ad apokalypsis.*

Construimos ciudades que no podremos habitar.

No es enteramente exacto.

Construimos las imágenes de lo inhabitable.

Estos son los espejos que salen de nuestras manos.

Somos orfebres locos, cazadores obsedidos por un cántico.

Mr. Pound con un mosquete al hombro junto a un árbol.

Paisaje de lianas, un sueño de Rogier Van der Weyden que se incluye sibilinamente en el cuadro, minúsculo, con un sombrero de castor a lo Robin Goodfellow.

Símbolos espejeantes.

La máscara debe estar escondida en algún lugar del bosque.

¿Pero dónde? ¿En qué refugio soleado de la boca inmensa que es el bosque, que es como decir el desierto, los inquietos anillos de dunas, las olas del mar transfinito?

¿Dónde? ¿Dónde? ¿Dónde?

Silencio. Por debajo de la masa de pelos asoma un hocico simpático.

Cuatro orificios dispuestos simétricamente. De eso hay en todas partes.

Son los cuatro orificios universales.

Son los cuatro elementos y las cuatro letras.

Son el Norte y el Sur, son el Este y el Oeste.

Etc. Etc. Etc.

Recoger piedras para clasificarlas sería más provechoso.

Hallar la fórmula una vez es imposible.

Hallar la fórmula siempre es todavía más imposible.

Philip the Beautiful: this is hell.

Someone quickly discovered it and profited.

Ahem. Be it said in his own words: *an American crime.*

Eliminating the *residuum* and placing it in the center of the circle:

A CRIME

So that as I would say this was the gesture of dancing on stairs.

Neither descending nor ascending, just dancing on stairs.

Because stairs, as Piranesi knew, are neither above nor beneath: *they're everywhere.*

This was Piranesi's madness.

The multiplication of stairs.

The proliferation of lilacs in spring.

The fiesta of death.

The world grows for the sake of solitude, *mundus ad apocalipsis.*

We construct cities that we cannot inhabit.

That's not it exactly.

We construct images of the inhabitable.

These are the mirrors that leave our hands.

We are crazy goldsmiths, hunters obsessed by a canticle.

Mr. Pound with a musket on his shoulder, next to a tree.

Landscape of lianas, a dream of a tiny Rogier van der Weyden mysteriously included in the painting, with a beaver hat like Robin Goodfellow.

Shining symbols.

The mask must be hidden somewhere in the forest.

But where? In what sunny refuge of the immense mouth that is the forest, that is like saying the desert, the restless rings of dunes, the waves of the transfinite sea.

Where? Where? Where?

Silence. Beneath the mass of hair a sympathetic snout.

Four orifices symmetrically disposed. These are commonplace.

The four universal orifices.

The four elements and the four letters.

North and South, East and West.

Etc. Etc. Etc.

To pick up stones to classify them would be more profitable.

To discover the formula once is impossible.

To discover the formula is always even more impossible.

Ja. Ja. Ja. Imposiblemente imposible.
Mr. Pound se ríe sentado en cuclillas sobre un cono.
Todo es real, todo es imaginario.
La risa del mono hace un remolino con las hojas plateadas.
El mono titubea pasándose un dedo por la boca.
Coloca una pirámide sobre el cubo y una esfera en el vértice de la pirámide.
La luna sobre el pico del abeto.
El mono se ríe con ganas, como un niño, y mira de soslayo el plátano que
    Mr. Pound le había prometido.
Luz que atraviesa los gruesos barrotes y proyecta una sombra
    enedimensional sobre el cuadrángulo.
La sombra se sacude rítmicamente al impulso de sus estremecimientos.
Es como una música de pequeñas campanas, como aquello con que termina
la suite *Los planetas* de Gustav Holst.
Din don din don din don din don din don.
Algo que no se oye, una especie de ideograma hecho con el silencio y la cal.
Como en la frase profunda de los gemelos siameses, donde uno es el
    asesino que escribe y el otro el asesino que escucha:

Todo fluye.

Ismael González Castañer

de Sábado

> *porque si hemos llegado a ese punto entonces no merecemos sobrevivir, y*
> *probablemente no sobreviviremos . . .*

en Solingen, el pasado 29 de mayo

Cinco mujeres turcas, que no tenían necesidad,
fueron terminadas.
Sin embargo, todo estaba claro. Era como abandonar
cada uno de los propios ritmos
por tender, como Wagner, a la *Gesamtkunstwerk*:
la obra de arte
        que reúne a las artes.

Ha. Ha. Ha. Impossibly impossible.
Mr. Pound laughs squatted on a cone.
Everything is real, everything is imaginary.
The monkey's laughter makes a whirlwind of silvery leaves.
The monkey hesitates, running a finger across its lips.
He places a pyramid on the cube and a sphere on the pyramid's apex.
Moon above the tip of the fir tree.
The monkey laughs gladly, like a child, and looks sidelong at the banana
   that Mr. Pound had promised him.
Light that passes through the thick bars projecting an n-dimensional
   shadow on the quadrangle.
The shadow shakes rhythmically to the beat of its trembling.
It's like a music of small bells, like the end of Gustav Holst's suite *The Planets*.
Ding dong ding dong ding dong ding dong ding dong.
Something that is not heard, a kind of ideogram made of silence and
   whitewash.
As in the Siamese twins' profound phrase, where one is the killer that
   writes and the other the killer that listens:

Everything flows.

Translated by Harry Polkinhorn

Ismael González Castañer

from Saturday

> *if this is the point we've come to then we don't deserve to survive, and probably*
> *won't . . .*

in Solingen, last May 29th

Five Turkish women, who didn't have to be,
were killed.
Nevertheless, everything was clear. It was like abandoning
each of their rhythms
so as to lean, like Wagner, toward the *Gesamtkunstwerk*:
the work of art
            that joins all arts together.

Yo, con toda solidaridad, se los iba a enseñar;
pero ahora me doy cuenta
                    de cómo podrían saberlo,
si parece—como antes / como siempre—
que no se va a escarmentar.

Empecemos a bien todos un día un poco a escarbar.
Bien. Es la arena irredenta de la blanca visión:
        Yo sí quiero la casa
        Yo sí quiero la playa
        Yo sí quiero la bata
            blanca.
¿Ven?, no hay quien diga "Yo no quiero la paz.
Entonces (porque sólo fue "entonces)
alemanes, españoles / italianos y franceses
comenzaron a llorar. Era una lloradera *lita*,
que no tenía bruces / cruces, y menos *cobalese*
(que no sé qué puede ser, hablando sinceramente.

VACACIONES EN EL MUNDO

living in a world like this

En un mundo como aquí
                    tengo vacaciones en el mundo
Nada más que existen las verdades en el mundo,
        nunca comentarios

y eso que estuvimos dando frutas
        —bastante y variedad—
para mejorar al órgano enfermo Hígado
cuando era justamente lo contrario /
        aunque no estoy seguro.
Vacaciones en el mundo / Yo era un gordo
y ahora es comprobado
                    que delgado va mucho mejor.

Estuvimos confundidos en el mundo
existiendo más de un engrasador muy bueno
—las bolitas resistentes de la caja
para que no haya rozamiento tan devastador

I, in complete solidarity, was going to teach it to them;
but now I understand
                    how they could have known it,
if it seems—as before/as always—
that the lesson wasn't to be learned.

For the better part of a day all did some digging.
OK. These are unredeemed sands of white vision:
          I do want the house
          I do want the beach
          I do want the white
               robe.
Do you get it? there's no one who'd say "I don't want peace."
Then (because it was only then)
Germans, Spaniards/Italians and French
began to cry. It was a sweet larval sobbing,
without rails/betrayals, and still less *cobalese*
(truthfully I don't know what that means).

A VACATION IN THE WORLD

                              living in a world like this

In a world like this one
                         I take a vacation in the world
There are only truths in the world
            never commentaries

even though we'd been offering fruit
        —voluminously and of all varieties—
to improve the condition of the sick organ the Liver
when it was exactly the opposite/
            though I'm not sure.
A vacation in the world/I was fat
and now there's proof
                       that skinny is better.

We were confused in the world
our existence due more than anything to a very good lubricant
—the hardy ball bearings
so that the friction won't be disastrous

y así los aparatos / aparatos del mundo
tengan recorrido tanto.

Aquí viviendo, donde hay prados . . .
y la hembra sólo quiere producir
y divertirse
a su modo antiguo. La seguimos /
Hoy presenta un *Modelage*
¡Vamos pronto al *Modelage* nuevo
y nada circunspectos.

MIRAR Y MIRAR POR LA VENTANA

uno come su pan e ignora al Atacante

No tengo idea de nada
sino del amor que perdí
y no se encuentra
También de la música, sé que es la música;
pero esto no hace
que abandone mirar y mirar por la ventana.

He escrito la frase "mirar y mirar por la ventana";
pero antes—recuerdo—la ventana era yo,
y el azul del cielo.
Y viajaba en las noches . . .
y volvía y decía a mi madre:
"He traído un país / El país tiene actores
de esos
que te harían ollantar /
Lo que se proponen sé / Sé que se proponen, madre:
pregúntame ya."

Escribí la palabra *ollantar*
sin saber lo que es,
porque sí creo saber lo que pudiera ser;
de hecho, lo que cualquier cosa
en un tiempo adelante
tuviera conversión
es de los Dominios . . .
No haría falta ser
la ventana para ello,

and the appliances / the world's appliances
will run and last.

Living here, where there are lawns . . .
and the female only wants to produce
                                        and have fun
in her timeless way. We follow her /
Today a *Collection* is shown
Let's hurry to the latest *Collection*
                                        carelessly.

LOOKING AND LOOKING THROUGH THE WINDOW

                        you eat your bread and ignore the Attacker

I haven't a clue about anything
            except for the love I lost
                        which can't be found
And all I know about music is that it's music;
but this doesn't
            keep me from looking and looking through the window.

I've written the phrase "looking and looking through the window";
But once—I recall—I was the window,
            and the blue of the sky
And I traveled by night . . .
            and returned and I said to my mother:
"I've brought a country / A country with actors
                        of the kind
            that would make you overyearn /
I know what they're up to / I know their plan, mother:
                        ask me, now."

I wrote *overyearn*
            with no idea what it means,
because I suspect what it might;
that anything
            that might be exchanged
                in a time to come
                        is of the Dominions . . .
You wouldn't need to be
            the window for this

y a mamá en modo alguno
  se le hubiera ocurrido preguntar
                           por lo Por-venir /
ella es la nube ella es el cielo.

Viendo construir un puente
      —la manera en que asentaban los pilotes—
puse al lado
      una o varias de las medidas Guerras
y no obtuve el preciado
           de los sentidos más nobles.
Así ni las formas—ni la ideológica forma—
    adquirieron su realce . . .

Todo esto que es arroyo, bisel, cultivo y aire
    (pena da el decirlo)
creo que ya estuvo antes—dije en la casa,
donde no están consecuentes
              sino bebiendo té.
Me dormí, me soñé, desperté
    y recogí la mañana sin saberme un nombre
        de las muchas plantas
            que la misma gente
              había regalado.
Ser chofer sería entonces   la mayor cosa del mundo.
Ser chofer, manejar algo, conducir alguna cosa es lo mejor.

—*Cómo te gustaría tu vida en el futuro?*
—*Viajes constantes; y en el reposo, una vida hogareña con hijos y amigos
siempre en fiesta*
—*Y si tuvieras que resumir todo lo aprendido en ésta hasta el momento,
¿qué dirías?*
—*Que nunca hay razón para hacer nada mal*—parlamento del cazador
de elefantes en la película de Eastwood.

and my mother would have thought
    somehow to ask
               about the What's-to-come /
she is the cloud she is the sky.

Watching them build a bridge
        —the way they drove the piles—
I put aside
        one or a few of the standard Wars
and gained nothing
           from the most noble feelings.
And neither the forms—nor the ideological form—
    achieved their splendor . . .

All this that is stream, bevel, farming and air
        (I'm ashamed to say)
I think was here before—I mentioned at home,
where they're never consistent
               except when they're sipping tea.
I slept, I dreamt, I awoke
      and I gathered the morning unaware of the names
          of the many plants
             that these same people
               had offered.
So to be a driver would be   the best thing in the world.
To be a driver, to control something, is the best of all.

—How would you like your life to be in the future?
—Constant travel; and in between, a home life with children and friends,
an endless party
—And if you had to condense everything you've learned so far, what would
you say?
—That there's never a reason to do something wrong—the elephant hunter's speech in Eastwood's film.

Translated by Todd Ramón Ochoa

Juan Carlos Flores

Tótem

B-u-e-y

En el centro del poema / comidos los bordes del poema / con ojos de buey
mira a la realidad / desde el centro del poema.

"—Doctor, las huellas de sus patas por los surcos eran el poema, donde caía
el agua de su nariz abrían sus dedos, sus cabezas las flores quemantes del
poema—"

B-u-e-y

Su cansancio es político / ya no se quiere levantar / no se quiere desposar /
comidos los bordes del poema / con ojos de buey mira a la realidad / desde el
centro del poema.

El secadero

Hay, al sur de La Habana, entre el verdor y el oro, un lugar destinado a los
juegos. Es un sitio tranquilo, dicen, muy bueno para las mutaciones. Yo, nunca
he ido a ese lugar, sólo por temor a no volver. Tú, nunca has ido a ese lugar,
sólo por temor a no volver. Él, nunca ha ido a ese lugar, sólo por temor a no
volver. Hay, al sur de La Habana, entre el verdor y el oro, un lugar destinado a
los juegos. Es un sitio tranquilo, dicen, muy bueno para las mutaciones.

Uno de los blues

(inspirado en la película Thelma and Louise*)*

La vida es un remake vivas allá o aquí te llames Peter te llames Pedro te
llames Thelma o te llames Louise / aventurarse y cruzar solas más allá de los
límites eso hicieron Thelma and Louise / en todos estos años a nosotros nos
ha venido sucediendo lo que a Thelma and Louise / cada cual de nosotros
ha intentado hacer cosas para que cambien nuestras vidas lo que hicieron
Thelma and Louise / pero nos detenemos siempre en las primeras escenas por
temor a acabar como acabaron Thelma and Louise.

Juan Carlos Flores

Totem

O-x

In the center of the poem / the poem's edges eaten away / observe reality through the eyes of an ox / from the poem's center.

"Doctor, their hoof prints between the furrows were the poem, where the fluid dripped from their noses their toes would open, their heads the poem's blazing flowers."

O-x

Its weariness is political / it no longer wishes to rise / or marry / the poem's edges eaten away / observe reality through the eyes of an ox / from the poem's center.

The Drying Shed

South of Havana, between the green and gold, there's a place set aside for games. They say it's a peaceful spot, excellent for making changes. Myself, I've never been there, for fear of not returning. You too have never been there, for fear of not returning. And he also has never been there, for fear of not returning. South of Havana, between the green and gold, there's a place set aside for games. They say it's a peaceful spot, excellent for making changes.

One of the Blues

(inspired by the film Thelma and Louise*)*

Life is a remake whether you live there or here call yourself Peter or Pedro or Thelma or Louise / what only Thelma and Louise did was to dare to pass beyond the limits / what happened to Thelma and Louise all these years happened to us as well / each of us like Thelma and Louise has resolved to do something to change our lives / but we always stop ourselves in the first scene for fear of ending up like Thelma and Louise.

Retrato de una (otra) dama

Escritora esquizotímida / con tendencia al suicidio / no soportando el simulacro de vida / que le ha tocado roer / encerrada dentro de caja negra / día tras día escribe / si lo escrito le parece bien / buena mercadería / pone en la grabadora música exótica / baila hasta que los pies no le pesan—

Apolítica, dice, pero paga su peaje

(realismo sucio: convertir la mierda en oro, o por lo menos en papel moneda, eso, ya estaba en Baudelaire)

Escritora esquizotímida / con tendencia al suicidio / no soportando el simulacro de vida / que le ha tocado roer / encerrada dentro de caja negra / día tras día escribe / si lo escrito le parece mal / mala mercadería / fuma / se acuesta / se deprime / mira al techo—

Apolítica, dice, pero paga su peaje

(unas veces soy César Vallejo, el mutilado de todas las guerras, que la visita en su casa. Otras, una piedra común que ella usa de pisapapeles)

El ciclista K

El ciclista K, otro de los segregados convertido en exegeta, todo el tiempo posible haciendo auto-stop entre ciudad y campo, o entre campo y montaña, sin encontrar solución al eterno problema, sin encontrar el necesario reposo del cuerpo . . . negroide, otro de los segregados convertido en exegeta, todo el tiempo posible haciendo auto-stop entre ciudad y campo, o entre campo y montaña, sin encontrar solución al eterno problema, sin encontrar el necesario reposo del cuerpo . . . me ha contado que al mirar allá adentro algo raro notó . . .

Sírvase Usted

Aunque sin ningún tipo de alegría particular, por tal hallazgo, sea de la gastronomía o no sea, carne, un subproducto, sírvase usted, si Guevara murió infecto, en hospital de Marsella, Rimbaud, asesinado, en Quebrada del Yuro, yo, mezcla explosiva y retazo, en los mismos lugares, exactamente ahora, y eso es preferible a limpiar, de sol a sol, día tras día la mierda de las ciudadelas,

Portrait of (Another) Lady

A schizotimid writer / with suicidal tendencies / unable to bear a sham of a life / that has begun to eat at her / shut inside a black box / day after day she writes / if the writing seems good to her / good merchandise / she plays a tape of exotic music / and dances until her feet are weightless—

Apolitical, she says, but she pays her price

(dirty realism: changing shit to gold, or at least to money, that's it, as it was in Baudelaire)

A schizotimid writer / with suicidal tendencies / unable to bear a sham of a life / that has begun to eat at her / shut inside a black box / day after day she writes / if the writing seems bad to her / bad merchandise / she smokes / goes to bed / gets depressed / stares at the ceiling—

Apolitical, she says, but she pays her price

(sometimes I am César Vallejo, he who was wounded in every war, who visited her at home. Other times, I'm a nondescript rock that she uses as a paperweight)

K the Bicyclist

K the bicyclist, another of the marginalized become an exegete, as often as possible hitch-hiking between city and country, or between country and mountain, without finding a solution to the eternal problem, without finding the necessary physical rest . . . negroid, another of the marginalized become an exegete, as often as possible hitch-hiking between city and country, or between country and mountain, without finding a solution to the eternal problem, without finding the necessary physical rest . . . told me that he noticed something odd when he looked within.

Help Yourself

Even if without any particular kind of happiness, by means of such a discovery, be it gastronomy or not, meat, a byproduct, help yourself, if Guevara had died of an infection, in a Marseilles hospital, and Rimbaud murdered in Quebrado del Yuro, I, an explosive mixture and a remnant, in the same places, exactly now, and it's preferable to clean up, sunup to sunup, day after day the shit of

cobrando un sueldo mínimo, aunque sin ningún tipo de alegría particular, por tal hallazgo, sea de la gastronomía o no sea, carne, un subproducto, sírvase usted,

La mosca

Un punto

donde dos soplos enemigos atracaron. "extranjera ya, ha venido a convertir mi plato en su dominio"

un punto

donde dos soplos enemigos se confunden. "extranjera ya, ha venido a convertir mi plato en su dominio"

un punto

donde a una llama que oscila le responde otra llama que oscila. "extranjera ya, ha venido a convertir mi plato en su dominio"

¿La aparto de un manotazo y continuo estibando?

Dijo el cara-tiznada: si a un lado de la pared hay lo mismo que al otro lado de la pared, ¿no podrías dejar de hacer más ruido y aprender a callar?

Pedro Llanes

Nombres de la casa invisible

I

He visto a la caída de la tarde los rostros de mis hermanos los leñadores. Marchaban a paso lento, como los cuerpos hacia el pozo, Señor. Aparecieron sobre el agua y luego fueron a parar donde los diablitos vienen taciturnos. He sabido que mis hermanos los leñadores se morían como las bestias de ojos de ángel en noviembre. Esperaban a la puerta, pero nadie salió a recibir-los. El viento soplaba en los andamios de las esquinas y las botellas. Yo salí y los besé y puse agua fresca para sus hombros. Se iban yendo paso a paso,

the citadels, collecting a minimal wage, even if without any particular kind of happiness, by means of such a discovery, be it gastronomy or not, meat, a byproduct, help yourself,

The Fly

A dot

where two enemy puffs of air attacked. "it's a stranger, and it's come to make my plate its domain"

a dot

where two enemy puffs of air mingle. "it's a stranger, and it's come to make my plate its domain"

a dot

where a flickering flame responds to another flickering flame. "it's a stranger, and it's come to make my plate its domain"

Do I push it aside with a slap and continue stuffing myself?

The black-face said: since it's the same on both sides of the wall, couldn't we stop making still more noise and learn to shut up?

Translated by Mark Weiss

Pedro Llanes

The Names of the Invisible House

I

I have seen the faces of my woodcutter brothers at sunset. They walked, Lord, slow as corpses toward a pond. They appeared upon the water and went to stand where mischief falls silent. I knew my brothers were dying like angel-eyed beasts in November. They waited at the door, but no one came out to greet them. The wind blew among the scaffolding at the corner and the bottles. I came out and kissed them and poured cool water on their backs. Slow step by slow step they left, their nightshirts and still their eyes

las camisolas y los ojos aun llenos de rencor. Se marcharon a la hora en que el níspero se recuesta a la luna grande de la cuaresma y la desolación golpea las puertas de la tierra.

II

En Cowley, una aldea de campesinos, hay una niña descalza que llora infinitamente y tiene las manos con el increíble olor del jazmín. La he visto embadurnada de lodo dormir junto a las aguas mientras la locomotora humea y los arroceros ponen a madurar las mieses. Anda por el viejo barrio como solo andan los inocentes. Quisiera enjugarle las lágrimas, regalarle una cintilla llena de figuras de bestias. La locomotora se va alejando con su extraña furia por los arrozales. Cae de pronto la maravillosa fragancia de la lluvia.

III

Se llevaron un arca, una sirena, unos espejos con el nombre inefable del pastor. El aire repicante hacía revolar la penumbra de tercia a lo largo de los naranjos.

IV

La abuela era menuda, de ojos castaños y de cabello muy claro. Una noche se fue sin decir palabra. Se fue silenciosamente y ya no la vimos más. Era la temporada del adviento cuando las aguas relumbran y crecen las siemprevivas. Si pasaras al lado de los muros de su casa, baja y arrodíllate junto a la tierra.

V

El padre está cerca de la hoguera, las manos y los ojos de síndico en el viento. He mirado sus arrugas, la espalda con el sudor humilde del laborero. Solo él sabe porqué bullen las aguas en el mayo intrincado y la hora en que abre la rosa. El plenilunio cae sobre sus ojos, sobre la hoguera, las bestias salen a deambular. Tuve un sueño y en el sueño mi padre era un jinete en lo oscuro.

VI

Juliana era tímida y dulce de corazón y tenía una niña y trabajaba duro como los labriegos para traerle el pan. En su casa de techo reblandecido había un canario, unas falsas frutas, una cupletista de cristal. Yo acaricié sus cabellos en el septiembre que es el mes en que el équite aparece por la pradera y las dalias comienzan a rebrillar. Se fue poniendo violácea, con los ojos que no decían nada, ya no la vi reír. Una tarde la despedimos para siempre y yo le rogué al Señor de la casa invisible y le pedí llorando que la llevara por sus caminos.

full of grudges. They left at the hour when the medlar leans against the big moon of Lent and desolation knocks upon the doors of earth.

II

In Cowley, a peasant village, there is a little barefoot girl who cries forever and whose hands give off the incredible odor of jasmine. I have seen her smeared with mud asleep by the water while the locomotive puffs and the rice farmers set the grain to ripen. She walks through the old quarter as only the innocent walk. I want to dry her tears and give her a strip of paper filled with animal drawings. The locomotive pulls away across the rice fields with its peculiar fury. Suddenly the marvelous fragrance of rain is coming down.

III

They took with them a coffer, a siren, some mirrors with the shepherd's ineffable name. The ringing air makes the shade of tierce fly again along the orange grove.

IV

Grandmother was little, with chestnut eyes and very pale hair. One night she went away without a word. She left silently and we never saw her again. It was during the Advent season when the water sparkles and the live-forever blossoms. If you pass by the walls of her house, drop down and kneel upon the ground.

V

Father is close to the bonfire, his working man's eyes and hands in the wind. I have seen his wrinkles, his back wet with the workman's humble sweat. Only he knows why the waters boil up in intricate May, and the hour when the rose opens. The full moon falls over his eyes, over the bonfire, the animals go out to wander. I had a dream and in the dream father was a horseman in the dark.

VI

Juliana was shy and soft-hearted and had a little girl and worked hard as a hired hand to bring her bread. In her house there was a canary, some wax fruit, a crystal figurine of a nightclub singer. I stroked her hair in September, which is the month when the horseman appears in the meadows and the dahlias begin to sparkle again. She became increasingly violet-colored, her eyes told nothing, I no longer saw her laugh. One day we said goodbye to her forever and I prayed to the Lord of the invisible house and asked him weeping to lead her upon his paths.

VII

Echa tu bendición sobre esta tierra, Señor, para que crezca junto al trébol la piedra blanca de tu reino. Llévanos por la pradera de la cuaresma donde hay una luna muy grande. Danos de tu agua y aleja de nosotros las tinieblas y sus guardadores.

VIII

En Arenas vive la chica de la afilada cintura de ciprés. Si ella sueña las flores de la tierra se deshojan y baja por el entrepuente el perfume. Si recoge el cabello de reina tiemblan como indistintas ajorcas el galán nocturno y la siempreviva. Quisiera verla asomada escuchar por el viento de témporas la música del agua porque así cimbra de manera inefable y siento que va quedando en la eternidad.

IX

El juglar del pueblo estuvo atento a sí mismo todo el tiempo, cubierto de un árbol demasiado frágil. Lo fuimos dejando en el dintel de la penumbra, embarrancado en el fuego. En un cuaderno hacia finales de año enumeró las torres, los naipes, la sibilancia de la lluvia. Lo encontramos de bruces contra el suelo con unos ojos insípidos, acusadores: Ve y duerme, hermano, ve y duerme, no despiertes de tu sueño.

X

El bebedor iba zigzaguente por los puestos de azafrán y los reductos. En otro tiempo tuvo esposa. Se le veía triste, con un hoyuelo relumbrante en la barbilla, la arena lo fue inundando: yo escuché su canción, la canción de Obiol, una tarde de agosto, de animales galopando por el polvo cuando mi hermana era novia y aun no conocía a Yanara.

XI

Un trirreme con una jarcia de oro y unos marineros broncos del color del aceite navega y nadie puede detenerlo, porque anda por el camino del fuego.

XII

Ya en el campo de amapolas me asediaron con la tierra mojada los recuerdos. Era una noche de luna muy cálida, soplaba el viento, el pertinaz y áspero viento de septiembre. Al amanecer cayeron algunas lloviznas, el patio parecía relumbrar. Cuando todo se puso melancólico y Amy llegó hasta la casa, yo le dije a la amada que recordara que éramos como el fuego y como la sombra.

VII

Put your blessing on this land, Lord, so that beside the clover the white stone of your kingdom will grow. Lead us through the meadows of Lent where there is an enormous moon. Vouchsafe us your water and take from us the darknesses and its keepers.

VIII

The pretty girl with a waist thin as cypress lives in the sand. When she dreams, the flowers of the earth shed their leaves and perfume flows down the tweendeck. When she gathers her queenly hair, the lover in the night and the live-forever tremble like indistinct bangles. I'd like to see her peeping out to listen through the wind of ember days for the music of the waters because then she waves a wand ineffably and I feel that she will remain in eternity.

IX

The village juggler was always careful of himself, covered by a fragile tree. We used to leave him under the lintel of the shade, stuck in the fire. Toward the end of the year he listed in a notebook the towers, the cards, the sibilance of the rain. We found him face down on the ground, with insipid, accusatory eyes: look, and sleep, my brother, look, and sleep, do not awaken from your dream.

X

The drinker went reeling between the saffron stands and the redoubts. In another time he had a wife. I saw him sad, with a dazzling dimple on his chin, the sand flooding him: I listened to his song, the song of Obiol, one August afternoon when animals were galloping through the dust, when my sister was engaged and I had not yet met Yanara.

XI

A trireme with gold rigging and rough crew the color of oil sails by and no one can stop it because it follows the path of fire.

XII

Memories besieged me in the wet field of poppies. It was a very hot moonlit night, the wind was blowing, the obstinate bitter wind of September. At dawn a fine rain fell, and the courtyard seemed to shine. When everything became melancholy and Amy arrived at the house I told my beloved to remember we were like fire and shadow.

XIII

He soñado con Amy (unos guardas y un precipicio, unos pases con su letra diminuta.) La he visto irse. Iba vestida de blanco con un alfiler de oro en el pecho.

XIV

Hoy enterramos a Simone. Era pelicastaña, muy joven, solo parecía dormitar. Los familiares iban cansinos, sin mucho dolor. Un airecillo sin fuerzas rebotaba en los panteones encristalados con una ligera música de cera.

XV

Me he levantado al mediodía. Tengo los ojos muy claros como los ojos de aquellos que han estado de personeros de un sótano. Cae la lluvia sobre el aire en la casa de afilados fantasmas y caracolas.

Sigfredo Ariel

La luz, bróder, la luz

Mirar caer la nieve en la oficina de registro
cuando uno es la señal con un pañuelo, un sauce
que huele a mar del trópico, un animal aislado.
Pudiera caer ahora mismo la nieve sobre los edificios
en copos graves
pudiera morirme si me viera en una cerrazón
que tumba la cabeza
hasta las manos de los padres
que esperan sentados en un parque
y que no saben nada.

Un hombre quitaría con una vieja pala esta ceniza.
Vagamente regresa a aquel lugar
donde llovía detrás de la cabeza
cuando tuvo otro nombre y una cicatríz en la barbilla
y era hipócrita y humano
como un pobre diablo.
Bebía en los circos de ocasión

XIII

I dreamed about Amy (some guard rails and a precipice, a few passes in her tiny handwriting). I saw her go. She went dressed in white with a gold brooch on her breast.

XIV

Today we buried Simone. She had chestnut hair and was very young, she seemed merely to be dozing. Her family moved tiredly, without much pain. A small breeze beat weakly among the glazed vaults in a light waxen tune.

XV

I got up at noon. My eyes are crystal clear, like the eyes of those who have been held prisoner in a cellar. The rain falls over the air in the house of thin ghosts and conchs.

Translated by Chris Brandt

Sigfredo Ariel

The Light, Brother, the Light

To gaze at the snow falling on the registry office
when one is the sign with a scarf, a willow
that smells like a tropical sea, an isolated animal.
The snow could fall right now on the buildings
in heavy flakes
I could die if I saw myself in an obstinate state
that knocks the head down
into the hands of the parents
who wait seated in a park
and who know nothing.

A man with an old shovel could remove these ashes.
He vaguely returns to that place
where it rains in the back of the head
when he had another name and a scar on his chin
and was hypocrite and human
like a poor devil.
He would drink at rundown carnivals

y tenía el bolsillo repleto de llaves inservibles
y un temor absoluto de la soledad.

Seré yo mismo acaso si fuera tenedor de libros
o fuera neerlandés y conociera la magia
y si en el extremo de mi vida la nostalgia
me pasmara las manos sobre el hielo.

Job pudo reposar sin violentarse
sobre este caracol marino
y las sabanas pudieran estar llenas de alfalfas
o de termas brillantes o de casas de troncos.
Quiénes seríamos entonces / calle abajo
acaso compraríamos el periódico de la mañana
cayéndonos de sueño
y las mandarinas y el pan dulce.

Estos años románticos los querrán los hijos de los hijos
y buscarán la letra en el registro, nuestros discos
los papeles sucios.
Voy a morir sin ver la nieve
qué hubiéramos adelantado bajo la nieve harinosa
esa pequeña aventura en nuestra luz:
el paso de un astro, la carrera de una estrella.

Estos días van a ser imaginados
por los dioses y los adolescentes que pedirán estos días
para ellos.
Y se borrarán los nombres y las fechas
y nuestros desatinos
y quedará la luz, bróder, la luz
y no otra cosa.

La vida ajena

Si este papel ya ha sido escrito
sobre otra mesa, debajo de otra oscuridad
que respiramos juntos, qué voracidad
por las palabras reúne las palabras que repito

aquí: he estado dando
palos de ciego / fabricando

and his pockets were full of useless keys
and an utter dread of solitude.

I'd be the same maybe if I were a bookkeeper
or if I were Dutch and knew magic
and if at my life's end nostalgia
passed my hands over the ice.

Job could rest without embarrassing himself
over this seasnail
and the savannas could be full of alfalfa
or bright thermal waters or log cabins.
Who would we be then / down the street
maybe we would buy the morning paper
falling asleep
and mandarins and sweet bread.

Our children's children will want these romantic years
and they will look for the letter in the registry, our records
the dirty papers.
I am going to die without seeing the snow
what advances we would have made under the flour-like snow
that small adventure in our light
an astral pass, the track of a star.

These days are going to be imagined
by the gods and the adolescents who will beg for these days
for themselves.
And the names and the dates will be erased
and our follies
and the light, brother, the light will remain
and nothing else.

The Other Life

If the writing on this paper was done
at another table, in another darkness
that we breathe together, what a hunger
for words is fulfilled in the words I repeat

here: I have been tapping my
way in the dark / fabricating

mi historia sobre estos canalizos, estoy
de nuevo dando calladas

a cambio de respuestas o es que voy
contigo en otras vidas: mucho antes
de haberse levantado esta ciudad

nos estuvo acechando con sus encrucijadas
y la inseguridad
que aleja y aproxima los seres semejantes.

La hora de comer

Éstos son los plátanos que ha mandado
mi hermana desde Oriente

y un poco de café porque imagina
que a la hora de comer cae la penuria

como un relámpago y la memoria
camina hacia los pueblos

buscando la señal, la cueva humana
con los perros ladrando alrededor

de las iglesias y los magos plomizos
entre el ruedo de mosquitos y la natividad.

A la hora de comer
cuando el plátano chirría

y la conserva da un golpe, mete su arponazo
en nuestra tarde brevemente histórica

una de estas en que llovizna siempre
la familia anterior espera nuestra prueba

un signo de calor en nuestra cueva humana
entonces uno apaga el globo de la luz

duerme como el hombre más viejo
como el príncipe

cansado de probar sus mejores caballos.

my history along these lines, I am
once again coming up with silence

in exchange for answers or that I'm
with you in other lives: long before
this city came about

it was lying in wait for us at its crossroads
and the insecurity
that separates and attracts similar beings.

Dinner Time

These are the plantains my
sister sent me from Oriente

and a little coffee because she imagines
that at dinner time poverty descends

like a lightning flash and memory
heads for the towns

looking for the signal, the human cave
with the dogs barking all around

the churches and the leaden wisemen
inside the ring of mosquitoes and the nativity.

At dinner time
when the plantain sizzles

and the preserves are perfect, harpooning
our brief historic afternoon

one of those drizzling afternoons
the family ahead waits for us to take our turn

a sign of warmth in our human cave
then one turns off the light bulb

and sleeps like the oldest man
like a prince

tired of trying out his best horses.

Translated by George Economou and Luis Cortest

Frank Abel Dopico

El correo de la noche

Mis piernas van tras el correo de la noche.
Un enemigo tiende su mano miserable, ayuda mi carrera, luego me hace
    polvo con su mano apagada.
Las casas huyen grises y una estrella abandona su casa de la noche
y anda con sus bártulos a cuestas. Una estrella vuelve
a su casa de la noche
y anda por el jardín, mediodormida.
El ciudadano que soy va tras su noticia. Apedreando al que fui.
Quiero saber cómo está Mayra, qué le hablan sus ojos al recuerdo.

El correo de la noche atraviesa edificios, irrumpe en plazas moribundas.
Sus remos son caballos silvestres como los ojos de Mayra.
Alguien cruza mordisqueando sus dedos. Alguien (y una carta) entró en la
    oscuridad.
Pasan los novios, humeantes cuerpos, y el reloj se clava sus agujas.
A dos cuadras de mí el anciano espera que esté completo su rebaño.
Un hombre esconde el espejo donde se va a mirar mañana.

Mis piernas siguen los ecos de la noche.
Soy un bufón, esquivo ese color dulce de la primavera
porque dentro llevo los charcos de su lluvia y puedo florecer,
y es indiscreto florecer, uno tan noble,
tan bueno que es uno así de solo,
con mi tierno diablo y mi dios tan solo y pobrecito.
Quiero poner la vida como trampa,
criar conmigo al rey que nunca seré, a los reyes sonámbulos, los que con
    cielo y pan hacen el amor sin manifiestos.
Busco una noticia, busco el puente que hicieron los héroes para mí,
y siempre está más lejos, está en el mismo sitio de los héroes,
debo hacer algo más que comerme estas naranjas,
debo inventar un flamboyán o algo amenazante,
el puente me espera, nos espera,
tantas flores mediocres aplastan los caballos
que el correo va lento, los caballos sangran pero yo los aplaudo.
Los caballos resbalan, rehenes de la luna,
dejan su lamido triste en mi pupila.

Frank Abel Dopico

Night Mail

My legs follow the night mail.
An enemy holds out his miserable hand, helps me on my way, then turns
me to dust with his dead hand.
Ashen, the houses flee, and a star steps from its house of night
and walks off with its things on its back. A star returns
to its house of night
and strolls in the garden, half asleep.
Citizen that I am I follow its news, stoning the one who left.
I want to know how Mayra is doing, what her eyes say when she remembers.

The night mail penetrates buildings, erupts in moribund plazas.
Its oars are wild horses like Mayra's eyes.
Someone crosses, chewing his fingers. Someone (and a letter) went into the
dark.
Lovers pass, smoldering bodies, and the clock nails down its hands.
Two blocks from me the old man waits for all his flock to gather.
A man hides the mirror where he plans to see himself tomorrow.

My legs follow the echoes of night.
I'm a fool, I shun the sweet color of spring
because within me I carry its puddles and I can flower,
and flowering is so indiscreet, I'm so noble,
so good alone,
with my tender devil, and my pitiful solitary god.
I'd like to set life like a trap,
to invent from my self the king I'll never be, sleepwalking kings who make
love not manifestos out of sky and bread.
I'm looking for news, I'm looking for the bridge the heroes built for me,
and it's always a little farther off, where the heroes are,
I ought to do something more than eat these oranges,
I ought to invent a flame tree, or something threatening,
the bridge awaits me, awaits us,
so many tacky flowers cake the horses
that the mail cart is slow, the horses bleed but I applaud them.
The horses slip, hostages of the moon,
they leave on my eye their sad tongues.

El correo de la noche puede ser asaltado
pero va con cicatrices que recuerdan al sol.

En un lugar de mi vida hay un revólver.

Mercadillo de máscaras

Recuerdo el mercadillo de máscaras.
Llegaban mujeres, niños, hombres, perros
desde todos los mundos conocidos.
Traían sus máscaras bajo el brazo
envueltas en periódicos, calientitas como panes.
La duda, el paso definitivo
era cruzar el umbral del mercadillo.
El himen.
Por eso, antes de dar el paso,
se pasaban un día y una noche borrachos y peleándose.
Despidiéndose.
Ensor, quien nunca decidió cruzar,
jugaba en las afueras con un aro dormido.
Un niño ordeñaba su reloj hasta sangrarle las manos.
Entonces, cuando estaban seguros,
compraban a la entrada del mercadillo
su boleto de ida.
Ni payasos ni noria ni pócimas oscuras:
sólo la tierra moja los pasos musicados.
Cada cual era el feriante de sí mismo
y ofrecía su máscara a cambio de otra máscara.
Recuerdo el mercadillo con sus praderas súbitas.

El regateo de ojos, de bocas, de narices, de orejas y de párpados.
El intercambio lento, el sudor de las máscaras.
El por favor. El exijo. Las estafas. El paseante. El ladronzuelo.

De cuando en cuando
conviene recordar el mercadillo.
No que estuviera mal.
No su clandestinidad.
Conviene recordar esa lúcida angustia
de ser otros.

The night mail could be attacked
but it goes on with scars that recall the sun.

Somewhere in my life there is a gun.

Mask Market

I remember the little market of masks.
Women, children, men, dogs came there
from all the known worlds.
They carried their masks under their arms
wrapped in newspapers, warm as fresh bread.
The doubt, the definitive step
was to cross the market's threshold.
Its hymen.
So, before taking that step,
they spent a day and a night drunk and fighting.
Saying goodbye.
Ensor, who never decided to cross,
played outside with a sleeping hoop.
A boy kept milking his clock til his hands bled.
Then, when they were ready,
they bought their ticket
at the market entrance.
No clowns, no ferris wheel, no dark potions:
only the ground dampens the musical steps.
Each was the fairgoer in the fair of himself
and offered to exchange his mask for another mask.
I remember the market with its sudden meadows.

The haggling over eyes, mouths, noses, ears and eyelids.
The slow exchange, the sweating masks.
The please. The demand. The scams. The passer-by. The thievery.

Once in a while
it's good to remember the little market.
Not that it was bad.
Not its secrecy.
It's good to remember that lucid distress
wanting to be someone else.

A mi padre

Quisiera morir como mi padre
enamorado.
Después de plantar
todos los árboles que pudo
—algunos le nacieron rosales,
otros le salieron hijos—,
siguió en el centro de mi madre,
quien le ha hecho viajar
a las estrellas.
Sabía, mi padre,
que cuando su corazón se detuviera,
no le iba quedar más corazón
que el de mi madre.
aferrado a sus labios,
pendiente de su voz de los domingos
como un astronauta que descubre
que ha sido el amor
y no la rabia
quien le llevó a los cielos.
No tenía más corazón que el de mi madre.
Y él lo conocía.
Sabía que podía quedarse allí
a vivir
toda su muerte.

Francois Villón

Quería escribir sed pero escribí aguacero
y, a partir de ahí,
mis manos se llenaron de hierbas
y abejorros
y desde la tierra emergió
un olor a espalda dulce
que me llamaba culpable
de su sed.
Abandoné el poema
y fui a expiar mi culpa.

To My Father

I'd like to die in love
like my father.
After he'd planted
all the trees he could
—some came up as roses,
others as children—
he stayed in my mother's center
and she made him travel
to the stars.
He knew, my father,
that when it was time for his heart to stop
he would have no other heart
but my mother's.
Fused to her lips,
hanging on her Sunday words
like an astronaut who discovers
that it was love
not rage
that raised him to the heavens.
He had no other heart but my mother's.
And he knew it.
He knew he could stay there
to live
all his death long.

François Villon

I meant to write thirst but I wrote cloudburst
and thereafter
my hands filled with grasses
and bumblebees
and up from the earth came
an aroma like a sweet back
that told me I was guilty
of its thirst.
I abandoned the poem
and went to expiate my guilt.

Cuando pasan los años

Entre los restos de un amor como entre los restos de un incendio
pueden aparecer naranjas medio buenas, silencios intocados,
respiraciones que el fuego no pudo atrapar y destejer.
La policía del olvido nos deja pasar y nos pregunta
si al menos algo se ha salvado y uno jura que no
pero buscando en los escombros encontramos un reloj vacío
y el banco de un parque donde las parejas jugaban a ser ciegos
y se miraban con manos y milagros.
Entre los restos de un amor quedan siempre las cosas
que no se pueden colgar como un teléfono
o romper como una foto.
Queda el giro de una mano señalando las ventanas
y el ladrido con que los perros hacen redonda la luna.
Si se vuelve al lugar de los hechos
de nada servirán los guantes blancos ni la mascarilla
ni la lógica ni el viejo abecedario de los hombres.
El lugar de los hechos siempre es una historia
y las historias de amor son estrellas fugaces,
fantasmas que atraviesan las mejillas del cielo
como si fueran la saliva de una lengua rotunda.
Como si fueran lágrimas.

Alberto Rodríguez Tosca

Ojos de perro azul

mira cuando puedas
escríbeme unas líneas en un vitral
de cualquier ciudad que digan más
o menos el mundo rota se marea o
los relojes adelantan el fin o
cuando pregunten por mí en cualquier
esquina donde tú estés esperando
una respuesta diles que estoy perdido
entre los humos las miradas los abrazos

When the Years Pass

Among the remains of a love as among what's left after fire
you might find half-good oranges, untouched silences,
breaths the fire could not trap and unravel.
The oblivion police lets us pass and asks us
if anything has been saved and we swear not,
but searching among the embers we find an empty clock
and a park bench where pairs of lovers used to play at being blind
seeing each other with hands and miracles.
In the ruins of a love there are always things
that can't be hung up like a telephone
or torn apart like a photograph.
Still there—the wave of a hand pointing to the windows
and the dogs barking that made the moon round.
If you return to the scene
neither the white gloves nor the mask will be of any use,
nor logic nor mankind's ancient spelling book.
The place where it happened is always a story
and love stories are shooting stars,
ghosts that fly across the cheeks of the heavens
like saliva from a fat tongue.
Like tears.

Translated by Chris Brandt

Alberto Rodríguez Tosca

Eyes of the Blue Dog

look when you can
write me a few lines on a stained-glass window
from any city saying more
or less that the world spins gets dizzy or
clocks bring the end closer or
when they ask about me on any
corner where you're waiting
for an answer tell them I'm lost
amid the smoke embraces glances

de esa misma ciudad en que tú escribiste
más o menos te amo pero que vuelvo diles
que vuelvo y diles también que el mundo
se marea rotan los relojes estallan en sus cajas.

cuando aprendas a delimitar un sueño
de una verdad avísame para olvidarte avísame
para soñar otro real espacio donde poner
la cabeza la alegría los instantes ávidos
de confundirlo todo la verdad el sueño.

cuando no sea tuya la gloria de la locura
y necesites dormir en paz con dios y conmigo
yo encontraré las palabras que escribiste para mí
en los mostradores de la ciudad y haré con ellas
adivinanzas mortales nadie nadie sabrá
qué dicen qué guardaron para después
adivina adivinador nadie sabrá que tú
te paseas por las costas del fin buscándome y yo
también me busco y no nos encontramos.

Suma transitoria

Ahora llegamos al momento
en que se abre una puerta
y aparece un fantasma
alegre y desnudo.

Vuelvo al lugar del crimen. Yo estuve ausente y todo pasó
pero más que eso: nada dejó de pasar. Yo
estuve ausente y no se inmutaron las lluvias, los cimientos,
la gente que debía morir, las palabras que se debieron decir,
los silencios fáciles y una conversación bajo un portal
de la calle República. Yo estuve ausente y todo pasó:
eso puede significar algo, aunque tal vez no sea más
que haber estado ausente . . .

Con una mano tendida sobre
el hombro de otro que
pregunta ¿pasó algo en mi
ausencia?

of the city in which you wrote
I love you more or less but I'm coming back tell them
I'm coming back and tell them also that the world
gets dizzy the clocks spin explode in their cases.

when you learn how to define a dream
of a truth tell me so that I can forget you tell me
so that I can dream another real space to rest
my head my joy excited moments
when everything the truth the dream is confounded.

when the glory of madness isn't yours
and you need to sleep in peace with god and me
I'll find the words you wrote for me
on the shop counters in the city and create with them
mortal riddles no one no one will know
when they say what they put aside for later
make a guess no one will know that you
stroll on the shores of the ending where you search for me
and I search for myself and we don't find each other.

Transitory Sum

> *Now we arrive at the moment*
> *when a door is opened*
> *and a happy naked*
> *ghost appears.*

I return to the scene of the crime. I was gone and everything happened,
but more important, nothing stopped happening. I
was gone and the rain, the foundations,
the people who should have died, the words that should have been said,
the easy silences and a conversation under a portal
on Calle Republica, carried on. I was gone and everything happened:
maybe that means something, or maybe only
that I'd been away . . .

> *With a hand*
> *on the shoulder of someone who*
> *asks, "Did something happen*
> *while I was away?"*

Cierro los ojos. Veo:
ésta es la nueva época. Animales nobles
e imaginarios pastan en los jardines de la misma
ciudad que un día pudo ser distinta; peces
sin alas rumian su locura entre las multitudes
que llegaron tarde a la repartición de las palabras verdaderas;
y eso también pudiera significar algo, si no fuera
porque significa: peces y animales coqueteando
con los primeros mensajes de la nueva época. Ésta es
(y fue puntual) la nueva época. Con su viento y su calle,
con su diario y su mapa: mírenla entrar al mismo cuerpo
que una vez se volvió para no oír cuando decía "yo soy
la nueva época". Porque una vez lo dijo y mi cuerpo tembló.
Y dijo que llegaría inesperadamente y mi cuerpo
no sólo tembló, sino que se abrió paso
entre los cuerpos que no oían y no dijo "yo soy el cuerpo
que oyó decir, que se puso a temblar cuando la nueva época
era todavía un rostro en el agua, una pregunta
en los labios . . . "

> *Y ningún diálogo fue más*
> *transparente.*

Y cuando cierro los ojos y veo,
descubro a otros cuerpos como el mío abriéndose paso,
ciegos y silenciosos, avergonzados de haberse reconocido
unos a otros y saludando al mismo tiempo con la mano
enferma: no estaban solos los cuerpos que, como el mío,
conocieron de antemano los puentes que habrían de devolverlos
a la aventura de cuyo origen alguna vez como locos escapamos.

> *Sí. Todo pasa en la ausencia*
> *del que pregunta.*

Pero yo estuve ausente y la noche pasó y la mañana pasó
y un tren cargado de pasajeros sin rumbo fijo pasó
y el maquinista sacó la cabeza por la ventanilla y me dijo
que yo nunca debí perder ese tren que pasaba . . . ¿Ya dije
que ésta es la nueva época? Entonces nadie se asombre
de que los trenes pasen y las noches y las mañanas pasen
y los maquinistas sean mis antepasados muertos
desfilando sobre mi conciencia y balbuceando palabras

I close my eyes. I see:
This is the new age. Noble imaginary
animals graze in the gardens of the city
that one day could have been different; fish
without wings mutter their madness among the crowds
that arrived late to the distribution of the true words;
which might also mean something, if it didn't
already mean merely fish and animals flirting
with the first messages of the new age. This is
the new age (and it arrived on schedule). With its wind and its street,
its newspaper and its map: look at it enter the body
that once turned away so as not to hear it announce "I am
the new age." Because it said that and my body trembled.
And it said it would arrive unforeseen and my body
not only trembled, but cleared a path
between bodies that heard not, nor did I say "I am the body
that heard, that began to tremble when the new age
was still a face on the water, a question
on its lips . . . "

> *And no dialogue was more*
> *transparent.*

And when I close my eyes and see,
I discover other bodies like mine clearing a path,
blind and silent, ashamed of having recognized
and greeted each other at the same time with a feeble
hand: the bodies were not alone and, like mine,
already knew the bridges that would bring them back
to the adventure from whose origin we once escaped like madmen.

> *Yes. Everything happens while the questioner*
> *is away.*

But I was away and the night passed and the morning passed
and a train full of passengers with no destination passed
and the engineer put his head out the window and told me
never to miss that train . . . Have I already said
that this is the new age? No one should be surprised
that trains pass and nights and mornings pass
and that the engineers are my dead ancestors
parading through my awareness muttering useless

inútiles . . . Ya lo dije: ésta es la nueva época, y soy
el mismo que lo ignora ¿Con cuál de los dos
quiere salir a recorrer el país? Será como adentrarse
en un espejo que dice la verdad . . . ¿pero a quién
le interesa un espejo que diga la verdad?
Ésta es, ésta no es, sino la insinuación
de un juego menos ingenuo que los otros: aquí el ausente,
aunque parte, aunque regresa, permanece en su puesto
como un soldado decidido a morir por el nombre de una mujer
escrito en el diario de campaña de su enemigo.

Omar Pérez López

Contribuciones a un idea rudimentaria de nación

En las volátiles noches de un invierno
que la naturaleza convalida con magnanimidad
el cubano se entrena para la diversión o para la amnesia,
muy injustamente se supone a veces que son la misma cosa
lleva dulces a Dios, fermenta los dialectos
combate la cirrosis con frutos en almíbar, hace comercio;
se dictamina entonces que El Cubano inventa.
En las pesadas coreografías de un verano
que la naturaleza autoriza, ya, con suspicacia
va el cubano hasta el océano con ofrendas y arpones,
muy injustamente se supone a veces que son la misma cosa
enumera con los dedos las bajas, ejerce la infracción
lleva las manos a los bolsillos, jura y compromete;
se diagnostica entonces que El Cubano inventa.
Asistamos al territorio improbable
donde el cubano y El Cubano conversan viril, pastosamente
allí conoceremos en qué travesías, en qué extraños parajes
en qué trueques
hemos contraído tanto ingenio.

words . . . As I said: this is the new age, and I'm
the one who doesn't know it. With which of the two
do you want to cross the country? It will be like
entering a mirror that tells the truth . . . But who is
interested in a mirror that tells the truth?
This is it, this isn't it, or rather, it's the hint
of a game that's less innocent than the others: in which he who was away,
whether he leaves or returns, stays at his post
like a soldier resolved to die for the name of a woman
written in his enemy's campaign diary.

Translated by Margaret Carson

Omar Pérez López

Contributions to a Rudimentary Idea of a Nation

In the volatile nights of a winter
affirmed magnanimously by nature
the cuban trains himself for amusement or amnesia,
sometimes unjustly thought to be the same
he carries sweets to God, arouses dialects,
combats cirrhosis with preserved fruit, does business;
that's why it's said that The Cuban fabricates.
In the heavy choreographies of a summer
authorized by nature, now, with deep mistrust,
the cuban goes to the ocean with offerings and harpoons,
sometimes unjustly thought to be the same
he counts casualties on his fingers, practices the infraction
raises his hands to his pockets, takes an oath and commits himself;
so the diagnosis is that The Cuban fabricates.
Let's attend the improbable territory
where the cuban and The Cuban talk man to man,
there we will learn to what crossroads, to what strange places,
to what exchanges
we have committed so much cleverness.

Cunda, el herrero . . .

Cunda, el herrero, en el bosquecillo de mangos
ofrece al Hombre Infinito algo que comer

platos moteados de leche
pimienta, anís estrellado

para quien siega el floreciente yo
posa su pie sobre el enano
de alas de mariposa

platos cruentos, así como la mano
no vacila ante los condimentos

para el Sentado mañana y tarde
en el cráter de los nenúfares

carne impura como siempre
es la carne, cocinada
con mis ojos en sus ojos

carne de animal salvaje
proscripto como el espíritu

Y he aquí que la va aceptando
sin decir esta boca es mía.

Imprecaciones, adivinanzas

No en balde ardía.

*

Se absorbe a veces con el humo perfumado
un poco de ceniza.

*

¿Mirar adónde antes de cruzar?
Atravesaré como un perro cansado.

*

En cuanto a mí
divino blasfemar.

*

Cunda, the blacksmith . . .

Cunda, the blacksmith, in the mango grove,
offers the Infinite Man something to eat

plates sprinkled with milk,
pepper, star anise

for he who harvests the flowering I
who rests his foot upon the dwarf
with butterfly wings

bloody plates, like the hand
that does not hesitate to offer condiments

morning and evening to the Seated One
in the bowl of water lilies

unclean meat as always
is the meat, cooked
my eyes in its eyes

meat of a wild beast
forbidden like the spirit

And there he is accepting it
without owning up.

Invocations, Riddles

I did not burn in vain.

*

a bit of ash is sometimes absorbed with perfumed smoke.

*

Looking both ways before crossing?
I will cross like a tired dog.

*

As for me
holy blasphemy.

*

Rutina del misterio
imposible sin ella.

*

Los gatos a la vía
los santos a su ataúd.

Saludo de los perros

Al llegado, al que produce llagas
al que las cura
tantos granos de maíz tostado en el cuenco de la luna
tantas luciérnagas en el tronco del flamboyán infectado
los perros, los olvidados príncipes
los guerreros echados de la casa del colibrí
no más guerra al cuerpo que tiembla sin comprender
al pensamiento que piensa sin especular
al hombre-perro en el espejo del corazón
no más tratados
estiremos el espinazo hasta la galaxia más próxima
orinemos al pie de los volcanes
para revivir el magma se dan hierbas amargas
un mechón de carretera antigua
una oración a la Virgen María Despalilladora
diecisiete centavos en un tazón de piedra.

Las instituciones místicas del decoro

Hay un tigre que mira la televisión
sabe mirar lo que en el ojo se aquieta:
el paso
miríadas de peces en el manto estelar
luna que se quiebra   como el pan de Cristo
comemos de ese pan y de la luna
y los supuestos sobre los cuáles
toda la vida se asienta y fija
allí orina el tigre
no para delimitar ni poseer

The habit of mystery
impossible without her.

*

Cats in the street
saints in their caskets.

The Dogs' Greeting

To he of the open sores, who causes
who cures them
so many kernels of corn toasted in the bowl of the moon
so many glow worms in the trunk of the infested flame tree
the dogs, forgotten princes
warriors evicted from the house of the hummingbird
no more war in the body that trembles without understanding
the thought that's thought without speculation
about the man-dog in the heart's mirror
no more treaties
let us stretch our spines to the nearest galaxy
let us piss at the base of volcanoes
to revive the magma bitter grasses are given
a thread of an old road
a prayer to Our Lady the Despalilladora
seventeen cents in a stone basin.

The Mystical Institutions of Decorum

There's a tiger watching television
he knows to watch what calms his eye:
the path
myriads of fish in the starry mantle
a moon broken   like the bread of Christ
we eat of this bread and of the moon
and those assumed to be above them
all his life he remains in place
and there the tiger pisses
not to mark boundaries or possession

fecunda el humus universal
siente el hocico de nueva criatura aproximarse
orina entonces.
A lomos de tigre la princesa Vida
cabalga la noche de pétalos
de azucenas, dices   o tal vez de aquellas mil
diminutas azucenas reunidas en tu mano
ellas también sin nombre. Mas a fuerza de nombrar
conozco, olvido, me aproximo:
vida, azucena, sangre   y patria aún
al combate corred como la espuma
¡Cómo! sonríes   yaguaza sobre tigre
candil en el sepulcro de los dioses   muchachita
patria es.

      •

Las puertas son del corazón las manos
no son herméticas, mi sangre
amplias, acuchilladas puertas
Uno, dos, tres   corazón aquí
haya un tercer corazón   ahora escucha.

      •

Padezco un decoro encendido
Nube, llévate mi luz
Hay tanta capacidad en la nube
para captar la luz
Luna, aquiétala
Magnolia   no recuerdo
mas si nos aproxima   sea.

      •

Goce de lo sublime
en árbol, pan, libro, escarcha
¿para qué?
el amor   anestesia.

      •

Escucha el tercer corazón   escucha
el mío   se desenvuelve en lirio africano

but to fecundate the universal humus
he senses the snout of a new beast approaching
and he pisses.
On the back of a tiger Princess Life
rides through the night of petals
of lilies, you call it   or perhaps of those thousand
tiny lilies, also nameless,
gathered in your hand. But by naming
I know, I forget, I approach myself:
life, lily, blood   and even homeland
oh rush like the foam into battle
Please! you smile   a stork on a tiger
an oil lamp in the tomb of the gods   a little girl
is the homeland.

Hands are the doors of the heart
they're not hermetic, my blood
wide, smooth doors
One, two, three   a heart here
may there be a third heart   now listen.

I endure a burning decorum
Cloud, carry my light away
there's enough space in the cloud
to catch the light
Moon, calm it
Magnolia   I don't remember
but if it approach us   be.

Enjoy the sublime
in a tree, bread, book, frost
why?
love   anaesthesia.

Listen to the third heart   listen
to mine   it unfolds in the African iris

en espuma de niños se concentra
Escucho el tuyo   playa retoza
camino de profundidad leñosa flor señala
en el vientre de encendida virgen
y encendida virgen nos contempla.

El loco

• *a Stéphane*

Yo traigo la avalancha del marinero
que por mucho que viaja no llega a puerto.
Nadie lo salva, nadie lo premia
nadie le paga la mercancía.

Mira cómo
viene soplando por la montaña.
Mira cómo
llega volando por la mañana.
Es anormal   entre los mortales.
Es inmortal   entre los normales.

Yo traigo la camisa de Fuenteblanca
y el paraíso tiene cinco banderas
una en el cielo, cuatro en la Tierra
dos en la nube. Tres en el agua.

Mira cómo
viene volando por la montaña.
Mira cómo
llega soplando por la mañana.
Es anormal   entre los mortales.
Es inmortal   entre los normales.

Si al loco se le ocurre no llegar a puerto
se queda en la excelencia de la cachimba
no tiene prisa en la encrucijada
si le parece no llega nunca.

Mira cómo
llega volando por la mañana.
Mira cómo

it is concentrated in the foam of children
Listen to your own   a frolicking beach
a path of woody depth marked by a flower
in the belly of a fiery virgin
and a fiery virgin watches us.

The Madman

• to Stéphane

I bring the avalanche of the sailor
who after long travels won't come to port.
No one saves him, no one rewards him
no one pays for the merchandise.

See how
he comes coursing down the mountain.
See how
he arrives flying through the morning.
He's abnormal   among mortals.
He's immortal   among the normal.

I bring the shirt from Fuenteblanca
and paradise has five flags
one in the sky, four on Earth
two in the cloud. Three in the water.

See how
he comes flying down the mountain.
See how
he arrives coursing through the morning.
He's abnormal   . among mortals.
He's immortal   among the normal.

If it occurred to the madman not to come to port
he would stay within the pipe's excellence
he doesn't hurry at the crossroads
if that's what he thinks he'll never come.

See how
he arrives flying through the morning.
See how

viene soplando por la montaña.
Es anormal   entre los mortales.
Es inmortal   entre los normales.

Antonio José Ponte

Un poco a la manera de Ismael

Se desprendió una nube, floreció el rododendro.
El estiércol humeaba en su nimbo de santo.
Saltó el gallo, la sangre,
se sublevó la lengua:
déjame echarte adentro mi moneda de leche.

Pasó el viento y abrió
las piernas de la hierba.
Se alzó el último oleaje del verano.
Déjame echarte adentro de mi moneda de leche,
llamarte perra arriba, llamarte alondra abajo.

Sobre el planeta

Una pluma caída y la cabeza
es el nido abandonado.

Una nube en la piel, un desgajado cirro
y tres gotas de lluvia tatuadas.

Un soplo hacia los pelos que aureolan la tetilla.
Cuero de otro animal que el sudor gasta.

Y un cabello de pubis, caprichoso dibujo,
como brizna de hierba entre los labios.

Canción

Pasé un verano entero escuchando ese disco.
Para que la emoción no se le fuera

he comes coursing along the mountain.
He's abnormal   among mortals.
He's immortal   among the normal.

Translated by Mark Weiss

Antonio José Ponte

Somewhat in the Style of Ismael

A cloud detached itself, the rhododendron bloomed.
The manure steamed in its saintly halo.
The rooster leapt, the blood as well,
the tongue rebelled:
let me drop my coin of milk inside you.

The wind passed by and spread
the legs of grass apart.
The final swell of summer rose.
Let me drop my coin of milk inside you,
call you she-dog above, call you skylark below.

Regarding the Planet

A fallen quill and the head
is the abandoned nest.

A cloud on the skin, a shredded cirrus
and three tattooed drops of rain.

Air blown at the hairs surrounding the nipple.
The skin of another animal corroded by sweat.

And a pubic hair, a fanciful sketch,
like a blade of grass between the lips.

Song

I spent a whole summer listening to that record.
To keep the feeling from disappearing

lo escuchaba una vez cada día.
Si me quedaba hambriento salía a caminar.

A su manera la luz cantaba esa canción,
la cantó el mar, la dijo
un pájaro.
Lo pensé en un momento:
todo me está pasando para que me enamore.

Luego se fue el verano.
El pájaro
más seco que la rama
no volvió a abrir el pico.

Un bosque, una escalera

En las ramas movidas a su paso hubo algo teatral,
hubo un presentimiento de escenario
y luego nada.
Se perdió entre dos árboles, bajaba una escalera,
tocó tu rostro con sus dedos finos llamándote Príncipe.

Si el minuto fuera ese escalón donde se han detenido
ustedes dos besándose
y sintieras aún el perfume que ha levantado el viento
cuando penetra ella entre dos árboles.

¿Qué ensaya el bosque con su cuerpo adentro,
sombra blanca entre ramas eléctricas?
¿Y qué haces tú sino amarla,
perseguir el minuto que ya no sabes dónde fue
—un bosque, una escalera—
pero que crece en ti casi hasta ahogarte?

La silla en escapada

En la silla dejamos nuestras ropas
y la silla escapó.
La doncella de hilo y el herrero sin cuerpo escapaban.
El techo estalló en nubes,
las paredes se hicieron fugitivos rebaños cardinales:
humo en el norte, nieve del este, ceniza al sur,
negrura hacia el ocaso.

I would listen to it once a day.
When I got hungry I would go for a walk.

In its own way, the light sang that song,
the ocean sang it, a bird
spoke it.
At one point I thought:
all this is happening to me so that I will fall in love.

Then summer disappeared.
The bird
drier than the branch
never opened its beak again.

A Forest, a Stairway

There was something theatrical in the rustling of branches
as she passed, there was a hint of a stage
and then nothing.
She disappeared between two trees, descended a flight of stairs,
touched your face with her slender fingers, calling you Prince.

If a minute were that stair on which the two of you have paused,
kissing each other,
and still you smelled the perfume stirred up by the wind
as she passes between two trees.

What is the forest rehearsing with her body inside,
white shadow among electrical branches?
And what are you doing but loving her,
pursuing the minute you can no longer trace
a forest, a stairway
but which grows inside you until you nearly choke?

Chair on the Run

We left our clothes on the chair
and the chair ran off.
The thread maiden and the bodiless blacksmith ran off.
The roof burst into clouds,
the walls turned to a compass of fugitive flocks:
smoke in the north, snow from the east, ashes to the south,
blackness westward.

Buscamos nuestras ropas—la doncella, el herrero—
en los bosques metálicos donde los grillos lijan.

Un animal con voz los había visto:
él celebraba su pelo inexistente,
ella en respuesta besaba sus tatuajes.
Volvieron las paredes,
se posó el techo,
regresaba la silla,
nada de los amantes.
Fueron tela huidiza que el río se lleva,
fueron manga en el aire.

Augurios

Mis manos entre las pocas frutas
palpan la tetilla en que terminan,
reconocen bajo la mesa al animal
que no adivina cuánto deseo sus entrañas.

Si a mí me hubieran hecho de aquel signo
que sólo es bueno para los de mi sangre,
no estaría entre frutas, entre moscas,
entre vasos de té reverenciando.

Tú me dices
"Una ciudad sucede a otra.
Un pez se moja en una y otra agua".
Yo que no tengo asco de las vísceras
yo que no juego sucio, abro su cuerpo.
Leo en su hígado hojas de té al fondo de los vasos.
Esas hojas dibujan un caballo destinado a pisar su propio estiércol,
a oler en las paredes sus bufidos.
Viene el caballo y dice
"Un pájaro canta en el muro del oriente.
El sol llega y me monta.
Un pájaro canta en el muro del poniente.
Vuelve la frialdad.
Un pájaro canta en el muro del oriente.
El sol me monta.
Oigo cantar desde el muro contrario".

We search for our clothes, the maiden, the blacksmith
in the metallic forests where crickets rub their sandpaper.

An animal with a voice had seen them:
he was praising her nonexistent hair,
she was kissing his tattoos in response.
The walls returned,
the rooftop perched,
the chair was on its way,
no word on the lovers.
They were fleeting fabric the river takes,
they were a sleeve in the wind.

Auguries

Amid the scattering of fruit my hands
squeeze the nipples at their tips,
recognize the animal under the table
that can't imagine how much I want its entrails.

If I had been created under that sign
that only benefits those of my blood,
I wouldn't be here offering reverence
amid fruit, flies, cups of tea.

You tell me
"One city follows another.
A fish swims through many waters."
I who am not disgusted by viscera,
I who never play dirty open its body.
I read in its liver tea leaves at the bottom of cups.
Those leaves reveal a horse destined to step in its own dung,
to smell its bellowing on the walls.
The horse comes and says
"A bird sings on the eastern wall.
The sun rises and mounts me.
A bird sings on the western wall.
The chill returns.
A bird sings on the eastern wall.
The sun mounts me.
I hear a song from the opposite wall."

Tú no conoces este ceño enemigo.
A ti la luz de agosto no hace más que mimarte.
Yo que nací en agosto no me siento tan dueño.
"Hay que apartar las hojas"
me dices.
"Esperar.
Enlaces y traiciones,
bautizos
y las mismas esperas,
las esperas de siempre".

Hemos hecho un oficio de beber agua parda,
de dorarnos,
de pasar entre cuerpos,
de dar con la cuchara en los costados.
Los pájaros que anunciarían tu ida
vuelan ahora frente al mar,
hacen sus círculos,
su fiesta aún sobre nosotros
como otros pájaros que vi dorándose en la tarde.
Otros pájaros un domingo
con la misma certeza de que nos dicen algo.

Asiento en las ruinas

Madrugadas en vilo de mil novecientos ochenta y ocho
donde acalladas mis vísceras remotas
tomóme la memoria de lo muerto,
memoria de familia vertical creciente.
¿Adónde iba mi infancia,
dónde estaban quienes prometieron segunda corona:
lo que el deseo no persiga,
lo que apenas intenten las palabras?
Madrugadas en que escribí
"¿Es necesario que yo escriba en verso
para apartarme del resto de los hombres?"
(Lautréamont)
Soplaba el viento de los manicomios,
¿dónde estaban quienes prometieron segunda corona:
lo que el deseo no persiga,
lo que apenas intenten las palabras?

You don't know this scowling enemy.
The August light does nothing but indulge you.
I who was born in August don't feel so confident.
"You must brush the leaves aside,"
you say.
"Wait.
Unions and betrayals,
baptisms
and the usual waiting,
the same old waiting."

We have become adept at drinking brown water,
at gilding ourselves,
at passing between bodies,
at sticking them in the side with a spoon.
The birds that would herald your departure
now fly at the edge of the sea,
they wheel about,
their celebration still above us
like other birds I've seen gilding themselves in the afternoon.
Other birds one Sunday
equally sure they are telling us something.

A Seat in the Ruins

Daybreaks poised in the air in nineteen hundred and eighty-eight
when my distant viscera were hushed
I was seized by the memory of the dead,
memory of a growing vertical family.
Where was my childhood going?
Where were those who had promised the second crown:
what desire does not pursue,
what words barely attempt?
Daybreaks when I wrote
"Must I write in verse
to separate myself from other men?"
(Lautréamont)
The wind from the madhouses was blowing.
Where were those who had promised the second crown:
what desire does not pursue,
what words barely attempt?

¿Es necesario apartarme de los hombres para escribir en verso?
Madrugadas en vilo de mil novecientos ochenta y ocho
con tu cabeza en mis manos.
Olía a bosque, nos maldecía un pájaro, era el fin de la tierra.
Cuántos paseos que haríanme más sabio,
cuánta luz, árbol, agua,
lo que una voz más justa llama vida,
ardió entonces para este entendimiento:
qué triste entre las manos,
como falsa plata que no morderé,
la cabeza de quien amaba.

Heriberto Hernández

Las paredes de vidrio

En este cuarto pesa demasiado la luz,
      las sombras son blanquísimas
      y no se pueden abrir las ventanas si aún no ha amanecido.
Una muchacha muy triste no podría sumergirse en las aguas,
      bordearlas,
      o decir que escucha una música transparente y muy húmeda.
Aquí no puede uno disfrazarse de ángel,
      no basta desnudarse.
A la mesa no pueden sentarse todos los que a veces no escuchan,
      no habrá comidas sobre manteles blancos,
      no vendrán juglares, ni citaristas, ni pájaros, ni peces.
La muchacha que estará tendida muy cerca de nosotros
      podrá estar desnuda, podrá estar dormida en la hierba
      o estar aún más desnuda si no se siente sola:
      pero nunca podría dividirse,
      pero no podría volar o ser una muchacha turbia,
      o tener nuestro pecho para decir que sueña;
      no podría soñar que habita un caracol y que a veces se pierde.
En este cuarto las sombras son muy blancas,
      algún día pudiesen pensar que son las nuestras y pedirles que canten,
      que se dejen caer.

Must I separate myself from men to write in verse?
Daybreaks poised in the air in nineteen hundred and eighty-eight
with your head in my hands.
It smelled like the forest, a bird cursed at us, it was the end of the earth.
How many outings that would make me wiser,
how much light, tree, water,
what a more virtuous voice calls life,
burning then for this understanding:
how sad between my hands,
like counterfeit coins I will not bite,
the head of the one I loved.

Translated by Mark Schafer

Heriberto Hernández

Glass Walls

In this room the light is too heavy,
  the shadows are bone-white
  and you can't open the windows before daylight.
The saddest of girls could not dive beneath these waters,
  skirt them,
  or declare she hears music transparent and soggy.
Here there's no impersonating an angel,
  and it's not enough to undress.
Those who sometimes don't listen may not sit at this table,
  there will be no dinners on white tablecloths,
  no jugglers, nor zither players, nor birds, nor fish.
The girl who will be lying down next to us
  might be naked, might be sleeping in the grass
  or nakeder still if she senses she's not alone:
  but she could never divide herself,
  nor fly nor be troubled,
  nor hold our breast to say she dreams;
  she couldn't dream she lives in a snail shell and sometimes loses
   her way.
In this room the shadows are very white,
  someday you might think they're ours and ask them to sing,
  to fall down.

Se pudiese pensar que a veces no dormimos,
  pero hablar del insomnio,
    eso puede impulsarnos a decir que la noche es un borde estrechísimo
en el que sólo se puede estar de espaldas.
Aquí alguna vez se habló de ciervos y figuras que lanzaban unas flechas muy
    curvas;
  pero todos pensaban en la música,
  pero todos querían animales más dóciles, figuras más heladas.
Una mañana trajeron una piedra,
  la pusieron muy alto, tan alto que a veces se volvía;
  nunca más pensamos en estar muy solos, muy oscuros,
  en tener unas ganas terribles de morder,
  un árbol parecido a esa forma en que a veces callábamos.
Entonces pensamos vender nuestra sonrisa,
  pero quién puede comprar algo que se deshace,
  pero quién puede morirse de tristeza con la sombra tan blanca.
En este cuarto pesa demasiado la luz,
  basta volverse,
  puede ser fácil soñar que estamos solos,
  que abrimos la ventana y nadie nos empuja, o nos recuerda lo dulce
    que fuera despeñarse.
Así, tan ebrios, pudiésemos pensar que somos los más desmemoriados
  y salir con el pecho del suicida, con la caja del músico;
  entonces estaríamos tranquilos
  aunque nadie contara que volvimos muy sucios,
  derribamos los muros, rompimos los pisos
  y gritamos a todos que la ventana fue una mentira muy dulce, muy azul;
  aunque nadie contara que tuvimos un poco de miedo,
  que el espejo
  empezaba a mostrarnos las sombras más oscuras.

Fábula del delfín y la sombra del pájaro

Sentado entre dos muertos, la sombra del pájaro en vuelo convertida, sombra
    sobre la sombra;
  como herida sentado entre dos muertos: la cerveza espuma oleada
    sobre el pecho
  y a nuestro lado dos muertos punzando los rostros de la conversación.
La verdad no es el vuelo del pájaro, es el plumaje penetrando la ambigüedad
    del canto,

One could think that sometimes we don't sleep,
    but to talk of insomnia,
        that might impel us to say the night is the narrowest of margins
    where we can exist only by turning away.
Once at this place they spoke of stags and shapes that loosed bent arrows;
    but everyone was thinking about music,
    everyone wanted tamer animals, shapes more frozen.
One morning they brought a stone,
    and set it very high, so high that from time to time it turned;
    never again did we think of being solitary, dark,
    of our terrible desire to bite,
    a tree like that shape where at times we stayed silent.
Then we thought about selling our smile,
    but who could buy something that can disappear,
    who could die of sadness when the shadows are so white.
In this room the light is too heavy,
    turning around would be enough,
    it could be easy to dream we're alone,
    that we open the window and no one pushes us or reminds us how
        sweet it would be to jump.
That way, drunk, we could imagine we are the least remembered
    and take off with the suicide's heart, the musician's box;
    then we'd be calm
    though no one would tell how we came back filthy,
    and threw down the walls, tore out the floors
    and shouted to all that the window was a sweet blue lie;
    though none would reveal that we'd been a little afraid,
    that the mirror
    was beginning to show us the darkest shadows.

Fable of the Dolphin and the Bird's Shadow

Seated between two corpses, the bird's shadow transformed into flight,
    shadow on shadow;
    seated like a wound between two corpses: beer foams up in a wave
    chest-high
    and by our side two corpses punching holes in the faces of
    conversation.
The truth is not the bird's flight, it's the plumage that penetrates the song's
    ambiguity,

el canto como un pequeño ruido acuchillado en el vacío del pecho.
En la jarra de los bebedores, la espuma de la cerveza como la voz del niño
      que entre dos muertes canta,
      es un ahuecamiento que va el doblez bordeando, un penetrar lento
      del plumaje en la oscura sordidez del sonido.
Viene el volatinero con las palabras del último golpearse, del último secreto
      impulso de estar ciego.
Todos alguna vez vimos su risa azul y el azul tras la risa del que sabe que ha
      recibido la última noticia;
      es el pañuelo, la estrella plateada en el pañuelo que ha lanzado el
      delfín, ahora busca en el agua la hendidura por la que ha de
      escapar,
      pero el niño ha dejado ya de abrirse el pecho, comienza a juntar los
      fragmentos del salto,
      pero ha vuelto a saltar y la vidriera se quiebra, cae como una lluvia
      de sal sobre los ojos.
Los bebedores alzan las jarras, beben largos sorbos de cerveza y de muerte,
      pero la canción ha cesado, el niño va guardando junto a su pecho
      los vidrios de colores,
      pero el delfín ha vuelto a saltar: cruza el pájaro, la sombra del
      pájaro en vuelo convertida,
      pero el delfín ha vuelto a saltar
      y el niño está tendido junto al agua con el pecho cubierto de hojas secas.
Cruza el pájaro, la verdad no es su sombra.

Pedro Marqués de Armas

Tú no irás a Troya

No irás a Troya a desmentir su sombra.
Como el amor, sólo ese cuerpo gotea y se recoge
y en él yaces tendido sin despertar,
que era la copa de tu amor lo que la alzaba,
el mar inclinado por la boca del otro rey soplando.
Un cielo agónico allá arriba.
Otra ciudad sitiada.

the song like a small sound stabbed into the chest's emptiness.
In the drinkers' glasses, the beer foam like the voice of the child who sings
    between two deaths,
    it's an excavation skirting along the crease, a slow penetration of
    plumage into the dark squalor of sound.
Here comes the acrobat with the words from the last time he misspoke, the
    last secret impulse to be blind.
Once we saw his blue laughter and the blue behind the laughter of one
    who knows he has received the latest news;
    it's the scarf, the silvered star in the scarf that launched the dolphin,
    now it seeks in the water the depths through which it must
    escape,
    but the child has already stopped opening his heart, he begins to
    join together the fragments of the leap,
    but it's already leapt again and the windowpane shatters, it falls like
    a rain of salt on the eyes.
The drinkers raise their glasses, take deep draughts of beer and of death,
    but the song has ceased, the child holds the stained glass windows
    to his chest,
    the dolphin has leapt again: the bird flies over, the bird's shadow
    transformed into flight,
    the dolphin has leapt again
    and the child is lying by the water, his chest covered with dry leaves.
The bird flies over, the truth is not its shadow.

Translated by Chris Brandt

Pedro Marqués de Armas

You'll Not to Troy

You'll not to Troy
to refute its shadow.
Like love,
its body just drips and collects
and you lie stretched out still wide-awake in it
that was the goblet of your love that I raised,
the sea pitching through the gusting mouth
of the other king.
A dying sky up above.
A walled city.

Mil puertas que no fugan.
Mil arcos donde ahora la nave colaría hacia el crepúsculo;
ola de albura inmóvil,
tibio el sitio en que mis labios parten como buques.
Brújula de hueso,
manto bermejo el sol ya se retira,
vuelve a fijar su lámina en el ojo.
Allí también su sombra, el agua en cuyo borde copio
esta aceitada desazón.

Ha oscurecido.
De pronto la ciudad no signa con tu fiebre.
Pero no vale el amor,
no vale la angustia de los días
que van sajando el alma.
Cada día penetra con su proa.
Cada proa se aleja con su angustia.
Otro destino vela tu orfandad,
acuna livideces a la orilla del muelle
mientras tu cabeza asoma su gran ojo de Cíclope
y ve que aun su cuerpo es toda el agua,
que pudo más un sueño,
que nunca irás a la lejana Troya.

Claro de bosque (semiescrito)

las puertas se abren hacia
dentro y
con *horror infinito*
hacia fuera los pensamientos
pienso
en una escritura-intensidad
pero no es escritura la palabra exacta
(exacto es claro de bosque)
ni siquiera la que más se aproxima
ya que
ninguna palabra es tan intensa

A thousand doors with no exit.
A thousand arches through which the ship now passes
towards the twilight;
a still white wave,
the warmer place in which lips set sail
like a vessel,
that was the goblet of your love . . .
The compass of bone,
the red mantled sun leaves now,
returns to fix its sheet in the eye.
Also there its shadow,
the water on whose rim I copy
this oily blandness.

It has grown dark.
Suddenly the city does not signal with your fever.
But love is not worth it,
not worth the anguish of the days
that cut the soul.
Each day pierces with its prow,
each prow distances itself with its anguish.
Another destiny watches over your orphaned state,
rocks your livid rages at the port's shore,
while your head looks out of its huge cyclopean eye
and sees that its body is still completely under water,
that a dream could do more,
that you will never go to faraway Troy.

Forest Clearing (Half-Written)

The doors open inwards and
with *infinite horror*
outwards the thoughts
I think
in an intense fit of writing
but writing is not the exact word
(the forest clearing is exact)
not even the one that comes closest
since
no word is so intense

para ser escrita
en el *horror infinito* de unos caracteres de tierra
en el cerebro *des*enterrado
de esas tierras al margen y
sin embargo
en algún punto o claro de bosque
calculado
(en la cabeza)
aunque el término *punto* también inexacto
y aún, todavía las rayas-excavan
cada uno de esos puntos dispersos
(pilar de lengua viva)
los caracteres se desprenden
al simple roce de las manos
así también la tierra
al borde de ciertos farallones o mantos de pizarra
ininterrumpidamente hacia
dentro y
con *horror infinito*
con (más) *horror infinito* hacia fuera luego
campos
cabezas
molinillos-organillos en Mandelstam,
Nietzsche (—¡que crujen!—)
y ahora
en la nunca espectral y absorbente cabeza de este Bernhard
con intensidad cada vez más creciente
más sin salida
hacia dentro y
fuera
lo mismo hacia la intersección
entre una idea, clara
de suicidio (sostenido a lo largo
de una existencia todo ella entregada al suicidio)
y el acto
al abrirse la puerta en la sima
—sismática
con fondo de hueso gris y libre
de todo *resto* de tejido humano
"allende los humanos"
así en las minas al aire libre de Serra Pelada

as to be written
in the *infinite horror* of some earthy characters
the *dis*interred brain
of those lands on the edge and
nevertheless
at some point or the forest clearing
calculated
(in one's head)
although the end point is inexact as well
and even now the rays excavate
every one of those scattered points
(column of living tongue)
the characters detach
at the simple touch of a hand
as does the earth
at the edge of certain cliffs or mantles of shale
continuously non-stop
inwards and
with *infinite horror*
with (more) *infinite horror* outwards then
fields
heads
hand-milled hurdy-gurdy in Mandelstam,
Nietzsche (let 'em creak!)
and now
in the never spectral and demanding head of this Bernhard
with ever increasing intensity
more with no exit
inwards and
outwards
in the same direction as the intersection
of a bright idea,
of suicide (sustained as long as
an existence devoted entirely to suicide)
and the act
upon opening the door to the abyss
—obsessive
with a base of gray and free bone
all from *remains* of human fabric
"beyond humans"
just as in the open air of the mines of Serra Pelada

400 kms al sur de Belén
donde los humanos
(moléculas rientes de negror corredizo)
han sustraído
en un corte sagital
la órbita de un ojo *infinitamente horrible*
semiescritos
emergen de la mina y
la tierra (pilar de lengua)
escala los bordes
reproducen el movimiento (ardoroso)
de la masa (de tierra)
que no va a ninguna parte
ningún pájaro atraviesa el aire libre
de estos yacimientos
el cielo ha perdido su *convexidad característica*
y, además
su oficios—y noble—*speculum*
como si en estas minas de oro
400 kms al sur de Belén
se hubiera operado ya
en la intersección
el *corte sagital del cerebro*
de manera
que
la cabeza y el ojo
el ojo y la cabeza y
así los *campus* (de ojos) y los *campus* (de cabezas)
expresen la superficie
(*ya,*
exclusivamente
*ext*irpada)
o sólo es,
exclusivamente,
el fondo de la mina
en uno y otro sentido *no debemos ceder*
          en la intensidad
así Bernhard
con horror infinito
ante el claro.

400 kms to the south of Belém
where humans
(laughing molecules of black slide)
have removed
with a sagittal incision
the orbit of an *infinitely horrible* eye
half-written
they emerge from the mine and
the earth (column of tongue)
scales the borders
reproducing the (arduous) movement
of the mass (of earth)
that goes nowhere
no bird crosses the fresh air
of these fields
the sky has lost its *characteristic convexity*
and, as well
its function—and noble—*speculum*
as if in these gold mines
400 kms to the south of Belém
would have already operated
in the intersection
the *sagittal incision of the brain*
in a way
that
the head and the eye
the eye and the head and
as the *campus* (of eyes) and the *campus* (of heads)
would express the surface
(*already*
exclusively
*ex*tirpated)
or is it only
exclusively
the bottom of the mine
in one sense and another *we must not give in
        to the intensity*
as Bernhard did
with infinite horror
before the clearing.

Translated by George Economou and Luis Cortest

Damaris Calderón

Con el terror del equilibrista

. . . las aguas del abismo
donde me enamoraba de mí mismo
QUEVEDO

Sobre el espanto del pozo
siempre pensé tocar el agua.
Nunca lavar las manos,
no mancharlas.
Sólo el pozo y mi sed.
Nunca las viejas bocas
ni los baldes usados en balde.
No el agua que titila
su confortable techo
y toda la pasión de sus ahogados.
Nunca
el ojo contemplativo.
Todo esto lo digo
con el terror del equilibrista.

Ésta será la única mentira en la que siempre creeremos

a fuerza de admitirla tantas veces.
Hoy
alguien intentará leer el ojo de un vecino
con el fin de saber si la tristeza
(esa muchacha indócil que va escupiendo amor)
es una amiga sádica de siempre
o un pez muerto nadando en la garganta.
Sería difícil disfrazar la felicidad.
(A ella siempre le quedaría corrido el maquillaje.)
Pero de todos modos tendrás que perdonarme
que no te ladre amor junto al oído.
Podrían despertarse muchos muertos
que están bajo nosotros.

Es una historia triste
jugar a ser perfectos.

Damaris Calderón

With the Terror of the Tightrope Walker

. . . the waters of the abyss
where I would fall in love with myself
QUEVEDO

There above the well
I thought only of touching the water.
Never of washing my hands there
of soiling them.
Only the well and my thirst.
Never of the old mouths
nor of the futile buckets.
Not of the water
gleaming against its comfortable roof
and the national passion of the drowned.
Never ·
the worried eye.
I speak in the voice
of the terrified tightrope walker.

This Will Be the Only Lie We'll Always Believe

by force of admitting it so many times.
Today
someone will try to read his neighbor's eyes
to find out if sadness (that headstrong girl
who goes about spitting love)
will be forever a sadistic friend
or a dead fish aswim in the throat.
Happiness wouldn't be easy to hide.
(Her make-up is always smeared).
But you'll have to forgive me anyway
if I don't bark love in your ear.
Too many of the dead beneath our feet
might be awakened.

This is a sad business
this playing at being perfect.

Astillas

♦ *(a mi madre)*

Mueres de día.
Sobrevives de noche.
Paisaje de guerra
de postguerra
paisaje después de la batalla.
Piedra sobre piedra
donde sólo se escuchan, en la noche, a los gatos,
a las parejas de amantes que no tienen dónde meterse,
chillando.
Basuras, hierbas ralas, trapos, condones,
aristas de latas con sangre.

Cuando salgo a la calle
como otro artista anónimo del hambre
más de algún cuerpo ha roto
la fingida simetría con un salto mortal.

Yo me sentaba en tus rodillas
no me daba vergüenza, Sulamita,
tu cabello de oro de ceniza.
Extranjeros ridículos colgando
sobre árboles inexistentes.

Hace frío.
Las cortezas sangrantes del otoño
aprietan como una mortaja.

Si me siento a la mesa
el vacío es demasiado inmenso
para poder rasparlo con una uña.

Huesos fuertes

El viento entra
por los huesos
una flauta
una cañería de desagüe.
      "Podrían tocar
      toda la noche

Splinters

◆ (to my mother)

You die by day sur-
vive by night.
A landscape of war
of postwar, a land-
scape of after-battle.
Stone upon stone where
only cats can be heard by night,
pairs of lovers with no place to go,
screaming.
Garbage, ratty grass, rags, condoms,
remains of bloody cans.

When I go out into the street
like any anonymous hunger artist
more than one body has broken
the pretense of symmetry with a fatal leap.

Once I sat on your knees
without shame, Shulamite,
your golden hair your ashen hair.
Ridiculous foreigners hanging
on nonexistent trees.

It's cold.
The bloody crusts of autumn
squeeze like a shroud.

If I sit at the table
the void is too vast
for a fingernail to scrape it away.

Strong Bones

The wind enters
through the bones
a flute
a drainpipe.
        "We could play
        all night

y pedir
durante tres generaciones.
Si se les mira
de cerca
no están hechos
para el trabajo
y ostentan su miseria
en carteles escritos
en lengua ajena."
Los rumanos
de los campos
de concentración
(y los otros)
escaparon
en vagones establos
falsificaron
pasaportes
caminaron
fueron devueltos
en las fronteras
limítrofes
del Este.
Lo intentaron de nuevo
(nos suicidaremos en masa).
Algunos
lo consiguieron
y llegaron
al Sur
(o a la muerte).

La máscara japonesa

Yo, Ito Toshitsugo
saqué mi cabeza de un agujero durante la noche
para comerme el cristal de un establecimiento comercial
en la Venecia japonesa.
Atraído por los cebos lumínicos
y los tubos de plástico.
Dos meses
como una anguila

and beg
for three generations.
Seen close up
they're not made
for work
and flaunt their poverty
in posters
written in a strange tongue."
The gypsies
from the concentration camps
(and the others)
escaped in cattle cars
they falsified
passports
walked, were
turned away at neighboring
eastern
borders.
They tried again
(we'll commit mass suicide).
Some succeeded
made it
to the South
(or death).

The Japanese Mask

I, Ito Toshitsugo
stuck my head from a hole all night
to devour the window of a business
in Japanese Venice.
Drawn out by the luminous lure
and plastic tubes.
Two months
eel-shaped

ante el pabellón dorado del bazar
permanecí extático.
Largo y delgado
estilizado por el hambre
una anguila de agua dulce
en el gran puerto marítimo.
Sesenta millones de personas
pasaron por mi lado
no me vieron.
          Sesenta millones
ocupadas en las compras navideñas
cegadas por la luz artificial
por las ramas (falsas)
del árbol donde recosté mi cuerpo.
Yo, Ito Toshitsugo
me convertí en el cadáver de un hombre de sesenta años
sin domicilio conocido
en uno de los barrios más populosos de Osaka.
Que alguien toque para mí la flauta de hierro.

Alessandra Molina

As de triunfo

Je reviendrai avec des membres de fer, la peau sombre, l'oeil furieux: sur mon masque, on me jugera d'une race forte. J'aurai de l'or (. . .)

RIMBAUD

No vas a decir una palabra inteligible
o vas a decirla
de modo que se retorcerá la antigua serpiente
que busca y lame su cola con deseos insaciables.
Ni álgebra ni filosofía
calmarán las palpitaciones de tu corazón;
opio ni barcos aliviarán la premura
por hacerte una persona confiable.
Nada. Todo será inútil.

I stood in ecstasy
before the golden pavilion of the bazaar.
Long and skinny
gaunt with hunger
a freshwater eel
in the saltwater port.
Sixty million people
passed by
without seeing me.
                    Sixty million
busy with Christmas shopping
blinded by the artificial lights
in the (artificial) branches
of the tree I leaned against.
I, Ito Toshitsugo
became the cadaver of a man of sixty
with no known residence
in one of Osaka's most crowded neighborhoods.
May somebody play the iron flute for me.

Translated by Joan Lindgren

Alessandra Molina

Trump Card

Je reviendrai avec des membres de fer, la peau sombre, l'oeil furieux: sur mon
masque, on me jugera d'une race forte. J'aurai de l'or . . .

RIMBAUD

You won't say an intelligible word
or you will say it
in such a way that the ancient snake that seeks its tail
and licks it with insatiable desire will writhe.
Neither algebra nor philosophy
will calm the beating of your heart;
neither opium nor bark will alleviate the pressure
to become trustworthy.
Nothing. Everything will be useless.

El barro acogerá tus manos
pero serán devueltas tan lánguidas
que no podrán sostener unas monedas.
Robarás a los desconocidos
cuando hayas robado lo más fácil,
los hurtos a la madre.
Adentro te tragará la hiedra de los muros,
lejos tropezarás con la flora silvestre,
y aún, ni álgebra ni filosofía
calmarán las palpitaciones de tu corazón.

¡Historias increíbles, los sintagmas tiranos!
confesarás con un instrumento de pasión y lástima
ante la pupila más vigilante,
envilecida para siempre.
Fingirás el suicidio. La cólera y la alegría
porque tendrás suicidios, cóleras y alegrías.
Al mediodía dormirás la noche
y durante la noche te preguntarás quién soy, quién soy.
Cuál nombre darás a tus trabajos
si habrás llegado a ellos por la expulsión del arte
y del arte no gozarás una figura
más que la serpiente
cuando se haya tragado
su muchas veces retorcida cola.

El alga y la fiebre,
la vigilia y la tierra,
la danza virtual y el contrabando . . .
Vagarás
por una belleza sin palabras
pero nada habrá calmado las palpitaciones de tu corazón.
Lo digo yo,
sentada sobre un contén ante el vano de una puerta
en una calle donde los autos modernos
se ensamblan milagrosamente a la arquitectura corroída
demasiado estrecha.
¡A tal punto ha llegado la previsión científica del comercio!
Las piernas inmóviles por el cansancio,
yo, nombrada la idiota, casi siempre ignorada;
que cuento una, dos, tres,
cuatro mil bolsas de nailon transparente
sin reliquias ni souvenirs,

The mud will welcome your hands
but they will become too languid
to sustain even a few coins.
After you have robbed the easiest,
thefts from the mother,
you will steal from strangers.
Inwardly you will swallow the ivy on the walls,
far away you will stumble upon a wildflower,
but neither algebra nor philosophy
will calm the beating of your heart.

Unbelievable stories, the tyrannical syntagmas!
you will make confession to an instrument of passion and pity
face to face with the most vigilant eye,
debased forever.
You will pretend to suicide. Anger and happiness
because you will have suicides, angers and happiness.
At midday you will dream the night
and at night you will ask yourself who am I who am I.
What name will you name your labors
if you have arrived at them by expelling art
and you will enjoy of art no form
more than the snake
after it has swallowed
its tail that writhed so often.

Seaweed and fever,
wakefulness and earth
virtual dance and contraband . . .
You will roam
through a wordless beauty,
but nothing will calm the beating of your heart.
I say this,
sitting on a curb in front of a doorway
in a street where cars of the latest design
are joined miraculously to the corroded, constricted
architecture.
To what point has the scientific forecasting of commerce arrived!
Legs immobile with exhaustion,
I, called The Idiot, almost always ignored;
I count one, two, three,
four thousand transparent nylon bags
that hold neither relics nor souvenirs,

llenas del aire lleno de cada una entre las otras.
Vientre de nailon que soy
y que ha parido al buscador de triunfos.

Herbolaria

• *Para Alicia, en su cumpleaños*

La hija más joven del boticario
salía en las mañanas vestida de escolar
por pétalo y raíz,
por junco y miel.
Como lo puede el amor
el miedo la hizo rastreadora,
bestia de la mirada y el olfato.
Hurtó, roció, imploró
a la tierra
que era también la tierra de los muertos.

Astro antiguo,
sol de ayer que pudre el polen de la flor,
que lo hace dulce,
por qué me has despertado
al bien y al sufrimiento de los otros
sin magia, sin labores,
sin el acto eficaz ni la virtud
con que la hija del boticario
ocultó un lenguaje,
se calló sus fórmulas.

Ronda infantil

De pestañas albinas
como espesor de polen a la luz
nace su propia alegría,
soplo de un estornudo.
Alérgica y albina
bien podría ser diosa
si al hincar con melindres lo que come
en la piel transparente le estallara lo púrpura,
se le hincharan los ojos,
si el golpe de la sangre fuera el de un sacrificio.

full rather of air that is full of each bag among the others.
Belly of nylon that I am
that has brought forth the seeker of triumphs.

Herbalist

• *for Alicia, on her birthday*

The pharmacist's youngest daughter
dressed like a schoolgirl set out each morning
for petal and root,
bullrush and honey.
Fear did what love could—it made her
a stalker, a beast of gaze and scent.
She stole, she watered, she begged
of the soil
that was also the soil of the dead.

Ancient star,
sun of other times that rots the flower's pollen,
that sweetens it,
why did you awaken me
to the good and the suffering of others
but without the magic, the spells,
the effective action or power
with which the pharmacist's daughter
hid a language,
kept secret her formulas.

A Childish Round

From albino lashes
no thicker than pollen in light
her personal allergy descends,
in the form of a sudden sneeze.
Allergic, albino, she could be a goddess
if despite her finicky eating
her transparent skin exploded in purple blotches,
and her eyes distended
as if the rush of blood were a sacrifice.

En este lugar sin estaciones, sin diosa antigua,
aquí donde no hay crímenes,
donde mejor que el crimen es la fábula,
ella cuenta lo que le cuenta una vecina,
un profesor de canto, un matrimonio,
el hombre de las cabras,
el joven novelista, la psicóloga . . .
Dicen ronda infantil de agudos que requiebran
y van más allá del canto
en proyecciones baratas del horror.
Dicen muñeca rota, pie de niña,
juguetería que cuelga entre las ramas;
de animales nocturnos dicen cópula.
En este lugar sin estaciones, sin diosa antigua
y sin legítimos crápulas.

Carlos A. Aguilera

B, Ce-

En casa de mis padres nunca hubo un gainsborough
el
permis-o
estatal,
o,
el lenguaj/e
cianótic
o
de
u
n
gainsborough
(deforme,
torcid-o,
como

In this place without seasons or ancient goddesses,
here where there are no crimes,
where a fiction is better than crime,
she recounts what a neighbor, a
voice teacher, the newlyweds, the goatherds, the young
novelist, the psychologist tell her.
They repeat a childish round of shrill stories that approach
and exceed the wildest of tales in their trashy
projections of horrors.
They speak of a broken doll, the foot of a girl,
a whole toy store hanging among the branches;
they speak of the copulation of nocturnal beasts.
In this place without seasons or ancient goddesses
or authentic toads.

Translated by Mark Weiss

Carlos A. Aguilera

B, Ce-

In my parent's house there was never a gainsborough
o
r
state
perm-is
sion,
or,
the
cyan-
otic
lan/guage
o
f
a
gainsborough
(de
formed,
twist-ed,
like

ciertos e-stamentos clínicos de Ce-,
o,
cierta-s notas
políticas
de
chopin

-estrategia
a-
proximativa d/el
sujeto plusváli
/co-):

Vertedero
Vertedero;

chopin pro-h-
ibido, o
, chopin
religioso (e
s decir: con la sotana negra de los que cortan la carne);

o: d-
o
nde
respira,

pro-
ces-o mecánic
o
p
ara
establecer
una
p-roducción mas-iva
d-el
Estado,
"ocupación y dinero"
(ha
dicho Ce-),

certain clinical cl-asses of Ce-,
or,
certain poli/itical
not-es
of
chopin

-a ro
ugh
policy
of
the
supply side sub
/ject-):

The Dump
The Dump;

banned
chop
in, or
, religious
chopin (that i
s to say: with the black c(ass)ock of those who cut meat);

or: w
he
re
he breathes,

mechanical pro-
cess in
or
der
to esta-
bl-ish
a
m
ass-ive State
p-rod-uction,
"jobs and money"
(so
said Ce-),

"test
í-c
ulo
amigdaloeconómico"
(ha
escrito Ce-),

o: donde
el gen tuberculoso
(lo que l-o convierte, de hecho, en un *infans* de novela)
s
e materia-liza
e-n
e-sa
forma
que-se-prolonga:
(gusanito-gusanito);

¿a
cuánt-o
asciende la carne podrida de un maestro en
alemania?,
¿a
cuán
to l
a caca pastosa
de un maelström en
alemania?;

costra ideológic
a
de *ese*
saber
que lee o no en editoriales,
que ob-
serva, en
las vidrier-as [cocaína de un profundo mental],
l-a(.)ovulación
(.)judía
(.)de(.)
lo
(.)que(.)se(.)
mueve

"a tonsilo-economical
test
ic
le"
(Ce- had
written),

or: where
the tuberculosis gene
(the one that turns him, in fact, into the *infans* of a novel)
materializes
in
a longer
l-as-ting
form
and thus prolonged:
(wormlet-wormlet);

or: h-
ow much
does the rotten meat of a master in germany
come to?
or h
ow much
the thick shit
of a maelstrom
in germany?;

the ideological *scab*
of *that person*
who knows
to read or not in editorials,
who ob-
serves, in
stain-ed glass wind-ows [cocaine is deep stuff],
the(.)ovulation
a(.)jewish woman
(.)of(.)
the thing
(.)that(.) moves(.) it
self

),
o: *metabolismus*;

        -froteur
        froteur-
        (lv, 6–7)

as(sssssss)co,
anular e
l proceso
(el-engranaje-totalitario-del-proceso,
el en-
granaje qu/e
con-viert-e
en
totalitario
al
proceso),
o: la
percepció-n
mítica del reich
contra
la
máqu-ina
(corta la res: distribuye,
corta la res: "el-dinero-en-la-banca"):

flesh/f
lesh/
fle-
sh/
como el que lasquea la te-o-ría factual de los
objetos
u-
sados;

"tu
excremento a-
necoico s-ulamita,
tu
cerebro
esquizoide m
argarita",

.),
or: *metabolismus*;

                    -froteur
                    froteur-
                    (lv, 6–7)

a/s(sssss)ick
ness
to an(n)ul
the process
(the-totalitarian-gear-of-the-process,
the gear wh/ich
becomes
tot
alitarian
in the
process),
or: the
mythical
percept-ion
of the reich
against
the
ma-chine,
(it cuts the beef: it distributes,
it cuts the beef: "money-in-the-bank"):

flesh/f
lesh/
fle-
sh/
like the one who slices up the factual the-or-y of
us-
ed objects;

"your
anechoic
excrement shu-lamite,
your
schizoid
brain mar
garete,"

cancioncilla ligera de un de-ter-mi-na-do
hábita-t
cerebralis;

o: torsssssssssssssssssssssssssssssssión,

sin
hacer per/ceptible la m
utación-
física-
permanent-e del agua,
en
relación
c
on las
condiciones
de
temperatura e-n el ambiente:
"z
ona *equis* d
e
poder"
(ha *dicho* Ce-),
a-vanzan-
do
con la premura fofa de un monje hacia el mercado donde
                                        revenden
                                                el
                                            arroz;

músculos:
dos
tres-d
os: haci-
a-a
bajo;

músculos:
dos
----
tres
----
dos:

a gentle ditty of a certain
cere,bra,l
environment;

or: twissssssssssssssssting,

without
making per/ceptible the perm
anent ph
ysical mut
ation of water,
in
relation t
o
the
temperature
c(o)nd
itions
in the environment :
"power z
one *x*"
(Ce- had *said*),
advancing
with the flabby haste of a monk toward the market where
                          they sell
                              rice;

muscles:
two
three-t
wo: do
wn-wa
rd ;

muscles:
two
----
three
----
two :

h-
acia ab-
ajo
con lentitu-d; c
itando frases de Wittgenstein y Pound),

músculos:
ha-ci-a-a-ba-jo,

(hac-ia
l
as
notas
políticas
(y, no encontradas)
de
u
n
Chopin
en
bucovina
("la tos, la tos:
cuidado con la tos"):

esputo.

Javier Marimón

Generación espontánea

1913. Joyce escribe Giacomo Joyce
el mismo año de la muerte de Saussure.
Alzo la vista y aquí estamos, la caterva de autistas y yo
camino al homenaje en zona de aeropuerto.
¿Es que puede homenajearse a una caja?
Pequeña, que trae
el reloj despertador llamado Joyce en la cajita que dice: *Frágil,*
y el casette (Saussure) con la canción que dice: *Fragile.*
Una sutileza diferenciadora bajo la cual se agazapan
las moscas de la generación espontánea.

dow
n war
d
slowly ; c
iting phras()es of Wittgenstein and Pound),

muscles:
d-own-war-d,

(to-war-d
the
political
notes
(and, lack of conflicts)
of
a
Chopin
in
bucovina
("the cough, the cough:
careful with the cough"):

sputum.

Translated by Gabriel Gudding

Javier Marimón

Spontaneous Generation

1913. Joyce writes Giacomo Joyce
in the year of Saussure's death.
I raise my eyes and here we are, an autistic mob and I
walk toward the airport to pay homage.
Can you pay homage to a box?
A small one, containing
the alarm clock called 'Joyce' in the little box marked: *Fragile*
and the cassette ('Saussure') with the song called: *Fragile*.
A differentiating subtlety under which the flies,
products of spontaneous generation, lie in wait.

Aceleradas en el deseo de pensamiento, crean
un oscuro cortejo por donde atravesamos los autistas y yo;
alfombras de transitorios reyes de las Estrictas Gramáticas Cumplidas.
Simetría, Simetría; festejamos los homenajeantes.
Entre franjas de datos descubro:
1892. La madre de Joyce muere siendo este un niño
El mismo año de la muerte de la madre de Saussure.
En el ambiente de su cama el niño Joyce sacrificado,
bajo un dominio espasmódico de moscas espontáneas.
Y ahora a mí me presienten, ven que comprendo; me acosan,
me piden el dedo índice para ellas.
Tengo que disfrutarlo todavía: señalo, señalo, señalo,
objetos dondequiera, transidos por el halo de la relación.
Señalo el camino de la playa.
Despertar entero el cúmulo relacionante.
¿Poner o no el reloj que han enviado, para despertar?
Aprovechando los trillos de la metáfora,
las moscas de la generación espontánea se propagan
por esa relación,
y por la materia de las subcajitas que contienen al reloj y al casette.
Y en el espacio sobrante del casette, que es una canción sola;
sinfonías de moscas allí dentro ejecutan.
Y debajo de la uña de irrealidad.
Oh, es fácil con el dedo, obtener relaciones sin nada que ofrecer.
Veo al salvavidas señalar con ese dedo índice a mí negado.
En el ámbito de mi dedo amputado las moscas de la generación espontánea
rellenan, abarcan el aspecto real.
Agárralo! Los sentidos simultáneos agazapados allí, ampliando en
elasticidades nuevas franjas de datos, luchas internas entre los datos
    significativos. ¡Dialéctica!
Un joven fránces, un Saussure, con sonrisa masticada: ¡Dialéctica!
Saussure definiéndose hacia fuera, emerge ahora *rey* del dato significativo;
(i) como nosotros: *reyes* transitorios de las Estrictas Gramáticas cumplidas
    (frágil-fragile).
Saussure, ¡Gramático!
(tenido eso como dato significativo).
O bien (ii): Oh, oh, y: francés, es Saussure quien dice: *fragile*, que es francés
(tenido eso como dato significativo).
Oh, inconcebible belleza de la simetría relacionando;
debo sin dudar entregarles mi dedo al hato de moscas.

Quickened by thought's desire, they forge
a dark cortege where the autistic and I cross;
rugs of the transitory kings of Strictly Executed Grammars.
Symmetry, symmetry; we worshipers celebrate it.
Among strips of facts I discover:
1892. Joyce's mother dies while he's still a boy,
The same year Saussure's mother dies.
By her deathbed Joyce was sacrificed
beneath the spasmodic dominion of spontaneous flies.
And now they sense me, they see I understand, they harass me,
they ask me to give them my index finger.
I still have use for it: I point, I point, I point
at objects wherever, stricken by the nimbus of relationship.
I point to the path to the beach.
To awaken the entire relational heap.
Should I set the clock they have sent to wake me?
Using the paths of metaphor
the flies of spontaneous generation propagate
through that relationship,
and through the matter of the sub-cartons containing watch and cassette.
And in the remaining space on the tape, which is just one song;
there they perform fly symphonies.
And beneath the fingernail of unreality.
Oh, how easy it is with a finger to achieve relationships with nothing to offer.
I see the lifeguard point with the finger denied me.
Around my amputated finger the flies of spontaneous generation
stuff themselves, embracing the real appearance.
Seize it! The simultaneous senses crouched there, enlarging in
elasticities new strips of data, internal struggles between significant facts.
    Dialectic!
A young Frenchman, a Saussure with a chewed-up smile: Dialectic!
Saussure, defining himself outward, now emerges, *king* of the significant fact;
(i) like us: transitory *kings* of Strictly Executed Grammar (fragile fragile).
Saussure, Grammarian!
(held on to, like a significant fact).
Or it could be (ii): Oh, oh, and: French, it is Saussure who says: *fragile,*
    which is French
(held on to, like a significant fact).
Oh, inconceivable beauty of symmetrical relationships;
I have no choice I must give my finger to the swarm of flies.

¡Qué bien entonces haber llamado al casette (de fragile): Saussure!
El joven Saussure incontinuado y yo,
Dos sacrificios en vida para el bulto negro de lo pensante.
Incontinuado: las moscas atacan sobre las nuevas relaciones, englobando,
disolviendo ahora la figura de Saussure-regente (i y ii) hacia
    Saussure regido.
¡Dialéctica!

Discurso del dedo ausente:
¿El pie que se adelanta deseoso de jugar con la niña
significa violación?
Ojillos saltones de las moscas reconocen,
no hay pensamiento que no se infiltre bajo esas estructuras.
Ausencia paulatina de un complejo de pensamientos en una sola dirección:
escrutan en el pie teórico que significa violar.
Escrutan en el pie abstracto que dice: jugar.
Pero no se deciden por ninguno,
su tarea es ese estado intermedio, de volar insistentes,
de dudar sobre el valor de esos elementos en relación,
de escrutar.
No, no hablo de un ridículo compuesto moral,
ellas remontan esos símbolos:
mi no dedo no es para ellas una garantía,
o el deseo inconfesado de violación;
Ocurre la recuperación del aspecto pensar desde otro inicio, un estímulo
en la práctica de las relaciones: *kiozaku*, tras lo cual
el espíritu se incorpora otra vez frente al muro,
pero sin obtener trascendencia: un cambio de elementos regidores,
un manchón de pensamiento en leves franjas acotejadas,
sin que sobresalgan unas sobre otras; sólo eso.
Un noble sacrificio; pasto de sus insatisfechas ventosas musculares.
Sobre el dedo abandonado en el paisaje
luchan las moscas de la generación espontánea.
No se han cansado aún. Rodean, instigan, siguen.
Habrá que agotar todas las deyecciones del pensamiento
y toda la materia relacionable,
para poder agotarlas también a ellas.
Y nada aún se ha preparado para eso.

How good indeed to have named the cassette (the fragile): 'Saussure!'
The young, discontinuous Saussure and I,
Two living sacrifices for the black bulk of that which thinks.
Discontinuous: the flies attack the new relationships, enclosing,
dissolving now the figure of Saussure—governing (i and ii) in Saussure's
    direction—governed.
Dialectic!

Discourse of the absent finger:
Does the foot that runs ahead eager to play with the girl
signify rape?
The flies' tiny bulging eyes acknowledge
that there is no thought that doesn't infiltrate those structures.
Gradual absence of a complex of thoughts in a single direction:
they scrutinize the theoretical foot that signifies rape.
They scrutinize the abstract foot that says: play.
But they don't choose either.
Their task is that intermediate state, of insistent flying,
of being unsure about the value of those elements in relationship,
of scrutinizing.
No, I am not talking about some ridiculous moral compound,
they overcome those symbols:
my no-finger is not a guarantee for them
nor is the unconfessed desire to rape;
The regaining of the thinking aspect from another beginning occurs, a
    stimulus
in the practice of relationships: *kyosaku*, after which
the spirit becomes flesh again before the wall
without achieving transcendence: a change of governing elements,
a large blot of thought arranged in slight strips,
without any standing out from the others: nothing more.
A noble sacrifice: fodder for their unsated muscular snouts
the flies of spontaneous generation fight
over the finger abandoned in the landscape.
They still haven't tired. They surround, they provoke, they follow.
All defecations of thought will have to be exhausted
before they're exhausted
and all relationable matter.
And nothing has yet been prepared for that.

Translated by Michael Kelleher

Biographies and Notes to the Poems

In the interest of brevity, the list of works given for each poet includes only poetry or books directly related to poetry, such as anthologies and critical writing. It is followed by a brief biography and notes to the poems and their translations. (All translations in the notes that are not otherwise credited are mine.)

Nicolás Guillén (Camagüey, 1902–Havana, 1989)

Motivos de son (Havana: Imp. Rambla, Bouza, 1930); *Sóngoro Cosongo. Poemas mulatos* (Havana: Úcar, García, 1931); *West Indies Ltd. Poemas* (Havana: Úcar, García, 1934); *Cantos para soldados y sones para turistas* (Mexico City: Masas, 1937); *España. Poema en cuatro angustias y una esperanza* (Mexico City: México Nuevo, 1937); *El son entero. Suma poética. 1929–1946* (Buenos Aires: Pleamar, 1947); *Elegía a Jesús Menéndez* (Havana: Páginas, 1951); *La paloma de vuelo popular. Elegías* (Buenos Aires: Losada, 1958); *Poesías* (Havana: Comisión Nacional Cubana de la UNESCO, 1962); *Poemas de amor* (Havana: La Tertulia, 1964); *Tengo* (Havana: Universidad Central de Las Villas, 1964); *El gran zoo* (Havana: Unión 1967); *El diario que a diario* (Havana: Unión, 1972); *Obra poética. 1920–1972* (Havana: Instituto Cubano del Libro, 1972–1973); *Poemas manuables* (Havana: Unión, 1975)

Best known in the United States for his *negrista* poetry of the 1930s, Guillén was the de facto poet laureate of Cuba after the Revolution. He had been active in politics since the early thirties and a member of the Communist Party since 1937, running for public office several times on the party ticket and traveling incessantly as its cultural representative. In 1953 he was refused reentry to Cuba and remained in exile, principally in Paris and Buenos Aires. He returned to Cuba in 1960. In 1961 he was founding president of UNEAC, the union of writers and artists of Cuba. He was also a minister plenipotentiary of the Cuban Foreign Service and a member of the Central Committee of the Cuban Communist Party.

ACONCAGUA

Aconcagua. Highest mountain in the Americas.

CLOUDS

Turquino. Highest mountain in Cuba.
Maritime Alps. A range of mountains in the south of France.
Pico Bolívar. Highest mountain in Venezuela.

ANNOUNCEMENT . . .

Patria o Muerte / Our Country or Death.   The slogan of the Cuban Revolution.

Eugenio Florit (Madrid, 1903–Miami, 1999)

> *32 poemas breves* (Havana: Hermes, 1927); *Trópico (1928–1929)* (Havana: Revista de Avance, 1930); *Doble acento. Poemas. 1930–1936* (Habana: Ucacia, 1937); *Reino (1936–1938)* (Havana: Úcar, García, 1938); *Cuatro poemas* (Havana: Úcar, García, 1940); *La estrella. Auto de Navidad* (Havana: Úcar, García, 1947); *Poema mío (1920–1944)* (Mexico City: Letras de México, 1947); *Conversación a mi padre* (Havana: Ayón, 1949); *Asonante final* (Bogotá: Revista de la Universidad Nacional de Colombia, 1950); *Asonante final y otros poemas (1946–1955)* (Havana: Orígenes, 1955); *Antología poética (1930–1955)* (Mexico City: Eds. de Andrea, 1956); *Siete poemas* (Montevideo: Cuadernos «Julio Herrera y Reissig», 1960); *Hábito de esperanza. Poemas (1936–1964)* (Madrid: Ínsula, 1965); *Antología penúltima* (Madrid: Plenitud, 1970); *De tiempo y agonía (Versos del hombre solo)* (Madrid: Revista de Occidente, 1974); *Versos pequeños* (New York: Eliseo Torres & Sons, 1977); *Donde habita el recuerdo* (Miami: Ultra Graphics Corp., 1984); *Momentos* (Miami: Ultra Graphics Corp., 1985); *Antología personal* (Huelva, Spain: J.R.J. Colección de Poesía, 1992); *Obras completas* (Lincoln, Neb.: Society of Spanish and Spanish-American Studies, 1983, 1993)

One of the pioneers of *conversacionalismo,* the conversational style. He migrated to Cuba at fifteen. In 1940, when he was thirty-seven, he moved to New York, where he worked for the Cuban consulate. In 1945 he became a professor of Spanish at Barnard College of Columbia University, where he taught until retirement, after which he lived in Miami.

POETS ALONE IN MANHATTAN

Alcides Iznaga.   Cuban poet (1914–).
Castillo de Jagua.   "The jagua's castle." A common name for Caribbean restaurants.
jagua.   A fruit tree native to Cuba, *Genipa americana.*
vicaria.   Author's note: "A Cuban plant, with white or violet flowers, very common." *Catharanthus roseus,* the common or Madagascar periwinkle.

BRUGES

Lake of Love.   A popular tourist destination in Bruges.

José Lezama Lima (Havana, 1910–1976)

> *Muerte de Narciso* (Havana: Úcar, García, 1937); *Enemigo rumor* (Havana: Úcar, García, 1941); *Aventuras sigilosas* (Havana: Orígenes, 1945); *La fijeza* (Havana: Orígenes, 1949); *Dador* (Havana: Úcar, García, 1960); *Órbita de Lezama Lima* (Havana: Unión, 1966); *Poesía completa* (Havana: Instituto del Libro, 1970); *Fragmentos a su imán* (Havana: Arte y Literatura, 1977), *Poesía completa* (Havana: Letras Cubanas, 1985); *José Lezama Lima: Selections* (Berkeley: University of California Press, 2005)

Cuba's most influential modern poet and essayist, and the first major practitioner of the *neobarroco.* Author, as well, of two seminal novels, *Paradiso* (Havana: Unión, 1966) and the posthumous *Oppiano Licario* (Mexico City: Ediciones Era, 1977), and editor of the *Antología de la poesía cubana* (Havana: Consejo Nacional de Cultura, 1965). His father, a colonel in the Cuban army, died when Lezama was nine, reducing the family to genteel poverty. Within a few years they moved to the modest apartment where he was to live for the rest of his life. His study of law at the University of Havana between 1930 and 1940 was sporadic, due to student political protests, in which he participated, which were followed by prolonged closures of the university. He supported himself in minor bureaucratic posts. In 1944 he founded and coedited, with the critic José Rodríguez Feo, the journal *Orígenes* (1944–1956), the most influential of several with which he was involved, which gave its name to a generation of poets, among them Piñera, Baquero, Diego, Vitier, García Marruz, and García Vega, as well as Feijóo and Jamís, and younger poets Pablo Armando Fernández and Roberto Fernández Retamar. From then until 1970 Lezama's modest apartment became one of the centers of Cuban intellectual and artistic life. In the beginning he was an enthusiastic supporter of the Revolution, and he held several important cultural posts under the new regime: director of the Department of Literature and Publications of the National Cultural Council, vice-president of UNEAC (Union of Cuban Writers and Artists), and director of the Library of the Economic Society of the Friends of Peace. After 1970, in the wake of his public opposition to the notorious persecution of the poet Heberto Padilla and the scandal occasioned by the explicit homosexuality of *Paradiso,* he was relieved of his posts and lived in relative seclusion, his new work unpublished and unavailable in Cuba. In his lifetime seven collections of his poetry, *Paradiso* (translated by Gregory Rabassa, 1974), and several collections of essays were published. A year after his death *Oppiano Licario* and the poetry collection *Fragmentos a su imán* were published. His influence continues to increase throughout Latin America.

THOUGHTS IN HAVANA

"l'étranger nous demande le garçon maudit."   "the stranger asks us for the cursed boy."
colibri.   hummingbird.

ODE TO JULIÁN DEL CASAL

Julián del Casal.   Cuban poet and journalist (1868–1893). The poem draws on his *Crónicas,* first published in the Havana journal *La Caricatura,* among others.
Teatro Tacón.   Havana's nineteenth-century theater and opera house, now called El Gran Teatro.
Clésinger.   Jean-Baptiste Clésinger (1814–1883). French sculptor.
opoponax.   A resinous incense.
Marquise of Polavieja.   Wife of Camilo García, marqués de Polavieja y del Castillo, Spanish governor of Cuba from 1890 to 1892.
Adonai.   Usually Adonis, as in English, a character in Greek mythology, though the spelling Adonai appears occasionally in Spanish. Adonai is Hebrew for the deity as lord. Lezama intends both to be understood here.

THE SEVEN ALLEGORIES

Licario.   Eponymous hero of Lezama's unfinished novel *Oppiano Licario.*

Virgilio Piñera (Cárdenas, 1912–Havana, 1979)

Las furias (Havana: Cuadernos Espuela de Plata, 1941); *La isla en peso* (Havana: Tipografía García, 1943); *Poesía y prosa* (Havana: Serafín García, 1944); *La vida entera* (Havana: Unión, 1969); *Una broma colosal* (Havana: Unión, 1988); *Poesía y crítica* (Mexico City: Consejo Nacional para la Cultura y las Artes, 1995); *La isla en peso. Obra poética* (Havana: Unión, 1998)

One of the founding members of the *Orígenes* group. Piñera's poetry until recently has been eclipsed by his plays and stories (he is arguably Cuba's greatest playwright and one of its finest writers of short fiction), but in recent years he has become an important influence on younger poets. He spent most of 1944 to 1958 in Buenos Aires, but remained closely involved with Cuba. He vehemently disagreed with Lezama's mystical bent and what he saw as his obscurantism, and in 1955 founded, with Lezama's erstwhile collaborator José Rodríguez Feo, the journal *Ciclón,* in competition with Lezama's *Orígenes.* Piñera and Lezama reconciled after the publication of *Paradiso* in 1968 and remained close until Lezama's death eight years later. After the Revolution, which he initially supported, Piñera joined the staff of the important weekly *Lunes de Revolución,* the cultural supplement to the official newspaper of Castro's July 26th Movement. He was also the director of the publishing house Ediciones R (1960–1964). He was jailed on October 11, 1961, the *Noche de las Tres Pes*—the Night of the Three Ps—the first of a series of roundups of suspected prostitutes, pimps, and pederasts, but was quickly released, as his considerable international reputation rendered his arrest a potential embarrassment to the government. In the aftermath of the Padilla Affair (see Introduction) and as a result of both his outspokenness and his overt homosexuality, Piñera was expelled from UNEAC and refused publication in Cuba and abroad, and his work was removed from libraries and bookstores. He continued to work as a translator. At his death the manuscripts that had accumulated in his apartment were confiscated by the authorities. The previously unpublished poems released for his posthumous books are suspected to be a fraction of the whole.

AT THE ONE-EYED CAT

The One-Eyed Cat.   A restaurant with live music and dancing and a major venue for the performance of *filin* (a popular song style), art exhibits, and poetry readings. Open from 1960 to 1970 and again from 1980 to 1985, it was a popular hangout for artists and writers. In 2001 it reopened as a tourist attraction.
feeling.   bolero con filin, a sentimental popular song genre.

A NIGHT

Zanja Street.   Main street of Havana's Chinatown.

Samuel Feijóo (San Juan de los Yeras, 1914–Santa Clara, 1992)

Camarada celeste (Havana: n.p., 1941); *Beth-el (1940–48)* (n.p., 1949); *Jiras guajiras (1937–38)* (Cuadernillo de la alegre noticia, 2, 1949); *Poeta en el paisaje* (Cienfuegos: n.p., 1949); *Gajo joven* (Sabaranamanga: Imp. El Zunzunito, 1950); *Carta en otoño* (Havana: Talleres Tipográficos de la Sociedad Colombista Panamericana, 1957); *Violas (1936)* (Havana: Úcar, García, 1958); *Poemas del bosquezuelo (1954) y Haz de la ceniza (1958–59)* (Havana: Úcar, García, 1960); *El pájaro de las soledades. Diario de un joven poeta enfermo (1937–40)* (Santa Clara: Universidad Central de Las Villas, 1961); *El girasol sediento (1937–48.) Edición definitiva* (Santa Clara: Universidad Central de Las Villas, 1963); *Cuerda menor (1937–1939)* (Santa Clara: Universidad Central de Las Villas,

1964); *Ser fiel (1948–62)* (Santa Clara: Universidad Central de las Villas, 1964); *Ser* (Havana: Letras Cubanas, 1984); *Poesía* (Havana: Letras Cubanas, 1984); *El pan del bobo* (Cienfuegos: Mecenas, 2002)

Feijóo was one of the few Cuban poets to remain in his native province instead of moving to Havana, spending most of his life in Las Villas (formerly Santa Clara Province). In addition to his work as a poet, he was a painter, folklorist, ethnomusicologist, novelist, short story writer, journalist, journal editor, and publisher. His work appeared in *Orígenes*.

THE MADMAN'S SON

son   A Cuban popular music genre, of African and Spanish derivation.

DEEP WITHIN THE CAONAO

Caonao.   A city, agricultural region, and river of Camagüey Province, Cuba.

Gastón Baquero (Banes, 1916–Madrid, 1997)

Poemas (Havana: Talleres de Serafín García, 1942); *Saúl sobre su espada* (Havana: Clavileño, 1942); *Poemas escritos en España* (Madrid: Cuadernos Hispanoamericanos, 1960); *Memorial de un testigo* (Madrid: Rialp, 1966); *Magias e invenciones* (Madrid: Instituto de Cooperación Iberoamericana, 1984); *Poemas invisibles* (Madrid: Verbum, 1991); *Autoantología comentada* (Madrid: Signos, 1992); *Poesía completa* (Salamanca: Fundación Central Hispano, 1995); *Antología (1937–1994)* (Bogotá: Norma, 1996); *Poesía completa* (Madrid: Verbum, 1998); *La patria sonora de los frutos. Antología poética* (Havana: Letras Cubanas, 2001)

One of the founding members of the *Orígenes* group. A child of rural poverty, Baquero trained as an agronomist, earning a doctorate in natural sciences from the University of Havana before turning to a career in journalism and literature. He was a close collaborator of Lezama Lima's on several journals preceding *Orígenes,* and the financial backer of *Orígenes* during its final two years. As an editor, journalist, and essayist he worked for several newspapers and journals closely connected to the Batista regime and was a member of Batista's appointed legislature. He left Cuba immediately after the Revolution, settling in Spain, one of the few Cubans to do so at the time. Thereafter he was officially nonexistent in Cuba: unpublished, written out of the history of Cuban poetry, his name removed from the captions of photographs. His poetry, including the work published after he left, was nonetheless known to poets on the island, and a visit to Baquero became a ritual of sorts for Cuban poets passing through Madrid. Since his death he has been "rehabilitated" and published on the island, and is once more publicly acknowledged as one of Cuba's major poets.

PAVANE FOR THE EMPEROR

[Musical composition].   Baquero assigned musical compositions, as a kind of commentary, to the poems in his *Autoantología comentada*. To *Pavana* he assigned Bach's *Italian Concerto*.

ON MONDAYS MY NAME WAS NICANOR

[Musical composition].   Mozart, *Symphony No. 40*.

FABLE

[Musical composition]. Haydn, *Country Dances.*

CHARADA FOR LYDIA CABRERA

Lydia Cabrera. Cuban ethnographer and fiction writer (1899–1991).
charada. *La charada cubana* is a divination game, used to convert dream imagery into lottery numbers. One hundred common objects are assigned numbers; the first three are horse, butterfly, and sailor.

MARCEL PROUST . . .

[Musical composition]. Rameau, *Castor and Pollux.*
The poem is structured around the title of the second volume of Proust's *A la recherche du temps perdu, A l'ombre des jeunes filles en fleur* (in Spanish, *A la sombra de las muchachas en flor*), literally, "in the shadow of the girls in flower." The standard English name of the book is *Within a Budding Grove.*

COUNT CAGLIOSTRO'S CAT

[Musical composition]. Mozart, *Adagio "The Veronese" [sic].* Perhaps the *Veronese Allegro*, K. 72a.
Cagliostro. Alessandro di Cagliostro (1743–1795), traveler, occultist, Freemason, and swindler.

THE TRAVELER

[Epigraph]. "I have built such lovely castles that their ruins would be enough for me." Jules Renard (1864–1910), French poet and novelist. From his *Journal 1887–1910* (Paris: Librairie Gallimard, 1960), p. 66.

Eliseo Diego (Havana, 1920–Mexico City, 1994)

En la Calzada de Jesús del Monte (Havana: Orígenes, 1949); *Por los extraños pueblos* (Havana: Orígenes, 1958); *El oscuro esplendor* (Havana: Belic, 1966); *Muestrario del mundo, o Libro de las maravillas de Boloña* (Havana: Instituto Cubano del Libro, 1967); *Versiones* (Havana: Unión, 1970); *Nombrar las cosas* (Havana: Unión, 1973); *Los días de tu vida* (Havana: Unión, 1977); *A través de mi espejo* (Havana: Unión, 1981); *Inventario de asombros* (Havana: Letras Cubanas, 1982); *Poesía* (Havana: Letras Cubanas, 1983); *Veintiséis poemas recientes* (Mexico City: Equilibrista, 1986); *Soñar despierto* (Havana: Gente Nueva, 1988); *Libro de quizás y de quién sabe* (Havana: Letras Cubanas, 1989); *Cuatro de oros* (Mexico City: Siglo XXI, 1990); *El silencio de las pequeñas cosas* (Havana: Letras Cubanas, 1993); *La sed de lo perdido* (Mexico City: Equilibrista, 1993); *En otro reino frágil* (Havana: Unión, 1999); *Aquí he vivido* (Havana: Instituto Cubano del Libro, 2000); *Poemas al margen* (Havana: Ateneo, 2000); *Obra poética* (Mexico City: Fondo de Cultura Económica, 2003).

One of the founding members of the *Orígenes* group. Married to Fina García Marruz' sister. As well as poetry, he published short stories, essays, and translations from several languages, including collections of children's literature and fairy tales. He was director of the Department of Children's Literature of the National Library of Cuba from 1962 to 1970, a vice president of UNEAC for many years, and editor of *Unión,* the journal and press of UNEAC, of whose publications commission he was a member. In his last years he traveled incessantly, and died while ostensibly on a trip to Mexico, although it is probable that he had quietly settled there. He is considered one of the great lyric poets of modern Spanish.

CARTAGENA OF THE INDIES
Cartagena de Indias.   Caribbean port of Colombia. One of the richest cities of colonial Spanish America, it was repeatedly attacked by pirates.

TO A GIRL
El Caballero de la Mano al Pecho.   Title of an El Greco portrait of an anonymous nobleman, but here imagined as a knight out of a tale of chivalry or a fairy tale.

Cintio Vitier (Cayo Hueso [Key West], 1921–)

Poemas (Havana: Úcar, García, 1938); *Sedienta cita* (Havana: Úcar, García, 1943); *De mi provincia* (Havana: Orígenes, 1945); *Extrañeza de estar* (Havana: Úcar, García, 1945); *Capricho y homenaje* (Havana: Úcar, García, 1947); *El hogar y el olvido* (Havana: Orígenes, 1949); *Sustancia* (Havana: Úcar, García, 1950); *Conjeturas* (Havana: Úcar, García, 1951); *Vísperas (1938–1953)* (Havana: Orígenes, 1953); *Canto llano* (Havana: Orígenes, 1956); *Escrito y cantado* (Havana: Úcar, García, 1959); *Testimonios (1953–1968)* (Havana: Unión, 1968); *La fecha al pie* (Havana: Unión, 1981); *Antología poética* (Havana: Letras Cubanas, 1981); *Viaje a Nicaragua* (Havana: Letras Cubanas, 1987), with Fina García Marruz; *Hojas perdidizas* (Mexico City: Equilibrista, 1988); *Poemas de mayo y junio* (Valencia, Spain: Pre-Textos, 1990); *Versos de la nueva casa* (Havana: Instituto Cubano del Libro, 1991); *Dama pobreza* (Valencia, Spain: Pre-textos, 1992); *Nupcias* (Havana: Letras Cubanas, 1993); *Antología de mis versos* (Mexico City: Oceano de México, 2002); *Antología poética* (Mexico City: Fondo de Cultura Económica, 2002); *Epifanías* (Havana: Letras Cubanas, 2004)

One of the founding members of the *Orígenes* group. Born in the United States to Cuban parents, he lived in Cuba from early childhood. He married Fina García Marruz in 1947. A poet, novelist, translator, critic, anthologist, and scholar, he was a major scholar of José Martí, the critical edition of whose *Poesía completa* (Havana: Letras Cubanas, 1985) he edited with Fina García Marruz and Emilio de Armas. He is president of the Centro de Estudios Martianos. He has been editor of numerous literary and scholarly journals, as well as a series of important anthologies, among them *Diez poetas cubanos* (Havana: Ediciones Orígenes, 1948); *Cincuenta años de poesía cubana, 1902–1952* (Havana: Dirección de Cultura del Ministerio de Educación, 1952); and *Poetas cubanos del siglo XIX* (Havana: Unión, 1969). He is author as well of the influential study *Lo cubano en la poesía* (Santa Clara: Universidad Central de Las Villas, 1958; Havana: Instituto del Libro, 1970, 1998) and the memoir *Para llegar a Orígenes. Revista de arte y literatura* (Havana: Letras Cubanas, 1994). He served as an appointed member of the National Assembly of the People's Power (Asamblea Nacional del Poder Popular). He lives in Havana.

BIRNAM WOOD
San Juan.   The San Juan River, which flows through Matanzas.
Teilhard.   Fr. Pierre Teilhard de Chardin, S.J. (1881–1955), French paleontologist and philosopher.

Thérèse of Lisieux.   Saint Thérèse de Lisieux (1873–1897), born Marie-Françoise-Thérèse Martin, Roman Catholic nun and saint.

Milanés.   José Jacinto Milanés (1814–1863), Cuban Romantic poet.

Fina García Marruz (Havana, 1923–)

Poemas (Havana: Úcar, García, 1942); Transfiguración de Jesús en el Monte (Havana: Orígenes, 1947); Las miradas perdidas, 1944–1950 (Havana: Úcar, García, 1951); Visitaciones (Havana: Unión, 1970); Poesías escogidas (Havana: Letras Cubanas, 1984); Viaje a Nicaragua (Havana: Letras Cubanas, 1987), with Cintio Vitier; Créditos de Charlot (Havana: Letras Cubanas, 1990); Los Rembrandt de l'Hermitage (Havana: Unión, 1992); Viejas melodías (Caracas, Fundarte, 1993); Nociones elementales y algunas elegías (Caracas: Fundarte, 1994); Habana del centro (Havana: Unión, 1997); Antología poética (Havana: Letras Cubanas, 1997); Décimas a Seboruco (Matanzas: Vigía, 1998); Antología poética (Mexico City: Fondo de Cultura Económica, 2002); Sin romper el silencio. Antología poética (Santiago, Chile: LOM, 2008)

One of the founding members of the Orígenes group, and its only female member. Married Cintio Vitier in 1947. A poet, essayist, and scholar, she edited, with Vitier and Emilio de Armas, the critical edition of José Martí's Poesía completa (Havana: Letras Cubanas, 1985).

VISITATIONS

Pilgrims of Emmaus.   Twelfth-century French liturgical drama.

Walter de la Mare.   English poet and novelist (1873–1956). The quotation is from "Autumn."

Amigo, el que yo más amaba . . . / Friend who most I loved . . .   From Al alva venid, buen amigo, an anonymous medieval Spanish poem.

Keats.   John Keats (1795–1821). The quotation is from "To Charles Cowden Clarke."

qui laetificat juventutem meam.   "who giveth joy to my youth." Ps. 42:4 in the Vulgate.

Lorenzo García Vega (Jagüey Grande, 1926–)

Suite para la espera (Havana: Orígenes, 1948); Ritmos acribillados (New York: Expublico, 1972); Poemas para penúltima vez, 1948–1989 (Miami: Saeta Ediciones, 1991); No mueras sin laberinto. Poemas (1998–2004) (Buenos Aires: Bajo la Luna, 2005)

Youngest founding member of the Orígenes group. A poet, essayist, and novelist, he wrote the important memoir Los años de Orígenes (Caracas: Monte Avila, 1979). He left Cuba in 1968, settling in Madrid until 1970. From 1970 to 1975 he lived in New York, after which he spent two years in Caracas, Venezuela. Since then he has lived in Miami.

OLD MALDOROR

Maldoror.   Eponymous speaker of Les chants de Maldoror, by the Comte de Lautréamont, pen name of Isidore Lucien Ducasse (1846–1870).

BY THE GOLF COURSE

Winn-Dixie.   A supermarket where the poet worked.

Carlos Galindo Lena (Caibarién, 1929–2004)

Ser en el tiempo (Havana: Belic, 1962); *Hablo de tierra conocida* (Havana: Belic, 1964); *Mortal como una paloma en pleno vuelo* (Havana: Letras Cubanas, 1988); *Rosas blancas para el apocalipsis* (Santa Clara: Capiro, 1991); *Últimos pasajeros en la nave de Dios* (Santa Clara: Capiro, 1996); *Aún nos queda la noche* (Santa Clara: Capiro, 2001)

One of the founders of UNEAC. An active member of the Partido Socialista Popular, the Communist party, in his native Las Villas Province, since the mid-1940s, he was a founder of the Milicias Nacionales Revolucionarias, which mobilized to resist the Bay of Pigs invasion and was involved in the elimination of counterrevolutionary guerrillas in Escambray Province. After ten years in Havana in the 1950s and 1960s, he returned to Las Villas, where he was a director of the literature division of the local branch of UNEAC.

YESTERDAY THE SEA WAS AN ABSENCE

Guillevic.   Eugène Guillevic (1907–1997), French poet. The epigraph is from "Les Charniers," in *Exécutoire* (Paris: Gallimard, 1947). Galindo Lena's translation, and the English, change the line order of the original.

Francisco de Oraá (Havana, 1929–)

Es necesario (Havana: Belic, 1964); *Por Nefas (1954–1960)* (Havana: Unión, 1966); *Con figura de gente y en uso de razón* (Havana: Unión, 1969); *Bodegón de las llamas* (Havana: Letras Cubanas, 1978); *Ciudad ciudad* (Havana: Unión, 1979); *Desde la última estación* (Havana: Letras Cubanas, 1983); *Haz una casa para todos* (Havana: Unión, 1986); *Bodas* (Havana: Letras Cubanas, 1989); *Mundo mondo* (Havana: Gente Nueva, 1989); *La rosa en la ceniza, 1947–1986* (Havana: Unión, 1990); *A la nada que actúa* (Havana: Unión, 2000); *Noche y fulgor* (Havana: Letras Cubanas, 2002)

Poet, novelist, translator, and essayist, as well as an active member of the Partido Socialista Popular, the Communist party, in Las Villas Province, where he spent his early years, since the mid-1940s. For six years following his move to Havana in 1960, he was librarian and teacher in the newly founded national school for art instruction. From 1966 to 1996 he was editorial secretary of *Unión*, the journal of UNEAC, and a member of the publication committee of its press.

A BOY'S LIFE

hierbabruja.   *Bryophyllum pinnatum:* a Caribbean plant with numerous local names, none of them current in North America.

ON THREE PHOTOS OF MELLA

Mella.   Julio Antonio Mella (1903–1929), a founder of the Cuban Communist Party. Assassinated in 1929, he is considered a martyr of the Revolution.

Roberto Branly (Havana, 1930–1980)

El cisne (Havana: Castor, 1956); *Las claves del alba* (Havana: Castor, 1958); *Firme de sangre* (Havana: Castor, 1962); *Apuntes y poemas* (Havana: Unión,

1966); *Poesía inmediata* (Havana: Unión, 1968); *Escrituras* (Havana: Unión, 1975); *Ya la orquesta triunfa sobre el aire* (Havana: Letras Cubanas, 1985)

Poet and scholar. In 1959 he coordinated the cultural affairs page of *Revolución*, the official newspaper of the July 26th Movement. As a member of the National Cultural Council he was publicity director of the Committee on Culture of the province of Havana and assistant director of literature and publications, as well as an official of the Pen Club of Cuba.

EVENING FALLS ON SAN ANASTASIO

The poem is set in the working-class Havana neighborhood of Lawton in the late 1930s.
Guiterista.   A follower of Antonio Guiteras Holmes (1906–1935), socialist leader and minister of the interior in the government of Ramón Grau San Martín. Assassinated by forces associated with Fulgencio Batista, he is considered a martyr of the Revolution.
yemas.   Yemas de Santa Teresa. A dessert made of egg yolks and caramelized sugar.

Pablo Armando Fernández (Las Tunas, 1930–)

Salterio y lamentaciones (1951–1953) (Havana: Úcar, García, 1953); *Nuevos poemas* (New York: Las Américas Publishing Company, 1955); *Toda la poesía* (Havana: Eds. R, 1961); *Himnos* (Havana: La Tertulia, 1962); *El libro de los héroes* (Havana: Casa de las Américas, 1964); *Un sitio permanente* (Madrid: Rialp, 1970); *Aprendiendo a morir* (Barcelona: Lumen, 1983); *Campo de amor y de batalla* (Havana: Letras Cubanas, 1984); *El sueño, la razón (1948–1983)* (Havana: Unión, 1988); *Ronda de encantamiento* (Venice: Centro Internazionale della Grafica, 1990); *Libro de la vida* (Seville: Renacimiento, 1997); *En otra estrella* (Sancti Spiritus: Luminaria, 1998); *De piedras y palabras* (Havana: Unión, 1999); *Pequeño cuaderno de Manila Hartman* (Santiago: Editorial Oriente, 2000); *Hoy la hoguera* (Las Tunas: Editorial Sanlope, 2001); *Reinos de la aurora* (Valladolid, Spain: Fundación Jorge Guillén, 2001); *Parábolas. Selección* (Oakville, Ont., Canada: Mosaic Press, 2001); *Escalas de ascenso* (Havana: Letras Cubanas, 2002); *En tiempos de ciega* (Santo Domingo, Dominican Republic: Carieva, 2002); *Lo sé de cierto porque lo tengo visto* (San Juan, Puerto Rico: Plaza Mayor, 2002); *Ser polvo enamorado (antología)* (Santo Domingo, Dominican Republic: Carieva, 2002); *Lo sé de cierto porque lo tengo visto. Antología poética (1947–2001)* (San Juan, Puerto Rico: Plaza Mayor, 2002); *Libro de los héroes y las armas son de hierro* (Madrid: Biblioteca Nueva, 2003)

Poet and novelist. He lived in New York from 1943 to 1959, returning to Cuba immediately after the Revolution, becoming assistant editor (to Cabrera Infante) of *Lunes de Revolución*. After its dissolution in 1961 he became a member of the editorial staff of Casa de las Américas, cultural attaché of the Cuban embassy in London (1962–1965), a member of the Publishing Council of the Cuban Academy of Science, and publications director of the Cuban National UNESCO Commission (1966–1971). He was for many years secretary of the Pen Club of Cuba and editor of *Unión*, the journal of UNEAC. He is a regular member of the Academia Cubana de la Lengua (Cuban Academy of Language) and corresponding member of the Real Academia de la Lengua (Royal Academy of the Spanish Language). Published in *Orígenes*. He lives in Havana.

Eggo. Also Igbo. Eshu, a member of the *santería* pantheon, in his aspect as the personification of *el monte.*

el monte/the wilderness. *El monte*, though usually translated as "mountain," in Cuba almost always means forest, scrubland, bush, or wilderness. It has a special significance in the practice of *santería* and is the subject of Lydia Cabrera's *El monte*, one of Cuba's great books. Here is her description:

> "Where you see a few herbs you'll find a remedy."
>
> There is no Black . . . who will not have recourse to the bush for the health of his body and soul: "We're herbalists," says Catalino, "by instinct. We hurl ourselves into *el monte!*"
>
> But the reader must not think that by the word *monte* or thicket—here no one ever says woods—is meant only a large, tree-covered expanse of uncultivated ground. In Havana, any overgrown lot is thought of as "a *monte*"—or even as a savannah!—any scrub-covered barren ground (just as one avocado or laurel tree is sometimes referred to as a grove). An empty lot of the most modest dimensions, because of the wild plants that grow there, is categorized as a thicket, and it will be called simply a *"monte"* or thicket. Any place with a dense growth of plants is an appropriate site for a "rogation," an *ebbo*, the offering destined for a saint. . . . So that a Black from the capital needn't go far to find *"el monte."*
>
> Most of the herbs that he habitually uses to cleanse himself of bad influences, to flush the floors of his dwelling, to burn as incense or for concocting simple home remedies, are easy to come by in these miniature, accessible *montes*, which are no less worthy of respect because of their size.

Lydia Cabrera, El monte, 4th ed. (Miami: Ediciones Universal, 1975), pp. 68–69

Eshu, Osain, Oggún, Obatalá, Elegguá. Orishas, members of the *santería* pantheon.

alúmamba. *Osmunda regalis,* the royal fern. Said by devotees of *santería* to grant clairvoyance. See Lydia Cabrera, *El monte,* 4th ed. (Miami: Ediciones Universal, 1975), p. 452.

Ibeyi. The divine twins, progenitors of mankind.

son (pl. *sones*). A Cuban popular music genre, of African and Spanish derivation.

Ocha. *Santería.*

anón (pl. *anones*). Tropical fruit; known in the anglophone Caribbean as sweetsop.

Roberto Fernández Retamar (Havana, 1930–)

Elegía como un himno (Havana: n.p., 1950); *Patrias (1949–1951)* (Havana: Úcar, García, 1952); *Alabanzas, conversaciones (1951–1955)* (Mexico City: El Colegio de México, 1955); *Vuelta de la antigua esperanza* (Havana: Úcar, García, 1959); *En su lugar, la poesía* (Havana: La Tertulia, 1959); *Con las mismas manos, 1949–1962* (Havana: Unión, 1962); *Historia antigua* (Havana: La Tertulia, 1964); *Poesía reunida, 1948–1965* (Havana: Unión, 1966); *Buena suerte viviendo* (Mexico City: ERA, 1967); *Que veremos arder* (Havana: Unión, 1970); *Cuaderno paralelo* (Havana: Unión, 1973); *Circunstancia de poesía* (Buenos Aires: Crisis, 1974); *Palabra de mi pueblo* (Havana: Letras Cubanas, 1980); *Juana y otros poemas personales* (Havana: Letras Cubanas, 1981); *Hacia la nueva* (Havana: Unión, 1989); *Hemos construido una alegría olvidada: poesías escogidas (1949–1988)*

(Madrid: Visor, 1989); *Algo semejante a los monstruos antideluvianos* (Havana: Letras Cubanas, 1994); *Las cosas del corazón* (Havana: Gente Nueva, 1994); *Aquí* (Caracas: Pomaire, 1995; Santa Clara: Capiro, 1996); *Versos* (Havana: Letras Cubanas, 1999); *Where's Fernández?* (Havana: José Martí, 2000); *Antología personal* (Buenos Aires: Instituto Movilizador de Fondos Cooperativos, 2000); *Felices los normales: poesías escogidas, 1949–1999* (Mexico City: Océano, 2002); *Décimas por un tomeguin* (Havana: Colección Clásicos de la Décima, 2003)

Poet, essayist, scholar, editor, and one of Cuba's most powerful cultural bureaucrats. A contributor to *Orígenes*, he edited the important anthology *La poesía contemporánea en Cuba (1927–1953)* (Havana: Orígenes, 1954). His essay *Calibán, apuntes sobre la cultura en nuestra América* (Mexico City: Diógenes, 1971) is widely taught both in the original and in English translation. He was a founder of UNEAC and a member of the editorial committee of its journal *Unión* from 1962 to 1964, and has edited the journal of the Casa de las Americas since 1965. He founded the Centro de Estudios Martianos in 1977 and was its director until 1986. He has been president of the Casa de las Américas since 1986. He is a deputy to the National Assembly of the People's Power (Asamblea Nacional del Poder Popular) and a member of the Council of State.

A MAN AND A WOMAN

Tirso.   Tirso de Molina (1579–1648), Spanish poet and dramatist.

BLESSÈD ARE THE NORMAL

Antonia Eiriz.   (1929–1995), Cuban painter.

BEING ASKED ABOUT THE PERSIANS

Matta.   Roberto Matta (1912–2002), Franco-Chilean surrealist painter.
Darío.   Rubén Darío (1867–1916), Nicaraguan poet.

Fayad Jamís (Zacatecas, Mexico, 1930–Havana, 1988)

Brújula (Las Villas: Imp. Wilfredo Rodríguez, 1949); *Los párpados y el polvo* (Havana: Orígenes, 1954); *Vagabundo del alba* (Havana: La Tertulia, 1959); *Cuatro poemas en China* (Havana: FJ, 1961); *La pedrada* (Havana: La Tertulia, 1962); *Por esta libertad* (Havana: Casa de las Américas, 1962); *Los puentes, Poesía: 1956–57* (Havana: Eds. R, 1962); *La victoria de Playa Girón* (Havana: Unión, 1964); *Cuerpos* (Havana: Unión, 1966); *Abrí la verja de hierro* (Havana: Unión, 1973); *Entre la muerte y el alba* (Havana: Unión, 1994); *Historia de un hombre* (Havana: Letras Cubanas, 1995); *La pedrada: selección poética (1951–1973)* (Havana: Letras Cubanas, 1981); *Sólo el amor* (Guadalajara, Mexico: Presente y Futuro, 1983)

Poet, painter, and editor. He and his family moved to Cuba when he was an infant. He spent 1955 to 1959 in Paris, returning to Cuba after the Revolution. Thereafter he edited several journals. Between 1964 and 1966 he was a member of the executive board of the literary section of UNEAC, and then a member of its secretariat. From 1973 until his death he was cultural attaché to the Cuban consulate in Mexico.

WANDERER OF THE DAWN

the war.   The 1956 Suez War.
la rue du Chat-qui-Pêche.   A narrow alley in Paris' Latin Quarter.

Escardó.   Rolando Escardó (1925–1960), Cuban poet.

Heberto Padilla (Pinar del Río, 1932–Auburn, Alabama, 2000)

Las rosas audaces (Havana: Los Nuevos, 1948); *El justo tiempo humano* (Havana: Unión, 1962); *La hora* (Havana: La Tertulia, 1964); *Fuera del juego* (Havana: Unión, 1968; Miami: Universal, 1998); *Por el momento* (Las Palmas: Inventarios Provisionales, 1970); *Provocaciones* (Madrid: La Gota de Agua, 1973); *Poesía y política. Poemas escogidos de Heberto Padilla / Poetry and Politics: Selected Poems of Heberto Padilla* (Madrid: Playor, 1974), bilingual; *El hombre junto al mar* (Barcelona: Seix Barral, 1981); *Legacies: Selected Poems* (New York: Farrar, Straus, Giroux, 1982), bilingual; *A Fountain, a House of Stone* (New York: Farrar, Straus, Giroux, 1991), bilingual

Poet, novelist, translator, and memoirist. He married Belkis Cuza Malé in 1967. He lived in the United States from 1949 to 1952 and 1955 to 1959, returning to Cuba after the Revolution, where he was involved in *Lunes de Revolución*. Subsequently he was sent to London and the Soviet Union as a correspondent for *Prensa Latina* and *Revolución* and as director of CUBARTIMPEX, which acquired foreign books for import to Cuba and exported Cuban books abroad. He returned to Cuba in 1968. That year UNEAC awarded *Fuera del juego* the prestigious Julián del Casal Prize, though the simultaneous condemnation of the book by the Department of Internal Affairs sparked what has come to be known as the Padilla Affair (see Introduction). As a consequence, he and his wife were briefly imprisoned in 1971. He was allowed to leave Cuba in 1980, and he settled in the United States, where he taught at Princeton, New York University, the University of Miami, and Auburn University and co-directed *Linden Lane Magazine* with Belkis Cuza Malé. His memoir *La mala memoria* (Barcelona: Plaza & Janés, 1989), translated as *Self-Portrait of the Other* (New York: Farrar, Straus, Giroux, 1990), is largely his account of the Padilla Affair and of literary relationships in postrevolutionary Cuba.

José Álvarez Baragaño (Pinar del Río, 1932–Havana, 1962)

Cambiar la vida (Paris: Le Soleil Noir, 1952); *El amor original* (Havana: Castor, 1955); *Poesía, revolución del ser* (Havana: Eds. R, 1960); *Himno a las milicias y sus poemas* (Havana: Guerrero, 1961); *Poemas escogidos* (Havana: Unión, 1963); *Poesía color de libertad* (Havana: Unión, 1977); *Himno a Camilo Cienfuegos* (Havana: Unión, 2004)

Baragaño lived in Paris from 1951 to 1954, where he was active in Surrealist circles. Upon his return to Cuba he became a columnist for *Revolución,* the newspaper of the July 26th Movement, and after the Revolution a part of the group that edited its literary supplement, *Lunes de Revolución.* He participated in the Playa Girón (Bay of Pigs) and Escambray campaigns. In 1961 he became UNEAC's first director of public relations.

*Donner un sens plus pur aux mots de la tribu/*To give a purer meaning to the words of the tribe.   From Stéphane Mallarmé, "Le tombeau d'Edgar Poe."

César López (Santiago, 1933–)

Silencio en voz de muerte (Havana: Unión, 1963); *Apuntes para un pequeño viaje* (Havana: La Tertulia, 1965); *Primer libro de la ciudad* (Havana: Unión, 1967); *La búsqueda y su signo* (Las Palmas, Spain: Inventarios Provisionales, 1971); *Segundo libro de la ciudad* (Barcelona: Ocnos, 1971); *Quiebra de la perfección* (Havana: Unión, 1983); *Ceremonias y ceremoniales* (Havana: Letras Cubanas, 1988); *Consideraciones, algunas elegías* (Madrid: Orígenes, 1990); *Doble espejo para muerte denigrante* (Havana: Extramuros, 1991); *Seis canciones ligeramente ingenuas* (Madrid: Taller Tórculo II, 1992); *Pasos, paseo, pasadizos* (Udine, Italy: n.p., 1996); *Tercer libro de la ciudad* (Seville: Renacimiento, 1997; Havana: Letras Cubanas, 1998); *Libro de la ciudad* (Havana: Unión, 2001); *Manos de un caminante* (Santiago: Editorial Oriente, 2005); *Paisaje, panorama* (Havana: Letras Cubanas, 2007)

Poet, short story writer, critic, and scholar. Active in clandestine revolutionary organizations before the Revolution. From 1960 to 1962 he was consul general of Cuba in Glasgow, Scotland. Upon his return until 1963 he served as head of the consular department for Western Europe in the Ministry of Foreign Affairs (1962–1963). He was coordinator of the literary section of UNEAC, of which he was a founding member, and activities secretary of the Pen Club of Cuba. Since 1972 he has worked in the translation department and in the Institute of Scientific and Technical Information of the Cuban Academy of Science. He is a member of the Academia Cubana de la Lengua and the Real Academia de la Lengua Española. He lives in Havana.

AS IN ANY RESPECTABLE CITY

Rilke.   Rainer Maria Rilke (1875–1926). The quotations are from his first and second "Duino Elegies."
Rafael Alberti.   Spanish poet (1902–1999). See his *Sobre los ángeles* (1929).

THE POET IN THE CITY

All of the quotations are adapted from poems and song lyrics. In order: "Apoyá en el quicio de la mancebía . . . encenderse las noches de mayo," from Rafael de León (1908–1982), "Ojos verdes"; "la soledad, la lluvia, los caminos," from César Vallejo (1832–1938), "Piedra negra sobre una piedra blanca"; "sorda a los ayes, insensible al ruego," from Gabriel de la Concepción Valdés (1809–1844), "A una ingrata"; "mudo y absorto y de rodillas," from Gustavo Adolfo Béquer (1836–1870), "Rima LIII"; "entra y sale un perro triste . . . ," from José Martí (1853–1895), "Los dos príncipes"; "aún guardo las dos blancas azucenas . . . ," from Pedro Flores Córdoba (1897–1979), "Blancas azucenas." "Quiebra de la perfección" is the name of one of López' books.
santera.   A female practitioner of *santería.*

Antón Arrufat (Santiago, 1935–)

En claro (Havana: La Tertulia, 1962); *Repaso final* (Havana: Eds. R, 1964); *Escrito en las puertas* (Havana: Instituto del Libro, 1968); *La huella en la arena* (Havana: Letras Cubanas, 1986); *Lirios sobre un fondo de espadas* (Havana: Letras Cubanas, 1995); *Celare navis y otros poemas* (Matanzas: Vigía, 1996); *El viejo carpintero* (Havana: Unión, 1999); *Antología personal* (Barcelona: Mondadori, 2000); *La huella en la arena. Poemas reunidos* (Havana: Unión, 2001).

Internationally recognized playwright and novelist, as well as a poet and editor. He returned to Havana from a two-year stay in New York immediately after the Revolution. From 1960 to 1965 he was editor of the journal of the Casa de las Américas. In 1968 his play *Los siete contra Tebas* (Havana: Unión, 1968) was awarded UNEAC's prize for drama and promptly condemned as counterrevolutionary. He edited his friend Virgilio Piñera's *La isla en peso. Obra poética* (Havana: Unión, 1998) and wrote the memoir *Virgilio Piñera: entre él y yo* (Havana: Unión, 1994). With Reina María Rodríguez he edits *Azoteas*, a magazine and small press. He lives in Havana.

FINAL REVISION 5

El monte/forest.   See note to "Birth of Eggo," page 573.

[*Oh*] *noche, sol del triste.*   From José Martí (1853–1895), *Águila blanca.* The poem melds Martí and *santería* ceremonies.

yagruma.   A common Caribbean tree, *Cecropia peltata.*

José Kozer (Havana, 1940–)

SELECTED BIBLIOGRAPHY: *Este judío de números y letras* (Tenerife: Católica, 1975); *Bajo este cien* (Mexico City: Fondo de Cultura Económica, 1983); *La garza sin sombras* (Barcelona: Llibres del Mall, 1985); *El carillón de los muertos* (Buenos Aires: Último Reino, 1987); *Carece de causa* (Buenos Aires: Último Reino, 1988); *et mutabile* (Xalapa, Mexico: Graffiti, 1995); *AAA1144* (Mexico City: Verdehalago–UAM Azcapotzalco, 1997); *La maquinaria ilimitada* (Mexico City: Sin Nombre, 1998); *Mezcla para dos tiempos* (Mexico City: Aldus 1999); *Rupestres* (Curitiba, Brazil: Tigre do Espelho, 2001); *Bajo este cien y otros poemas* (Barcelona: El Bardo, 2002); *Rosa cúbica* (Buenos Aires: Tsé-tsé, 2002); *No buscan reflejarse* (Havana: Letras Cubanas, 2002); *Ánima* (Mexico City: Fondo de Cultura Económica, 2002); *Un caso llamado FK* (Mexico City: Editorial Sin Nombre, 2002); *Una huella destartalada. Diarios* (Mexico City: Aldus, 2003); *Y del esparto la invariabilidad* (Madrid: Visor, 2005); *Ogi no mato* (Mexico City: UACM, 2005); *Stet: Selected Poems* (New York: Junction Press, 2006), bilingual; *Trasvasando* (Caracas: Monte Ávila, 2006)

The child of Eastern European Jewish immigrants, Kozer first left Cuba in 1958 to study at NYU. He returned after the Revolution but left definitively in 1960, working in New York City at menial jobs while completing his education. From 1967 to 1997 he taught at Queens College in New York. After retirement he lived in Spain for two years, after which he and his wife settled in Hallandale, north of Miami, Florida. He has written over thirty-five books of poetry, which have been published in virtually every Latin American country and in Spain. With Roberto Echavarren and Jacobo Sefamí he edited *Medusario: Muestra de la poesía latinoamericana* (Mexico City: Fondo de Cultura Económica, 1996), a defining anthology of *neobarroco* poetry of the 1980s and 1990s. *No buscan reflejarse* (2002) was the first poetry collection by a living Cuban exile to be published in Cuba since the early 1970s.

ANIMA

Guadalupe.   The poet's wife.

DANZONETE

danzonete.   A Cuban musical and dance genre of the 1930s.

Miguel Barnet (Havana, 1940–)

La piedrafina y el pavorreal (Havana: Unión, 1963); *Isla de güije* (Havana: El Puente, 1964); *La sagrada familia* (Havana: Casa de las Américas, 1967); *Orikis y otros poemas* (Havana: Letras Cubanas, 1980); *Carta de noche* (Havana: Unión, 1982); *Claves por Rita Montaner* (Matanzas: Centro de Información Ecuménica «Augusto Coto», 1987); *Viendo mi vida pasar* (Havana: Letras Cubanas, 1987); *Mapa del tiempo* (Havana: Letras Cubanas, 1989); *Poemas chinos* (Havana: Unión, 1993); *Con pies de gato* (Havana: Unión, 1993); *Actas del final* (Havana: Letras Cubanas, 2000); *When Night Is Darkest* (Havana: José Martí, 2002), translated by Charles Dean Hatfield, bilingual; *Cuaderno de París* (Matanzas: Vigía, 2003)

Poet, novelist, ethnographer, and screenwriter, best known for a series of "ethnographic novels." He was a founding member and vice president of UNEAC, becoming its president in 2008, and one of the founders of the Cuban Academy of Science and the Fundación Fernando Ortiz (Cuba's major ethnographic institute), which he has directed since its inception in 1995. In 1996 he was appointed a member of the executive council of UNESCO. He is a member of the National Assembly of the People's Power (Asamblea Nacional del Poder Popular).

DEATH'S LIKE THAT

Castillo de la Punta.   Castillo de San Salvador de la Punta, a sixteenth-century fortress guarding the entrance to Havana harbor.

santero.   A male practitioner of *santería.*

Oggún Arere.   One of the Orishas.

Paseo del Prado.   A mile-long street with a broad island running down its center, on the edge of Havana's old quarter. Popular for evening strolls, but also a longtime cruising ground for homosexuals and prostitutes.

bar of chocolate.   Cuban slang: black penis.

CUBAN SUITE

Committee of Defense.   Committees for Defense of the Revolution serve as neighborhood arms of the internal security apparatus but also as neighborhood advocates for goods and services.

Orlando de la Rosa.   Cuban singer-songwriter of *boleros de filin* (1919–1957).

Malecón.   The seawall that runs the length of Havana, and the boulevard that parallels it.

danzón.   A traditional Cuban dance music genre, of European derivation.

Valenzuela.   Raimundo (1848–1905) and Pablo (1859–1926), composers and conductors of *danzones.*

Mariana Gamborino.   Either Manuela Gamborino or Mariana Galino, Spanish dancers and courtesans, active in Havana in the 1810s and 1820s. See Alejo Carpentier, *La música en Cuba* (Havana: Letras Cubanas, 1988), p. 150.

marimbula.   A Caribbean folk instrument similar to a very large African kalimba.

WALKING THE CITY

Vedado.   One of Havana's better neighborhoods.

Julián del Casal.   Cuban poet and journalist (1868–1893). See Introduction, p. 6.

son.   A Cuban popular music genre, of African and Spanish derivation.

Teodora Ginés.   Freed slave who is said to have invented the *son* at the end of the sixteenth century.

volunteers for the harvest.   City dwellers who helped bring in the crucial sugar crop during the early years of the Revolution.

Belkis Cuza Malé (Guantánamo, 1942–)

El viento en la pared (Santiago: Universidad de Oriente, 1962); *Los alucinados* (Santiago: Unión, 1962); *Tiempos de sol* (Havana: El Puente, 1963); *Cartas a Ana Frank* (Havana: Unión, 1966); *Juego de damas* (Havana: Unión, 1971; Cincinnati: Termino Editorial, 2002)

Poet, essayist, and journalist. She married Heberto Padilla in 1969 and was jailed briefly in 1971, at which time her just-published book *Juego de damas* was withdrawn from circulation. She left Cuba in 1979 and currently lives in Fort Worth, Texas, where she directs La Casa Azul, the Heberto Padilla Cuban Cultural Center. She is also editor of *Linden Lane Magazine*, a quarterly literary journal which she founded with Padilla in 1982.

Nancy Morejón (Havana, 1944–)

Mutismos (Havana: El Puente, 1962); *Amor, ciudad atribuida* (Havana: El Puente, 1964); *Richard trajo su flauta y otros argumentos* (Havana: Unión, 1967); *Parajes de una época* (Havana: Letras Cubanas, 1979); *Octubre imprescindible* (Havana: Unión, 1982); *Elogio de la danza* (Mexico City: UNAM, 1982); *Cuaderno de Granada* (Havana: Casa de las Américas, 1984); *Piedra pulida* (Havana: Letras Cubanas, 1986); *Baladas para un sueño* (Havana: Unión, 1991); *Poemas de amor y muerte* (Toulouse, France: Revista Caravelle, 1993); *Paisaje célebre* (Caracas: Fondo Editorial Fundarte, 1993); *Elogio y paisaje* (Havana: Unión, 1996); *El río de Martín Pérez y otros poemas* (Matanzas: Vigía, 1996); *La Quinta de los Molinos* (Havana: Letras Cubanas, 2000); *Cántico de la huella* (Matanzas: Vigía, 2002); *Cuerda veloz. Antología poética, 1962–1992* (Havana: Letras Cubanas, 2002); *Looking Within: Selected Poems, 1954–2000 / Mirar adentro: poemas escogidos, 1954–2000* (Detroit: Wayne State University Press, 2003), bilingual; *Carbones silvestres* (Havana: Letras Cubanas, 2005); *Estos otros argumentos* (Santiago: Santiago, 2005)

Poet, translator, ethnographer, and critic. Director of Caribbean Studies of the Casa de las Américas from 1986 to 1993, and again from 2000 to the present. From 1995 to 2000 she was an advisor to the governing body of the National Theater of Cuba. In 1999 she became a member of the Cuban Academy of Science.

Luis Rogelio Nogueras (Havana, 1944–1985)

Cabeza de zanahoria (Havana: Unión, 1967); *Las quince mil vidas del caminante* (Havana: Unión, 1977); *Imitación de la vida* (Havana: Casa de las Américas, 1981); *El último caso del inspector* (Havana: Letras Cubanas, 1983); *Nada del otro mundo* (Havana: Letras Cubanas, 1988); *La forma de las cosas que vendrán* (Havana: Letras Cubanas, 1989); *Las palabras vuelven* (Havana, Unión, 1994); *Encicloferia. Antología poética* (Mexico City: Mucuglifo/Fin de Siglo, 1999); *Hay muchos modos de jugar. Poesía completa* (Havana: Letras Cubanas, 2006)

Poet, novelist, editor, and filmmaker. He worked in various editorial jobs at the Instituto Cubano del Libro from 1960 to 1979, and in 1966–1967 edited the newly formed *Caimán Barbudo*. A member of ICAIC, he worked as an animator, cameraman, director, and screenwriter. In 1980 he became editor of the review *Cine cubano*.

DON'T LOOK BACK, LONESOME BOY

Zenea.   Juan Clemente Zenea (1834–1871), Cuban poet and a martyr of the war for independence against Spain. The quote is from his poem "Fidelia."

(INTERRUPTED IAMBS)

Jean Sénac.   Algerian poet and novelist of French extraction (1926–1973), hero of the Algerian struggle for independence, and minister of education in the first post-independence government. Assassinated in 1973. The quote appears to be from a translation of his poem "Citoyens de beauté."

LOSS OF THE LOVE POEM CALLED "MIST"

Luis Marré.   Cuban poet (1926–).

PRAYER FOR THE SON WHO WILL NEVER BE BORN

In *El último caso . . .* , ascribed to Miki Taisuke:

> Miki Taisuke was born in Yeddo (now Tokyo) in 1784. In her brief life, this important poet wrote twenty-four long works in verse and a treatise on martial arts. She practiced haiku (poems consisting of seventeen syllables) in the style of Master Shida Noha (1663–1740).
>
> Only daughter of the powerful daimyo of Izunohara and an extraordinary and famous beauty (when she was sixteen her portrait was drawn by the great Katsushika Hokusai), she scorned her numerous suitors and divided her time between *belles lettres* and *zu/yu/the* (a kind of karate). To her father's displeasure, she held numerous public combats with expert *senseis* (masters) of judo, jiujitsu, and karate/do. She also mastered fencing (kendo).
>
> Despite her aristocratic origin, Miki Taisuke denounced harshly in her works the miserable lives of the people.
>
> The poetess died in Yokkaichi, in 1805, in a duel with the legendary *gokenin* (samurai in service to the Shogun) Kiba Fukagawa.
>
> The poems of Miki Taisuke were collected in book form for the first time at the late date of 1926, under the title of *Hogu Zuka* (Paper Tumulus).

A POEM

In his book *El último caso del inspector* Nogueras gathered together a group of poems, most of which had been published independently under his own name, as an "anthology," complete with biographies of their fictional authors. For "A Poem" he supplied the following:

> Anonymous.
> "A poem" was written by a soldier of the Sandinista Front for National Liberation in the final days of the uprising against the tyranny of Anastasio Somoza. We include it here not only for its literary quality, but as a brotherly homage to courageous Nicaragua. As well, it's not easy to find another text that expresses as forcefully as this the mystery of artistic inspiration, that indirect, dialectical relationship between word and man.

THE DETECTIVE'S LAST CASE

In *El último caso . . .* ascribed to Joe Bell:

For lack of evidence, we have no alternative but to accept as legitimate the thesis that the English critic Thomas Hogarth more than thirty years ago forcefully put forward: that "Murder" was written by Joe Bell, a former grammar instructor of Conan Doyle's, whose sharp face, extravagant tastes, and curious facility for noticing certain details was a partial inspiration for Sherlock Holmes.

Very little is known about Bell. Even Hogarth can offer little concrete information about this enigmatic model for the immortal Holmes. The trump card that the English critic raised to defend his thesis is a brief note, appearing on the page corresponding to Tuesday, February 11, 1888, in the account book of the defunct London periodical *Express*, in which is noted: "17 guineas paid to Mr. Joe Bell, author of the poem 'Murder,' which appeared signed by William Eliot pseud[onym] in the edition of 8–2 [February 8]."

Hogarth affirms that the director of *Express,* Sir Gilbert Cuff, was a close friend of Doyle's, and that it was probably he who submitted his old instructor's poem for publication.

The translation (in free verse) of "Murder" was provided by Samuel Spade, who preferred the title "The Inspector's Last Case."

VOYAGE

All references are to Boris Pasternak's *Dr. Zhivago.*

Lina de Feria (Santiago, 1945–)

Vocecita del alba (Santiago: D.N.P., 1961); *Casa que no existía* (Havana: Unión, 1967); *A mansalva de los años* (Havana: Unión, 1990); *Espiral en la tierra* (Havana: Unión, 1991); *A la llegada del delfín* (Havana: Unión, 1998); *El mar de las invenciones* (Havana: Letras Cubanas, 1999); *El rostro equidistante* (Santiago: Editorial Oriente, 2001); *Omisión de la noche* (Matanzas: Matanzas, 2003); *País sin abedules* (Havana: Unión, 2003); *Absolución del amor* (Havana: Unión, 2005)

Poet, playwright, and essayist. She succeeded her friend Luis Rogelio Nogueras as editor of *El Caimán Barbudo* (1968–1971). In 2005 she illegally crossed the border from Mexico into the United States, causing a considerable stir in the exile community. She spent two months with her son in Miami and returned to Cuba. She claimed that she had wanted to be present at the birth of her grandchild. She lives in Havana.

Delfín Prats (Holguín, 1945–)

Lenguaje de mudos (Madrid: El Puente, 1970); *Para festejar el ascenso de Ícaro* (Havana: Letras Cubanas, 1987); *El esplendor y el caos* (Holguín: Holguín, 1991); *Cinco envíos a Arboleda* (Holguín: Holguín, 1991); *Abrirse las constelaciones* (Havana: Unión, 1994); *El esplendor y el caos* (Havana: Unión, 2002)

Poet. Resident in Holguín.

NEVER RETURN TO THE SCENES OF YOUR HAPPINESS

First published in *Para festejar el ascenso de Ícaro* (1987). The second, third and fourth lines don't appear in print until *El esplendor y el caos* (2002), from which this version was drawn.

IN CELEBRATION OF THE ASCENT OF ICARUS

First published as the title poem *of Para festejar el ascenso de Ícaro* (1987), lineated, and dedicated "A Yuri Gagarin." The current version is drawn from *El esplendor y el caos* (2002).

Icarus. According to Greek myth, Icarus flew on wings of his father's devising, attached to his shoulders with wax, which melted when he flew too close to the sun. Aetna. The mountain in Sicily where Icarus began his flight.

Patmos. Site of the visions recorded by Saint John in the *Book of Revelation*. *Civitas Dei*. *The City of God*, by Saint Augustine.

Excilia Saldaña (Havana, 1946–1999)

Soñando y viajando (Havana: Gente Nueva, 1980); *Cantos para Mayito y una paloma* (Havana: Unión, 1983); *Kele Kele* (Havana: Letras Cubanas, 1987); *La noche* (Havana: Gente Nueva, 1989); *El refranero de la Víbora* (Havana: Gente Nueva, 1989); *Mi nombre: antielegía familiar* (Havana: Unión, 1991); *In the Vortex of the Cyclone* (Gainesville: University Press of Florida, 2002), bilingual; *Mi nombre* (Havana: Unión, 2003)

Poet, author of children's books, editor, essayist, and translator. She taught at several Cuban universities and held important editorial positions, including that of children's book publisher at Editorial Gente Nueva. She was a member of the Cuban committee of the International Board on Books for Young People and president of the children's literature section of UNEAC.

Jorge Berroa. Cuban composer (1938–).

Raúl Hernández Novás (Havana, 1948–1993)

Da capo (Havana: Unión, 1982); *Enigma de las aguas* (Havana: Universidad de Havana, 1983); *Los ríos de la mañana* (Havana: Juventud Rebelde, 1984); *Embajador en el horizonte* (Havana: Letras Cubanas, 1984); *Animal civil* (Havana: Unión, 1987); *Al más cercano amigo* (Havana: Letras Cubanas, 1987); *Sonetos a Gelsomina* (Havana: Unión, 1991); *Atlas salta* (Havana: Letras Cubanas, 1995); *Amnios* (Havana: Ateneo, 1998); *Poesía* (Havana: Casa de las Américas, 2006)

Poet, scholar, and critic. As a scholar he worked for the Center for Literary Research of the Casa de las Américas. Among other works of scholarship and criticism he edited César Vallejo, *Poesía completa* (Havana: Centro de Investigaciones Literarias, Casa de las Américas, 1988).

Author's note: "This poem is based loosely on images and characters from the film *One Flew Over the Cuckoo's Nest*, by Milos Forman." The film in turn was based on the novel by Ken Kesey (New York: Viking Press, 1962).

Translations of the epigraphs from Lezama's "Pensamientos en la Habana" are, with minor changes, from James Irby's version on page 61 of this volume. Several popular English-language songs are quoted, in the following order: "I'll Be Back" (Lennon/McCartney), "If I Were a Carpenter" (Tim Hardin), "Let 'Em In" (Paul McCartney), "The Sound of Silence" (Paul Simon), "Let the Sunshine In" (Gerome Ragni and James Rado), "Let It Be" (Lennon/McCartney), and "Let It Bleed" (Jagger/Richards).

rio manzanares . . . déjame pasar / manzanares river . . . let me cross over.   The first
line and title of a song by José Antonio López Mata (1920?–1971).

Amando Fernández (Havana, 1949–Miami, 1994)

Herir al tiempo (Miami: SIBI, 1986); *Perfil de la materia* (Miami: SIBI, 1986);
Azar en sombra (Miami: SIBI, 1987); *Rostrum* (n.p., 1987); *Pentagrama* (c. 1988);
El ruiseñor y la espada (Córdoba, Spain: Diputación Provincial, 1989); *Los siete
círculos* (León, Spain: Ayuntamiento de León, 1990); *Materia y forma* (Badajoz,
Spain: Departamento de Publicaciones de la Diputación Provincial de Badajoz,
1990); *Espacio mayor* (Huelva, Spain: La Diputación, 1991); *Antología personal*
(Lima, Peru: Jaime Campodónico, 1991); *Museo natural* (Coral Gables, Fla.:
Arenas, 1993); *Lingua franca* (Coral Gables, Fla.: Arenas, 1993); *El mino-
tauro* (Coral Gables, Fla.: Arenas, 1993); *El riesgo calculado* (Cáceres, Spain:
Colección Cocodrilo Verde, 1994); *Ciudad, isla invisible* (Coral Gables, Fla.:
La Torre de Papel, 1994); *La rendición, La túnica dorada, Las miradas de jano*
(León, Spain: Institución "Fray Bernardino de Sahagún," 1995)

Fernández left Cuba with his family in 1960. He and his family lived in Madrid until
1980, when they moved to Miami. He taught at the Interamerican Campus of Miami
Dade College.

Soleida Ríos (Santiago, 1950–)

De la sierra (Santiago: Uvero, 1977); *De pronto abril* (Havana: Unión, 1979);
Entre mundo y juguete (Havana: Letras Cubanas, 1987); *Un soplo dispersa los
límites del hogar* (Matanzas: Vigía, 1995); *El libro roto* (Havana: Unión, 1995);
Libro cero (Havana: Letras Cubanas, 1999); *El texto sucio* (Havana: Unión,
1999); *El libro de los sueños* (Havana: Letras Cubanas, 1999); *Fuga. Una
antología personal* (Havana: Unión, 2004)

Poet and fiction writer. She edited an anthology of young Cuban women poets, *Poesía
infiel* (Havana: Abril, 1989). A participant in Reina María Rodríguez' *azotea*. She lives
in Havana.

THE WITCH'S BIRD

El monte/forest.   See note to "Birth of Eggo," page 573.

MALEVA AND THE CHILDREN IN PARADISE

J. L. Borges.   Jorge Luis Borges (1899–1986), Argentine poet and fiction writer. The
quotation is from *La cifra*.

GATHERING LEMONS

Asteroide.   The poet's apartment.

Lourdes Gil (Havana, 1950–)

Neumas (New York: Senda Nueva de Ediciones, 1977); *Vencido el fuego de la
especie* (Somerville, N.J.: Slusa Editores, 1983); *Blanca aldaba preludia* (Madrid:
Editorial Betania, 1989); *Empieza la ciudad* (Coral Gables, Fla.: La Torre de
Papel, 1993); *El cerco de las transfiguraciones* (Coral Gables, Fla.: La Torre de
Papel, 1996); *Ánima vagula* (Madrid: Verbum, 2007)

Poet, teacher, editor, and journalist. She left Cuba in 1961 in the Pedro Pan airlift and has lived in New Jersey since then. She teaches at Baruch College of the City University of New York and the Tenafly Adult School of New Jersey. She was co-director of the literary magazines *Lyra* and *Románica*. In 1994 she was guest editor of *Brújula*, the magazine of the New York Institute of Latin American Writers.

THE BIRDS' INSOMNIA LAST NIGHT

[Epigraph]. Heberto Padilla, "Estado de sitio," in *Fuera del juego* (Havana: UNEAC, 1968).
Los montes/wastelands. See note to "Birth of Eggo," page 573.

FATA MORGANA

Jesús Díaz. Cuban novelist and filmmaker (1942–2002). Founder of the journal *Encuentro*.

Reina María Rodríguez (Havana, 1952–)

La gente de mi barrio (Havana: Universidad de La Habana, 1975); *Cuando una mujer no duerme* (Havana: Unión, 1982); *Para un cordero blanco* (Havana: Casa de las Américas, 1984); *En la arena de Padua* (Havana: Unión, 1991); *Páramos* (Havana: Unión, 1995); *Ellas escriben cartas de amor* (Havana: Unión, 1998); *La foto del invernadero* (Havana: Casa de las Américas, 1998); *Como un extraño pájaro que viene del sur* (Paris: Fourbis, 1998); . . . *Te daré de comer como a los pájaros . . .* (Havana: Letras Cubanas, 2000); *Otras cartas a Milena* (Havana: Unión, 2003); *Una muchacha loca como los pájaros. Antología personal* (Mexico City: Ediciones Coyoacán, 2003); *Violet Island and Other Poems*, translated by Kristin Dykstra and Nancy Gates Madsen (Los Angeles: Green Integer, 2004), bilingual; *Bosque negro* (Havana: Extramuros, 2005); *Time's Arrest/La detención del tiempo*, edited and translated by Kristin Dykstra (San Diego, Calif.: Factory School, 2005); *El libro de las clientas* (Havana: Letras Cubanas, 2005); *Catch and Release* (Havana: Letras Cubanas, 2006)

Poet and novelist. Since the late 1980s her *azotea*, or rooftop apartment, has been both a gathering place and a salon for artists and writers, among them Antón Arrufat, Omar Pérez, Antonio José Ponte, Pedro Marqués de Armas, Carlos Aguilera, Javier Marimón, Alessandra Molina, Juan Carlos Flores, and Ismael González Castañer. She directs the small press Torre de Letras and, with Arrufat, publishes and edits *Azoteas*, a journal. Since 1998 she has edited the poetry column "La Azotea de Reina" in the important ezine *La Habana Elegante*.

A GIRL MAD AS BIRDS

Dylan Thomas. Welsh poet (1914–1953). The quotation is from his "Love in the Asylum."

FISHERMEN (ROUGH)

J. A. Miralles. Jorge Miralles (1967–), Cuban fiction writer and translator.

Abilio Estévez (Havana, 1954–)

Manual de las tentaciones (Havana: Letras Cubanas, 1989)

Novelist, playwright, screenwriter, and poet. He has been living in Barcelona for the past several years.

Iraida Iturralde (Havana, 1954–)

Hubo la viola (Hoboken, N.J.: Viento y Marea, 1979); *Tropel de espejos* (Madrid: Betania, 1989); *Discurso de las Infantas* (Coral Gables, Fla.: La Torre de Papel, 1997); *La isla rota* (Madrid: Verbum, 2002)

Poet, translator, and editor. She left Cuba in 1962 in the Pedro Pan airlift. She was co-director of the literary magazines *Lyra* and *Románica*. President of the Cuban Cultural Center of New York. She lives in New Jersey.

Ruth Behar (Havana, 1956–)

Poemas que vuelven a Cuba / Poems Returned to Cuba (Matanzas: Vigía, 1995); *Todo lo que guardé / Everything I Kept* (Matanzas: Vigía, 2001), monolingual English

Ethnographer, fiction writer, filmmaker, and poet. She left Cuba with her family in 1961 and arrived in New York in 1962, after a year in Israel. The author of several important ethnographic studies, she also edited the anthologies *Bridges to Cuba* (Ann Arbor: University of Michigan Press, 1995) and *The Portable Island: Cubans at Home in the World* (New York: Palgrave MacMillan, 2008), with Lucía M. Suárez. She wrote, directed, and produced *Adio Kerida / Goodbye Dear Love: A Cuban Sephardic Journey* (2002), a feature-length documentary. She is professor of anthropology at the University of Michigan and a recipient of a MacArthur Foundation Award.

Ángel Escobar (Guantánamo, 1957–Havana, 1997)

Viejas palabras de uso (Havana: Unión, 1978); *Epílogo famoso* (Havana: Letras Cubanas, 1985); *Allegro de sonata* (Havana: Unión, 1987); *La vía pública* (Havana: Letras Cubanas, 1987); *Malos pasos* (Havana: Letras Cubanas, 1991); *Todavía* (Havana: Unión, 1991); *Abuso de confianza* (Santiago, Chile: Kipus 21, 1992; Havana: Letras Cubanas, 1994); *Cuando salí de La Habana* (Zaragoza, Spain: Olifante, 1996; Havana: Unión, 1997); *El examen no ha terminado* (Zaragoza, Spain: Galería Lausín & Blasco, 1997; Havana: Letras Cubanas, 1999); *La sombra del decir* (Zaragoza, Spain: Galería Lausín & Blasco, 1997; Havana: Unión, 2003); *Poesía completa* (Havana: Unión, 2006)

Poet, fiction writer, and dramatist.

Ramón Fernández Larrea (Bayamo, 1958–)

El pasado del cielo (Havana: Unión, 1987); *Poemas para ponerse en la cabeza* (Havana: Abril, 1989); *El libro de las instrucciones* (Havana: Unión, 1991); *Manual de pasión* (Guadalajara, Mexico: Universidad de Guadalajara, 1993); *El libro de los salmos feroces* (Havana: Extramuros, 1994); *Terneros que nunca mueran de rodillas* (Santa Cruz de Tenerife: Nuestro Arte, Ayuntamiento, 1998); *Cantar del tigre ciego* (Guadalajara, Mexico: Arlequín, 2001); *Nunca canté en Broadway* (Barcelona: Linkgua, 2005)

Poet, essayist, and fiction writer. Between 1989 and 1991 he produced *El Programa de Ramón*, a weekly broadcast on Radio Ciudad de Havana. He writes the weekly satirical *Columna de Ramón* for *Encuentro en la Red* (www.cubaencuentro.com). He left Cuba in 1995 for Barcelona. Currently he lives in Miami.

Victor Rodríguez Núñez.   Cuban poet, resident in Ohio (1955–).

SINGING WITH MY GRANDMOTHER ON MY LAP
"alánimo . . . la fuente se rompió" / "Courage! . . . the fountain is broken."   First line
of a popular children's song.
The two quotations in italics are from the lyrics to "Eleanor Rigby" (Lennon/
McCartney) and "Rain" (Lennon/McCartney).

THE LAND OF ELVES
Email from the poet: "I left Cuba in June of 1995 with a phony invitation from a Span-
ish organization, supposedly to direct some documentaries. I had been abroad at vari-
ous times: in 1985–86 in the Angolan War; in 1986 in the former German Democratic
Republic; in 1990 in Czechoslovakia. The following year I was in France, where I
thought to remain, but decided otherwise. And in 1993 I lived in Guadalajara, Mexico,
for several months, but I returned to the island. By '95 [my] situation was insupport-
able and unsustainable. Out of all this weariness comes the 'damn' *[cojones]* of 'The
Land of Elves,' which is something like 'the promised future, idyllic communism.'"

Roberto Méndez (Camagüey, 1958–)

   Carta de relación (Havana: Letras Cubanas, 1988); *Manera de estar solo*
   (Havana: Unión, 1989); *Desayuno sobre la hierba con máscara* (Havana:
   Unión, 1993); *Música de cámara para los delfines* (Havana: Letras Cubanas,
   1994); *Soledad en la plaza de la Vigía* (Matanzas: Vigía, 1995); *Cuaderno de
   Aliosha* (Camagüey: Ácana, 2000); *Viendo acabado tanto reino fuerte* (Havana:
   Letras Cubanas, 2001); *Libro del invierno* (Havana: Letras Cubanas, 2002);
   Autorretrato con cardo (Havana: Unión, 2004)

   Poet, fiction writer, and art critic. He lives in Camagüey.

THE STELLAR
[Epigraph].   From a letter dated "end of January 1964" to Carlos M. Luis, reprinted
   in *deLiras* 11 (April 2001): 38. Luis (1932–) is a Cuban artist, poet, and essayist,
   resident in the United States since 1962.

Rolando Sánchez Mejías (Holguín, 1959–)

   Collage en azul adorable (Havana: Letras Cubanas, 1991); *Derivas* (Havana:
   Letras Cubanas, 1994); *Cálculo de lindes (1986–1996)* (Mexico City: Aldus,
   2000)

   Poet and writer of short fiction. He left Cuba in 1997 and currently lives in Barcelona.
   From 1997 until 2002 he edited, with Carlos Aguilera, the influential photocopy jour-
   nal *Diáspora(s)*. He also edited the anthologies *Mapa imaginario* (Havana: Embajada
   de Francia en Cuba/Instituto Cubano del Libro, 1995), which defined the then-emerg-
   ing Generation of the 80s, and *Nueve poetas cubanos del siglo XX* (Madrid: Mondadori,
   2000). He teaches at the Ateneu Barcelones.

Rogelio Saunders (Havana, 1963–)

Polyhimnia (1988–1990) (Havana: Abril, 1996); *Observaciones* (Havana: Extramuros, 1999)

Poet, fiction writer, novelist, and essayist. A participant in Reina María Rodríguez' *azotea* and a member of the *Diáspora(s)* group. He left Cuba in 1998 and lives in Sabadell, near Barcelona.

VATER POUND

Email from the poet:

Aside from the fact that it's at least sixteen years since I wrote "Vater Pound" and that I tend to forget very quickly the source of everything in a poem (when I'm writing it I know everything; when I'm finished, nothing), it's perhaps best if I tell you a couple of things about how I write. The objects in a poem are something like objects in a dream: they have no previous or subsequent existence. Which is to say that a poem is a world (or a slice of a world) in itself that retains only a distant resemblance to "reality" (or that order of things we call reality). Perhaps, for example, there is no painting by Rogier van der Weyden to which this line refers. And perhaps Gustav Holst's suite *The Planets* doesn't (or may not) end, as in the poem, with the pealing of bells. When I begin to write I have no idea how the poem is going to continue, and the confused and mistaken offer me a second chance. Only occasionally a strange scruple forces me to rectify some too obvious incoherence. But in dreams (as in jazz) there's no way to revise. The confused acquires a form, and it's done. It's not a mistake, it's something new.

As to that emblematic "Rogier van der Weyden," I think I remember an apple thief in a tree, and a hunter watching him (hence the musket), but the truth is that at this moment I have no idea if such a painting even exists, and if it does, if it's by Rogier. It could just as easily be by Hieronymus, as you have noticed. What's not in the poem (what's not on its surface) exists nowhere. They're glimpses attracted by glimpses. Words attracted by words. Better, they are instances that arrive in the place where only what I call an invisible ceremony can be performed. The lianas, Pound with a musket, the possible painting by Rogier, Robin Goodfellow who is also a robin, the woods, ancient Celtic tales, etc. etc. etc. As the poem says, "shining symbols." But we can't do anything with them. We wander in a forest of symbols and can't find the key or the path. (And Pound, the surrogate father of contemporary poetry, is also like this). Because there is no key or path. We were lost before we set out. We think we see signs, but it's our own reflection or a spot of light. Something that attracts us as Pinocchio's classmates were attracted. There's no signified, no painting of Rogier's to shelter us, there's nothing at all. That's why the poem says "we are crazy goldsmiths, obsessed by a canticle." From this distance in time, I speak as a reader, because the moment of the poem can't be reproduced. And anyone can make of it what he can.

I know that for a translator (I am one as well) this may not be helpful, but it's how I see it.

Sextus Empiricus.   Second century A.D. Roman philosopher.

ínfero / inferus.   Latin: the below-ground, hell.

Piranesi.   Giovanni Battista Piranesi (1720–1778), Italian etcher and architect. The stairs in the following lines are a reference to his series of *Carceri d'invenzione,* imaginary prisons.

Ismael González Castañer (Havana, 1961–)

Canciones del amante todavía persa (Havana: Taller Experimental de Gráfica, 1991); *Mercados verdaderos* (Havana: Unión, 1998); *La misión* (Havana: Letras Cubanas, 2005)

Poet, fiction writer, and essayist. A participant in Reina María Rodríguez' *azotea* and a member of the *Diáspora(s)* group.

FROM *SATURDAY*

[Epigraph]. Author's note: "William Faulkner, in an interview in the *Paris Review*," no. 12 (Spring 1956): 51. Faulkner was commenting on the killing of Emmett Till. The full text reads: "Maybe the purpose of this sorry and tragic error committed in my native Mississippi by two white adults on an afflicted Negro child is to prove to us whether or not we deserve to survive. Because if we in America have reached that point in our desperate culture when we must murder children, no matter for what reason or what color, we don't deserve to survive, and probably won't."

"FIVE TURKISH WOMEN . . ."
Author's note of dedication: "For Alia"
cobalese. A nonsense word.

LOOKING AND LOOKING THROUGH THE WINDOW
Author's note of dedication: "Bárbara Castañer"
ollantar/overyearn. Neologism. According to the poet, in conversation with the translator, "*Ollantar* has to do with being emotionally touched in a meditative way. Like a nostalgia for the future, for a future you want to return to."

"WATCHING THEM BUILD A BRIDGE . . ."
Author's note: "In Cojímar with Alius and Tumbaga to see Maya."
—*How would you like . . .* Author's note: "From an interview on Radio Metropolitana—Harold" (probably Haroldo de Campos).
Eastwood's film. White Hunter, Black Heart (Warner Brothers, 1990).

Juan Carlos Flores (Havana, 1962–)

Los pájaros escritos (Havana: Unión, 1994); *Distintos modos de cavar un túnel* (Havana: Unión, 2003)

A participant in Reina María Rodríguez' *azotea.*

Pedro Llanes (Placetas, Villa Clara Province, 1962–)

Diario del ángel (Havana: Abril, 1993); *Sibilancia* (Havana: Unión, 1996); *Sonetos de la estrella rota* (Santa Clara: Sed de Belleza, 2000); *Partitura hecha por el sinsonte* (Matanzas: Matanzas 2001)

Poet, novelist, playwright, and critic. An editor at Editorial Capiro and editor of the journal *Umbral* (Villa Clara, Cuba), he lives in Placetas.

THE NAMES OF THE INVISIBLE HOUSE
innocent. The word can mean an innocent, a young child, or a mentally retarded person, or any combination of the three.

Sigfredo Ariel (Santa Clara, 1962–)

Algunos pocos conocidos (Havana: Unión, 1987); *El enorme verano* (Havana: Abril, 1996); *El cielo imaginario* (Matanzas: Vigía, 1996); *Las primeras itálicas* (Málaga: Miguel Gómez, 1997); *Hotel Central* (Havana: Unión, 1999); *Los peces & la vida tropical* (Havana: Letras Cubanas, 2000); *Manos de obra* (Havana: Letras Cubanas, 2002); *Escrito en playa amarilla* (Matanzas: Matanzas, 2004); *Born in Santa Clara* (Havana: Unión, 2006)

Poet, filmmaker, music producer, and visual artist, as well as a writer and director of cultural programs for Cuban radio and television and a producer of recordings of traditional and popular Cuban misic. He was an advisor for the film *Buena Vista Social Club* (1998). He lives in Santa Clara.

DINNER TIME

Oriente.   Oriente Province, Cuba

Frank Abel Dopico (Santa Clara, 1964–)

Poemas del adolescente (Havana: Ministerio de Educación, 1983); *Noticias de lo increíble* (Havana: Ministerio de Cultura, 1985); *La casa a cuesta* (Havana: Ministerio de Cultura, 1986); *El correo de la noche* (Havana: Unión, 1989); *Algunas elegías por Huck Finn* (Havana: Ministerio de Educación, 1989); *Expediente del asesino* (Santa Clara: Capiro, 1990); *Las islas del aire* (Santa Clara: Capiro, 1999); *El país de los caballos ciegos* (La Palma, Islas de las Canarias, Spain: Ediciones La Palma, 2006)

Dopico left Cuba in the late 1990s. He currently lives in Alicante, Spain.

MASK MARKET

Ensor.   James Ensor (1860–1949), Belgian expressionist painter and printmaker.

Alberto Rodríguez Tosca (Artemisa, 1962–)

Todas las jaurías del rey (Havana: Unión, 1988); *Otros poemas* (Havana: Unión, 1992); *El viaje* (Santiago, Colombia: Ediciones Catapulta, 2003); *Escrito sobre el hielo* (Bogotá: La Pobreza Irradiante, 2006); *Las derrotas* (Havana: Unión, 2007)

Poet, fiction writer, journalist, and writer and director of radio programs. He established the Cuban radio program *Hablar de poesía*. He has lived in Colombia since 1994, where he teaches at the International Institute of Film and Television "Isla de Mediodía" and is editor in chief of the journal *La Sangrada Escritura*.

EYES OF THE BLUE DOG

Eyes of the Blue Dog.   A story by Gabriel García Márquez, from the book of the same name (Esplugas de Llobregat: Plaza & Janes, 1974).
Adivina adivinador.   "Guess guesser": a formula from a children's guessing game.

Omar Pérez López (Havana, 1964–)

Algo de lo sagrado (Havana: Unión, 1995); *Oíste hablar del gato de pelea?* (Havana: Letras Cubanas, 1998); *Canciones y letanías* (Havana: Extramuros, 2002)

Poet, translator, and essayist. In recent years he has divided his time between Europe and Cuba, where he participates in Reina María Rodríguez' *azotea*.

CUNDA, THE BLACKSMITH . . .
Based on the story of the Buddha's last meal as told in the Kammaraputta Sutta.

THE DOGS' GREETING
he of the open sores. San Lázaro, the leper, who is always portrayed accompanied by dogs.
despalilladora. Cubanism. In cigar factories the *despalilladora's* job is to remove the coarse central vein of the tobacco leaf.

Antonio José Ponte (Matanzas, 1964–)

Trece poemas (n.p., 1988); *Poesia, 1982–1989* (Havana: Letras Cubanas, 1991); *Asiento en las ruinas* (Havana: Letras Cubanas, 1997)

Fiction writer, poet, essayist, and screenwriter. He trained as a hydraulic engineer and practiced as such for several years. A participant in Reina María Rodríguez' *azotea*. He is author of the important collection of critical essays *El libro perdido de los origenistas*, and two of his short story collections have been translated by Cola Franzen. He currently lives in Madrid, where he co-edits the journal *Encuentro de la Cultura Cubana*.

SOMEWHAT IN THE STYLE OF ISMAEL
[Title]. Email from the poet: "I'm referring to Ismael González Castañer. I don't know what made me think (when even Ismael himself denied it) that this poem had any similarity to those that Ismael wrote back then. Several readers have since told me that it didn't. And I can't guarantee it myself, because you know what Maurice Blanchot said about writers: that tattooed on their foreheads they wear the inscription *noli me legere.*"

A SEAT IN THE RUINS
Lautréamont. Comte de Lautréamont, pen name of Isidore Lucien Ducasse (1846–1870). The quotation is from Maxim 142: "Faut-il que j'écrive en vers pour me séparer des autres hommes?"

Heriberto Hernández (Camajuaní, Las Villas, 1964–)

La patria del espejo (n.p., 1987); *Poemas* (Matanzas: Matanzas, 1991); *Discurso en la montaña de los muertos* (Havana: Unión, 1994); *La patria del espejo* (Havana: Unión, 1994); *Los frutos del vacío* (Matanzas: Matanzas, 1997)

Poet, novelist, and art critic. He studied architecture at the Universidad Central de Las Villas. Subsequently he lived in Matanzas. In 1997 he left Cuba for Peru. Since 2001 he has lived in Miami, where he works as an architect.

Pedro Marqués de Armas (Havana, 1965–)

Fondo de ojos (Havana: Extramuros, 1988); *Los altos manicomios (1987–1989)* (Havana: Abril, 1993); *Cabezas* (Havana: Unión, 2002)

Poet and scholar. A psychiatrist by profession. He left Cuba in 2003 and currently lives in Coimbra, Portugal. He was a participant in Reina María Rodríguez' *azotea* and a member of the *Diaspora(s)* group.

FOREST CLEARING (HALF-WRITTEN)
Mandelstam. Osip Mandelstam (1891–1938), Russian poet and essayist.
Serra Pelada. A region of Brazil, site of a gold rush in the 1980s.
Bernhard. Thomas Bernhard (1931–1989), Austrian playwright and novelist.

Damaris Calderón (Havana, 1967–)

Con el terror del equilibrista (Matanzas: Matanzas, 1987); *Duras aguas del trópico* (Matanzas: Matanzas, 1992); *Guijarros* (Havana: El Túnel, 1994); *Babosas. Dejando mi propio rastro* (Santiago, Chile: Las Dos Fridas, 1997); *Duro de roer* (Santiago, Chile: Las Dos Fridas, 1999); *Se adivina un país* (Havana: Unión, 1999); *Sílabas, ecce homo* (Santiago, Chile: Editorial Universitaria, 2000); *Parloteo de sombra* (Matanzas: Vigía, 2004); *Los amores del mal* (Mexico City: El billar de Lucrecia, 2006)

Poet, fiction writer, and essayist. Since 1995 she has lived in Santiago, Chile.

WITH THE TERROR OF THE TIGHTROPE WALKER
Quevedo. Francisco de Quevedo (1580–1645), Spanish poet. The quotation is from his *Heráclito cristiano*, psalm VII.

SPLINTERS
Shulamite, / your golden hair your ashen hair. Reference to and quotation from Paul Celan's "Todesfuge" ("Death Fugue").

Alessandra Molina (Havana, 1968–)

Anfiteatro entre los pinos (Havana: Extramuros, 1998); *As de triunfo* (Havana: Unión, 2001)

Poet. She left Cuba in 2001, settling in New Orleans until Hurricane Katrina. A former participant in Reina María Rodríguez' *azotea*, she currently lives in Rome.

TRUMP CARD
[Epigraph]. "I will return with iron limbs, dark skin, a furious eye: because of my mask they will think me a member of a superior race. I will have gold . . . " From *Un saison en enfer (A Season in Hell)*, by Arthur Rimbaud (1854–1891).
triunfo. The poet uses the word in both of its meanings, "triumph" and "trump."

Carlos A. Aguilera (Havana, 1970–)

Retrato de A. Hooper y su esposa (Havana: Unión, 1996); *Das kapital. Primera entrega, 1992–1993* (Havana: Abril, 1997)

Poet and essayist. From 1997 until he left Cuba in 2002 Aguilera edited, with Rolando Sánchez Mejías, the influential photocopy journal *Diáspora(s)*. He also edited *Memorias de la clase muerta. Poesía cubana, 1988–2001* (Mexico City: Aldus, 2002), an anthology of the core group represented in the journal. He was a frequent participant in Reina María Rodríguez' *azotea*. He lives in Dresden.

B. Gottfried Benn (1886–1956), German poet and novelist who had been a member of the Nazi Party.

Ce-. Paul Celan (1920–1970), Romanian Jewish poet and Holocaust survivor, who wrote primarily in German.

Javier Marimón (Matanzas, 1975–)

La muerte de Eleanor (Havana: Abril, 1998); *Formas de llamar desde Los Pinos* (Havana: Letras Cubanas, 2000); *El gran lunes* (Matanzas: Vigía, 2000); *El gatico vasia (como engane al subito)* (Matanzas: Aldabón, 2001); *Himnos urbanos* (Havana: Letras Cubanas, 2002)

Marimón left Cuba in 2004 and currently lives in Texas, where he is studying for a doctorate in Hispanic Studies at Texas A&M. He was a frequent participant in Reina María Rodríguez' *azotea.*

SPONTANEOUS GENERATION

Saussure. Ferdinand de Saussure (1857–1913), Swiss linguist. He is often considered the founder of modern linguistics.

fragile. The distinction between the French *fragile* and the Spanish *frágil,* a repeated motif of the poem, does not translate easily into English.

kyosaku. In Zen meditation practice, the wooden stick with which the master wakes people when they fall asleep or their attention strays.

Translators

Chris Brandt teaches writing and literature at various New York City colleges and in prisons and job training programs. His poetry and translations have appeared in journals in Spain, Mexico, France, and the United States. He is also a cabinetmaker and furniture designer. He has been the recipient of Shubert and NBC Fellowships.

Margaret Carson is a freelance translator of Latin American fiction, poetry, and plays. Her translation of Virgilio Piñera's *Electra Garrigó,* as well as her translations of five other plays, appeared in the anthology *Stages of Conflict: A Reader of Latin American Theatre and Performance* (Ann Arbor: University of Michigan, 2008).

Luis Cortest was chair of the Department of Modern Languages, Literatures, and Linguistics at the University of Oklahoma, where he is associate professor of Spanish, from 1992 to 1999. He has written and edited numerous studies of the literature and culture of the *siglo de oro,* among them *Sor Juana Inés de la Cruz: Selected Studies* (Asunción, Paraguay: CEDES, 1989).

Kristin Dykstra is the translator of three books by Reina María Rodríguez: *Violet Island and Other Poems* (Los Angeles: Green Integer, 2004), with Nancy Gates Madsen; *Time's Arrest/La detención del tiempo* (San Diego, Calif.: Factory School, 2005); and *The Winter Garden Photograph,* an edition of Reina María Rodríguez' *La foto del invernadero* (Los Angeles: Green Integer, forthcoming). She also translated Omar Pérez' 1995 *Algo de lo sagrado,* as *Something of the Sacred* (New York: Factory School, 2007). She edits, with Roberto Tejada, *Mandorla: New Writing from the Americas/Nueva escritura de las Américas.*

George Economou, professor emeritus of English at the University of Oklahoma, is the author of nine books of poetry. He is the translator of *Acts of Love: Ancient Greek Poetry from Aphrodite's Garden* (New York: Random House, 2006), Constantine Cavafy's *I've Gazed So Much* (London: Stop, 2003) and *Half an Hour* (London: Stop, 2009), and William Langland's *Piers Plowman* (Philadelphia: University of Pennsylvania Press, 1996), editor and translator of *Ananios of Kleitor: Poems and Fragments* (Exeter, U.K.: Shearsman Press, 2009), and editor of of the definitive edition of the late Paul Blackburn's troubadour translations, *Proensa* (Berkeley: University of California Press, 1986). He was a founding editor of *The Chelsea Review* and co-founder of *Trobar* and Trobar Books. A Rockefeller Fellow at Bellagio, he has received two NEA Fellowships in Poetry.

Cola Franzen is the translator of ten volumes of poetry and thirteen of prose, including two by Antonio José Ponte: *In the Cold of the Malecón and Other Stories* (San Francisco: City Lights, 2000), with Dick Cluster; and *Tales from the Cuban*

Empire (San Francisco: City Lights, 2002). She has been the recipient of the Harold Morton Landon Translation Award from the Academy of American Poets and the Gregory Kalavakos Award from the PEN American Center.

Gabriel Gudding is the author of two books of poetry. He is a recipient of *The Nation* Discovery Award and the Agnes Lynch Starrett Poetry Prize of the University of Pittsburgh Press. He is assistant professor of English at Illinois State University.

James Irby is professor emeritus of Latin American literature at Princeton and editor and translator, with Donald Yates, of Jorge Luis Borges' *Labyrinths: Selected Stories and Other Writings* (New York: New Directions, 1964).

Michael Kelleher is the author of two collections of poems. He lives in Buffalo, New York, where he is artistic director for Just Buffalo Literary Center and literary editor of *Artvoice*.

Joan Lindgren (d. 2007) was the translator of Magda Santonostasio, *Letters to an Owl* (San Diego: Brighton Press, 1985); Francisco Morales Santos, *The Task of Telling* (Portland, Ore.: Trask House, 2000); and *Unthinkable Tenderness: Selected Poems of Juan Gelman* (Berkeley: University of California, 1997), among others. She was the recipient of a Fulbright Fellowship and a residency at the the International Centre for Literary Translation in Banff, Canada.

Nancy Gates Madsen translated Reina María Rodríguez' *Violet Island and Other Poems* (Los Angeles: Green Integer, 2004), with Kristin Dykstra. She teaches Spanish and Latin American literature at Luther College in Decorah, Iowa.

Todd Ramón Ochoa is a postdoctoral fellow in the Department of Anthropology at the University of California, Berkeley, where he has recently completed a manuscript on Cuban-Kongo sacred societies. His translations have appeared in *Mandorla* and the Cuban review *Diaspora(s)*.

Harry Polkinhorn is internationally recognized as a visual poet and for his work on the U.S.-Mexican border. Professor of English and comparative literature at San Diego State University and director of its press, he has edited and translated numerous books on the border and its literature, authored ten books of poetry, four books of prose, and three books of visual poetry. In addition, he edited and translated *Visual Poetry: An International Anthology* (Providence: Visible Language, 1994), and edited, with Mark Weiss, *Across the Line / Al otro lado: The Poetry of Baja California* (San Diego: Junction Press, 2002).

Mark Schafer is the translator of Virgilio Piñera, *Cold Tales* (Hygiene, Colo.: Eridanos, 1988) and *René's Flesh* (Boston: Eridanos, 1989); Eduardo Galeano, *The Book of Embraces* (New York: W. W. Norton, 1990), with Cedric Belfrage; Alberto Ruy Sánchez, *Mogador: The Names of the Air* (San Francisco: City Lights, 1992); Jesús Gardea, *Stripping Away the Sorrows of This World* (Mexico City and San Francisco: Aldus and Mercury House, 1998); Gloria Gervitz, *Migrations* (San Diego: Junction Press, 2004); and *Before Saying Anything: Selected Poetry of David Huerta* (Port Townsend, Wash.: Copper Canyon Press, 2009). He has been awarded two NEA Fellowships, a grant from the Fund for Culture Mexico–USA, and the Robert Fitzgerald Translation Prize.

Cindy Schuster translated *Cubana: Contemporary Fiction by Cuban Women* (Boston: Beacon, 1998), with Dick Cluster; and Raúl Henao, *La vida a la carta: Poemas selectos /*

Life a la Carte: Selected Poems (Medellín, Colombia: Ediciones Festival de Poesía de Medellín, 1998), with Edgar Knowlton, Philip West, and Ricardo Pau-Llosa. She is the recipient of a translation fellowship from the National Endowment for the Arts.

Rebecca Seiferle is the author of four books of poems. Among her translations are two books by César Vallejo, *Trilce* (New York: Sheep Meadow, 1992) and *The Black Heralds* (Port Townsend, Wash.: Copper Canyon, 2003). She edits the e-zine *The Drunken Boat* (www.thedrunkenboat.com).

Michael Smith is the author of seven books of poetry and the translator of sixteen, including works of Neruda, Machado, Quevedo, Góngora, and Lorca. His most recent translations are César Vallejo, *Trilce* (Exeter, U.K.: Shearsman, 2005), *The Complete Later Poems, 1923–1938* (Exeter, U.K.: Shearsman, 2005), *Selected Poems* (Exeter, U.K.: Shearsman, 2005), and *The Black Heralds and Other Early Poems* (Exeter, U.K.: Shearsman, 2007), all with Valentino Gianuzzi; and Vicente Huidobro, *Selected Poems* (Exeter, U.K.: Shearsman, 2007). In 2001, he was the first Irish recipient of the European Academy Medal for distinguished work in the translation of poetry, awarded by the European Academy of Poetry.

Nathaniel Tarn has published over thirty books of poetry, among them *Selected Poems: 1950–2000* (Middletown, Conn.: Wesleyan University Press, 2002), and five books of anthropology, including *Scandals in the House of Birds* (New York: Marsilio, 1997). His translations have included, among others, three books of Pablo Neruda's work and one of Victor Segalen's. He edited the bilingual *Con Cuba: An Anthology of Cuban Poetry of the Last Sixty Years* (London and New York: Cape Goliard and Grossman, 1969).

Mónica de la Torre is the author of two books of poetry. She is editor and translator of *Gerardo Deniz: Poemas/Poems* (Mexico City: Ditoria; Providence: Lost Roads, 2000) and editor, with Michael Wiegers, of the multilingual anthology *Reversible Monuments: Contemporary Mexican Poetry* (Port Townsend, Wash.: Copper Canyon, 2002).

Jason Weiss is author or editor of a novel and four books of nonfiction, among them *The Lights of Home: A Century of Latin American Writers in Paris* (Routledge, 2003). His translations include Luisa Futoransky, *The Duration of the Voyage: Selected Poems* (San Diego: Junction, 1997); and Marcel Cohen, *Mirrors* (Los Angeles: Green Integer, 1998).

Mark Weiss is the author of six books of poetry. He translated Javier Manríquez, *Cuaderno de San Antonio/The San Antonio Notebook* (La Paz: Universidad Autónoma de Baja California Sur, 2005); edited and translated José Kozer, *Stet: Selected Poems* (New York: Junction Press, 2006); and translated Gaspar Orozco, *Notas del país de Z/Notes from the Land of Z* (Chihuahua, Mexico: Universidad Autónoma de Chihuahua, 2009). He edited, with Harry Polkinhorn, *Across the Line/Al otro lado: The Poetry of Baja California* (San Diego: Junction Press, 2002).

Christopher Winks is assistant professor of comparative literature at Queens College of the City University of New York. He is translator and editor of *Lorenzo García Vega: Selected Poems* (New York: Junction Press, forthcoming 2010) and author of *Symbolic Cities in Caribbean Literature* (New York: Palgrave MacMillan, 2009). His reviews, articles, and translations from French, German, and Spanish have appeared in numerous publications.

Acknowledgments

More than most books, this anthology would have been impossible without the help of a great many people. The poets, heirs of poets, and translators have been unstinting in their generosity. Rolando Sánchez Mejías, Antonio José Ponte, Josefina de Diego, and Reina María Rodríguez, as well as Francisco Morán, Efraín Rodríguez Santana, Enrique Saínz, Daniel García, and especially Jorge Luis Arcos, assisted in the often difficult task of locating poets and heirs. Iraida Iturralde, Lourdes Gil, Rogelio Saunders, Ramón Fernández Larrea, Ismael González Castañer, Frank Abel Dopico, Omar Pérez López, and Alessandra Molina tolerated with good humor my often naive questions about their work.

Finding Cuban books is no easy matter, and I owe a debt to Lesbia O. Varona and her staff at the University of Miami's Cuban Heritage Collection. Also invaluable has been the consummate sleuthing of Elliot Klein, one of the few foreign booksellers working in Cuba.

Margaret Carson, Cindy Schuster, Rebecca Seiferle, Chris Brandt, and Mónica de la Torre, among the translators, as well as Dick Cluster and César Pérez, pulled my hand out of the fire more often than they are probably aware of.

James Irby deserves special mention as a model for all of us who work as scholars and translators.

Kim Eherenman, Candice Ward, Roberto Fernández Retamar, Miguel Barnet, Ruth Behar, Ambrosio Fornet, Pío Serrano, Jorge Accame, Barbara Jamison, Alina Camacho Gingerich, Forrest Gander, Regla Albarran, Ned Sublette, and Peter Riley were instrumental in getting this project off the ground.

A small group who helped in all the ways mentioned above, as well as bearing with my complaints and being there in the darkest nights, could truly be called my mentors: Jerome Rothenberg, Jacobo Sefamí, Tom Miller, Jason Weiss, Christopher Winks, and especially José Kozer, my passport to all things Cuban.

I owe a special note of thanks to my friend and colleague Joan Lindgren, now no longer with us.

My editors at University of California Press, Laura Cerruti and Rachel Berchten, deserve a medal for patience and understanding, as well as astute advice. Anne Canright, my copyeditor, and Rose Vekony, my project editor, were industry itself, repairing my own failures of attention.

My thanks to the Foundation of Yaddo, which afforded me a crucial month of undisturbed labor.

Finally, I wish to thank the governments of the United States and Cuba, for policies that helped make this anthology necessary.

Credits

The following individuals and publishers have graciously granted permission to include the indicated material in this anthology.

Carlos A. Aguilera: "B, Ce-." By permission of the poet. Translation by permission of Gabriel Gudding.

José Álvarez Baragaño: "Los distritos sonoros," "Yo oscuro," "Los muertos," "Revolución color de libertad," "Nuestro nombre no está escrito . . ." By permission of the estate of José Álvarez Baragaño. Translations by permission of Christopher Winks.

Sigfredo Ariel: "La luz, bróder, la luz," "La vida ajena," "La hora de comer." By permission of the poet. Translations by permission of George Economou and Luis Cortest.

Antón Arrufat: selections from "Repaso final." By permission of the poet. Translations by permission of Rebecca Seiferle.

Gastón Baquero: "Breve viaje nocturno," "Pavana para el Emperador," "El viento en Trieste decía," "Los lunes me llamaba Nicanor," "El héroe," "Fábula," "Charada para Lydia Cabrera," "Marcel Proust pasea en barca por la bahía de Corinto," "El gato personal del conde Cagliostro," "El viajero." By permission of the estate of Gastón Baquero.

Miguel Barnet: "Así, la muerte," "Suite cubana," "Caminando la ciudad," "Con pies de gato," "Memorándum XIV," "En el barrio chino." By permission of the poet.

Ruth Behar: "Carta," "Ofrenda," "El mundo," "Un deseo para el año que viene." By permission of the poet.

Roberto Branly: "Atardecer sobre San Anastasio." By permission of the estate of Roberto Branly. Translation by permission of Todd Ramón Ochoa.

Damaris Calderón: "Con el terror del equilibrista," "Ésta será la única mentira en la que siempre creeremos," "Astillas," "Huesos fuertes," "La máscara japonesa." By permission of the poet. Translations by permission of the estate of Joan Lindgren.

Belkis Cuza Malé: "Las cenicientas," "La fuente de plata," "Caja de Pandora," "Crítica a la razón impura," "El ombligo del mundo." By permission of the poet. Translations by permission of Jason Weiss.

Lina de Feria: "Poema para la mujer que habla sola en el Parque de Calzada," "No es necesario ir a los andenes," "Preámbulo." By permission of the poet. Translations by permission of Michael Smith.

Francisco de Oraá: "Yo no sé cómo voy a no sé donde," "De cómo fue la muerte hallada dentro de una botija," "En uso de razón," "Ahora quita el agua y pon el sol," "Vida de niño," "Ahogado en el serón," "Sobre las cosas que, si miras bien,

ves en el cielo," "Dos sueños con un ave," "Aventura entre niños," "Del pescador,"
"De tres fotos de Mella." By permission of the poet. Translations by permission of
Christopher Winks.

Eliseo Diego: "Bajo los astros," "El oscuro esplendor," "En memoria," "Cartagena de
Indias," "Versiones," "La casa del pan," "Riesgos del equilibrista," "La niña en el
bosque," "La casa abandonada," "Oda a la joven luz," "Testamento," "Mi madre
la oca," "Comienza un lunes," "A una muchacha." By permission of the estate of
Eliseo Diego.

Frank Abel Dopico: "El correo de la noche," "Mercadilla de máscaras," "A mi padre,"
"Francois Villón," "Cuando pasan los años." By permission of the poet. Transla-
tions by permission of Chris Brandt.

Ángel Escobar: "Las puertas," "El pulgar y el índice," "Hospitales," "Los cuatro cuen-
tos," "Otro," "La sombra del decir," "La guardería infantil," "Quién le teme a Franz
Kafka," "Frente frío." By permission of the poet. Translations by permission of
Mónica de la Torre.

Abilio Estévez: "Las pequeñas cosas," "Frente al río," "Visita del abuelo." By permis-
sion of the poet. Translations by permission of Cola Franzen.

Samuel Feijóo: "En la muerte por fuego de Gladys, la joven de los canarios," "Tumba
con palmas," "Tres blues," "Son del loco," "Caonao adentro." By permission of the
estate of Samuel Feijóo. Translations by permission of Michael Smith.

Amando Fernández: "Descenso de la agonía," "El capitán," "La estatua." By permission
of the estate of Amando Fernández. Translations by permission of Cindy Schuster.

Pablo Armando Fernández: "Nacimiento de Eggo," "Rendición de Eshu," selections
from "Suite para Maruja." By permission of the poet. Translations of "Nacimiento
de Eggo" and "Rendición de Eshu" by permission of Nathaniel Tarn.

Ramón Fernández Larrea: "Poema transitorio," "Cantando con mi abuelita sobre las
piernas," "El país de los elfos." By permission of the poet.

Roberto Fernández Retamar: "Un hombre y una mujer," "Felices los normales," "Le
preguntaron por los persas." By permission of the poet. Translation of "Le pregun-
taron por los persas" by permission of Nathaniel Tarn.

Juan Carlos Flores: "Tótem," "El secadero," "Uno de los blues," "Retrato de una (otra)
dama," "El ciclista K," "Sírvase usted," "La mosca." By permission of the poet.

Eugenio Florit: "Los poetas solos de Manhattan," "Juego," "Brujas," "El eterno," "La
niebla." By permission of the estate of Eugenio Florit. Translations by permission
of Jason Weiss.

Carlos Galindo Lena: "Qué hacer si he perdido las llaves . . . ," "Siempre es bueno
recordar a Tebas . . . ," "Ayer el mar era una ausencia." By permission of the estate
of Carlos Galindo Lena. Translations by permission of Michael Smith.

Fina García Marruz: "Visitaciones," "El momento que más amo," selections from
"Gramática inglesa." By permission of the poet.

Lorenzo García Vega: "Variaciones," "En las lágrimas de las focas," "Túnel," "El santo
del Padre Rector," El viejo Maldoror," "Con una advertencia," "Texto martiano,"
"Buscándome el vacío," "Ilusión venido a menos," "Arañazo mediúmnico," "El
extraño rigor," "Colosal olvido," "Manuscrito para la cajita," "No, vano discurso no
es vacío," "Junto al campo de golf," "Revisando la visión," "Caluroso el día," "Un
mandala." By permission of the poet. Translations by permission of Christopher
Winks.

Lourdes Gil: "Desvelo de los pájaros anoche," "Fata Morgana." By permission of the poet. Translations by permission of Gabriel Gudding.

Ismael González Castañer: selections from "Sábado." By permission of the poet. Translations by permission of Todd Ramón Ochoa.

Nicolás Guillén: Selections from *El gran zoo*: "El caribe," "Guitarra," "La pajarita de papel," "La Osa Mayor," "El Aconcagua," "Los ríos," "Señora," "La sed," "El hambre," "Las nubes," "Los vientos," "El tigre," Ciclón," "Ave Fénix," "Lynch," "KKK," "Las águilas," "Luna," "Tenor," "Reloj," "Aviso." By permission of the estate of Nicolás Guillén. Translations by permission of Rebecca Seiferle.

Heriberto Hernández: "Las paredes de vidrio," "Fábula del delfín y la sombra del pájaro." By permission of the poet. Translations by permission of Chris Brandt.

Raúl Hernández Novás: "Quién seré sino el tonto," "Sobre el nido del cuco." By permission of the estate of Raúl Hernández Novás.

Iraida Iturralde: "Claroscuro," "El rostro de la nación," "Exilio, la sien." By permission of the poet.

Fayad Jamís: "A veces," "Las bodas del hormiguero," "Vagabundo del alba," "Charlot y la luna," "Por esta libertad." By permission of the estate of Fayad Jamís. Translations by permission of Jason Weiss.

José Kozer: "Te acuerdas, Sylvia," "Rebrote de Franz Kafka," "La dádiva," "Jerusalén celeste," "Última voluntad," "Ánima," "Reino," "La casa de enfrente," "Danzonete." By permission of the poet.

José Lezama Lima: "Pensamientos en la Habana," "Oda a Julián del Casal," "Atraviesan la noche," "Las siete alegorías." By permission of the estate of José Lezama Lima. Translations of "Pensamientos en la Habana" and "Oda a Julián del Casal" by permission of James Irby.

Pedro Llanes: "Nombres de la casa invisible." By permission of the poet. Translations by permission of Chris Brandt.

César López: "Como en cualquier ciudad . . . ," "El poeta en la ciudad." By permission of the poet. Translations by permission of Rebecca Seiferle.

Javier Marimón: "Generación espontánea." By permission of the poet. Translation by permission of Michael Kelleher.

Pedro Marqués de Armas: "Tú no irás a Troya," "Claro de bosque (semiescrito)." By permission of the poet. Translations by permission of George Economou and Luis Cortest.

Roberto Méndez: "Fábula peligrosa," "Ensayo sobre la tristeza," "Lo estelar." By permission of the poet.

Alessandra Molina: "As de triunfo," "Herbolaria," "Ronda infantil." By permission of the poet.

Nancy Morejón: "Parque Central alguna gente (3:00 P.M.)." By permission of the poet. Translation by permission of Nathaniel Tarn.

Luis Rogelio Nogueras: "Mujer saliendo del armario," "Un tesoro," "Canta," "Don't look back, lonesome boy," "(Yambos interrumpidos)," "Pérdida del poema de amor llamado 'niebla'," "Oración por el hijo que nunca va a nacer," "Un poema," "El último caso del inspector," "Una muchacha," "Viaje." By permission of the estate of Luis Rogelio Nogueras.

Heberto Padilla: "En tiempos difíciles," "El discurso del método," "Oración para el fin de siglo," "Los poetas cubanos ya no sueñan," "Para aconsejar a una dama," "Poética," "Paisajes," "El lugar del amor." By permission of the estate of Heberto Padilla. Permission to translate "En tiempos difíciles," "Oración para el fin de siglo," "Para aconsejar a una dama," and "El lugar del amor" courtesy of Farrar, Straus and Giroux, holder of English language rights. Translations by permission of Jason Weiss.

Omar Pérez López: "Contribuciones a un idea rudimentaria de nación," "Cunda, el herrero . . . ," "Imprecaciones, adivinanzas," "Saludo de los perros," "Las instituciones místicas del decoro," "El loco." By permission of the poet.

Virgilio Piñera: "Los muertos de la Patria," "Nunca los dejaré," "En la puerta de mi vecino . . . ," "Testamento," "En el Gato Tuerto," "Pin, pan, pun," "Quien soy," "Una noche," "Bueno, digamos," "Y cuando me contó," "Reversibilidad," "Isla." By permission of the estate of Virgilio Piñera.

Antonio José Ponte: "Un poco a la manera de Ismael," "Sobre el planeta," "Canción," "Un bosque, una escalera," "La silla en escapada," "Augurios," "Asiento en las ruinas." By permission of the poet. Translations by permission of Mark Schafer.

Delfín Prats: "No vuelvas a los lugares donde fuiste feliz," "Para festejar el ascenso de Ícaro," "Fábula del cazador y el ciervo," "Viento de Patmos." By permission of the poet.

Soleida Ríos: "Pájaro de La Bruja," "Maleva y los niños en el paraíso," "El texto sucio," "Recogí limones," "El camino del cementerio." By permission of the poet.

Reina María Rodríguez: "Ellas escriben cartas de amor," "Una mujer se desnuda frente a un profesor estupefacto," "Una muchacha loca como los pájaros," "Pescadores (crudo)." By permission of the poet. Translations of "Ellas escriben cartas de amor," "Una mujer se desnuda frente a un profesor estupefacto," "and "Una muchacha loca como los pájaros" by permission of Kristin Dykstra and Nancy Gates Madsen. Translation of "Pescadores (crudo)" by permission of Kristin Dykstra.

Alberto Rodríguez Tosca: "Ojos de perro azul," "Suma transitoria." By permission of the poet. Translations by permission of Margaret Carson.

Excilia Saldaña: "La mujer que ríe y llora." By permission of the poet.

Rolando Sánchez Mejías: "Cálculo de lindes." By permission of the poet.

Rogelio Saunders: "Vater Pound." By permission of the poet. Translation by permission of Harry Polkinhorn.

Cintio Vitier: "El bosque de Birnam," "Plegaria." By permission of the poet. Translations by permission of Jason Weiss.

designer Lia Tjandra
compositor BookMatters, Berkeley
text 10.25/13 Adobe Garamond
display Adobe Garamond and Berthold Akzidenz Grotesk
printer and binder Maple-Vail Book Manufacturing Group